BIBLIOTECA DI SCIENZE RELIGIOSE

187

TRANSCENDING BOUNDARIES

Contemporary Readings of the New Testament

Essays in Honor of Francis J. Moloney

Edited by

Rekha M. CHENNATTU and Mary L. COLOE

LAS - ROMA

The cover design is a painting of the Nativity by Australian Aboriginal artist Matthew Gill. To see other works and artists from the Central Desert region of Australia go to:
http://www.balgoart.org.au/art_center/balgo/art_center_pages/mainframeabout.htm
http://www.aboriginalartprints.com.au/ab_susiebootjabootja.cfm

© 2005 by LAS - Libreria Ateneo Salesiano
Piazza dell'Ateneo Salesiano, 1 - 00139 ROMA
Tel. 06 87290626 - Fax 06 87290629 - e-mail: las@ups.urbe.it - http://las.ups.urbe.it

ISBN 88-213-0565-1

Elaborazione elettronica: LAS ❑ *Stampa:* Tip. Istituto Salesiano Pio XI - Via Umbertide, 11 - Roma (Febbraio)

CONTENTS

Chapters

PREFACE

The painting of the Nativity on the front cover is the work of an artist from Balgo Hills, a small aboriginal community in the Great Sandy Desert of central Australia. Using the earthy reds, yellow ochres, and black and white of traditional cave drawings, the artist portrays the infant Jesus in the center, with Mary and Joseph on either side. Aboriginal art often depicts a scene from directly overhead giving it such a unique iconic perspective. The crescent shapes are the traditional ways of representing seated figures, showing the imprint their bodies leave in the sand. The child rests in a coolomon, which is a shallow, hollowed-out wooden vessel used for gathering seeds and berries. Mothers also use coolomons as baby carriers.

The painting reflects the theme of this collection of essays written in honor of Francis J. Moloney: *Transcending Boundaries*. The Incarnation was that boundary shattering moment when heaven met earth, when Word became Flesh that flesh might become glory. The painting melds an ancient tribal culture of Australia with the younger tradition of Western Christianity. Its theological and cultural transcendence suggests the rich ministry of Francis J. Moloney as biblical scholar and teacher during his more than thirty years of priesthood. In thinking of a title for this work, we chose *Transcending Boundaries* since, throughout Frank's ministerial and academic life, he has continually been open to new ideas and always ready to address new issues. Frank has never "rested on his laurels" nor let the *status quo* or political correctness restrict his vision. Boundaries are challenges to be tackled, not walls to confine.

Like many of the scholars contributing to this volume, Frank's first methodological training was in Historical Criticism. Some of his early articles and his doctoral thesis, *The Johannine Son of Man*, show his mastery of this approach. But Frank has been able to move beyond this method; in his work in the late 80's and the 90's, he shifted towards the new literary critical methods. His major study of the Gospel of John, in the Sacra Pagina Series, is the first commentary in that series to fully integrate narrative and historical methods. After this outstanding accomplishment, he turned to the Gospel of Mark and produced two excellent studies.

As anyone who has flown across the Pacific realizes, Melbourne is a long way from other centers of biblical research. Frank's large "island home" can present a formidable boundary to a truly international participation in current scholarship. Frank has crossed the seas to be "at home" in Oxford, Rome, Jerusalem, and currently Washington. His writings demonstrate cross-cultural awareness as well as an appreciation of different hermeneutical approaches.

Frank has placed his biblical scholarship at the service of the wider Church, not only through his work on various theological commissions and his service within the Salesian Congregation, but also through his willingness, in his writings and public lectures, to address contemporary issues, such as religious life, women, Christian discipleship, the Eucharist, and new medical technologies. As both disciple and prophet, he has pushed the boundaries of theological thinking, bringing academic skill to sensitive pastoral concerns.

Frank's 65th birthday is a fitting opportunity to celebrate and honor his extensive contribution to biblical scholarship. The contributors of this Festschrift are some of his former students, his colleagues, and friends from across the globe who want to express their appreciation of him and his work.

The opening chapter by Tony Kelly situates Frank's biblical work within the broader context of theology. He ponders the conjunction of Theology and Exegesis and how, in this fruitful nexus, we may come to a deeper understanding of God's most gracious designs. Words such as "biblical" or "systematic" are descriptors, not boundaries. Following this general theological introduction, Dorothy Lee and Gail O'Day examine the theme of *Friendship* in the Fourth Gospel and the uniqueness of the Gospel's presentation when compared with the Greco-Roman literature on this theme. Though taking different approaches, both develop the Johannine insight into the manner of Jesus' relationship with his initial disciples and with all believers. Friendship dissolves boundaries while respecting the integrity of difference.

The next seven chapters examine specific Johannine passages and issues. Martin Asiedu-Peprah's study on "internal analepsis" draws on the narrative chronology of the Gospel to show how the "timelessness" of the Father, bears witness in time, to the person and ministry of Jesus. With the Incarnation, our constructs of space and time are transcended. Continuing this notion of transcending space and time, Mary Coloe's analysis of the Johannine anointing draws upon Israel's distinctions between the sacred and profane and how they are ritualized in the closing Sabbath prayers. Her reading of John 12:1-8 offers new insights into this scene. Readers frequently stop short when they come to 12:40, one of *John's* "hard sayings." The text appears to say that God wills the unbelief of some of Jesus' listeners, thus making their present response predetermined by the past. John Painter's lucid exposition of the literary and theological context surrounding 12:40 offers a way of reading this difficult text that allows "time" to have its proper freedom and *kairos* opportunity.

Rekha Chennattu presents the Old Testament covenant motif as a key to the structure and interpretation of John 15–16. She defines Johannine discipleship as a covenant relationship that implies an ever-deeper experience of God's abiding love and that calls for a commitment to collaborate with God's creative and life-giving works. This notion of discipleship transcends all ethnic and religious boundaries in its invitation to all to become "children of God" (1:12-13). Robert Kysar addresses the particular way Frank translates and interprets the phrase παρέδωκεν τὸ πνεῦμα in 19:30b, that Jesus "handed over the Spirit." Kysar appreciates the ambiguity of the phrase from a reader's perspective and extends it to include *both* Jesus' human spirit *and* the divine Spirit. He demonstrates the possibility of doing New Testament theology without recourse to the history behind the texts. The start perhaps of further fruitful dialogue! Raymond Collin's essay on the beatitude (20:29) illustrates the way John's Gospel transcends the boundaries of narrative time and reaches out to believers beyond the world of the text. The believers whom Jesus proclaims as "blessed" include the characters in the story, members of the Johannine Community, and contemporary readers, all of whom are promised eternal life (20:31). Francis Gignac concludes the section with a study of the Johannine literary device of expressing the same idea in two or more Greek verbs (e.g., πέμπω ἀποστέλλω, ἀγαπάω–φιλέω). While some exegetes see different theological nuances in the different usages of the Greek words, he argues that they are used synonymously and ought not to be given any distinctive theological weight.

Keeping to the "boundlessness" of our theme, the next chapters extend into the New Testament literature beyond the Fourth Gospel. Since his latest ventures into *Mark*, even Frank must now acknowledge this world outside *the* text! Frank Matera examines the way both *Mark* and *John* present Jesus as Messiah, but in a way that transcends the usual expectations associated with this title. He proposes that, rather than starting with Israel's expectations, the early Christian communities started with the death and resurrection of Jesus and reinterpreted Israel's messianic traditions. Brendan Byrne offers a finely argued case for interpreting the rending of the Temple veil in Mark as an allusion to Israel's Day of Atonement. Drawing on Paul's use of the term ἱλαστήριον, he shows how Paul and *Mark* share a common understanding of the death of Jesus as an act of atonement for sin. While interpreting Jesus' death in terms of Israel's Temple activity, Byrne maintains that the act of atonement on Calvary transcends all Israel's cultic rituals, as this atonement has universal consequences for all people.

The following chapter by Elaine Wainwright shifts from atonement to healing. She proposes that the healing stories in *Mark* render healing not only to the characters within the story, but also offer healing to those who hear and tell the story today. The power of the healing story reaches outside the limits of narrative time and place to impact on listeners and readers. As Wainwright reminds us, our world today has need of such healing stories.

Joseph Fitzmyer addresses the way Luke reformulates Paul's teaching on justification. He presents with great clarity the rich complexity of this concept of Paul, which has various connotations. However, when Paul's speech in Pisidian Antioch is related by Luke (Acts 13:16b-41), the emphasis is on forgiveness of sin, which has economic or social aspects that are not included in Paul's understanding of justification. The differences between Luke and Paul not only reveal something of their collaborative relationship, but also raise the question of how well Luke really understood Paul.

In the next chapter Timothy Friedrichsen focuses on the commissioning of the women in Matthew 28:9-10 and compares this to the commissioning of the Eleven in Matthew 28:16-20. The scene of the meeting between Jesus and the women is a Matthean redaction that changes the nature of the women's testimony. They are no longer merely messengers, but become witnesses, thus taking on a role similar to the male disciples (vv. 16-20), although the male disciples have a more expansive task "to all nations."

Frank's teaching, public speaking, and writing went well beyond the biblical text and into broad theological analysis. Following the impetus of

Vatican II, he applied his biblical skills to retrieving the evangelical counsels which are the basis of formal religious life. Veronica Lawson honors this aspect of Frank's ministry when she writes on Tabitha, disciple and prophet for her community. She applies a hermeneutic of suspicion and a hermeneutic of retrieval to her re-reading of Acts 9:36-43 and draws this woman from her silent place in the text.

Our final contributor, William Loader, takes us outside the canonical texts of the Bible to other Jewish/early Christian literature in *The Testaments of the Twelve Patriarchs*. His discussion of sexuality, within the philosophical and religious context of Judaism and the Hellenistic Roman world, enlightens any reading of the New Testament treatment of this topic. Verses from the Gospel and Paul can be better understood if read within a far broader discussion of earlier understandings of anthropology and human sexuality. Such informed reading is essential to avoid rigid fundamentalist interpretations.

The editors thank the contributors for their generous response to the invitation to be part of this volume. We also express our gratitude to the people who assisted us in preparing this book. In particular we thank our two religious congregations, the Presentation Sisters of Victoria and the Religious of the Assumption. Our Sisters by their interest and appreciation have generously supported our scholarship over many years and contributed significant funding, allowing us time and opportunities for theological research. In the final flurry of gathering chapters, editing, proofing, and meeting deadlines, we could not have managed this project without the financial support and released time provided to Mary by the Australian Catholic University and the Australian Research Council and to Rekha by the Catholic University of America and her Religious Congregation. This book would not have been produced without the financial backing of a dear friend, who wishes to remain anonymous. While the name may be missing, our thanks are not. We gratefully acknowledge the generous and valuable contribution of Nerina Zanardo F.S.P., the director of Pauline Books and Media, Adelaide, Australia, who proofread these pages, as she has for most of Frank's writing.

Finally, a word to Frank himself.

We hope this book gives you the pleasure that we have enjoyed in its preparation. While your natural Aussie humor and humility may like to brush aside such honors, we hope that you will take time to savor not only the written words, but also the spirit of appreciation and love in which they have been offered by all our contributors. Perhaps a word from *John* can best bring this preface to an end. "If you remain in my word, you are truly my disciples; you will know the truth and the truth will make you free" (John 8:32).

Frank, we your colleagues and friends salute and applaud you for your commitment to the Word, your faithful discipleship, your dedication to truth and scholarship, and your freedom and grace in transcending so many boundaries, thereby opening pathways for others.

MARY and REKHA

CONTRIBUTORS

Martin Asiedu-Peprah, D.Theol., Professor of New Testament, St. Peter's National Seminary, Ghana, West Africa

Brendan Byrne, S.J., D.Phil., Professor of New Testament, United Faculty of Theology, Melbourne, Australia

Rekha M. Chennattu, R.A., Ph.D., Head, Department of Scriptural Studies, Jnana-Deepa Vidyapeeth, Pontifical Institute of Philosophy and Religion, Pune, India

Raymond F. Collins, S.T.D., Warren-Blanding Professor of Religion, Professor of New Testament, The Catholic University of America, Washington, DC, USA

Mary L. Coloe, P.B.V.M., D.Theol., Senior Lecturer, School of Theology, Australian Catholic University, Brisbane. Director of Biblical Studies, St Paul's Theological College, Brisbane, Australia

Joseph A. Fitzmyer, S.J., Ph.D., Professor Emeritus of New Testament, The Catholic University of America, Washington, DC, USA

Timothy A. Friedrichsen, S.T.D., Assistant Professor of New Testament, The Catholic University of America, Washington, DC, USA

Francis T. Gignac, S.J., D.Phil., Professor and Director, Biblical Studies, The Catholic University of America, Washington, DC, USA

Anthony J. Kelly, C.Ss.R., D.Theol., Professor of Theology, Australian Catholic University, Brisbane, Australia

Robert Kysar, Ph.D., Bandy Professor Emeritus of Preaching and New Testament, Emory University, Atlanta, GA, USA

Veronica Lawson, R.S.M., Ph.D., Senior Lecturer, Australian Catholic University, Brisbane, Australia

Dorothy A. Lee, Ph.D., Professor of New Testament, United Faculty of Theology, Parkville, Australia

William Loader, D.Theol., Professor of New Testament; Head, School of Social Inquiry, Murdoch University, Western Australia

Frank J. Matera, Ph.D., Professor of New Testament, The Catholic University of America, Washington, DC, USA

Gail O'Day, Ph.D., Associate Dean of Academic Affairs and A.H. Shatford Professor of New Testament and Preaching, Candler School of Theology, Emory University, Atlanta, GA, USA

John Painter, Ph.D., Professor of Theology, Charles Sturt University, NSW, Australia

Elaine M. Wainwright, Ph.D., Foundation Professor of Theology, University of Auckland, New Zealand

FRANCIS JAMES MOLONEY, S.D.B.

Cursus Vitae

1940   Born in Melbourne, Victoria, Australia.

1957   Graduated from St. Bernard's Christian Brothers College, Essendon.

1958   First Year of a Bachelor of Arts Course, University of Melbourne.

1959-60 Salesian Congregation formation program.

1961-62 Philosophical Studies and Teacher Training.

1963-66 Full-time teacher in the senior secondary section of Salesian College "Rupertswood," Sunbury, Victoria.

1966-70 Theological studies at the Salesian Pontifical University, Rome, Italy.

1969   Awarded Bachelor's Degree (B.A.), *magna cum laude*.

1970   Awarded Licence in Sacred Theology (S.T.L.), *magna cum laude*.

1970   Ordained Priest in Melbourne by James Cardinal Knox, Archbishop of Melbourne (July 11).

1970-72 Biblical studies at the Pontifical Biblical Institute, Rome. Licence in Sacred Scripture (S.S.L.), *magna cum laude*.

         (a) Licence Paper: "The Suffering Servant and the Son of Man in Mark 10:45"

         (b) Thesis: "The Christological Re-interpretation of Psalm 8."

1972-75 Faculty of Theology, University of Oxford, England. Doctoral research carried out under the direction of Prof. Morna D. Hooker. Doctoral thesis: *The Johannine Son of Man*. Defended before Prof. C. K. Barrett and Rev. J. L. Houlden (July).

1976   Doctor of Philosophy (D. Phil. [Oxon]) conferred on 17th January.

1976   Appointed by the Australian Episcopal Commission on Ecumenical Affairs to the Roman Catholic - Uniting Church of Australia working party.

1976-94 Lecturer in New Testament Studies at Catholic Theological College, Clayton, Victoria, Australia.

1979   Appointed by Pope John Paul II as a Consultor to the Secretariat for Christian Unity. Reappointed in May 1984 for a further quinquennium. Reappointed in May 1989 for a further quinquennium.

1982   Appointed Head of the Biblical Studies Department, Catholic Theological College, Clayton, Victoria, Australia.

1982-88   Member of the Provincial Council of the Australian Salesian Province. Councillor responsible for formation of personnel.

1982-88   Rector the Salesian Theological College, Oakleigh, Victoria.

1983-88   Vice Provincial of the Australian Salesian Province.

1986   Appointed by Pope John Paul II as a member of the International Theological Commission to the Holy See.

1988   Founding Editor of *Pacifica. Australian Theological Studies.*

1988   Appointed Visiting Professor to the École Biblique et Archéologique Française de Jérusalem for 1989-90.

1990   Elected a Fellow of the Australian Academy of the Humanities (F.A.H.A.). "Fellows shall be persons of the highest distinction in scholarship in the field of the humanities whose domicile at the time of their election is in Australia" (*The Australian Academy of the Humanities*, By-law 4 [I]).

1991   Appointed to give the triennial Melbourne College of Divinity public lectures. Series: *Beginning the Good News.*

1992   Appointed a Member of the General Division of the Order of Australia (A.M.) for Service to Religion.

1992   Reappointed by Pope John Paul II to the International Theological Commission to the Holy See.

1992   Appointed Visiting Professor to the Pontifical Biblical Institute, Rome, for 1993-94.

1994   Appointed Foundation Professor of Theology, Australian Catholic University.

1999   Appointed Professor of New Testament, The Catholic University of America, Washington, DC, USA.

2001   Elected a Member of group: "Biblical Theologians."

2001   Elected the President of the Catholic Biblical Association of America.

2002   Appointed to the Katherine Drexel Chair of Religious Studies, The Catholic University of America, Washington, DC, USA.

2003   Appointed Dean of the School of Theology and Religious Studies, The Catholic University of America, Washington, DC, USA.

2004   Awarded Doctorate in Sacred Theology, Honoris Causa, St Mary's Seminary and University, Roland Park, Baltimore, MD, USA.

Visiting Professor at:

- Salesian Pontifical University, Rome, Italy (Regular).
- Gregorian University, Rome, Italy (1976-77).
- Pontifical Institute "Regina Mundi," Rome, Italy (1976-77).
- Yarra Theological Union, Box Hill, Victoria, Australia (Regular).
- United Faculty of Theology, Parkville, Victoria, Australia (1993).
- National Pastoral Institute, Gardenvale, Victoria, Australia (1989).
- Assumption Institute, Rosanna, Victoria, Australia (Regular).
- École Biblique et Archéologique Française, Jerusalem, Israel (1989-90).
- Pontifical Biblical Institute, Rome Italy (1993-94).

Membership in Professional Societies

- Catholic Biblical Association of America (Vice President 2000-2001; President 2001-2002). The first non-USA citizen ever to be elected to this position.
- Society for Biblical Literature.
- Australian Catholic Biblical Association (President, 1980).
- Fellowship for Biblical Studies (President, 1985).
- Societas Novi Testamenti Studiorum.
- Associazione Biblica Italiana.
- Fellow of the Australian Academy of the Humanities.
- Biblical Theologians Association.

A Bibliography of Published Works: 1976-2004

Books

1976   *The Johannine Son of Man.* Biblioteca di Scienze Religiose 14. Rome: Libreria Ateneo Salesiano, 1976. 2d ed. Rome: Libreria Ateneo Salesiano, 1978.

1977   *The Word Became Flesh.* Theology Today Series 14. Dublin/Cork: Mercier Press, 1977.

1980   *Disciples and Prophets. A Biblical Model for the Religious Life.* London: Darton, Longman & Todd, 1980/New York: Crossroad, 1981.

1981   *Discepoli e Profeti. Un Modello Biblico per la Vita Religiosa.* Torino: Elle di Ci, 1981.

Free to Love. Poverty-Chastity-Obedience. London: Darton, Longman and Todd, 1981.

Woman in the New Testament. Homebush: St Paul Publications, 1981.

1983   Edited translation from the original Italian of E. Corsini: *The Apocalypse. The Perennial Revelation of Jesus Christ.* Good News Studies 5. Wilmington: Michael Glazier, 1983.

1984   *A Life of Promise. Poverty-Chastity-Obedience.* Consecrated Life Series 1. Wilmington: Michael Glazier, 1984/London: Darton, Longman & Todd, 1985/Homebush: St Paul Publications, 1985. Repr. Eugene, OR: WIPF and Stock, 2001.

1985   *Woman: First among the Faithful. A New Testament Study.* Melbourne: Dove Communications, 1985/London: Darton, Longman & Todd, 1985/Indiana: Ave Maria Press, 1986. Published under the title *Woman in the New Testament.* Manila: Saint Paul Publications, 1985.

1987   *The Living Voice of the Gospel. The Gospels Today.* Melbourne: Collins-Dove, 1987/London: Darton, Longman & Todd, 1987/New York: Paulist Press, 1987.

1989   *Mary: Woman and Mother.* Homebush: St Paul Publications, 1988/Collegeville: Liturgical Press, 1989.

La Donna: Prima tra i Fedeli. Collana Varia. Torino: Società Editrice Internazionale, 1989.

1990   *A Body Broken for a Broken People. Eucharist in the New Testament.* Melbourne: Collins-Dove, 1990/London: Collins/San Francisco: Harper & Row/Quezon City [Manila]: Claretian Publications, 1991. 2d rev. ed. Peabody: Hendrickson, 1997.

1991   *This is the Gospel of the Lord. Reflections on the Gospel Readings. Year C.* Homebush: St Paul Publications, 1991.

1992   *Beginning the Good News. A narrative approach.* Biblical Studies 1. Homebush: St Paul Publications, 1992/Collegeville: Liturgical Press, 1993.

Quattro vangeli una parola. Collana Varia. Turin: Società Editrice Internazionale, 1992.

This is the Gospel of the Lord. Reflections on the Gospel Readings. Year A. Homebush: St Paul Publications, 1992.

1993   *Belief in the Word. Reading John 1-4.* Minneapolis: Fortress Press, 1993.

This is the Gospel of the Lord. Reflections on the Gospel Readings. Year B. Homebush: St Paul Publications, 1993.

1995 *Reading John. Introducing the Johannine Gospel and Letters.* Melbourne: Harper-Collins, 1995.

1996 *Signs and Shadows. Reading John 5-12.* Minneapolis: Fortress Press, 1996.

1998 *Glory not Dishonor. Reading John 13-21.* Minneapolis: Fortress Press, 1998.

The Gospel of John. Sacra Pagina 4. Collegeville: The Liturgical Press, 1998.

1999 *From James to Jude.* The Peoples' Bible Commentary. Oxford: Bible Reading Fellowship, 1999.

2001 *"A Hard Saying." The Gospels and Culture.* Collegeville: The Liturgical Press, 2001.

2002 *The Gospel of Mark. A Commentary.* Peabody: Hendrickson Publications, 2002.

2003 *The Experience of God in the Johannine Writings.* In collaboration with Anthony J. Kelly. Mahwah: Paulist Press, 2003.

R. E. Brown, *Introduction to the Gospel of John.* Edited, completed and updated by Francis J. Moloney. ABRL. New York: Doubleday, 2003.

2004 *Mark: Storyteller, Interpreter, Evangelist.* Peabody: Hendrickson Publications, 2004.

Articles

1974 "Why Community?" *Supplement to Doctrine and Life* 49 (1974): 19-31.

"The Communities of the Early Church." *Supplement to Doctrine and Life* 50 (1974): 24-30.

"Community Life and the Paschal Mystery." *Supplement to Doctrine and Life* 53 (1974): 29-34.

1975 "The Targum on Psalm 8 and the New Testament." *Salesianum* 37 (1975): 326-336.

"Asking the Scriptures about Religious Life." *Supplement to Doctrine and Life* 58 (1975): 3-12.

"John 6 and the Celebration of the Eucharist." *The Downside Review* 93 (1975): 243-51.

1976 "The Johannine Son of God." *Salesianum* 38 (1976): 71-86.

"The Johannine Son of Man." *Biblical Theology Bulletin* 6 (1976): 177-89.

1977   "A Johannine Son of Man Discussion?" *Salesianum* 39 (1977): 93-102.

"The Gospel of John: A Survey of Current Discussion." *Scripture Bulletin* 11 (1977): 20-25.

"The Fourth Gospel's Presentation of Jesus as 'the Christ' and J. A. T. Robinson's' 'Redating'." *The Downside Review* 95(1977): 239-53.

1978   "The Fullness of a Gift which is Truth (John 1:14, 16-17)." *Catholic Theological Review* 1 (1978): 30-33.

"From Cana to Cana (Jn 2:1 - 4:54) and the Fourth Evangelist's Concept of Correct (and Incorrect) Faith." *Salesianum* 40 (1978): 817-43. Also published in E. A. Livingstone (ed.), *Studia Biblica* 1978. II. Pages 185-123 in *The Gospels: Sixth International Congress on Biblical Studies.* Oxford 3-7 April 1978. JSNTMS 2. Sheffield: JSOT Press, 1980.

1979   "Matthew 19:3-12 and Celibacy. A Redactional and Form Critical Study." *Journal for the Study of the New Testament* (1979): 42-60.

"The Infancy Narratives. Another View of Raymond Brown's 'The Birth of the Messiah'." *The Clergy Review* 64 (1979): 161-66.

1980   "Revisiting John." *Scripture Bulletin* 11 (1980): 9-15.

"The End of the Son of Man?" *The Downside Review* 98 (1980): 280-90.

1981   "The Reinterpretation of Psalm VIII and the Son of Man Debate." *New Testament Studies* 27 (1981): 656-72.

"La preghiera dell'ora di Gesù (Gv. 17)." *Parole di Spirito e Vita* 3 (1981): 167-78.

"The Vocation of the Disciples in the Gospel of Mark." *Salesianum* 43 (1981): 487-516.

"Resurrection and accepted exegetical opinion." *The Australasian Catholic Record* 58 (1981): 191-202.

"Faith in the Risen Jesus." *Salesianum* 43 (1981): 305-16.

"Woman in the New Testament." *Compass* 15 (1981-82): 10-18.

1982   "Dating the Fourth Gospel." *Emeth* 11 (1982): 25-35.

"John 17: The Prayer of Jesus' Hour." *The Clergy Review* 67 (1982): 79-83.

"John 20: A Journey Completed." *The Australasian Catholic Record* 59 (1982): 417-32.

"When is John Talking about Sacraments?" *Australian Biblical Review* 30 (1982): 10-33.

"The infancy narratives in Luke." Pages 1-10 in *The Year of Luke.* Edited by H. McGinlay. Melbourne: Desbooks/Joint Board for Christian Education, 1982.

1983 "John 1:18: 'In the Bosom of' or 'Turned towards' the Father?" *Australian Biblical Review* 31 (1983): 63-71.

"The infancy narrative in Matthew." Pages 1-9 in *The Year of Matthew*. Edited by H. McGinlay. Melbourne: Desbooks/JBCE, 1983.

1984 "Biblical Perspectives on Peace." *Word in Life* 32 (1984): 4-7.

"The Way of the Son of Man (Mark 8:22 to 10:52)." Pages 50-63 in *The Year of Mark*. Edited by H. McGinlay. Melbourne: Desbooks/JBCE, 1984.

1985 "The First Days ... from Cana to Cana (John 1:19 to 4:54)." Pages 9-17 in *The Year of John*. Edited by H. McGinlay. Melbourne: Desbooks/JBCE, 1985.

1986 "'The Living Voice of the Gospel' (*Dei Verbum* 8): Some Reflections on the Dynamism of the Christian Tradition." *The Australasian Catholic Record* 63 (1986): 264-79. Repr. *Salesianum* 48 (1986): 225-54.

"The Structure and Message of John 13:1-38." *Australian Biblical Review* 34 (1986): 1-16.

1987 "The Structure and Message of John 15:1-16:3." Pages 35-49 in *Australian Biblical Review* 35: Studies in Honour of Professor Eric Osborne. Edited by I. Breward - M. O'Brien. 1987.

"To be 'orthodox' in Australia today." *Compass* 21/3 (1987): 1-4.

1988 "Jesus Christ: The question to cultures." *Pacifica* 1 (1988): 15-43.

"A New Testament Reflection on Mary." Pages 9-21 in *Mary: The Great Wave of Mercy*. Edited by F. O'Loughlin. Melbourne: Diocesan Liturgical Center, 1988.

"Jesus and Woman." Pages 53-80 in *Virgo fidelis. Miscellanea di studi mariani in onore di Don Domenico Bertetto, S.D.B.* Edited by M. Cimosa - F. Bergamelli. Bibliotheca "Ephemerides Liturgicae Subsidia" 43. Rome: Edizioni Liturgiche, 1988.

"A Theology of Multiculturalism." Pages 133-46 in *Discovering an Australian Theology*. Edited by P. Malone. Homebush: St Paul's Publications, 1988.

"Whither Catholic Biblical Studies?" *The Australasian Catholic Record* 65 (1988): 83-93.

1989 "The Eucharist as Jesus' Presence to the Broken." *Pacifica* 2 (1989): 152-75.

"Mary in the Fourth Gospel: Woman and Mother." *Salesianum* 51 (1989): 421-40.

"The Motherly Intervention of Mary." Pages 15-40 in *Parola di Dio e Carisma Salesiana*. Edited by C. Bissoli. Rome: Editrice S.D.B., 1989.

"Johannine Theology." Pages 1417-26 in *The New Jerome Biblical Commentary*. Edited by R. E. Brown - J. A. Fitzmyer - R. E. Murphy. Englewood Cliffs: Prentice Hall, 1989.

"The Prophetic Presence of Religious in Australia." Pages 19-80 in *Refounding the Religious Life*. Sydney: Australian Conference of Major Superiors, 1989.

"La Parola di Dio nella vita della Chiesa e nella vita salesiana." *Quaderni di Spiritualità Salesiana* 5 (1989): 5-10.

1990   "Jesus of Nazareth and the Resurrection." Pages 20-26 in *The Cross our Glory*. Edited by F. O'Loughlin. Melbourne: Diocesan Liturgical Center, 1990.

"Jesus of Nazareth and the Resurrection." *Priests and People* 4 (1990): 125-29.

"Reading John 2:13-22: The Purification of the Temple." *Revue Biblique* 97 (1990): 432-52.

"Jesus de Nazaré e a ressurreição." *Communio. Revista Internacional Católica* 7 (1990): 128-36.

1991   "A Sacramental Reading of John 13:1-38." *The Catholic Biblical Quarterly* 53 (1991): 237-56.

"Reading Eucharistic Texts in Mark." *Proceedings of the Irish Biblical Association* 15 (1991): 7-24.

"Reading Eucharistic Texts in Luke." *Proceedings of the Irish Biblical Association* 15 (1991): 25-45.

"Narrative Criticism of the Gospels." *Pacifica* 4 (1991): 181-201.

"The Dead Sea Scrolls and the Story of Jesus." Pages 1-21 in *St Albert's Lecture 1991*. The University of New England, 1991.

"La Eucaristía come presencia de Jesús para los rotos." *Phase* 31 (1991): 183-202.

"To Stand at the Periphery." *Compass* 25/4 (1991): 26-27.

"Beginning the Gospel of Matthew." *Salesianum* 54 (1992): 341-59.

1992   "Women priests: What the New Testament Says." *The Catholic Leader* (February 16, 1992): 13.

"Seeking the Living among the Dead." *Eureka Street* 2/3 (April 1992): 4-5.

"John's Message ... for Today." *The Catholic Leader* (April 22, 1992): 11.

"The Strangeness of Jesus Christ." Pages 112-17 in The Australian Catholic Bishops' Committee for Migrant Affairs - Australian Council of Churches Refugee and Migrant Services, *Proceedings of the "Welcome Stranger" National Forum On Refugees*. Sydney 19th-21st June 1992. Canberra: Research Department Australian Catholic Bishops Conference, 1992.

"Who is 'The Reader' in/of the Fourth Gospel?" *Australian Biblical Review* 40 (1992): 20-33.

1993   "Catholic Biblical Scholarship - Fifty Years On." *The Australasian Catholic Record* 70/3 (1993): 275-88.

1994   "John 18:15-27: A Johannine View of the Church." *The Downside Review* 112 (1994): 231-48.

"Biblical Reflections on Marriage." *Compass* 28 (1994): 10-16.

1995   "The Direction of Theology at Australian Catholic University." *Compass* 29 (1995): 6-9.

"The Johannine Passion and the Christian Community." *Salesianum* 57 (1995): 25-61.

"The Faith of Martha and Mary. A Narrative Approach to John 11:17-40." *Biblica* 75 (1994): 471-93.

"Life, Healing, and the Bible: A Christian Challenge." *Pacifica* 8 (1995): 315-34.

1996   "Refinishing Martha and Mary: A Literary Approach to John 11:17-40." Pages 29-53 in M. Griffith and J. Tulip (eds.), *Religion, Literature and the Arts. Conference Proceedings. 2nd Australian International Conference 1995.* Sydney: RLA Project, 1996.

"Eucharist in the Year of Tolerance. What are we doing in Memory of Jesus?" Pages 1-19 in *Victor J. Couch Lecture.* North Sydney: Australian Catholic University, 1996.

"La sequela di Cristo." Pages 69-76 in *Parola di Dio e Spirito Salesiano. Ricerca sulla dimensione biblica delle Costituzioni della Famiglia Salesiana.* Edited by J. Bartolomé and F. Perrenchio. Torino: Elle di Ci, 1996.

1997   "To Make God Known. A Reading of John 17:1-26." *Salesianum* 59 (1997): 463-89.

"The Function of Prolepsis in the Interpretation of John 6." Pages 129-48 in *The Interpretation of John 6.* Edited by R. A. Culpepper. Biblical Interpretation Supplement Series; Leiden: E. J. Brill, 1997.

"Who is 'The Reader' in/of the Fourth Gospel?" Pages 219-33 in *The Interpretation of John.* Edited by J. Ashton. Studies in New Testament Interpretation; 2d ed. Edinburgh: T&T Clark, 1997.

1998   "The Function of John 13-17 within the Johannine Narrative." Pages 43-66 in *"What is John?" Volume II: Literary and Social Readings of the Fourth Gospel.* Edited by F. F. Segovia. Symposium 7. Atlanta: Scholars Press, 1998.

"To Teach the Text: The New Testament in a New Age." *Pacifica* 11 (1998): 159-80.

"A Response to Mark Brett's 'Response'." *Pacifica* 11 (1988): 316-23.

1999   "An Adventure with Nicodemus." Pages 97-110 in *The Personal Voice in Biblical Interpretation*. Edited by I.-R. Kitzberger. London: Routledge, 1999.

"The Johannine Paraclete and Jesus." Pages 213-28 in *Dummodo Christus annuntietur. Studi in Onore del Prof. Jozef Heriban*. Edited by A. Strus and R. Blatnicky. BibSciRel 146; Rome: LAS, 1998.

"Salesians Beyond 2000." *Journal of Salesian Studies* 10 (1999): 1-18.

2000   "The Fourth Gospel and the Jesus of History." *New Testament Studies* 46 (2000): 42-58.

"Where Does One Look? Reflections on some recent Johannine scholarship." *Salesianum* 62 (2000): 223-51.

"The Scriptural Basis of Jubilee, Part I: The First Testament – the End of Servitude." *Irish Theological Quarterly* 65 (2000): 99-110.

"The Scriptural Basis of Jubilee, Part II: The Second Testament – at What Price?" *Irish Theological Quarterly* 65 (2000): 231-44.

"Joseph A Fitzmyer, S. J., Celebrating Eighty Years." *CBQ* 62 (2000): 607-8.

"Books, Articles and Reviews by Joseph A. Fitzmyer, S. J. Published since 1985." *CBQ* 62 (2000): 609-20.

2001   "'He is going before you into Galilee': Mark 16:6-8 and the Christian Community." Pages 108-21 in *Be My Witnesses. Essays in Honour of Dr. Sebastian Karotemprel SDB*. Edited by J. Varickasseril and M. Kariapuram. Shillong: Vendrame Institute Publications, 2001.

"Mark 6:6b-30: Mission, the Baptist, and Failure." *CBQ* 63 (2001): 647-63.

2002   "L'Écriture Sainte et le Magistère: une relation mouvementée." Pages 493-505 in *La Responsabilité des Théologiens. Mélanges offerts à Joseph Doré*. Edited by F. Bousquet, H.-J. Gagey, G. Médevielle, and J.-L. Souletie. Paris: Desclée, 2002.

"'He is going before you into Galilee.' Mark 16:6-8 and the Christian Community." Pages 64-75 in *Charism. Leadership and Community*. Proceedings of the Second Annual Convention of the Catholic Biblical Association of the Philippines; Tagaytay City, 20-22 July, 2001; Manila: CBAP, 2002.

"The Twelve, Mission and Failure in Mark 6:6b-30." Pages 159-89 in *Prophecy and Passion: Essays in Honour of Athol Gill*. Edited by D. Neville; Melbourne: Australian Theological Forum, 2002.

"Narrative and Discourse at the Feast of Tabernacles: John 7:1-8:59." Pages 155-72 in *Word, Theology and Community in John. Studies in Honor of Robert Kysar*. Edited by J. Painter, R. A. Culpepper and F. F. Segovia. St Louis: Chalice Press, 2002.

"Telling God's Story: The Fourth Gospel." Pages 107-22 in *The Forgotten God: The God of Jesus Christ in New Testament Theology: Essays in Honor of Paul J. Achtemeier on the Occasion of his Seventy-fifth Birthday.* Edited by A. A. Das and F. J. Matera. Louisville: Westminster John Knox Press, 2002.

"'The Jews' in the Fourth Gospel: Another Perspective." *Pacifica* 15 (2002): 16-36.

"John and the Lectionary." *The Bible Today* 40 (2002): 72-79.

"Israel, the People and the Jews in the Fourth Gospel." Pages 351-64 in *Israel und seine Heilstraditionen im Vierten Evangelium.* Edited by A. Strotmann, M. Labahn and K. Scholtissek. Paderborn: Schöningh, 2002.

2003 "Conversion in the Bible." Pages 4:231-34 in *The New Catholic Encyclopedia.* Edited by B. R. Marthaler. Washington, DC: The Catholic University of America, 2003.

"John, Apostle, St." Pages 7:895-97 in *The New Catholic Encyclopedia.*

"Johannine Comma, The." Pages 7:891-92 in *The New Catholic Encyclopedia.*

"John, Epistles of." Pages 7:897-902 in *The New Catholic Encyclopedia.*

"John, Gospel according to." Pages 7:902-13 in *The New Catholic Encyclopedia.*

"Johannine Writings, The." Pages 7:892-95 in *The New Catholic Encyclopedia.*

"Salesians." Pages 12:614-15 in *The New Catholic Encyclopedia.*

"Literary Strategies in the Markan Passion Narrative (Mark 14,1-15,47)." *Studien zum Neuen Testament und seiner Umwelt* 28 (2003): 5-25.

"Can Everyone be Wrong? Reading John 11:1-12:8." *New Testament Studies* 49 (2003): 505-27.

Book reviews

1973 G. Kulicke - K. Matthiae - P. Sänger (eds.), *Bericht von der Theologie. Resultate, Probleme, Konzepte.* In *Regulae Benedicti Studia* 3 (1973): 144-45.

1975 M. D. Hooker - C. Hickling (eds.), *What about the New Testament? Essays in Honour of Christopher Evans.* In *The Downside Review* 93 (1975): 237-38.

J. McHugh, *The Mother of Jesus in the New Testament.* In *The Epworth Review* 3 (1975): 123-24.

1976 B. Chudoba, *Of Time, Light and Hell. Essays in Interpretation of the Christian Message.* In *Salesianum* 38 (1976): 186.

P. von der Osten Sacken, *Römer 8 als Beispiel paulinische Soteriologie.* In *The Catholic Biblical Quarterly* 38 (1976): 125-27.

L. Oberlinner, *Historische Überlieferung und christologische Aussage: Zur Frage der*

"Brüder Jesu" in der Synopse. In *The Catholic Biblical Quarterly* 38 (1976): 582-83.

A. Nissen, *Gott und der Nächste im antiken Judentum. Untersuchungen zum Doppelgebot der Liebe.* In *Salesianum* 38 (1976): 416-18.

J. Alberto Soggin, *Old Testament and Oriental Studies.* In *Salesianum* 38 (1976): 427-28.

N. Gill, *The Social Context of Theology: A Methodological Enquiry.* In *Salesianum* 38 (1976): 428-30.

G. Fischer, *Die himmlischen Wohnungen. Untersuchungen zu Joh 14,2f.* In *Salesianum* 38 (1976): 701-2.

R. Mahoney, *Two Disciples at the Tomb. The Background and Message of John 20,1-10.* In *Salesianum* 38 (1976): 702-4.

U. B. Müller, *Die Geschichte der Christologie in der Johanneischen Gemeinde.* In *Salesianum* 38 (1976): 704-5.

W. Resenhöft, *Der Tag des Menschensohnes. Die Geschichte Jesu im Wortlaut der Urquellen.* In *Salesianum* 38 (1976): 705-6.

R. Schnackenburg, *Das Johannesevangelium, III. Teil, Kommentar zu Kap 13-21.* In *Salesianum* 38 (1976): 706-8.

G. Vermes, *The Dead Sea Scrolls in English.* In *Salesianum* 38 (1976): 708.

A. Vögtle - R. Pesch, *Wie kam es zum Osterglauben?* In *Salesianum* 38 (1976): 708-10.

W. Barclay, *The Gospels and Acts.* In *Salesianum* 38 (1976): 965-67.

J. Bodson, *Regards sur L'Évangile de Saint Jean.* In *Salesianum* 38 (1976): 967.

J. Hainz (ed.), *Kirche im Werden. Studien zum Amt und Gemeinde im Neuen Testament.* In *Salesianum* 38 (1976): 968-69.

M. Lattke, *Einheit im Wort. Die Spezifische Bedeutung von "agape" und "filein" im Johannes-Evangelium.* In *Salesianum* 38 (1976): 969-70.

J. T. Sanders, *Ethics in the New Testament.* In *Salesianum* 38 (1976): 973-74.

1977   E. Arens, *The ELTHON-Sayings in the Synoptic Tradition: A Historico-critical Investigation.* In *The Catholic Biblical Quarterly* 39 (1977): 272-73.

1978   R. E. Brown, *The Birth of the Messiah.* In *Salesianum* 40 (1978): 684-86.

Jan-A. Bühner, *Der Gesandte und sein Weg im 4. Evangelium.* In *Salesianum* 40 (1978): 686-87.

M. Hengel, *Der Sohn Gottes.* In *Salesianum* 40 (1978): 691-92.

V. Salmon, *The Fourth Gospel. A History of the Textual Tradition of the Original Greek Gospel.* In *Salesianum* 40 (1978): 693-94.

J. P. Miranda, *Die Sendung Jesu im vierten Evangelium.* In *Salesianum* 40 (1978): 964-65.

1979   M. L. Appold, *The Oneness Motif in the Fourth Gospel*. In *Salesianum* 41 (1979): 556-57.

S. A. Panimolle, *Lettura Pastorale del Vangelo di Giovanni,* Vol. I. In *Biblica* 60 (1979): 279-81.

S. S. Smalley, *John: Evangelist and Interpreter*. In *Scripture Bulletin* 9 (1979): 324-25.

J. D. M. Derrett, *Studies in the New Testament,* Vol. I. In Salesianum 41 (1979): 557.

J. D. G. Dunn, *Jesus and the Spirit*. In *Salesianum* 41 (1979): 557-58.

D. Marzotto, *L'unità degli uomini nel Vangelo di Giovanni*. In *Salesianum* 41 (1979): 558-59.

A. Serra, *Contributi dell'antica letteratura Giudaica per l'esegesi di Giovanni 2,1-12 e 19,25-27*. In *Salesianum* 41 (1979): 562-63.

A. Sicari, *Matrimonio e verginità nella rivelazione*. In *Salesianum* 41 (1979): 563-64.

W. S. Towner, *How God Deals with Evil*. In *Salesianum* 41 (1979): 565.

J. R. W. Stott, *Christ the Controversialist. A Study of the Essentials of the Evangelical Religion*. In *Salesianum* 41 (1979): 565.

D. R. Griffin, God, *Power and Evil: A Process Theodicy*. In *Salesianum* 41 (1979): 571.

1980   C. K. Barrett, *The Gospel According to St. John*. In *Scripture Bulletin* 10 (1980): 38.

C. K. Barrett, *The Gospel According to St. John*. In *The Catholic Biblical Quarterly* 42 (1980): 261-62

M. de Dreuille, *From East to West. Man in Search of the Absolute*. In *Scripture Bulletin* 11 (1980): 25.

R. E. Brown, *The Community of the Beloved Disciple*. In *The Downside Review* 98 (1980): 164-65.

C. Brown (ed.), *History, Criticism and Faith. Four Exploratory Studies*. In *Salesianum* 42 (1980): 669-70.

J. Ernst, *Herr der Geschichte: Perspektiven der lukanischen Eschatologie*. In *Salesianum* 42 (1980): 929.

J. Carmignac, *Le Mirage de l'Eschatologie*. In *Australian Biblical Review* 28 (1980): 64-65.

A. George, *Études sur L'Oeuvre de Luc*. In *Scripture Bulletin* 11 (1980): 38-39.

J.-M. Guillaume, *Luc interprète des anciennes traditions sur la résurrection de Jésus*. In *Scripture Bulletin* 11 (1980): 39-40.

1981   A. Y. Collins, *The Apocalypse*. In *The Catholic Biblical Quarterly* 43 (1981): 125-26.

W. Langbrandtner, *Weltferner Gott oder Gott der Liebe*. In *Salesianum* 42 (1980): 935-36.

A. A. Trites, *The New Testament Concept of Witness*. In *Salesianum* 42 (1980): 942.

E. Leidig, *Jesu Gespräch mit der Samaritanerin und weitere Gespräche im Johannesevangelium*. In *The Catholic Biblical Quarterly* 43 (1981): 649-50.

1982 A. Q. Morton - J. McClennan, *The Genesis of John*. In *The Catholic Biblical Quarterly* 44 (1982): 519-20.

P. Garnet, *Salvation and Atonement in the Qumran Scrolls*. In *Salesianum* 44 (1982): 556.

S. Safrai - M. Stern (eds.), *The Jewish People in the First Century*, Vol. 2. In *Salesianum* 44 (1982): 587-88.

A. Oppenheimer, *The 'Am Ha-'Aretz. A Study in the Social History of the Jewish People in the Hellenistic-Roman Period*. In *Salesianum* 44 (1982): 814-15.

F. T. Fallon, *The Enthronement of Sabaoth. Jewish Elements in Gnostic Creation Myths*. In *Salesianum* 44 (1982): 839.

U. Mauser, *Gottesbild und Menschwerdung. Eine Untersuchung zur Einheit des Alten und Neuen Testament*. In *Salesianum* 44 (1982): 845.

A. Polag, *Die Christologie der Logienquelle*. In *Salesianum* 44 (1982): 848-49.

1983 X. Léon-Dufour, *Le partage du pain eucharistique: Selon le Nouveau Testament*. In *The Catholic Biblical Quarterly* 46 (1984): 350-52.

1984 S. Brown, *The Origins of Christianity. A Historical Introduction to the New Testament*. In *The Advocate* (8th November, 1984): 8.

P. S. Minear, *Matthew: The Teacher's Gospel*. In *The Advocate* (8th November, 1984): 8.

J. A. Grassi, *Rediscovering the Impact of Jesus' Death: Clues from the Gospel Audiences*. In *Pacifica* 1 (1988): 223-24.

W. Loader, *The Christmas Stories*. In *Pacifica* 1 (1988): 345-46.

1989 H. Bloem, *Die Ostererzählung des Matthäus*. In *The Catholic Biblical Quarterly* 52 (1989): 739-40.

V. C. Pfitzner, *The Gospel According to St John*. In *Lutheran Theological Journal* 23 (1989): 87-89.

J. L. Staley, *The Print's First Kiss. A Rhetorical Investigation of the Implied Reader in the Fourth Gospel*. In *Australian Biblical Review* 37 (1989): 75-77.

T. Okure, *The Johannine Approach to Mission. A Contextual Study of John 4:1-42*. In *Australian Biblical Review* 37 (1989): 77-80.

1990 I. de la Potterie, *The Hour of Jesus*. In *Pacifica* 3 (1990): 97-99.

S. Freyne, *Galilee, Jesus and the Gospels: Literary Approaches and Historical Investigations*. In *Pacifica* 3 (1990): 240-42.

M. Hengel, *The Zealots: Investigations into the Jewish Freedom Movement*. In *Pacifica* 3 (1990): 340-41.

J. L. Staley, *The Print's First Kiss. A Rhetorical Investigation of the Implied Reader in the Fourth Gospel*. In *Revue Biblique* 97 (1990): 617-18.

T. Okure, *The Johannine Approach to Mission. A Contextual Study of John 4:1-42*. In *Revue Biblique* 98 (1990): 290-92.

J. Murphy-O'Connor - J. Taylor, *The École Biblique and the New Testament. A Century of Scholarship (1890-1990)*. In *Revue Biblique* 97 (1990): 466-70.

K.-J. Kuhn, *Christologie und Wunder. Untersuchungen zu Joh 1,35-51*. In *Revue Biblique* 97 (1990): 618-19.

1991   G. van Belle, *Johannine Bibliography 1966-1985. A Cumulative Bibliography on the Fourth Gospel*. In *The Catholic Biblical Quarterly* 53 (1991): 348-49.

W. Loader, *The Christology of the Fourth Gospel*. In *Pacifica* 4 (1991): 108-10.

1992   B. Witherington, III, *The Christology of Jesus*. In *Pacifica* 5 (1992): 229-32.

D. R. A. Hare, *The Son of Man Tradition*. In *Pacifica* 6 (1993): 214-16.

Association Catholique Française pour l'Etude de la Bible, *Origine et postérité de l'évangile de Jean*. In *The Catholic Biblical Quarterly* 54 (1992): 606-7.

B. Byrne, *Lazarus. A Contemporary Reading of John 11:1-46*. In *Pacifica* 5 (1992): 324-25.

1993   F. Manns, *L'Évangile de Jean à la lumière du Judaïsme*. In *Revue Biblique* 100 (1993): 120-24.

J. Painter, *The Quest for the Messiah. The History, Literature and Theology of the Johannine Community*. In *Pacifica* 6 (1993): 106-9.

D. Burkett, *The Son of the Man in the Gospel of John*. In *The Journal of Theological Studies* 44 (1993): 259-61.

D. Burkett, *The Son of the Man in the Gospel of John*. In *Pacifica* 6 (1993): 109-12.

J. C. Thomas, *Footwashing in John 13 and the Johannine Community*. In *Pacifica* 6 (1993): 212-14.

F. F. Segovia, *The Farewell of the Word. The Johannine Call to Abide*. In *The Catholic Biblical Quarterly* 56 (1994): 150-52.

1994   M. Davies, *Rhetoric and Reference in the Fourth Gospel*. In *The Journal of Theological Studies* 45 (1994): 233-37.

U. Schnelle, *Antidocetic Christology in the Gospel of John*. In *Pacifica* 7 (1994): 246-48.

A. J. Malherbe - W. A. Meeks (eds.), *The Future of Christology. Essays in Honor of Leander E. Keck*. In *Pacifica* 7 (1994): 240-41.

A. Link, *"Was redest du mit ihr?" Eine Studie zur Exegese-, Redaktions- und Theologiegeschichte von Joh 4,1-42.* In *The Journal of Theological Studies* 45 (1994): 664-69.

1995 D. Burkett, *The Son of the Man in the Gospel of John.* In *Australian Biblical Review* 40 (1995): 85-87.

C. Niemand, *Die Fusswaschungserzählung des Johannesevangeliums. Untersuchungen zu ihrer Entstehung und Überlieferung im Urchristentum.* In *The Catholic Biblical Quarterly* 57 (1995): 184-86.

M. Hengel, *Die johanneische Frage. Ein Lösungsversuch mit einem Beitrag zur Apokalypse von Jörg Frey.* In *Biblica* 76 (1995): 270-75.

F. Andersen, *Jesus: Our Story.* In *Pacifica* 8 (1995): 360-61.

G. Goosen and M. Tomlinson, *Studying the Gospels: An Introduction.* In *Pacifica* 8 (1995): 361.

C. Hill, *Jesus and the Mystery of Christ: An extended Christology.* In *Pacifica* 8 (1995): 361.

G. O'Collins, *Experiencing Jesus.* In *Pacifica* 8 (1995): 361-62.

R. Leonard, *Beloved Daughters: 100 Years of Papal Teaching,* in *Pacifica* 8 (1995): 362.

A. Murray (ed.), *The New Catechism: Analysis and Commentary.* In *Pacifica* 8 (1995): 362-63.

E. S. Malbon and E. V. McKnight (eds.), *The New Literary Criticism and the New Testament.* In *Australian Biblical Review* 43 (1995): 91-92.

1996 The Bible and Culture Collective, *The Postmodern Bible.* In *Pacifica* 9 (1996): 98-101.

D. H. Juel, *A Master of Surprise: Mark Interpreted.* In *Pacifica* 9 (1996): 104-6.

G. Korting, *Die esoterische Struktur des Johannesevangeliums.* In *The Catholic Biblical Quarterly* 58 (1996): 159-60.

K. Berger, *Jesus and the Dead Sea Scrolls: the Truth under Lock and Key?* In *Pacifica* 9 (1996): 117-18.

1997 C. R. Koester, *Symbolism in the Fourth Gospel: Meaning, Mystery, Community.* In *The Catholic Biblical Quarterly* 59 (1997): 162-64.

1998 R. Hardiman (ed.), *The Years of the Year: The Paschal Mystery Celebrated in Christian Worship.* In *Pastoral Liturgy* 28:2-3 (1998): 7.

A. Obermann, *Die christologische Erfüllung der Schrift im Johannesevangelium: Eine Untersuchung zur johanneischen Hermeneutik anhand der Schriftzitate.* In *The Catholic Biblical Quarterly* 60 (1998): 375-77.

L. D. McIntosh, *Religion and Theology: A Guide to Current Reference Resources.* In *Pacifica* 11 (1998): 115-16.

P. N. Anderson, *The Christology of the Fourth Gospel: Its Unity and Disunity in the Light of John 6*. In *Pacifica* 11 (1998): 335-38.

D. M. H. Tovey, *Narrative Art and Act in the Fourth* Gospel. In *Pacifica* 11 (1998): 333-35.

A. Obermann, *Die christologische Erfüllung der Schrift im Johannesevangelium: Eine Untersuchung zur johanneischen Hermeneutik anhand der Schriftzitate*. In *Pacifica* 11 (1998): 83-85.

B. Byrne, *Romans*. In *Pacifica* 11 (1998): 85-88.

M.-E. Boismard, *Le Martyre de Jean L'Apôtre*. In *AusBR* 46 (1998): 91.

1999   C. Dietzfelbinger, *Der Abschied des Kommenden: Eine Auslegung der johanneischen Abschiedsreden*. In *Pacifica* 12 (1999): 90-93.

A. J. Köstenburg, *The Missions of Jesus and the Disciples according to the Fourth Gospel. With Implications for the Fourth Gospel's Purpose and the Mission of the Contemporary Church*. In *Pacifica* 12 (1999): 93-95.

J. Lieu, *The Gospel of Luke*. In *Pacifica* 12 (1999): 227-29.

J. Painter, *Just James. The Brother of Jesus in History and Tradition*. In *Australian Biblical Review* 47 (1999): 87-88.

2000   M. Lang, *Johannes und die Synoptiker: Eine redaktionsgeschichtliche Analyse von Joh 18-20 vor dem markinischen und lukanischen Hintergrund*. In *The Catholic Biblical Quarterly* 62 (2000): 364-66.

2001   F. Lozada, *A Literary Reading of John 5. Text as Construction*. In *The Catholic Biblical Quarterly* 63 (2001): 554-56.

2002   M. Sasse, *Der Menschensohn im Evangelium nach Johannes*. In *Journal of Theological Studies* 53 (2002): 210-15.

K. Scholtissek, *In Ihm sein und bleiben. Die Sprache der Immanenz in den johanneischen Schriften*. In *The Catholic Biblical Quarterly* 64 (2002): 394-95.

C. R. Koester, *Revelation and the End of All Things*. In *New Theology Review* 15/4 (2002): 87-88.

S. Hamid-Khani, *Revelation and Concealment of Christ. A Theological Enquiry into the Elusive Language of the Fourth Gospel*. In *Journal of Theological Studies* 53 (2002): 643-49.

2003   R. Kysar, *Preaching John*. In *New Theology Review* 16 (2003): 92-93.

A. C. C. Ndayango, *Wunder Glaube und Leben bei Johannes. Eine exegetisch-hermeneutische Studie am Beispiel von Joh 3 im Hinblick auf die Inkulturationsaufgabe*. In *The Catholic Biblical Quarterly* 65 (2003): 296-97.

2004   J. S. Webster, *Ingesting Jesus: Eating and Drinking in the Gospel of John*. In *The Catholic Biblical Quarterly* 66 (2004): 333-34.

Tape and video recordings

1979　*The Evangelical Counsels: The Vows of Poverty, Chastity and Obedience.* Melbourne: St Paul Publications, 1979. 3 audio cassettes.

　　Introduction to Mark's Gospel. Melbourne: Pastoral Formation Center, 1979. 1 audio cassette.

　　Saint John's Gospel. Melbourne: Pastoral Formation Center, 1979. 6 audio cassettes.

1981　*Mary: A Gospel Portrait.* Melbourne: St Paul Publications: 1981. 2 audio cassettes. Also published in Canfield, Ohio: Alba House Cassettes, 1983.

　　Introduzione generale alla lettura della Bibbia. Melbourne: Centro Italiano di Rinnovamento Cattolico, 1981. 3 audio cassettes.

1982　*To Follow Jesus: Discipleship according to the Gospel of Mark.* Melbourne: St Paul Publications, 1982. 2 audio cassettes.

　　Introduzione al Pentateuco. Melbourne: Centro Italiano di Rinnovamento Cattolico, 1982. 1 audio cassette.

　　Il linguaggio umano della Bibbia. Melbourne: Centro Italiano di Rinnovamento Cattolico, 1982. 1 audio cassette.

　　La Bibbia è Parola di Dio: in che senso? Melbourne: Centro Italiano di Rinnovamento Cattolico, 1982. 1 audio cassette.

　　Il canone dell'Antico e del Nuovo Testamento. La Bibbia Cattolica e le Bibbie protestanti sono diversi? Melbourne: Centro Italiano di Rinnovamento Cattolico, 1982. 1 audio cassette.

1983　*Happy are those who hear the Word of God and Keep it. Small Group Reflection* on *Luke's Gospel.* Melbourne: Catholic Adult Education Center, 1983. 2 audio cassettes.

1985　*Out of His Treasure things New and Old. Small Group Reflection Program on Matthew's Gospel.* Melbourne: Catholic Adult Education Center, 1985. 2 audio cassettes.

　　But you, who do you say that I am? Small Group Reflection on Mark's Gospel. Melbourne: Catholic Adult Education Center, 1985. 2 audio cassettes.
　　The Vows in the Life of an Apostolic Religious. Homebush: Daughters of St Paul, 1985. 2 audio cassettes.

1986　*Camminando con Gesù. Vangelo secondo Marco.* Homebush: Daughters of St Paul, 1986. 4 audio cassettes.

1986　*We have seen his Glory. Stories from John's Gospel.* Melbourne: Catholic Adult Education Center, 1986. 2 audio cassettes.

Reading Mark's Gospel Today. Melbourne: Pastoral Formation Center, 1986. 1 audio cassette.

1989   *The Living Voice of John.* Canberra: Catholic Institute for Ministry, 1989. 4 audio cassettes.

ABBREVIATIONS

AB	Anchor Bible
ABD	*Anchor Bible Dictionary*
ABR	*Australian Biblical Review*
ABRL	The Anchor Bible Reference Library
ACNT	Augsburg Commentary on the New Testament
AJP	*American Journal of Philology*
An Bib	*Analecta biblica*
ANTC	Abingdon New Testament Commentaries
APOT	*The Apocrypha and Pseudepigrapha of the Old Testament.* Edited by R. H. Charles. 2 vols. Oxford, 1913
AUUHR	Acta Universitatis Upsaliensis, Historia Religionum
BBC	Blackwell Bible Commentaries
BDAG	Bauer, W., F. W. Danker, W. F. Arndt, and F. W. Gingrich. *Greek-English Lexicon of the New Testament and Other Early Christian Literature.* 3d ed. Chicago, 1999
BDF	F. Blass and A. Debrunner, *A Greek Grammar of the New Testament and Other Early Christian Literature.* Revised and translated by R. W. Funk. Chicago: University of Chicago Press, 1961
BELS	Bibliotheca Ephemerides Liturgicae, Subsidia
BeO	*Bibbia e oriente*
BETL	Bibliotheca ephemeridum theologicarum lovaniensium
Bib	*Biblica*
BibIntS	Biblical Interpretation Series
BibVC	*Bible et vie chrétienne*
BNTC	Black's New Testament Commentaries
BSac	*Bibliotheca sacra*
BSR	Biblioteca di Scienze Religiose
BT	The Bible Translator
BTB	*Biblical Theology Bulletin*
BZ	*Biblische Zeitschrift*
BZNW	Beihefte zur Zeitschrift für die neutestamentliche Wissenschaft
CahRB	Cahiers de la Revue biblique
CBQ	*Catholic Biblical Quarterly*
CentBib	Century Bible
CNT	Companions to the New Testament

CTAP	Cahiers Théologiques de l'Actualité Protestante
EB	Études Bibliques
EDNT	*Exegetical Dictionary of the New Testament.* Edited by H. Balz, G. Schneider. E. T. Grand Rapids, 1990-1993
EKKNT	Evangelisch-katholischer Kommentar zum Neuen Testament
EstBib	*Estudios biblicos*
ETL	*Ephemerides theologicae Lovanienses*
EvQ	*Evangelical Quarterly*
EWNT	*Exegetisches Wörterbuch zum Neuen Testament*
ExAud	*Ex auditu*
ExpTim	*Expository Times*
FF	Foundations and Facets
FilNeot	*Filologia Neotestamentaria*
FTS	Frankfurter Theologische Studien
GBS	Guides to Biblical Scholarship
GPT	Growing Points in Theology
GNC	Good News Commentaries
GRRS	Graeco-Roman Religion Series
GTS	Gettysburg Theological Studies
HeyJ	*Heythrop Journal*
HNT	Handbuch zum Neuen Testament
HT	Helps for Translators
HTCNT	Herders Theological Commentary on the New Testament
HTR	*Harvard Theological Review*
HTS	*Harvard Theological Studies*
IBC	Interpretation: A Biblical Commentary for Teaching and Preaching
IBT	Interpreting Biblical Texts
ICC	International Critical Commentary
IJPCP	*International Journal of Personal Construct Psychology*
IkaZ	*Internationale katholische Zeitschrift*
Int	*Interpretation*
ISPCK	Indian Society for Promoting Christian Knowledge
JAOS	*Journal of the American Oriental Society*
JBL	*Journal of Biblical Literature*
JECS	*Journal of Early Christian Studies*
JPJRS	*Jnanadeepa: Pune Journal of Religious Studies*
JSNT	*Journal for the Study of the New Testament*
JSNTSup	Journal for the Study of the New Testament: Supplement Series
JSOTSup	Journal for the Study of the Old Testament: Supplement Series
JTS	*Journal of Theological Studies*
LAS	Libreria Ateneo Salesiano
LCL	Loeb Classical Library
LTMP	Louvain Theological and Pastoral Monographs
MelT	*Melita theological*
MNTC	Moffat New Testament Commentary
MSR	*Mélanges de Science Religieuse*
NC	Narrative Commentaries

NCB	New Century Bible
NEchtB	Die Neue Echter Bibel
Neot	*Neotestamentica*
NICNT	New International Commentary on the New Testament
NIB	*The New Interpreter's Bible*
NIGTC	New International Greek Testament Commentary
NovT	*Novum Testamentum*
NovTSup	Supplements to Novum Testamentum
NTAbh	Neutestamentliche Abhandlungen
NTD	Neue Testament Deutsch
NTM	New Testament Message
NTOA	Novum Testamentum et Orbis Antiquus
NTS	*New Testament Studies*
ÖTBK	Ökumenischer Taschenbuchkommentar zum Neuen Testament
OTP	*Old Testament Pseudepigrapha.* Edited by J. H. Charlesworth. 2 vols. New York, 1983
PG	Patrologia graeca
PGC	Pelican Gospel Commentaries
PSTJ	*Perkins School of Theology Journal*
PTMS	Pittsburgh Theological Monograph Series
PVTG	Pseudepigrapha Veteris Testamenti Graece
RB	*Revue biblique*
RTP	*Revue de théologie et de philosophie*
Sal	*Salesianum*
SANT	Studien zum Alten und Neuen Testaments
SBFA	Studium Biblicum Franciscanum Analecta
SBLDS	Society of biblical Literature Dissertation Series
SBLMS	Society of biblical Literature Monograph Series
SBLRBS	Society of Biblical Literature Resources for Biblical Study
SBLSymS	Society of Biblical Literature Symposium Series
SBLTT	Society of biblical Literature Texts and Translations
ScEs	*Science et esprit*
SedB	*Sedos Bulletin*
SJT	*Scottish Journal of Theology*
SNTMS	Society for New Testament Studies Monograph Series
SNTW	Studies in the New Testament and its World
SO	Symbolae Osloenses
SP	Sacra Pagina
Str-B	Strack, H. L., and P. Billerbeck. *Kommentar zum Neuen Testament aus Talmud und Midrash.* 6 vols. Munich, 1922-1961
SupDL	*Supplement to Doctrine and Life*
SVTP	Studia in Veteris Testamenti pseudepigraphica
TC	Thornapple Commentaries
TDNT	*Theological Dictionary of the New Testament*
TE	*The Theological Educator*
ThTo	*Theology Today*
TS	*Theological Studies*

TSNS	Texts and Studies New Series
TT	Texts and Translations
TWNT	*Theologische Wörterbuch zum Neuen Testament*
UBT	Understanding Biblical Themes
VEWS	Vidyajyoti Education and Welfare Society
VJTR	*Vidyajyoti: Journal of Theological Reflection*
WBC	Word Biblical Commentary
WMANT	Wissenschaftliche Monographien zum Alten und Neuen Testament
WTJ	*Westminster Theological Journal*
WUNT	Wissenschaftliche Untersuchungen zum Neuen Testament
ZNW	*Zeitschrift für die neutestamentliche Wissenschaft und die Kunde der älteren Kirche*
ZTK	*Zeitschrift für Theologie und Kirche*

1. DIMENSIONS OF MEANING: THEOLOGY AND EXEGESIS

Anthony J. KELLY

In gladly accepting the invitation to contribute to this *Festschrift*, I am, of course, one of the many theologians who have found Frank Moloney's work in New Testament studies singularly luminous over the years. Admittedly, in the company of the exegetes and biblical scholars represented in this volume, I am the odd man out. My own specialization, despite an interest in interdisciplinary studies in these past decades, has been in what is unsatisfactorily termed "systematic theology." Still, the opportunity arose to collaborate with Frank in our recent publication *Experiencing God in the Gospel of John.*[1] I would like to contribute, therefore, some methodological reflections on this particular collaborative experience.

The Methodological Context

In my approach to this collaborative project a major influence has been Lonergan's methodological writings. His *Method in Theology*[2] has addressed the question of how the ever-pullulating specializations of this historical era might find common cause – but without each losing its own integrity, or, for that matter, pretending to a totalitarian self-sufficiency. Lonergan identified some eight "functional specialties"[3] in his concern to present a "framework of collaborative creativity."[4] His method is designed to be

---

[1] A. J. Kelly and F. J. Moloney, *Experiencing God in the Gospel of John* (New York: Paulist, 2003).

[2] B. J. F. Lonergan, *Method in Theology* (London: Darton, Longman and Todd, 1971).

[3] Lonergan, *Method*, 125-48.

[4] Lonergan, *Method*, xi.

quite specific yet sufficiently flexible to enable researchers, exegetes, historians – those concerned mainly with the data of the past (Research, Interpretation, History, Dialectics) – to share one enterprise with those whose main concern is the self-appropriation of the believer faced with the demands and possibilities of culture today (Foundations, Doctrines, Systematics, Communications). Obviously, Frank's expertise is most evident in the philological, exegetical, historical and hermeneutical treatment of the Johannine writings. To that degree, he is an eminent practitioner in areas relevant to Lonergan's first four specializations. My contribution, presupposing an immersion in the Johannine texts and Moloney's commentaries, deals more with the foundational viewpoint, and the doctrinal and theological elaboration of the data with an eye to the present cultural situation – Lonergan's second set of specializations. I should say, nonetheless, that Frank's scholarship is characterized by a firm grasp of theological issues and a deep pastoral and spiritual sense of the relevance of his biblical work. His scholarship is never antiquarian.

I should stress, therefore, that Lonergan's methodological framework, far from imposing an intrusive philosophical or epistemological or doctrinal framework on the challenge to mediate the texts of Christian tradition to contemporary culture, appeals to something much closer to home. Such a method invites scholars, whatever their specific concerns, to take notice of the workings of their own minds, and to attend to the "intentionality" – the conscious experience – of their coming to know anything at all. This generalized empirical method is analogically applicable to any area of investigation. In its theological specification it necessarily focuses on the data of, say, Christian experience and tradition. Yet it does this by being firmly based on an anthropological datum, namely, the self-transcendence of the conscious subject.[5] In this regard, human consciousness unfolds through the four inter-related levels of experience, understanding, judgment and decision, none of which is irrelevant to the work of Moloney, the exegete, or to Kelly, the theologian, collaborating on this project.[6]

I make mention of this larger context to explain, in a rather cursory manner, something of the methodological underpinnings of the work in question. It is a partial exploitation of the possibilities of a much larger collaboration. It could have involved many other kinds of specializations, especially in terms of history (the reception of John's Gospel in different

[5] Lonergan, *Method*, 6-19.
[6] Lonergan, *Method*, 13-19.

eras), dialectics (as in ecumenical theology), foundations (including the experience of faith and spirituality), doctrines (an evaluative judgment on the emergence of classic Church doctrines on the incarnation and the Trinity) and communications (how the fruits of this kind of reading can be presented to the cultural complexity of our day).[7]

The Proximate Context: Meaning

While such methodological matters are largely implicit in *Experiencing God*, the category of meaning figures quite explicitly throughout this book.[8] The nature of meaning, though a pervasive category in the human sciences, may seem so obvious and general to the exegete as to scarcely merit attention. Yet, just as obviously, the Gospel of John is a textual field of meaning. It emerges from the past to witness to a once lived and still living field of meaning arising out of singular events and encounters. The biblical writer had once to ask not only, "What does all this mean?" but also, "How shall I best mean it?" In some striking sense, Jesus Christ "meant the world" to those early communities. The totality of their experience was affected by the all-meaningful Johannine *Logos*. The meaning of the Word informed their relationship to God, to their fellow believers, to the world at large and its future. The labors of exegesis and theology today continue this meaningful activity, to explore in different ways the manner in which what was meant back then can still be meaningful for believers at this far distant time.

If "in the beginning was the Word" (John 1:1), that creative, enlivening and enlightening Word (John 1:3-4) "became flesh and dwelt among us" (John 1:14), it enters into the world of human meaning. In the course of the Gospel narrative, the meaning of the Word incarnate is expressed linguistically as, say, a question (e.g., John 1:38), a conversation (e.g., John 1:47-51), a command (e.g., John 13:34), judgment (e.g., John 5:27) and prayer (e.g., John 17). It is carried in symbols such as light (John 8:12), bread (John 6:35), the good shepherd (John 10:11), the true vine (John

---

[7] For other possibilities, especially regarding history, see B. F. Meyer, *Reality and Illusion in New Testament Scholarship. A Primer in Critical Realist Hermeneutics* (Collegeville: Liturgical Press, 1994) and A. J. Kelly, "The Historical Jesus and Human Subjectivity: A Response to Recent Suggestions," in *Australian Lonergan Workshop II* (ed. M. C. Ogilvie and W. J. Danaher; Drummoyne: Novum Organum Press, 2002), 151-79.

[8] Kelly and Moloney, *Experiencing God*, 55-60; 92-96; 136-40; 395-405.

15:1), to name but some. It is dramatically instanced in works of healing as with the man born blind (9:13-39) and in interpersonal gestures such as Jesus washing the disciples' feet (John 13:1-11). It generates its own art as in the prologue to the Gospel and in the discerning arrangement of Gospel narrative itself. This complex of meaning culminates in the subversive glory of the Cross as it incarnates the meanings of all the words, gestures, relationships and symbols that anticipated it.

The Johannine Context of Meaning

The theology of John unfolds as the thoroughgoing effort to bring out the meaning of everything in terms of the incarnate *Logos*. In this regard, it suggests its own "*Log*-ic." It intensifies, in a dramatic fashion, the general category of self-transcendence. What it inspires is not simply the ongoing demand to search for unconditional truth and goodness (the transcendentals of philosophical tradition) as might be too easily deduced early in the Gospel when the Father is depicted as seeking out genuine worshipers "in spirit and truth" (John 4:23-24). For John, however, true adoration is made concrete through humble service of the other in accordance with the supreme example of Jesus himself washing his disciples' feet (John 13:14-15). Not only is it a matter of service of others but of laying down one's life for them (John 15:13-14; 1 John 3:16-17). This aspect of dying to this present individual life or of dying into the realm of communal and eternal life is likened to the grain of wheat falling into the ground to bring forth much fruit (John 12:24). The dynamics of self-transcendence are shared by all genuine searchers, be that search religious, philosophical, artistic or scientific. It is the source of meaning for such terms as meaning, truth, life and goodness. But this general movement is given a special intensity in John's understanding of faith, love and discipleship. The unfolding horizon is not simply that of ultimate self-realization, or even of self-transcendence, but of "true life." The form of this true and endless life is the self-giving love that Jesus reveals, incarnates and inspires.

The Johannine experience of true life is expressed in a distinctive narrative form. Even the prologue, taken as the "abbreviated" Gospel, is not without its narrative development. Nor is a narrative context absent from the more theological distillation of 1 John. Inscribed into the movement of that narrative are, we might suggest, seven key terms: Father, Son, cross, resurrection, Spirit, community and eternal life. Not one of these terms can be omitted without mutilating the basic Johannine narrative. They can of course have equivalent expressions, and be ordered in different sequences; but each is necessary, for each is an expression of an essential, telling aspect of the communicative reality of God as life, light and love. Accordingly, the Kelly-Moloney book concluded with a reflection on these terms specifically in relation to the great Johannine affirmation, "God is love" (1 John 4:8, 17).[9] We could summarize it in the following manner.

God is love in that the *Father* is the source and exemplar of love (1 John 4:10). Faith operates in an horizon of pure gift from a source not of this world.

Secondly, God is love in the intimate self-giving and self-expressiveness manifest in the giving of his only *Son.*[10] So intimately connected is the Son to the Father's self-revelation, that 1 John can state: "No one who denies the Son has the Father; everyone who confesses the Son has the Father also" (1 John 2:23).

Thirdly, God is love to an unconditional extreme marked by the *cross.* The power of divine love works in the maximal experience of evil. It is a love that keeps on being love, "to the end" (John 13:1b). Death is thus transformed into an occasion of love, a condition of limitless loving into which believers themselves are drawn: "We know love by this that he laid down his life for us – and we ought to lay down our lives for one another" (1 John 3:16).

Fourthly, God is revealed as love in the *resurrection* of Jesus. With the transformative vindication of the Crucified, God's love has not been defeated. Jesus has returned to his own as "the resurrection and the life" (John 11:25).

Fifthly, God is love by giving into human history the permanent presence of the *Spirit.* The Paraclete guides those who follow the way of love into an ever-fuller realization of the form of true life. The coming of the Spirit is the "advantage" that would follow the departure of Jesus from the earthly scene (John 16:7). It is evocatively linked to the last breath of the Crucified (John 19:30) and the first breath of the Risen One (John 20:22).

Sixthly, God is love through an historical embodiment in a *community* of mutual love and common mission. The gathering of believers, identified

[9] Kelly and Moloney, *Experiencing God*, 389-394.
[10] See John 1:18; 3:16; 8:19, 38; 10:17, 30; 12:45, 50; 14:7, 10-11; 16:28.

by their celebration of baptism (cf. John 3:5) and the Eucharist (cf. John 6:32-35), is sent into the world with its own distinctive mission, thus continuing the mission that Jesus himself has received from the Father (John 20:21). Their unity, as it participates in the primordial unity of the Father and the Son, witnesses to the world the love that has been made known (John 17:23, 26).

Seventhly, God is love as leading to an eschatological consummation, even while the stream of *eternal life* has already begun to flow (John 4:14). Yet Jesus' desire is still to be fulfilled: "Father, I desire that those also whom you have given me, may be with me where I am, to see my glory…" (John 17:24. Cf. 6:40).

John's use of these key terms enables him to give a meaningful answer to the questions necessarily occurring within the Gospel's field of meaning, as to the source, form, present realization and future consummation of "the way, and the truth and the life" (John 14:6) that Jesus embodies. Indeed, so intimate and unreserved is the self-communication of the Father through his Son (John 3:16) and Spirit (John 3:34), that the Gospel narrative touches on something approaching the "autobiography" of God in which disciples and future believers are given their part to play (cf. John 17).

Four Dimensions of Meaning

The Johannine writings richly exemplify the complexity and manifold character of the experience from which they arise. But when the phrase "experiencing God" appears in the title of a book, the critical reader might be forearmed with all kinds of misgivings against the elusive term, "experience." Can the interpreter express anything more than what the Johannine writings say *about* God; for example, about how Jesus is related to the Father, how the Spirit is related to them both, how the consequent doctrine was received by various groups. I would suggest, however, that such a reader should be cautioned about having too abstract a notion of experience, as though it were detachable from meaning in some elemental way. Experience is always potentially or actually meaningful – creative of meaning, recognized by meaning and even shaped by it. Otherwise, the experience could not be registered, known or spoken of. On the other hand, to reduce the data of the Johannine experience merely to a catalogue of objective truths or to new doctrines about God (*cognitive* meaning) would be rather jejune. There are elements of personal transformation (*constitutive* meaning), new imperatives toward community (*communicative* meaning) and new forms of ethical conduct (*effective* meaning) inherent in the experience.

Following Lonergan's sketch of these four dimensions of meaning,[11] I suggest that such a manifold of inter-related dimensions of meaning is a useful tool in elaborating the compact experience of the truth of God as found in the Johannine writings. These various dimensions point to the density of past experience of the Johannine community to suggest ways in which it can be personally appropriated now and so transposed into the present cultural situation – as I hope we can briefly indicate.

The Word becomes flesh; and so enters into the world of human meaning, with its questions, answers, conflicts, fears, failures and hopes. The first words of the Word in the Gospel are a question, "What are you looking for?" (John 1:38). The believing community continues to feel the multiple resonances of this question. It must ask: What is the ultimate truth that summons and judges us in the chiaroscuro of our experience of the world? In this it would be inquiring into the *cognitive* meaning of its experience. Yet it can ask: Who are we in this conflict of light and darkness? In this regard, it would be seeking to objectify its *constitutive* meaning. It can reflect further: How do we most radically belong together? Then, it would be expressing its *communicative* meaning. Finally, it is impelled to ask: What should we be by our way of acting and responding in this present age? And that would be to deliberate on the *effective* meaning of the Gospel.

Cognitive Meaning

While not implying any temporal ordering of these dimensions of meaning and the questions related to each, we can first treat the most obvious dimension of meaning, namely, the *cognitive*. The adult no longer lives in a child's world of immediacy. What is real is not reducible to what is already out there to be seen. Reality is known through the actuation of all our capacities to experience, imagine, understand, reflect and judge. Knowing is, therefore, a compound of activities, including yet transcend-

---

[11] Lonergan, *Method in Theology*, 76-81. See also his "Dimensions of Meaning," in *Collection: Collected Works of Bernard Lonergan* (ed. F. E. Crowe and R. M. Doran; vol. 4; Toronto: University of Toronto Press, 1993), 232-243.

ing what sense, imagination, feeling and their various projections can deliver. The cognitive dimension of meaning implies a definable content grasped in an objective judgment. It is inherent in faith's answer to the questions: Who is the one true God? How is this God revealed? How is the divine will to be discerned? In this cognitive dimension, the Word enters our experience as an objective *datum*, provoking questions, and demanding an assent to the reality of the God Jesus reveals. In this regard, it can recognize things known that were previously unknown (e.g., John 16:29), and come to the realization of the need for further illumination (John 16:12-14; 1 John 3:2).

As the Gospel leads its readers further into the depth and breadth of the Christian experience of God, it moves along lines shaped by the disconcerting otherness that Jesus brings into the situation. It looks back and upward – to his origin with the Father – and out, – to the scope of what the Father is bringing about. Yet the experience of God works toward an enriched *cognitive* sense of the God of Christian faith. Take one example drawn from John 5. Though the one God of Israel is working in all that happens, the singularity of Jesus' witness to this "one God" discloses a unique form of communication and communion between the Father and the Son. It presumes a reciprocity of consciousness between the Father who unceasingly works and the Son who also works. Not unexpectedly, such an implication provoked theological outrage (John 5:17). Undifferentiated monotheism allows for no self-communication either within the divine realm, or beyond it to the world. God is not only one, but ultimately alone. To the degree such a presupposition goes unquestioned, the Jesus' filial experience of God is a scandal. As a result, "the Jews" see him not only as a breaker of the Sabbath law, but also as blasphemously making himself God's equal by "calling God his own Father" (John 5:18).

This charge occasions the expression of a cognitively rich and nuanced theology on the part of the Johannine author. His frame of reference always includes the utterly "Father-ward" relationality of Jesus' existence and action (John 5:19, 30, 43). And yet the Father's "Son-ward" communication is stated in various ways: "The Father loves the Son and shows him all he himself is doing" (John 5:20). This "showing" includes the "work" of raising the dead and giving life "to whom he will" (John 5:21, 26). Still, it is not only a matter of the Father's *showing*, but *giving* to the Son: the gifts of "all judgment" (John 5:22), of having "life in himself" (John 5:26), and the "authority to execute judgment" (John 5:27), along with "the works" that are his to accomplish (John 5:36). While Jesus bears witness to the Father from whom he comes, the Father both sends and bears witness to the Son (John 5:37). Even though he receives all from the Father and is unreservedly surrendered to the Father's will, Jesus remains a free agent; and his relationship to the Father is acted out in freedom (John 5:17). In one respect, the Father "rests" while the Son "works," for "the Father judges no one, but has given all judgment to the Son" (John 5:22). In this regard, the Father not only gives, but also yields, to the Son the properly divine activity of judging. In yielding and giving over judgment to the Son, the divine purpose is "that all may honor the Son, even as they honor the Father" (John 5:23).

The intentional reciprocity and the mutuality of relationships here described will give rise, in the centuries to come, to a full-blown Athanasian trinitarianism of the post-Nicene doctrine. Here it is sufficient to observe the striking cognitive development in John's presentation. Jesus' personal action and authority cannot be considered apart from the Father who sends, loves, shows, gives and even yields to the Son. In this, the Gospel transforms former religious and philosophical notions of undifferentiated divine unity.

In terms of 1 John, the distinctive Johannine accent falls on the truth, and the criteria for judging it. The subjectivity of Johannine faith is marked with a kind of salvific objectivity concerning the reality of God, and what is divinely revealed and willed. In this regard, we note the vigorously objective rhetoric with which the letter begins. It recaptures the revelatory language of the Gospel and sets the tone for the treatment of its own themes. What God has revealed from the beginning has been seen, gazed upon, touched and heard (1 John 1:1-3a). This privileged immediacy is characteristic of the foundational witnesses: "truly our fellowship is with the Father and with his Son Jesus Christ" (1 John 1:3b). The joyous conviction of the past is communicated to the present generation of faithful through the force of an original and transforming truth (1 John 1:4).

In their receptivity to the divine light, love and life, the faithful are anointed by the Holy One, and "have all knowledge" and "know the truth" (1 John 2:20-21, 27). Yet such a knowledge does not place believers in some kind of Gnostic heaven; for it is always beholden to the incarnate reality of God's only Son, Jesus Christ. Indeed, to confess the incarnate reality of the Son is the essential condition for knowing and "having" the Father as well (1 John 2:23), for dwelling in both (1 John 2:24), thus to enjoy the promised eternal life (1 John 2:25). Faith lives from the conviction that the love of the Father has already brought about a transformation: "Beloved, we are God's children now" (1 John 3:2a), even as it awaits the full evidence concerning both God and the children of God, "when we will be like him, for we will see him as he is" (1 John 3:2b).

From this perspective, the God-given Spirit is the medium and assurance of the believer's knowledge of God's indwelling presence (1 John 3:24b; 4:13; 5:6-8). The Spirit is received as coming "from God" and being "of God" in that it leads to the confession that "Jesus Christ has come in the flesh" (1 John 4:2). Moreover, since "God is love" (1 John 4:8), since love is from God, the divine life can be lived and the true God can be known only by loving (1 John 4:7-8). The possibility of reducing the agapeic and properly divine extent of love to the measure of human subjectivity is carefully precluded. The divine initiative acknowledges no human conditions, neither that of a prior human loving search for God ("... not that we loved God"), nor even that of a prior innocence in those who have been so loved, for all have sinned ("...to be the atoning sacrifice for our sins" [1 John 4:10]). As they participate in the reality of divine *agape* through mutual love, believers are drawn by the invisible God into the divine life; and the self-communicating love of God achieves its purpose (1 John 4:12). Both the gift of the Spirit and the sending of the Son (1 John 4:13-15) figure in the Letter's presentation of the originating and life-giving nature of God's love: "so we have known and believe the love that God has for us" (1 John 4:16a). *Our* knowing depends on God's action; and the reality of *our* loving derives from Love's initiative, as the Father gives of his Spirit and sends his Son to be the Savior of the world. Where 1 John ends, theology must always begin anew, noting the cognitive challenge implicit in those last words, "Little children, keep yourselves from idols!" (1 John 5:21).

Constitutive Meaning

Secondly, meaning functions in a *constitutive* manner. The meaning of the Word affects the experience of human identity. In this dimension, the Word of God "informs" the sense of self. It not only speaks about God, but also forms a Godly identity in its light. This meaning "constitutes" believers in an awareness of being "the children of God," and recipients of the gift of the truth. The believer enters into the divine meaning to find a new self in the light of what God is. The whole horizon of Christian existence is radically affected. Living this identity-shaping dimension of meaning, we can read the Gospel with the question: What new identity do we have as believers in the light of the God who is self-revealed in Jesus Christ?

First, an instance from the Gospel. Although the Spirit will come as gift, witness, and guide to serve the Father's communication to the world, the disciples still have to contend with their own confusions and sorrow. While the work of God is still in progress, they still have little sense of the unity and direction of the divine purpose and the phases of its timing (John 16:15-19). Their experience is still being determined by the opaque finality of death – the silence, darkness, defeat, and terminal separation from the Jesus who is leaving them by going to the Father. Still outside of the Father's house and lacking the benefit of the Spirit's guidance, they interpret any promised "little time" as the long time of death – when the dead stay dead, and human fate is wrapped in dread and obscurity. They have no eyes to look forward to that visibility of the glorified Jesus that will result from his going to the Father. They cannot comprehend his promised return to be the source of life from beyond the limits of death. In the history of faith, they are not the last to express the limitations of both their vision and their patience: "we do not know what he means" (John 16:18b).

The dispirited sadness of the disciples is met with the assurance of Jesus as he moves toward his goal. At the depths of apparent defeat, and in the face of the world's celebration of victory, a great transformation will occur. The glorification of Jesus will mean a transformation of the consciousness and very imagination of the disciples: "Amen, amen I say to you, you will weep and lament, but the world will rejoice; you will be sorrowful, but your sorrow will turn into joy" (John 16:20). A world-transforming birth is about to occur. For, in the hour determined by the Father, new life is being brought forth. Genuine believers, modeling their faith on the Mother of Jesus (John 2:4-5), will participate in a joyous birth. Their present sorrows are not symptoms of terminal distress but signs of the travail connected with being born from above to abundant life (John 10:10). Despite the inevitable darkness of history, the light will bring its joyous evidence. The cross will reveal the glory of God; and the life that streams from the Crucified will lead to its consummation in perfect joy. The followers of Jesus will experience their lives unfolding in the sight of Jesus – "I will see you again" (John 16:22) – in a kind of eye-to-eye contact unclouded by the darkness of death and failure. The experience of joy is not moved indefinitely into the future. The journey of faith in time, whatever its conflicts, will unfold in the presence of the gracious Father. Believers will no longer experience themselves as outsiders to the communion existing between the Father and the Son, needing to address Jesus in order to contact the Father. Through Jesus they will be drawn into an immediate relationship with the Father, "for the Father himself loves you" (John 16:27). They will have peace in Jesus and in his victory over the world (John 16:33). Christian identity is based on intimacy with God and in the joy and peace of Jesus. In the joy of life as it has been revealed, believers will come to know themselves as involved in the conversation of heaven, as when Jesus prays to the Father: "They are yours and you gave them to me" (John 17:6).

Then, in terms of 1 John, the features of Christian self-awareness are further developed. Christian consciousness is illumined by the light that God is (1 John 1:5), so that believers walk in the light (1 John 1:7), and, by loving their fellows, live in it (1 John 2:10). In the light of him who is "faithful and just" (1 John 1:9), "righteous" (1 John 2:29) and "pure" (1 John 3:3), they are offered the assurance of being forgiven, cleansed, purified, justified and confirmed in sinless-ness (cf. 1 John 1:9; 2:2; 3:3, 7, 9; 5:16, 18).

Fundamental to Christian identity is a sense of being "beloved" (1 John 2:7; 3:2; 4:1, 7, 11), animated by a conviction of knowing the revealed truth. The root of this conviction is the "christening" and interior witness of the Spirit of God, who is the truth (1 John 2:20, 26; 3:24b; 5:6, 10). Hence, believers understand themselves to abide in the Father and the Son (1 John 2:24; 3:24). And so they already participate in the eternal life (1 John 2:25; 3:14; 5:11-13), as it is found in the Son (1 John 5:11-12), and is what God is (1 John 5:20). Even though they must live in hope, the "beloved" are already God's children (1 John 3:2-3) aware of God's love manifest to them and abiding within them (1 John 3:17; 4:9-10, 16a).

Consequently, believers face the world in the consciousness of being "from God," and with the assurance of a final victory over all evil (1 John 4:4; 5:4). As the faithful are conformed to God who is love (1 John 4:8, 16b), they are born of God, live in God and know God (1 John 4:7, 16b). In this awareness, they enjoy an unreserved freedom with God. It builds an assurance that casts out all fear (1 John 2:20; 4:18) and inspires unconditional confidence in prayer (1 John 5:14). In this way, the meaning of God constitutes Christian identity by informing the believer's consciousness with a new self-understanding: "…as he is, so are we in this world" (1 John 4:17).

Communicative Meaning

Thirdly, the meaning of the Word is *communicative*. A community of common experience, conviction and identity is the outcome of communication in the ultimately meaningful. The followers of Christ are "meant" into a co-existence founded in their shared experience of God. The communicative dimension of meaning is clearly of prime importance in all the New Testament, as well as in the Johannine writings. The very choice of the name "the Word" in the first verse of the prologue of the Gospel underlines its communicative meaning, pervading the Gospel right to its end (John 20:31). At a moment of climactic intensity, Jesus asks the Father that the disciples and their successors be one as he and the Father are one (John 17:20-24).

The communicative dimension of meaning is elaborated even further in 1 John. It witnesses to a communion, the *koinonia*, which unites present believers with the witnesses of the past ("...from the beginning" [1 John 1:1; 3:11]), with communities in other places (2 and 3 John), and, most of all, with the Father and the Son (1 John 2:23-24). The field of communication in question has historical,[12] geographical,[13] interpersonal,[14] intergenerational,[15] transcendent,[16] and cosmic[17] dimensions. The communicative meaning of God in 1 John includes past witnesses, present relationships with those both near and far, communion with the Father and the Son, and, more implicitly, a relationship with the world itself.

Effective Meaning

Lastly, the meaning of the Word is *effective*. Jesus Christ, and the God revealed through him, means Christians to transform the world in new and hopeful ways. The experience of God is effectively expressed in the supreme example of Jesus washing the feet of his disciples (John 13:1-11), and in the new commandment to love as he loved (John 13:34). The effective meaning of God entails following him who is "the way" (John

---

[12] Cf. 1 John 1:1-3; 2:1, 7, 8, 12, 21, 26; 4:6; 5:13.
[13] Cf. 2 John 1, 10-11; 3 John 1, 5-8.
[14] As in 1 John 1:7; 4:20.
[15] 1 John 2:12-14.
[16] See 1 John 1:3; 2:23-24; 5:11-12.
[17] Cf. John 3:16; 1 John 2:2; 4:9, 14; 5:4-5.

14:6), as it affects every aspect of existence. So central to the Johannine experience of God is this effective dimension that the three other dimensions of divine meaning would collapse if the meaning of faith is not effective. To pretend to love God while hating a member of the community is to be in darkness (1 John 2:9, 11). We cannot love the invisible God without loving the all-too visible human other (1 John 4:20). Hence, the exhortation, "Let us love one another, because love is from God. Everyone who loves is born of God and knows God" (1 John 4:7). Believers must walk in the light (1 John 1:7), confess their sins (1 John 1:9). They must obey the commandments (1 John 2:3; 5:2-3) and do the Father's will (1 John 2:17).

All this is to suggest that these classic texts of Christian faith "word" the experience of God in accord with these four dimensions. They are interwoven and interpenetrate in a holographic manner within the density of faith's experience of divine life, love and communication. If ignoring this manifold meaning would result in being locked into a literalism of an extreme kind, these dimensions of meaning can never constrict the utter originality of the Word to the limited dimensions of human meaning. On the other hand, a consideration of these four dimensions may well find them to be a valuable tool in interpreting the experience of God as attested in the Johannine writings.

Conclusion

It would be of special interest, given the context of these reflections, to hear Francis Moloney's own response to this kind of collaborative project. No doubt this will occur in due course. In the meantime, I conclude by noting the further task implicit in the dimensions of meaning as I have outlined them. It can be crystallized in the question: How can this rich and manifold context of meaning be transposed into the present context of Church and world? In this we would be exploring the manner in which our present experience of the God of Jesus Christ could be shaped by the meaningful experience of Christians in a world far different from our own.

The wider cognitive context has been immeasurably extended. Our knowledge of the world, for instance, has now to include data pointing to the fifteen billion years of cosmic emergence, and to the four and a half billion year evolution of life on this planet. The planet circles a sun, a medium-sized star in a galaxy of some hundred billion such stars said to shine, in a cosmos of perhaps a hundred billion galaxies. Moreover, our known world includes religions and spiritual paths beyond the imagination of the Johannine world. When Mt Gerizim in Samaria and the Temple of Jerusalem were significant markers in the religious geography of the Gospel, what now of Benares or Mecca or Nairobi or Kyoto or New York, or the forty-thousand year history of Aboriginal inhabitation of Frank Moloney's native land? How is the Johannine *Logos* the all-creative, enlightening and life-giving utterance of God? How does it dwell among us when "we" are an inexpressibly larger community?

Then, the constitutive meaning of Christian identity with characteristics of peace and joy, life and communion with God has moved into a new context. Once Darwin, Marx, Nietzsche, Freud and evolutionary biology have had their say and communicated their respective "suspicions," in what does our deepest identity reside? Given the phenomenon of the "unemployed self" of the technological world of our experience, where does "the Father" find those worshipers in "spirit and truth" (John 4:23) he is seeking out?

The evidence suggested that those early Johannine communities suffered a special grief, and felt beleaguered and isolated, at enmity with the world – which, however hostile, was still understood to be the object of God's love. Those small, fragile communities have now died into the Great Church, which, in turn, is located in an unimaginably greater world – of both promise and threat. How does the light and truth of the Gospel continue to communicate, inspiring – and risking – modes of communication and solidarity in ways that would have been too much to bear for those early Christian generations?

Finally, the inescapable imperatives of Christian love, which are such a striking aspect of the way of life witnessed to in the Johannine writings, have now to develop into a much broader effectiveness. Loving one's fellow believers must meet not only the (more Synoptic) challenge of loving one's suffering neighbor, but also of loving the "neighborhood" in this time of threatened ecology and pressing environmental concern.

In an expanding theology,[18] each of the dimensions of meaning inherent in the Johannine witness will be included and extended. The task is barely begun. But when you can call on the splendid work of scholars such as Francis Moloney, the way seems more hopeful.

---

[18] See A. J. Kelly, *An Expanding Theology. Faith in a World of Connections* (rev. ed.; Sydney: E. J. Dwyer, 2003).

2. FRIENDSHIP, LOVE AND ABIDING IN THE GOSPEL OF JOHN

Dorothy LEE

It seems particularly appropriate to be writing of friendship in the Fourth Gospel in a work such as this, dedicated to honoring the scholarly work of Francis J. Moloney. My experience of Frank may well be summed up by the notion of friendship, a friendship that (as many others have found) is personal as well as collegial and scholarly. As one of the many whom Frank has mentored over the years, I value this opportunity to express gratitude for his continuous support, his warmth and encouragement, and his helpful criticism. Frank is a fine scholar and a warm human being who loves the Fourth Gospel, not in a dispassionate, uncommitted way but from the perspective of what the Gospel reveals about God and what it has to teach the Church. He has succeeded in transmitting that love and nurturing the scholarly aspirations of many in a way that demonstrates his profound commitment to the values of this most friendly and loving of Gospels.

Introduction

Friendship, love and abiding are closely related themes in the Gospel of John. God's self-revelation imparts a vision of intimacy and communion at the heart of the created world, manifest in the incarnation (John 1:14). The love of Father and Son in the Fourth Gospel flows out to embrace the world (3:16). Resting in that divine friendship is the meaning of salvation, a salvation that draws human beings into a community of faith extending across heaven and earth. Becoming children of God means returning to that condition of primordial love, which is the ground of creation (1:12-13). The Johannine imagery of abiding and friendship offers a radically new way of living in affinity with God and others. This is a pertinent theme in view of contemporary theological concerns – among feminist theologians and others – to rediscover the trinitarian and intrinsically relational nature of God. Friendship offers a compelling model in which to understand divine-human relations, life in community and even kinship with the earth.[1]

Love and Friendship

The Johannine imagery of love and friendship spans two word groups. The verb ἀγαπᾶν ("to love") occurs thirty-seven times, nearly three times as often as the synonymous φιλεῖν ("to love"). Both are used with little or no difference in meaning. The standard epithet for the Beloved Disciple, for example, is the one "whom Jesus loved," the verbal form being either ἠγάπα (13:23; 19:26; 21:7, 20) or ἐφίλει (20:2); similarly, the two verbs are used synonymously of the Father's love (e.g., φιλεῖν, 3:16; 5:20; 16:27; verb ἀγαπᾶν, 3:35; 10:17; 14:23). The abstract noun ἀγάπη ("love") appears seven times, and the noun φίλος ("friend/beloved") occurs six times. Most of this usage congregates around the Farewell Discourse, where love and friendship are major themes.[2]

Friendship was a popular theme among ancient writers, and in the Græco-Roman world highly prized. The term "friendship" (φιλία, *amicitia*) was used of different kinds of relationship: allies, lovers, followers of political leaders, members of philosophical groups, and the relationship between patrons and clients.[3] Personal friendship in the ancient world was to be built on integrity, equality, maturity, intimacy, love and affection, honesty, constancy, reciprocity and self-sacrifice.[4] Aristotle observes that

---

[1] Further on the symbolism of abiding, love and friendship, see D. A. Lee, *Flesh and Glory. Symbolism, Gender and Theology in the Gospel of John* (New York: Crossroad, 2002), 88-109.

[2] Similar usage is to be found in the Johannine Epistles, with the addition of the adjective ἀγαπητός ('beloved').

[3] G. Stählin, 'φιλέω, καταφιλέω, φίλημα, φίλος, φίλη, φιλεῖν φιλία' *TDNT*, IX, 147, 151-154.

[4] See, in particular, Cicero, *De Amicitia* (LCL; London: Heinemann, 1953); also Aristotle, *The Nicomachean Ethics* (LCL; Cambridge: Harvard University Press, 1982), Books VIII & IX and Plutarch, 'De Multitudine Amicorum' in *Moralia* (LCL; London: Heinemann, 1971), II, 93-97.

"without friends no-one would choose to live, even possessing all the other good things of life."[5] Although the Old Testament is not explicit in extolling the virtues of friendship, preferring the language of covenant and kinship, there are remarkable examples: Ruth and Naomi, for example, or David and Jonathan (Ruth 1:14-18; 2 Sam 1:17-27). Philo uses the ancient Græco-Roman proverb "between friends all is common" (κοινὰ τα φιλῶν, *amicorum communia omnia*), but applies it not just to human friendships but also to friendship with God (e.g., Moses and Abraham, Gen 18:1-33; Exod 32:7-14), a friendship that for him is grounded in worship.[6] In later Old Testament traditions, *Sophia* ("Wisdom") gathers a community of friends, bound by mutual love (Prov 8:17; Sir 4:12; Wis 6:12); she has the capacity to "enter into holy souls," making them "friends of God" (Wis 7:27-28).

Love, like friendship, "sounds a persistent beat from the beginning to the end" of the Gospel.[7] It has several dimensions that are not strictly separate but intertwined. First and foremost is the love within the divine being, which is the fundamental basis of the Father-Son relationship.[8] The friendship between them is eternal and mutual (e.g., 10:17; 14:31; 15:9, 10; 17:23-26) and, by implication, this love incorporates also the Spirit. The second is the love of the Father for the created world, a love that results in the sending of the Son into mortal flesh (3:16). The third is the love of Jesus for his disciples (13:1, 34; 14:21; 15:9, 12, 13), a love that manifests itself in the revelation of divine glory in his life and death; this love is shared by the Father who also loves the disciples (14:21, 23; 16:27; 17:23). The fourth is the love disciples have for Jesus in response to God's self-giving glory disclosed in Christ (14:15, 21, 23-24, 28; 16:27). Last of all, the same love is to be the basis of the community's life; being drawn into the trinitarian circle of love, believers are to live out the love-command, by loving each other with Christ's own life-giving love (13:34-35; 15:12, 17).

As a central feature of community, love is also used of individual disciples: most notably, the Beloved Disciple.[9] The Beloved Disciple plays a

---

[5] Aristotle, *Nicomachean Ethics*, VIII.1.

[6] Philo, *Vit. Mos.*, I, 156. The saying, quoted in Plato (*Laws* 5.739b-c), Cicero (*De Officiis* 1.16.51) and other ancient authors, is said to have had its origins in Pythagoras.

[7] S. H. Ringe, *Wisdom's Friends: Community and Christology in the Fourth Gospel* (Louisville: Westminster John Knox, 1999), 93.

[8] It is arguable that the fatherhood symbol in the Fourth Gospel is anti-patriarchal in its focus on relinquishing power and drawing outsiders into the divine relationship; see Lee, *Flesh and Glory*, 110-34.

[9] See John 13:23-26; 19:25-27; 20:2-10; 21:7, 20, 23-24; also 1:37; 18:15; 19:35. For a

representative role, particularly in the second half of the Gospel, where he stands as the witness of the Gospel's tradition and exemplar of the love of Christ for the disciples. His place of honor at the Last Supper is emblematic of the household of faith which resides in the same place, enjoying the same intimacy with Jesus, a love that has its source in the union Jesus shares with the Father. Just as the Beloved Disciple reclines "on the breast of Jesus" (κόλπος, 13:23; στῆθος, 13:25),[10] so the Word, being "turned towards" God (1:1-2), exists "in the bosom of the Father" (κόλπος, 1:18).

Jesus' relationship with the Beloved Disciple is "embedded in a wider love relationship" between Jesus and his followers.[11] For example, the group of friends and "beloved disciples" decidedly includes women. The mother of Jesus enjoys a privileged position in the Gospel and frames the opening and closing of Jesus' ministry (2:1-11; 19:25-27). The love between her and the Beloved Disciple, through the indwelling Paraclete, forms the basis of the post-Easter community. The same could be said of the Samaritan woman in her conversation with Jesus (4:1-42); and also of Mary Magdalene, present at the foot of the cross, who searches for the body of Jesus as a grief-stricken friend, recognizing his presence when her name is spoken, and greeting him in love and joy (19:25; 20:1-18). The Bethany sisters are named explicitly as Jesus' friends (11:5; cf. 11:3); their love for Jesus is confirmed in the feast they provide after their brother is restored to life. Mary of Bethany exemplifies the mutuality of true friendship, mirroring the costliness of Jesus' love with the costly anointing of his feet (12:1-8): "It is the love of Mary, anticipated in her response to the voice of Jesus in 11:28-32, that fills the house with fragrance."[12] The Last

---

survey of the material on the Beloved Disciple, see especially J. H. Charlesworth, *The Beloved Disciple: Whose Witness Validates the Gospel of John?* (Valley Forge: Trinity Press International, 1995), esp. 127-224, and R. A. Culpepper, *John, the Son of Zebedee. The Life of a Legend* (Columbia: University of South Carolina Press, 1994), 56-88. On the gender issue, see S. M. Schneiders, *Written that You May Believe. Encountering Jesus in the Fourth Gospel* (New York: Crossroad, 1999), 211-32. On the Beloved Disciple as a figure outside the circle of the Twelve, see R. E. Brown, *The Community of the Beloved Disciple. The Life, Loves, and Hates of an Individual Church in New Testament Times* (London: Geoffrey Chapman, 1979), 31-34.

[10] On 'turned towards' as a translation of the preposition πρός at 1:1-2, see I. de la Potterie, 'L'emploie de εἰς dans Saint Jean et ses incidences théologiques,' *Bib* 43 (1962) 366-87; also F. J. Moloney, *Belief in the Word. Reading John 1-4* (Minneapolis: Fortress, 1993), 28, and *The Gospel of John* (SP 4; Collegeville: Liturgical Press, 1998), 35.

[11] S. van Tilborg, *Imaginative Love in John* (Leiden: Brill, 1993), 131.

[12] Moloney, *John*, 349. Moloney argues for a contrast between Mary's extraordinary action and what he sees as Martha's more limited response in the Raising of Lazarus (327-330).

Supper, moreover, is not necessarily confined to the Twelve, the narrator leaving open the question of whether a wider group of friends, including women, is present (cf. Mark 14:17 pars.).[13]

Male disciples also share the same intimacy with Jesus. The word φίλος ("friend") first appears in relation to John the Baptist who identifies himself as "the friend of the bridegroom" (3:29). His role is secondary to that of the bridegroom, yet there is an intimacy between the groom and the "best man" that indicates close friendship (3:30). In the Raising of Lazarus, Jesus identifies Lazarus, like his sisters, as "our friend" (ὁ φίλος ἡμῶν, 11:11; 11:3, 5, 36). Though Martha and Mary reproach Jesus for abandoning his friend (11:21, 32), Jesus proves his love by the authoritative voice which summons Lazarus from the tomb, freeing him from the trappings of death (11:38-44; cf. 5:25-29). In this narrative, we see Jesus laying down his life for his friends (11:45-53).

The language of friendship intensifies in the symbolism of the vine and the branches.[14] In the explanation that follows this Johannine symbol, Jesus discloses that the relationship between himself and believers is one of friendship, a friendship that has its archetype in the love of Father and Son (15:12; cf. 13:34-35). The imagery is not concerned with power relations among believers – although it has political implications – but exemplifies shared knowledge, trust and openness in relationship to Jesus who acts as the true friend, revealing that "greater love" for his friends by dying for them (15:13).[15] The connection between Jesus and believers, typified in the vine and the branches, is a deep and lasting friendship that includes intimacy, personal knowledge and self-giving love.

The final explicit mention of love is Peter's encounter with the risen Christ in a narrative that many regard as a later addition to the Gospel (21:15-19).[16] The variations in language that describe love (and also the

---

[13] Van Tilborg suggests a wider, all-male group (*Imaginative Love*, 111-112), but there is no reason to assume that, if a wider group were present (in John's understanding), it would exclude those women who have been among Jesus' closest and most percipient followers.

[14] See S. M. Schneiders, 'The Foot Washing (John 13:1-20): An Experiment in Hermeneutics' *ExAud* 1 (1985), 140-143; also van Tilborg, *Imaginative Love*, 110-68, esp. 148-54.

[15] The language parallels that of the Good Shepherd who knows his sheep by name (10:3), offers them life and protects them (10:9-10), shares knowledge with them (10:14), and lays down and takes up his life for them (10:15-18).

[16] E.g., R. E. Brown, *The Gospel According to John* (AB 29-29A, 2 vols.; Garden City: Doubleday, 1966), II: 1077-82; R. Schnackenburg, *The Gospel According to St John* (trans. K. Smyth et al. 3 vols.; HTCNT. London: Burns & Oates, 1968-82), 3: 341-51, F. J. Molo-

sheep) are stylistic rather than substantial.[17] More important is the reiter-ating of Jesus' question and Peter's increasing distress at the implications of this repetition (21:17b). From the viewpoint of the drama, the scene re-plays Peter's threefold denial of Jesus where he has been proved faithless in his friendship with Jesus (18:15-18, 25-27). For the reader, the resur-rection scene rehabilitates Peter as Jesus' faithful friend, while functioning also to assign Peter a significant place in the community of friends. The leadership role which he assumes – to shepherd the flock of the Good Shepherd – is to be grounded in love. Like Jesus, Peter is called to lay down his life for his friends (21:18-19).[18]

At the same time, there is an ironical element to friendship in the Fourth Gospel. During the trial before Pilate, the authorities manipulate the Roman governor into taking action against Jesus, playing on his fear and ambition. When "the Jews" accuse Pilate of being "no friend to Cae-sar" (οὐκ εἶ φίλος τοῦ Καίσαρος, 19:12), Pilate chooses friendship with Caesar over friendship with God, giving the Roman *imperium* precedence over the divine βασιλεία manifest in Jesus (18:36-37). Faced with so ulti-mate a decision, Pilate makes judgment against his true "king" and con-demns Jesus to death (19:13-16a). His choice of friendship reveals both his own misjudgment and also the radical nature of Jesus' love for "his own" (13:1). In a similar way, the Evangelist condemns those who love darkness rather than light (3:19); those who love and cling to their own life (12:25); and those who love human glory more than the glory of God (δόξα, 12:43). Such people belong to the κόσμος, the realm of unbelief, which "loves its own" and thus hates the believing community, just as it has hated Jesus (15:18-19).

---

ney, *Glory not Dishonor. Reading John 13-21* (Minneapolis: Fortress, 1998), 182-192, and *Gospel of John*, 545-47, 562-66. Others, such as P. S. Minear, argue for the literary unity of John 20-21 ('The Original Functions of John 21' *JBL* 102 [1983], 85-98). A mediating position admits the disjunction between John 20 and 21, yet argues also for the impor-tance of John 21 in completing the Johannine narrative. See also R. A. Culpepper, *The Gospel and Letters of John* (Nashville: Abingdon Press,1998), 244-45.

[17] This view now represents the majority among commentators; see Moloney, *John*, 559.

[18] For a study of the relationship between Peter and the Beloved Disciple, see K. Quast, *Peter and the Beloved Disciple. Figures for a Community in Crisis* (Sheffield: JSOT Press, 1989).

The Imagery of Abiding

Overlapping with images of love and friendship, the word "to abide" (μένειν) is scattered throughout the Fourth Gospel, appearing some forty times. Most instances are found in the Farewell Discourse,[19] along with the cognate μονή ("abiding-place," 14:2). "Abiding" is an important Johannine term, often occurring in the formula "to abide in/on" (μένειν ἐν); it is also used in the colloquial sense of "stay" or "remain."[20] In its theological sense, apart from notions of friendship and love, the imagery is linked with other Johannine conceptions such as unity, oneness, and indwelling. Abiding is particularly related to the Johannine understanding of disciples as "friends" of Jesus, as we have observed – an image that, like abiding, is expressed in the symbol of the vine.

Abiding first appears in the opening narrative where it is used to denote the Spirit's presence with Jesus. John the Baptist witnesses to Jesus as the Lamb of God (1:29, 35), the One on whom the Spirit descends and rests ("abides," 1:32-33).[21] The ensuing dialogue between Jesus and the Baptist's two disciples operates on two levels, the literal and symbolic (1:37-40). In response to the question, "What do you seek?" the disciples respond with another question, equally evocative: "where do you abide?" (ποῦ μένεις; 1:38).[22] At Jesus' invitation to "come and see" – words that are suggestive of discipleship (1:50-51; 3:3; 12:21; 20:8) – the disciples "saw where he stayed ["abode"] and remained ["abode"] with him that day" (1:39). Although John, like the Synoptics, describes discipleship as following Jesus,[23] the Fourth Gospel sees it also in terms of abiding, an abiding that is dependent on the Spirit.

As the Gospel progresses, the symbolic meaning of abiding unfolds. In the story of the Samaritan woman, Jesus invites the woman's hospitality (4:7) and offers his own in its place (4:10), a hospitality that crosses

---

[19] See F. Hauck, μένω, *TDNT* 4.574-74, and Brown, *John*, 1:510-11; also J. Heise, *Bleiben. Meinen in den Johanneischen Schriften* (Tübingen: J.C.B. Mohr [Paul Siebeck], 1967), 22-28. Two Old Testament themes provide the background: that God abides for ever (e.g., LXX Ps 9:8; 111:3, 9; Isa 40:8; Wis 7:27) and God's indwelling in Zion (e.g., LXX Ezek 43:7; Zech 2:11; Joel 4:17; Sir 24:4).

[20] Further on the two meanings of μένειν, see Heise, *Bleiben*, 47-103.

[21] In the Synoptics, the declaration of Jesus' divine sonship comes not from the Baptist but the divine voice (Mark 1:11 pars.).

[22] X. Léon-Dufour, *Lecture de l'Évangile de Jean* (4 vols.; Paris: Éditions du Seuil, 1988-1996), 1:189.

[23] See Mark 1:16-20; 8:34; 10:32; John 1:37, 43; 8:12; 10:4, 27; 12:26; 21:19-22.

boundaries to reach her. Recognizing him as "the Savior of the world" (4:42), the villagers extend their hospitality to Jesus, both literally and symbolically. Like the woman, they enter a relationship of abiding with him, evident in his "abiding" with them for two days (4:40).[24] The theme of hospitality is taken further in the Bread of Life narrative where, particularly towards the end, μένειν takes on sacramental overtones (6:53-58). The Eucharist is a symbolic enactment of the reciprocal and covenantal abiding between Jesus and believers (6:56): the "Son of Man" both *gives* and *is* the food that "abides to eternal life" (6:27). The one eating the flesh of Jesus abides in him and will "have life" (6:57). Like friendship, abiding symbolizes a new relationship with Jesus that is life-giving, transcending the power of death. The relationship between Jesus and disciples – whether in regard to abiding or friendship – is influenced by the Old Testament portrait of *Sophia* who draws companions to her table and feeds them with her wisdom (Prov 9:2-5; Sir 15:3; 24:21).[25]

In the Farewell Discourse, abiding is both a present and future reality. The imagery is linked to that of "place" (τόπος, 14:2b; cf. 4:20-24).[26] Abiding in Jesus is the pathway that takes believers to the eschatological abode of the Father (14:6). Later, the imagery is inverted: now it is the Father and Son who journey into the heart of the believer (14:22-23). In either case, abiding symbolizes the indwelling Father and Son who together make their home in the believer. As Jesus has already indicated, abiding is actualized in the community after his glorification through the "other Paraclete," the Spirit of truth, who "abides with you and will be in [among?] you" (14:17). Jesus' abiding will continue even in his absence through the Spirit-Paraclete who makes real the abiding of Father and Son (16:7).[27]

As a symbol of discipleship, abiding is most powerfully visible in the

---

[24] Léon-Dufour, *Jean*, 1:243.

[25] M. E. Willett, *Wisdom Christology in the Fourth Gospel* (San Francisco: Mellen Research University Press, 1992), 112. On the Wisdom overtones of 'abiding', see M. Scott, *Sophia and the Johannine Jesus* (JSNTSup 71; Sheffield: JSOT Press, 1992), 157-159.

[26] On the eschatology of the Farewell Discourse, see Brown, *John*, 2:601-603; also M. L. Coloe, *God Dwells With Us: Temple Symbolism in the Fourth Gospel* (Collegeville: Liturgical Press, 2001), 157-78.

[27] Moloney defines the Paraclete as 'the ongoing presence of Jesus even in his absence' and sees the gift of the Spirit-Paraclete as inaugurating 'a new era' which will be 'marked by love, the keeping of the commandments of Jesus, and the promise of a future time when the Father and the Son will abide forever with the disciple' (*John*, 401).

"extended metaphor" of the vine and the branches (15:1-17),[28] in which the metaphor "serves as a vehicle to articulate the importance of abiding."[29] The language of abiding multiplies, being used eleven times, arising from the core symbol of the vine which, as it transpires, underlies the theological usage of earlier chapters. The passage falls into two sections, linked by the motif of abiding, and interweaves images of love, fruit-bearing, the love-command and friendship (15:1-10, 11-17). The symbolism highlights the desirability of connection to Jesus, a theme that is integral to the Farewell Discourse.[30] Disciples are dependent on Jesus for life, just as branches "abide on" the vine in order to have life (15:1-8). Like the bond between mother and child, where the infant is dependent for life on its mother's body, so attachment to Jesus is the way to life.[31] The eucharistic overtones of the vine recall the Wedding at Cana, expressing the *jouissance* of union, a union that is fecund and life-giving (15:11, 16:20-22).[32] The image of fruit-bearing makes clear that abiding is not static but dynamic and vital.[33] The vine is a symbol of fecundity and growth, revealing the flourishing of the believing community in its relationship with God (cf. 1 Cor 12:12-27).[34]

---

[28] F. F. Segovia, *The Farewell of the Word. The Johannine Call to Abide* (Minneapolis: Fortress, 1991), 123-35. The vine is a Johannine 'parable' with allegorical elements (cf. Ps 80:9-16; Isa 5:1-7; Jer 2:21; Ezek 15:1-8; 19:10-14; also Cant 8:11-12; Sir 14:16-21). Judaism makes no absolute distinction between parable and allegory (so B. Witherington, *John's Wisdom. A Commentary on the Fourth Gospel* [Cambridge: Lutterworth Press, 1995], 257-58); see also Brown, *John*, 2:668-672, and D. M. Smith, *John* (Abingdon NT Commentaries; Nashville: Abingdon, 1999), 279-280.

[29] Moloney, *John*, 417.

[30] Some have argued convincingly that John 13-17 has a chiastic structure, despite the literary unevenness at a number of points. See, for example, Moloney, *John*, 24, 370-481, and W. Brouwer, *The Literary Development of John 13-17. A Chiastic Reading* [Atlanta: SBL, 2000]). For Moloney, the center of the chiasm is 15:1-16:3, with its opposition of love and hate; for Brouwer, the center of the Johannine 'macro-chiasm' is 15:1-17, with the theme: 'Abide in me!' (9-10, 117-118).

[31] On maternal imagery for Christ in the Fourth Gospel, see Lee, *Flesh and Glory*, 148-50, 154-59.

[32] For possible parallels with the rites of Dionysius, see J. A. Sanford, *Mystical Christianity. A Psychological Commentary on the Gospel of John* (New York; Crossroad, 1995), 284-285.

[33] It is doubtful whether the language here is mission-oriented, as Witherington argues (*John's Wisdom*, 258), since fruit-bearing is concerned primarily with growth in love.

[34] On the ecclesiology of the imagery, see G. R. Beasley-Murray, *John* (WBC 36; Waco: Word Books, 1987), 272; also Augustine, *In Joannis Evangelium Tractatus CXXIV*, in J.-P. Migne (ed.), *Patrologiae Cursus Completus. Series Latina* (Vols. 34-35; Paris: Garnier, 1846-1891), LXXX.2.

Individuals in the community will prosper only insofar as they recognize themselves as members of an organic unit. No individual is a free agent, but is one branch of an encircling and intertwining vine whose fruitfulness depends on abiding with Jesus.[35]

Whereas the friendship language does not, of itself, include any reference to judgment, the imagery of pruning extends abiding to include purification. The verb καθαίρειν can mean "cleanse" as well as "prune," and John exploits both meanings (cf. 13:10). Pruning is the process of removing what is dead for the plant to flourish, paralleling the washing away of impurity in the heart. For the Evangelist, abiding is a matter of life and death, distinguishing the community from the κόσμος, the latter characterized by hatred and rejection (15:18-16:4a). For the reader, there is a simple choice: "One of the two the branch must be united with, either the vine, or the fire: if it is not on the vine, it will be in the fire: so that therefore it may not be in the fire, it must be on the vine."[36] Yet pruning is necessary for *all* disciples.[37] All the branches are cut back, even if not all are cut off. This "purification" is the work of the vine-dresser, its purpose being to lead disciples to a deeper knowledge of God (15:9-10). Pruning thus suggests the necessity of growth through suffering, both of which are necessary for the community to thrive. In the mutual abiding formula, true disciples are those who abide in Jesus as the source of life and in whom Jesus himself reciprocally abides (see also 1 John 3:24; 4:13, 15-16). The language coheres with the Beloved Disciple and the mother of Jesus being given to each other at the foot of the cross (19:25-27). In the context of the Passion, suffering and death are a kind of "pruning" or "cleansing" that bring life (cf. 12:24). The discipleship of abiding and friendship has as its heart the reality of the cross.

Not only disciples but also Jesus himself shares in the mutuality of abiding. Jesus' place in the divine "household" as Son is an abiding one, as distinct from the household slave (8:35). The Father abides in Jesus in a relationship of intimacy and union (14:10); Jesus abides with the disciples only because the Father abides in him (15:9-10). The unity he shares with

---

[35] G. R. O'Day, "John," in C. A. Newsom & S. H. Ringe (eds.), *The Women's Bible Commentary* (expanded ed.; London: SCM, 1998), 303.

[36] Augustine, *In Joannis Evangelium*, LXXXI.3.

[37] T. L. Brodie speaks of 'breaking free from the world with all its enslaving habits, values, and relationships' (*The Gospel According to John: A Literary and Theological Commentary* [Oxford: Oxford University Press, 1993], 475).

the Father is the ground of this relationship which expresses "mutual or reciprocal immanence" (see 3:35; 6:57; 10:30, 38b; 14:9-11, 20; 17:20-23).[38] Abiding has a vertical dimension that is theologically prior to the horizontal, though the two are ultimately inseparable. The abiding of Father and Son is the archetype of believers' abiding, a centripetal force drawing them into the divine communion.[39] Believers do not manufacture their own abiding but are gathered into that which already exists, already flourishes, is already redolent with love and life.[40]

At the same time, John uses μένειν in an ironical sense. God's anger is said to "abide" on those who reject the Son and knowingly choose death over life (3:36); while this is the expression of divine judgment, it is also the result of the individual's own choice (cf. 3:19). In usage that coheres with abiding as the expression of discipleship, Jesus declares that God's word *fails to abide* on the religious authorities in Jerusalem (5:38). In the story of the man born blind, the sin of the Pharisees *abides* because of their illusion of sight (9:41). The seed which will not submit to "death and burial" is unable to bear fruit; it is said to *abide alone*, solitary and infertile (12:24). Whereas abiding means openness to light and life, the failure to abide means being closed to the light. To reject true abiding is to be condemned to isolation and detachment – everything that is the opposite of life, affiliation, and community. Those who reject life encounter instead an ironical "abiding," a sense of separation and darkness (cf. 1 John 3:14-15). Following the imagery of the vine, we read of the hatred of the "world" (15:18-16:4a),[41] which is the other face of abiding. Images of friendship, union and love are now replaced by the language of hatred, rejection and persecution.[42] The community that abides in love is hated by the "world"

---

[38] C. H. Dodd, *The Interpretation of the Fourth Gospel* (Cambridge: Cambridge University Press, 1953), 187; see also Brown, *John*, 1:511.

[39] Throughout his discussion of the Last Discourse, Moloney refers to the fragility of the disciples, particularly in view of his impending departure, a situation that the Johannine Jesus directly addresses. Thus, for example in John 17, Jesus 'expresses his desire that the gulf be bridged between the Father-Son oneness and the ambiguous situation of fragile disciples and believers *in the world* but not *of the world*' (*John*, 475).

[40] This reciprocity is expressed in the Great Prayer in synonymous terms. Disciples are gathered into the 'I in you and you in me' of Jesus' affinity with the Father: 'I in them' and 'they in us' and 'I in them and you in me' (17:23; see 6:56; 15:5). Jesus is the symbol of both dimensions, divine and human, since in his flesh he is the abiding-place of God among people (1:14; cf. Rev 21:3b).

[41] See Segovia, *Farewell of the Word*, 179-212.

[42] Commenting on 17:9, Barrett captures the nuanced Johannine sense of the 'world': 'John, having stated (3:16) the love of God for the κόσμος, does not withdraw from that

and suffers because it belongs to the light.[43] The solidarity of believers, while cutting across the boundaries of community (16:2), is strengthened so that opposition becomes a catalyst for abiding, creating ironically the parameters in which love and intimacy thrive.

Like friendship, abiding is a quality of the divine realm, symbolized in the relationship between Father and Son. Discipleship is not a self-generating relationship but entry into a divine, pre-existing communion through the Spirit. To be a disciple means to be in union with Jesus and through Jesus with God – a union that is mutual and oriented towards community, the antithesis of isolation and seclusion. Abiding is not based on human achievement, but derives from a divine source, an indwelling that is intimate and personal. The symbolism of the vine signifies growth and fecundity, mutuality and reciprocity, friendship and self-giving. Yet abiding, as a force for life, does not bypass suffering and death: such friendship requires a love that will go "to the end" (εἰς τέλος, 13:1), even to death. Yet paradoxically this death is itself the source of life. Abiding does not end with death; on the contrary, love and intimacy blossom in the ultimate expression of divine, self-giving love.

Worship and Obedience

The Fourth Gospel employs other imagery for relationships in the household of faith, imagery that either overlaps with abiding and friendship or co-exists in some tension. For example, the Gospel draws on images derived from the family.[44] These symbols begin in the Father-Son relationship, and extend to disciples as children of God, born of the Spirit through Jesus, the incarnate Son (1:12-13; 3:1-8). In the Tabernacles' Discourse, disciples are free members of the household, children rather than slaves, their status dependent on the Son who "abides for ever" (8:35-36). The risen Christ reveals to Mary Magdalene the inauguration of a new,

---

position in favour of a narrow affection for the pious... But to pray for the κόσμος would be almost an absurdity, since the only hope for the κόσομς is precisely that it should cease to be the κόσμος' (*John*, 506).

[43] See D. Rensberger, *Overcoming the World. Politics and Community in the Gospel of John* (London: SPCK, 1988), 15-36.

[44] J. van der Watt sees the family as fundamental to the Fourth Gospel's symbolic structure, pervading the narrative like a web (*Family of the King. Dynamics of Metaphor in the Gospel According to John* [BibIntS 47; Leiden: Brill, 2000]).

covenant community in which disciples are ἀδελφοί to one another:[45] "Go to my brothers and sisters and tell them: 'I am ascending to my Father and your Father, my God and your God'" (20:17).[46] Maternal imagery is arguably implicit in the portrayal of both Jesus and the Spirit, while the mother of Jesus possesses a symbolic, maternal role in the community after Jesus' death, a role that transcends Jesus' immediate family (cf. 7:5).[47] Familial images are important in the Fourth Gospel to designate the intimacy lying at the core of faith.

In addition, John's Gospel uses imagery derived from the wider Græco-Roman household. The master-slave/servant paradigm is common in the NT, where its usage represents an overturning of social expectations.[48] In the Synoptics, Christ is the servant-leader who comes "not to be served but to serve" (e.g., Mark 10:45; par. Luke 22:7). In line with this symbolism, Paul sometimes refers to himself as a "slave of Jesus Christ" (Rom 1:1; Phil 1:1), a paradoxical state of voluntary "slavery" in which the apostle ironically finds true freedom (1 Cor 9:19). The Fourth Gospel is sparing in its use of such imagery. The tone is set in the Footwashing, where Jesus takes on the role of a servant/slave, washing the disciples' feet to indicate that union in his sacrificial death and mutual love are to be the basis of true community (13:12-16; cf. 12:26).[49]

Nevertheless, the Evangelist has a decided preference for the language of abiding and friendship over other models. In the discourse on abiding, John favors the imagery of friendship, unfolding the innermost meaning of the vine: "No longer do I call you slaves (δοῦλοι), since the slave does not know what the lord is doing; but I have called you friends (φίλοι), since everything which I have heard from my Father I have made known to you" (15:15). These words demonstrate the mutuality of friendship that

[45] Given the Evangelist's relative disinterest in the Twelve, there seems no reason to interpret ἀδελφοί as meaning only 'brothers'. Against this, cf. A. Fehribach, *The Women in the Life of the Bridegroom. A Feminist Historical-Literary Analysis of the Female Characters in the Fourth Gospel* (Collegeville: Liturgical Press, 1998), 165-66.

[46] John's language is nuanced, indicating both commonality and differentiation in the relationship of Jesus and of disciples to the Father. See M. M. Thompson, *The Promise of the Father: Jesus and God in the New Testament* (Louisville: Westminster John Knox, 2000), 135-36, 144, and *The God of the Gospel of John* (Grand Rapids: Eerdmans, 2001), 70-71, 96-97.

[47] Lee, *Flesh and Glory*, 143-47, 152-57.

[48] See also Mark 13:32-37; par. Luke 12:35-48; 17:1-10; Tit 1:1; James 1:1; 2 Peter 1:1; Rev 1:1; 19:2, 5.

[49] The primary symbolic meaning of the footwashing, however, is union with Christ and cleansing through his death (13:8-10); see Lee, *Flesh and Glory*, 78-81.

shares knowledge, secrets and plans, a friendship based on understanding and trust.[50] Indeed, the most perfect form of love in this Gospel is not the love of enemies (cf. Matt 5:44-48), but the life-giving love of friends even to the point of death (15:13), a love exemplified in Jesus himself.

Yet in showing preference for friendship, the Fourth Gospel does not necessarily discount other models. The familial imagery crosses over into that of friendship, extending the household well beyond blood relations.[51] The master-slave model appears to be rejected yet the friends of Jesus are called paradoxically to "do as I command you" (15:14): the disciples "are no longer δοῦλοι depending on the wishes and the whims of a master, but φίλοι, intimate and equal associates of Jesus who loves them without limit."[52] In contemporary terms, friendship and obedience do not easily cohere. The language of friendship stretches beyond its normal reach, almost to breaking point, qualifying what is meant by this divine-human friendship: "The friendship is not ordinary friendship, but friendship with the unique Son."[53] Perhaps it is significant that the normal verb "obey" (ὑπακούειν) is not used in this context. Jesus speaks in the Farewell Discourse of "keeping my word" (14:23-24; 17:6) and "keeping my commands" (14:15, 21; 15:10, 20), where the Johannine verb τερεῖν ("to keep, guard") suggests guarding or holding what is precious and life-giving. While the Johannine Jesus does not invite servile obedience, disciples are drawn into a divine sovereignty that seeks their allegiance and commitment, as well as providing freedom and insight.[54]

A further aspect – though not explicit in the vine and branches – is that of worship. Here too the imagery of friendship expands beyond its normal limits. Jesus reveals to the Samaritan woman the need to "worship the Father in spirit and truth" (or "Spirit of truth," 4:23). Towards the end of the Gospel, Thomas acclaims the risen Christ as "my Lord and my God" (20:28). The relational model behind the language of worship is covenantal: "I will be their God, and they shall be my people." The

---

[50] The knowledge which Jesus shares with his 'friends' relates to his identity as the divine Son, the love and purpose of the Father's sending, the ongoing presence of the Spirit, and the glorification which is the true meaning of Jesus' life and death.

[51] Friends can be seen in the ancient world as part of one's household (οἶκος; van Tilborg, *Imaginative Love*, 149).

[52] Moloney, *Glory not Dishonor*, 65-66.

[53] Van der Watt, *Family of the King*, 367. See also Philo, *Plant.*, 90.

[54] Augustine distinguishes between a servitude based on fear (the opposite of love) and a servitude without fear, although the latter retains a sense of 'holy fear' that is perfectly compatible with love (*In Joannis Evangelium*, LXXXV.2).

friends of Jesus offer worship and adoration to the Father, through Jesus, as their part of the covenant, a worship that produces in disciples life, growth, and fruit. Indeed, Augustine regards the cultivation imagery of John 15 as both mutual yet differentiated in this way:

> For we cultivate God, and God cultivates us. But we do not cultivate God in such a way as to make him better for our cultivating. For we cultivate him in adoring, not in ploughing. But he cultivates us as a farmer the fields. Because therefore he cultivates us, he makes us better.[55]

Friendship and abiding do not dissolve the distinction between divine and human. Disciples are friends of Jesus, abiding in love, but they remain disciples, followers of the *Kyrios* who is the source of their love and worship. Friendship and obedience, in this case, do not cancel each other out. They exist in dialectical relationship, both equally necessary in defining the profound relationship between disciples and the one who is their Lord and Friend.

The friends of God are those who abide on the vine, who live as adult children in the household of faith. Worship and obedience are required of them, but only as these arise from the freedom of love. Disciples are not kept in the dark nor treated as servile and childish, but given access to understanding and insight, so that the allegiance they render is intelligent and perceptive. The only instruction they are called to observe is the love-command, a command that draws them into the Father's love for the Son (14:15; 21-24). Like the spokes of a wheel, the closer they come to the center, the closer they move toward one another. This ecclesiological vision is very different from legalism and servility. Disciples are called to abide in Jesus: to be friends of the One whose love and friendship for them is beyond anything they are capable of returning.

Conclusion

There are vital theological implications that flow from the Fourth Gospel's perspective on love and friendship that this essay can only touch upon. The Johannine vision of community challenges the individualism and detachment of Western culture, an individualism that is in large part the product of the Enlightenment, though largely unchallenged by post-

---

[55] Augustine, *In Joannis Evangelium*, LXXXVII.1.

modern thinking. Writing from an Orthodox perspective that is close to the Johannine worldview, John Zizioulas argues that the objectification of one human being by another is the consequence of the sinful denial of communion. Such denial allows the created world "to posit its being ultimately with reference to itself and not to an uncreated being."[56] The separation of *being* from *communion* means that our relationship to God becomes secondary or derivative rather than prior and intrinsic. As a result we are divorced from that divine communion which constitutes our being – disconnected also from communion with one another and the created world. In this sense, for Zizioulas, God's own being is itself "identical with an act of communion."[57] Such a viewpoint derives originally from the Cappadocian Fathers, with their stress on God as a communion of "persons," among whom no hierarchy or subordination exists but only the mutuality of love.[58]

Viewed from this perspective, the Fourth Gospel's focus on abiding and friendship is of immense significance. The Johannine symbolism dissolves the subject-object relation between the divine and the human that is characteristic of the Enlightenment. This dissolution begins in the divine realm, which is the archetype of all relations in the Johannine worldview. Abiding is an expression of the divine life, revealed in the Johannine Jesus who lives in union with the One who is the source of all being and whose nature is immanent and relational, as well as transcendent and holy. The trinitarian shape of revelation is not self-sufficient and isolating, but the source of intimacy. Into this friendship human beings are drawn, as subjects capable of loving response in freedom of heart. God is not paternalistic and condescending. The Father's love for the world is vulnerable and self-giving (1:11-12; 3:16), calling disciples to intimacy with God. Through the indwelling Spirit, human beings stand before God as subject to subject, I-Thou, drawing the world from isolation into love and community.

By dissolving the subject-object relation between divine and human, John's theological understanding includes the relationship between human

---

[56] J. Zizioulas, *Being as Communion. Studies in Personhood and the Church* (New York: St. Vladimir's Seminary Press, 1985), 102.

[57] Zizioulas, *Being as Communion*, 44.

[58] C. M. LaCugna argues that contemporary theology needs to recover the Cappadocian understanding of the Trinity (*God For Us. The Trinity and Christian Life* [San Francisco: Harper, 1991], esp. 53-79, 243-317; also 'God in Communion with Us' in C. M. LaCugna [ed.], *Freeing Theology: The Essentials of Theology in Feminist Perspective* [San Francisco: Harper, 1993], 85-88).

beings. Abiding in the love and friendship of God is never in isolation. Separation and autonomy are overcome in a vision of communion that encompasses heaven and earth, promoting freedom and personhood. Being drawn into friendship with God, human beings become friends to one another. To abide in love with others is to live in a community that works to overcome alienation and isolation, individualism and the ranking of human life.[59] It is mutual rather than condescending, co-operative rather than competitive, self-giving rather than status-oriented. As Mary Grey has argued, right relations lie at the heart of redemption; for her, we need to discern "those deeper patterns of affiliation and mutuality" which are part of the original fabric of the world.[60]

From this perspective, it is important to recover a renewed sense of the communion of saints (*communio sanctorum*), a concept that has been largely forsaken in modern industrialized society with its denial of death and material empiricism. Elizabeth Johnson sees the communion of saints consisting of the "friends of God and prophets" of Wis 7:27, who are "freely connected in a reciprocal relationship characterized by deep affection, joy, trust, support in adversity, and sharing life."[61] This communion of "friends and prophets" derives from the Johannine understanding of friendship in which the believing community abides in loving relation to one another. Johannine symbols of friendship and abiding support contemporary theological concerns to develop inclusive community over against individualistic segregation and isolation.

There is a further dimension that takes us beyond the immediate Johannine text, though not against its spirit. Abiding and friendship can be extended to kinship with a wounded creation, a creation exploited by Enlightenment anthropocentrism. Grey argues that creation itself is part of redemption and that relationship extends to all living things: "The theological meaning of Easter night, the night of redemption, symbolizes the renewal of the cosmos, with every aspect of creation drawn into the mystery of the resurrection."[62] Similarly, Johnson believes that the communion of saints embraces nature as well as human beings.[63] The Johannine

---

[59] O'Day, "John," 303.

[60] M. Grey, *Redeeming the Dream. Feminism, Redemption and Christian Tradition* (London: SPCK, 1989), 31.

[61] E. A. Johnson, *Friends of God and Prophets. A Feminist Theological Reading of the Communion of Saints* (London: SCM, 1998), 41.

[62] Grey, *Redeeming the Dream*, 51.

[63] Johnson, *Friends of God*, 217-218.

language of love and friendship has the potential to overcome alienation at every level, disclosing the pathway from isolation to intimacy with God and empathy with all created things.

The Johannine imagery of abiding in Jesus offers the basis for a renewed understanding of relationship. Divine friendship in the Fourth Gospel is grounded in the abiding of Father and Son, an abiding manifest through the incarnation, ministry, death and resurrection of Jesus. For contemporary theology, this central aspect of Johannine theology presents a powerful challenge to Enlightenment polarities, bestowing communion and intimacy in place of a rationalist and objectivist view of the world. John's imagery of love and friendship gives hope of an abiding-place where women and men belong in friendship with God and with each other, and also – by extension – in harmony with a re-made creation. For the reader of the Gospel, the symbolism makes possible a transfiguring awareness of personhood and communion, grounded in the love of the Spirit. This transforming experience of the life of God, symbolized in the Fourth Gospel as a communion of persons, is the inner meaning of salvation and the goal of all existence.

3. JESUS AS FRIEND IN THE GOSPEL OF JOHN

Gail R. O'DAY

"No one has greater love than this, to lay down one's life for one's friends" (John 15:13).

"Hannah is my best friend." So says my seven-year-old neighbor about the eight-year-old girl who lives two doors down from her. I do not know the exact meaning of that phrase to Solveig, or how she would define friendship. I do know, though, that Solveig acts out her friendship when she walks to school with Hannah every morning, takes a special trip to the town library with her on Wednesday, and plays with her at least one weekend day each week. Their friendship is apparent when Hannah and Solveig fall into each other's arms almost every time they see one another.

Yet Solveig and Hannah's friendship is much more than a sweet diversion and something about which the adults in their lives can wax sentimental. The formation of friendship bonds is one of the first acts of socialization that a child makes outside of its family. We choose our friends in ways that we do not and cannot choose our families, and so the formation of friendships is essential to the creation of social community. The ability and inclination to establish friendship bonds is key to the formation of a social network later in life. Friendship moves a person from being a private individual to a member of a social group based on something beyond kinship.[1]

Friendship, then, is not simply about affection but also about social roles and responsibilities. Friendship is not defined exclusively by what

---

[1] The wildly popular television show "Friends" builds on this social reality. For all the absurdities of its plots and of the economic ease with which its protagonists live in New York City, the show has created a world in which community is defined and built by the bonds of friendship, not family.

the individual "feels" for another, although affection is definitely a part of friendship. Friendship is at least as much about the social responsibilities that accompany friendship as it is about how people choose their friends.[2] Even as seven and eight year olds, Hannah and Solveig learn about social expectations and obligations through their friendship and also learn how to put their feelings of affection for one another into practice. Hannah and Solveig are trying on new identities in their friendship for one another. In their friendship, they are not simply defined as someone's daughter or someone's sister. The roles of daughter or sister are given to them, but the role of friend is one that they can create. Friendship places these two girls in a new world defined by relationship and mutual accountability.

This combination of affection, social choice and obligation, and practice has made friendship a perennially intriguing topic. In recent years, friendship has become an important category of theological reflection, especially among feminist theologians who are drawn to the patterns of reciprocity found in friendship.[3] God as friend and the Christian community as a community of friends are important themes that emerge. Friendship as a social and theological motif has been given considerable attention by NT scholars in recent years as well,[4] because it is a motif that the NT shares with the Greek and Roman cultures in which the early church took shape and the NT documents were written. Friendship was an especially popular topic in ancient Greece and Rome, as philosophers and storytellers attempted to define the social and moral virtues and the characteristics of a good society. When the NT talks about friends (φίλοι), it is using a vocabulary current in its cultural context.

---

[2] Say, e.g., on the morning of Hannah's birthday party, Solveig announces, "I don't want to go to Hannah's party. I don't like her – she wasn't nice to me yesterday." Solveig's mother then explains to her that she has to go to the party, because she and Hannah are friends, regardless of Solveig's feelings of the moment.

[3] See, e.g., S. McFague, *Metaphorical Theology: Models of God in Religious Language* (Philadelphia: Fortress, 1982); E. Johnson, *She Who Is: The Mystery of God in Feminist Theological Discourse* (New York: Crossroad, 1994); C. M. LaCugna, *God for Us: The Trinity and Christian Life* (San Francisco: Harper San Francisco, 1991); E. Moltmann-Wendel, *Rediscovering Friendship*, tr. J. Bowden (London: SCM, 2000).

[4] See, e.g., the two collections of essays edited by J. T. Fitzgerald, *Greco-Roman Perspectives on Friendship*, SBLRBS 34 (Atlanta: Scholars Press, 1997); and *Friendship, Flattery, and Frankness of Speech*, NovTSup LXXXII (Leiden: Brill, 1996).

Friendship in Greek and Roman Antiquity[5]

It is important to begin by noting that even though there is a consistency of vocabulary across the centuries used to discuss friendship in antiquity, there is not a consistency of emphasis or definition.[6] Because friendship is a socially embedded phenomenon, as the social fabric of a culture shifts, so does the understanding of the role and place of friendship in society. Each ancient writer, including the NT writers, worked variations on the friendship traditions depending on that writer's own community setting. The NT writers, and later Christians, can be read as shaping the discussion of friendship in antiquity, not simply dependent on following its conventions.[7]

The social dimension of friendship has long been recognized by ancient writers, especially philosophers. The particular context in which that social dimension was enacted shifted depending on the particular moment in history. For classical Greek philosophers in Athens in the 5th and 4th centuries BCE, for example, most notably Aristotle, "friend" or φίλος played a pivotal social role in the maintenance of the πόλις, the city-state. Aristotle devoted two out of ten books in the *Nicomachaen Ethics* to friendship,[8] a considerable portion of this treatise. For Aristotle and classical philosophers who followed him, friendship was not an incidental relationship. It exemplified, rather, the mutual social obligation on which the πόλις depended.[9] In the democratic ideal of the Athenian πόλις, the relationship between friends, φίλοι, was a relationship between equals contributing together to the public ethos of citizenship. To be a good friend was by definition also to be a good citizen.[10] To the philosophers, the success of the Athenian democracy depended on the enactment of friendship

---

[5] Most of this essay first appeared in *Int* 58 (2004): 144-57.

[6] For a discussion of the range of meaning of φίλος, see D. Konstan, "Greek Friendship," *AJP* 117 (1996) 71-94.

[7] A. C. Mitchell, "'Greet the Friends by Name': New Testament Evidence for the Greco-Roman *Topos* on Friendship," in *Greco-Roman Perspectives on Friendship*, 225-62, esp. 261-62. See D. Konstan, "Problems in the History of Christian Friendship," *JECS* 4 (1996): 87-113, for the contributions of later Christian writers to the concept of friendship in antiquity.

[8] Books 8 and 9.

[9] F. M. Schroeder, "Friendship in Aristotle and Some Peripatetic Philosophers," in *Greco-Roman Perspectives on Friendship*, 36.

[10] Konstan, "History of Christian Friendship," 90.

and the related virtues of courage and justice by its citizenry.[11] The following quote from Aristotle illustrates this well:

But it is also true the virtuous man's conduct is often guided by the interests of his friends and of his country, and that he will if necessary lay down his life in their behalf. …And this is doubtless the case with those who give their lives for others; thus they choose great nobility for themselves.[12]

The ideal city-state that Athens represented no longer existed after Philip of Macedon's conquest of Greece in 338 BCE and the empire building of Alexander the Great that followed. The establishment of the Hellenistic empire created a much more diverse and complex population. The sweep of Hellenism and the Hellenistic empire replaced the democratic ideal of the Athenian city-state as the social context for friendship. This shift continued with Rome's conquest of the Hellenistic empire in the second century BCE and the subsequent establishment of the Roman empire in 31 BCE. As a result of this shift in the political and social landscape, philosophical reflections on the meaning and value of friendship also shifted. Friendship remained a social virtue and moral value but was enacted in a different arena.

In the Hellenistic age and the Roman empire, for example, friendship was no longer viewed primarily through the lens of democratic citizenship. The classical perspectives remained touchstones for later philosophers, but Hellenistic philosophers took their reflections in new directions. In the Hellenistic period, the classical ideal of friendship met the realities of political pragmatism, and philosophical discussions of friendship reflected both realities.

In particular, a new sphere of friendship, patron-client relationships, entered the public arena. In the classical period, for example, a false friend was one who was not available in a time of crisis, but in the Hellenistic age discussions of false friends began to focus on those who have only their

---

[11] See, e.g., M. Nussbaum, *The Fragility of Goodness: Luck and Ethics in Greek Tragedy and Philosophy* (Cambridge: Cambridge University Press, 1986); Schroeder, "Friendship in Aristotle"; L. S. Pangle, *Aristotle and the Philosophy of Friendship* (Cambridge: Cambridge University Press, 2003). Athens was a small slice of the ancient world, even the Greek world, and the other city-states did not share the Athenians' enthusiasm for democracy. Sparta, for example, was more of a military state, whose military defeated Athens in the Peloponnesian War (431-404 BCE).

[12] *Nicomachaen Ethics* 9.8.9 (translation, LCL).

own betterment in view.[13] Among Roman philosophers like Plutarch and Cicero, discussions of friendship concerned not only what it means to be a friend but how to distinguish between a true friend and its opposite, the flatterer, κόλαξ.[14] As Plutarch wrote:

[T]he friend is always found on the better side as counsel and advocate, try-ing, after the manner of a physician, to foster the growth of what is sound and to preserve it; but the flatterer takes his place on the side of the emotional and irra-tional.[15]

Philosophers advised the patron on how to recognize social contacts who were not friends–those who did not have the patron's interests at heart but their own. One of the main distinguishing marks was the use of "frank speech" (παρρησία). "Frankness of speech, by common report and belief, is the language of friendship especially (as an animal has its peculiar cry), and on the other hand, that lack of frankness is unfriendly and igno-ble. ..."[16] Friendship was at least as much about one's private dealings as it was about public obligations.

Another Hellenistic social context in which discussions of friendship played a pivotal role was the philosophical schools. In many ways, these schools can be seen as reclaiming the classical ideal of a community of equals from the more pragmatic realities of patron-client relationships and the political expediency of "friends of the emperor."[17] This is clearly the case with the Neopythagoreans, who shaped themselves around the values of harmony and friendship first articulated by Pythagorus of Samos in the sixth century BCE.[18] The philosophical schools of the Epicureans and Stoics also gave a prominent role to friendship in their reflections on the meaning of the good life, the proper education and conduct of the good

[13] D. Konstan, "Friendship, Frankness and Flattery," in *Friendship, Flattery, and Frank-ness of Speech*, 8-12.

[14] See, e.g., Plutarch, *How to Tell a Flatterer from a Friend (Quomodo adulator ab amico inter-noscatur)*; Cicero, *On Friendship (Laelius; De amicitia)*.

[15] Plutarch, *How to Tell a Flatterer from a Friend*, 61.

[16] Plutarch, *How to Tell a Flatterer from a Friend*, 51.

[17] See the use of this expression in John 19:12.

[18] See Pythogorean sayings collections, e.g., H. Chadwick, *The Sentences of Sextus: A Contribution to the History of Early Christian Ethics* (Texts and Studies n.s. (new series) 5; Cambridge: Cambridge University Press, 1959) and J. C. Thom, *The Pythagorean Golden Verses: With Introduction and Commentary* (Religion in the Greco-Roman World 123; Leiden: Brill, 1995), and biographical traditions, *Iamblichus; On the Pythagorean Way of Life* (SBLTT 29; Atlanta: Scholars Press, 1991).

person, and the nature of community life.[19] The language of friendship provides language for talking about the construction of a community of like-minded people, informed by a particular set of teachings.

Early Christian understandings of friendship took shape in this diverse social context with its intentional reflection on friendship. Many different motifs from the Hellenistic conversations can be detected in the NT writings. For example, a well-known friendship maxim, attributed to Pythagorus and the Neopythagoreans, was that friends had all things in common.[20] Luke portrays the early Christian community in Acts as living out this value (e.g., Acts 2:44-47), and so this maxim provides a promising entry point for a discussion of friendship and community in Acts.[21] But not all NT writers are drawn to the same motifs; holding all things in common plays no role in the Johannine discussion of friendship, for example. The varieties of understandings of friendship that one finds in other Hellenistic writings are also found in the NT.

Friendship in John

The Gospel of John is a pivotal text for the discussion of friendship in the NT, as the vocabulary of friendship, especially the noun φίλος and the related verb φιλέω, occurs at key moments in the narrative.[22] As we will see below, friendship is one of the ways in which the revelation of God in Jesus is extended beyond the work of Jesus to the work of the disciples. One of the pivotal texts in Jesus' words of instruction and farewell to his disciples is John 15:12-17, in which Jesus calls the disciples "friends" and enjoins them to acts of friendship.

---

[19] For a careful discussion of one Stoic perspective on friendship, see C. E. Glad, "Frank Speech, Flattery, and Friendship in Philodemus," in *Friendship, Flattery, and Frankness of Speech*, 21-60.

[20] "Again, the proverb says, 'Friends' goods are common property,' and this is correct, since community is the essence of friendship" (*Nicomachaen Ethics*, 8.9.2).

[21] See A. C. Mitchell, "The Social Function of Friendship in Acts 2:44-47 and 4:32-47," *JBL* 111 (1992): 255-72.

[22] See three recent book-length studies of friendship and John: E. Puthenkandathil, *Philos: A Designation for the Jesus-Disciple Relationship. An Exegetico-Theological Investigation of the Term in the Fourth Gospel* (Frankfurt: Peter Lang, 1993); J. M. Ford, *Redeemer–Friend and Mother. Salvation in Antiquity and in the Gospel of John* (Minneapolis: Fortress, 1997); S. Ringe, *Wisdom's Friends: Community and Christology in the Fourth Gospel* (Louisville: Westminster John Knox, 1999).

The word "friend" in John carried many associations for most of John's first readers. Modern readers cannot completely recapture those associations for their own reading, but can at least recognize that John is not creating the theme of friendship out of whole cloth.[23] Awareness of cultural embeddedness helps modern readers see that friendship is not a universal term that means the same things in all times and cultures. Most contemporary friendship greeting cards, for example, adorned with roses, kittens, and butterflies, do not exhort the card's recipient to "lay down one's life for a friend," so that Jesus' words in John 15:13 seem completely unprecedented for a modern friend. As the above quote from Aristotle shows, however, Jesus' saying has precedent as a model for the ultimate friend in antiquity. This does not mean, of course, that any more people laid down their lives for their friends in the first century than are inclined to do so today – but that the possibility of doing so belonged to the ancient rhetoric of friendship.

In looking for interaction with Greco-Roman friendship motifs in John, one can look for the attributes and virtues that are associated with friendship in the Hellenistic world, as well as for the specific vocabulary of "friend" (φίλος *ktl.*). For example, in the NT period, the distinction between the friend who employs frank speech (παρρησία) and the flatterer (κόλαξ) was prominent in discussions of friendship. While the word κόλαξ does not occur in John, its opposite, frankness or boldness (παρρησία), does (7:4, 13, 26; 10:24; 11:14, 54; 16:25, 29; 18:20), suggesting a possible connection with these friendship conventions.

One can also look for stories in the Gospel in which friendship and its values are enacted. In the philosophical treatises on friendship, the virtues of friendship were often illustrated by reference to traditional pairs of friends (e.g., Achilles and Patroclus), suggesting that friendship is not simply an abstract social and moral virtue, but achieves its real worth when it is modeled and embodied in practice. In addition, Hellenistic narratives often recounted tales of friends and acts of friendship.[24] The most well-known of these may have been Lucian's *Toxaris*, in which two men tell each other competing stories about the practice of friendship to demonstrate the superiority of the people of their respective nations.[25]

---

[23] Of the three recent books on friendship and John cited above, two, Ford and Ringe, are attentive to the first-century social and rhetorical context.

[24] See R. F. Hock, "An Extraordinary Friend in Chariton's *Callirhoe*: The Importance of Friendship in the Greek Romances," in *Greco-Roman Perspectives on Friendship*, 145-62.

[25] Even if, as R. Pervo suggests ("With Lucian: Who Needs Friends? Friendship in

Our study of John will begin with the character of Jesus, looking for the vocabulary and attributes of friendship, as well as stories in which Jesus embodies friendship. From there, we can consider if Jesus as friend in John has any implications for contemporary theology. Two friendship motifs from the Greco-Roman world provide a promising framework for looking at Jesus as friend in John: Jesus' love for others that is embodied in his death and Jesus' boldness in speech and action.

Friendship, Love, and Death

The first motif, the offer of Jesus' life, receives the most attention in studies of friendship in John.[26] It is widely recognized among Johannine scholars that the notion of laying down one's life for one's friends is resonant with one of the classical motifs of friendship.[27] Plato's *Symposium* ("Only those who love wish to die for others") is widely cited as evidence of this aspect of friendship in antiquity.[28] Interestingly, it is not clear that this connection between friendship, love, and death in antiquity has had much real influence on the way Christian theology and piety interpret the death of Jesus in John. Perhaps it is feared that this resonance with the friendship conventions of John's time somehow diminishes the significance of Jesus' teaching about his own death or routinizes the death itself.[29]

In fact, the opposite is more likely the case – the connection with a well-known convention enhances John's presentation of Jesus. For the

---

the *Toxaris*," in *Greco-Roman Perspectives on Friendship*, 163-80), Lucian intended this work as a parody of the friendship tales of romances, the friendship *topoi* embodied by these stories had to have been widely recognized for the parody to be effective.

[26] E.g., both Ringe (*Wisdom's Friends*) and Ford (*Redeemer–Friend and Mother*) discuss this motif and its relationship to the love commandment (13:33-35 and 15:12), but neither of them even allude to the motif of boldness.

[27] E.g., R. E. Brown, *The Gospel According to John* (AB 29-29A; Garden City: Doubleday, 1966, 1970), 2: 664.

[28] *Symposium* 179B, also 208D. See also Aristotle, *Nicomachaen Ethics*, 9.8.9; Lucian, *Toxaris* 36; Epictetus, *Dissertations*, 2.7.3; Seneca, *Epistulae morales* 9.10. In the NT, see Rom 5:6-8.

[29] It is also the case that the distinctive soteriology of the Gospel of John is often subsumed under the models of vicarious suffering or Jesus' death as a ransom for sins. John does not subscribe to either of those dominant understandings of the death of Jesus, but those perspectives so dominate most Christian theology and piety that the Johannine voice is not heard. See G. R. O'Day, *John: Introduction, Commentary, and Reflections* (NIB IX; Nashville: Abingdon, 1995), 713-15.

first readers of John's Gospel, the link with friendship motifs helped to create a context for what John was teaching about Jesus' death. Since both classical and popular philosophy held up the noble death as the ultimate act of friendship,[30] Jesus' teaching in John fits a recognizable pattern. Jesus' words in John 15:13, for example, could be a friendship maxim from any philosophical treatise on friendship, as there is nothing distinctly Christological in their formulation: "No one has greater love than this, to lay down one's life for one's friends." In the teachings about laying down one's life for a friend, the Gospel's first readers would recognize that Jesus is evoking a world in which the greatest moral good prevails.

What distinguishes John 15:13 from other teachings on friendship and death is that Jesus does not merely talk about laying down his life for his friends. His life is an incarnation of this teaching. Jesus did what the philosophers only talked about – he lay down his life for his friends, and this makes all the difference in appropriating friendship as a theological category. The pattern of Jesus' own life and death moves the teaching of John 15:13 from the realm of abstract philosophical maxim to an embodied promise and gift.

John 10:11-18 well illustrates the transition from maxim to promise. In these verses, which form a central section of the Good Shepherd discourse, Jesus combines figurative and discursive language to evoke the type of friendship he offers the community. In 10:11a, Jesus says, "I am the good shepherd," but immediately moves away from first person language to describe more generalized activities of "the good shepherd." The good shepherd "lays down his life for the sheep" (v. 11b), as opposed to the hireling who would put the sheep at risk rather than risk his own life (vv. 12-13). This mini-parable could be taken as an illustration of the classical distinction between the true and the false friend – the false friend will not be around in a time of crisis, but the true friend will be.[31]

What moves Jesus' teaching here from maxim to promise is his return to first person language ("I lay down my life for the sheep" v. 15) and his move away from figurative language to talk directly about his own life and death: "For this reason the Father loves me, because I lay down my life in

---

[30] For an excellent discussion of "noble death" and its connections to John, see J. Neyrey, "The 'Noble Shepherd' in John 10: Cultural and Rhetorical Background," *JBL* 120 (2001): 267-91. Oddly, Neyrey never explicitly links the noble death motif with the motif of friendship, even though both John and Greco-Roman philosophers do.

[31] E.g., Lucian, *Toxaris* 36 ("Just so in calm weather a man cannot tell whether his sailing master is good; he will need a storm to determine that").

order to take it up again. No one takes it from me, but I lay it down on my own accord" (vv. 17-18a). The first person language makes clear that Jesus is not speaking generally about the gift of one's life for others but making a specific promise about his own life. Jesus has already pointed figuratively toward his death earlier in the Gospel narrative (e.g., 3:14; 8:28). What is new here is his direct speech about his death and the element of volition that he highlights. Jesus announces that he will choose to give his life for the sheep. His words are no longer generalized friendship teachings but are about the conduct of his own life.

The stories of Jesus' arrest and death show that his promises about the gift of his life can be trusted. The scene of the arrest in the garden has interesting echoes of John 10. Jesus leads his disciples into an enclosed garden, recalling the shepherd and the sheepfold of John 10:1-5; there is a thief in the garden (Judas, 18:2; described as κλέπτης in 12:7), like the bandit in the sheepfold (κλέπτης, 10:1). Against the backdrop of these echoes, Jesus' act of volition, in which he steps forward to meet those who come to arrest him (18:4-6),[32] can only be read as showing the truth of his announcement and promise in 10:17-18: he lays down his life of his own accord. At 18:11, Jesus states explicitly that he chooses the death that is before him ("the cup that the Father has given me"; cf. 12:27). Jesus' life is not taken from him, but he willingly chooses the ultimate act of friendship. Jesus also directly links the offer of his life to his care for his "sheep" (cf. 10:11-13), because his offer of himself is accompanied by the protective instruction to "let these men go."[33]

Jesus' free offer of his life for his friends is also illustrated in the quiet dignity of his death scene (19:28-30). Jesus announces the end of his own life and work ("It is finished"). The description of Jesus' moment of dying positions him as the actor in laying down his life, not as one acted upon: "Then he bowed his head and gave up his spirit."

The arrest and crucifixion narratives confirm that Jesus' words about laying down his life for others are much more than the articulation of the ideal situation. In the life and death of Jesus, the friendship convention of loving another enough to give one's life moves from philosophical or moral possibility to incarnated actuality. Jesus' words about laying down his life articulate the very real choices that he makes for his own life and

---

[32] Jesus does not wait for Judas to identify him with a kiss in John, thereby robbing the "thief" of any access to the shepherd and his flock.

[33] Neyrey, "Noble Shepherd," 291.

that guide his relationships in the world. What once was recognizable to at least some of John's readers as a standard part of philosophical rhetoric loses its conventional quality and becomes a distinctive description of who Jesus is. Jesus does not merely talk the language of friendship; he lives out his life and death as a friend.

Equally important, the convergence of Jesus' words with his actions shows that his words and promises can be trusted. Jesus does what he says. There is complete unanimity between what Jesus says about laying down his life and what Jesus does. Because Jesus is the Word-made-flesh, speaking and doing are inextricably linked in John (e.g., 14:10). Jesus both says and does what he receives from God: he speaks God's words and he does God's works (5:19-24; 10:38; 12:49-50; 17:7-8). Jesus' teaching about laying down one's life in John 10 is a reliable promise because his subsequent enactment of these words shows that Jesus' promises can be trusted.

The reliability of Jesus' promises and the integration of his speaking and acting set the context for his teachings about the disciples' own conduct as friends in John 15:12-17. Jesus' own life and death is what gives the teaching of John 15:13 its meaning. The maxim of 15:13 is inseparable from the commandment that precedes it, "Love one another as I have loved you." The Fourth Evangelist has told the reader that Jesus loved his own "to the end" (13:1). "To the end" (εἰς τέλος) can mean simultaneously "to the end of time" and "to the full extent of love," and both of these ways of loving carry over into Jesus' commandment to his disciples. Jesus' incarnation of limitless love moves the teaching of John 15:13 from the realm of the general (e.g., "Only those who love wish to die for others") into the very specific. Jesus' disciples are urged to live the same way Jesus has lived, to be the kind of friend that Jesus has been. He is not simply asking them to be good citizens or moral exemplars. He is commanding them to embody the very promises that he has embodied for them (15:14, 17).

The title "friend" is never used to describe Jesus in the Fourth Gospel. Throughout John, Jesus has been the incarnation of friendship without the explicit appellation. But in speaking of his disciples' future lives, Jesus makes the explicit connection between his life of love and the conduct of friends. Jesus calls the disciples his "friends" (φίλοι), if they enact his commandment (15:14) – to love one another as Jesus has loved them (v. 12), to lay down their lives for their friends (v. 13). Jesus' gift of his life for others embodies friendship's highest attribute and defines the meaning and extent of "love."

For Jesus' disciples, the title "friend" becomes something into which Jesus invites them to grow. The name "friend" and the relationship of friendship is a gift from Jesus to them,[34] just as his life is a gift to them. The disciples begin with the explicit appellation, "friend," and the challenge for them is to enact and embody friendship as Jesus has done. The disciples know how Jesus has been a friend; they are called to see what kind of friends they can become. Jesus' friendship is the model of friendship for the disciples, but it is more than that. Jesus' friendship also makes any subsequent acts of friendship by them possible, because the disciples themselves are already the recipients of Jesus' acts of friendship.

Friendship as Boldness of Speech and Action

As noted above, the theme of frankness or boldness of speech (παρ-ρησία) emerged as an important friendship motif in the Hellenistic period.[35] There were several social contexts in which this theme appeared. One, alluded to above, was the patron-client/monarch-subject relationship, in which the benefactor needed to be on the lookout for whether "friends" were speaking honestly and openly, or whether they were engaging in flattery to further their own ends. Another context where παρ-ρησία played a role was in the instruction of the philosophical schools, where frank speech was encouraged as a mark of honest instruction, dialogue, and training. To be someone's friend was to speak frankly and honestly to them and to hold nothing back. A third context, also associated with philosophical schools, used παρρησία to speak of the importance of freedom of speech, even when using that freedom meant taking unpopular positions and speaking openly against the authorities.[36]

Perhaps because this friendship motif does not have the same emotional resonance that is associated with language about love and laying down one's life, most studies of friendship in John have not lingered on this topic.[37] Given the importance of speech and speaking in the Gospel

---

[34] So R. Schnackenburg, *The Gospel according to St. John* (3 vols.; New York: Crossroad, 1982), 3:110. See also the language of election in 15:16, "You did not choose me but I chose you."

[35] See the collection of essays, *Friendship, Flattery, and Frankness of Speech.*

[36] See the essay by W. Klassen, "ΠΑΡΡΗΣΙΑ in the Johannine Corpus," in *Friendship, Flattery, and Frankness of Speech,* 227-54. This essay, while solidly grounded in the Hellenistic context, does not provide a very subtle reading of the Johannine material.

[37] See n. 23 above. Klassen's essay studies παρρησία but does not link it with friend-

of John, however, a friendship motif that focuses on the nature of speaking seems worthy of study. Moreover, the word παρρησία occurs nine times in the Gospel of John (7:4, 13, 26; 10:24; 11:14, 54; 16:25, 29; 18:20), more times than in any other book of the NT.

The first aspect of παρρησία, the distinction between flattery and direct speech, is not overt in the portrait of Jesus as friend in John. It is intriguing, however, to wonder if there are nonetheless some resonances of this aspect. The preceding discussion about death, love, and friendship showed how Jesus gave his life openly for others, with no hesitation. Jesus' free gift of his life provides the context for Jesus' words in 12:27 ("And what should I say – 'Father, save me from this hour?' No, it is for this reason that I have come to this hour. Father, glorify your name"). These words seem to be a play on the "agony" of the Gethsemane tradition from the Synoptic Gospels (e.g., Matt 26:39), in which Jesus asks that the cup pass from him, if that is God's will. John 12:27 acknowledges this piece of Jesus tradition, but transforms it to conform to the Gospel's understanding of the death of Jesus.

Yet there may be another reason why John handles the Gethsemane tradition the way that he does here. The words of the Synoptic tradition (e.g., "yet not what I want but what you want," Matt 26:39) could be read as the words of someone attempting to curry favor with a "patron." In John, God and Jesus are true friends ("The Father loves [φιλεῖ] the Son" 5:20); their relationship is not that of patron-client, but one of full reciprocity and mutuality ("The Father and I are one" 10:30). The revisioning of the Gethsemane tradition here makes clear that Jesus does not attempt to flatter God for his own purposes but seeks only God's glory.

A similar link to the flattery/direct speech contrast may also provide a context for Jesus' words in 11:41-42 ("Father, I thank you for having heard me. I knew that you always hear me, but I have said this for the sake of the crowd standing here, so that they may believe that you sent me"). These words, spoken by Jesus prior to calling Lazarus from the tomb, have always puzzled commentators, because they seem to interrupt the movement of the story and raise questions about the function of Jesus' prayer.[38] Read in the light of friendship conventions, however, it is possible that John includes Jesus' commentary on his own prayer here in

---

ship. Schnackenburg, *St. John*, 111, alludes to the connection between παρρησία and friendship in John 15 (see discussion below) but does not develop it.

[38] E.g., A. Loisy, *Le Quatrième Évangile* (Paris: Alphonse Picard, 1903), 651.

order to highlight that Jesus is not currying favor with God at this critical moment. He is not attempting to please God with a prayer and positive words. Rather, Jesus speaks in order to turn a moment that could look like flattery into a moment of open testimony, so that the crowd can see God at work in what Jesus does.

The second motif of παρρησία as a direct and open speech plays a more explicit role in the image of Jesus as friend in John. Of the nine occurrences of παρρησία in John, three refer to his instruction of the disciples (11:14; 16:25, 29). The first, 11:14, seems relatively straightforward and as such its potential significance for understanding friendship is overlooked. At 11:11, Jesus tells his disciples that "our friend (ὁ φίλος ἡμῶν) Lazarus has fallen asleep (κεκοίμηται)." "To fall asleep," in Greek as in English, can function as a euphemism for death. Jesus' disciples do not recognize Jesus' words as a euphemism, and so do not understand why Jesus should put himself at risk by returning to Judea if Lazarus is only sleeping (v. 12). The narrator explains the euphemism to the Gospel's readers, drawing attention to the disciples' lack of understanding (v. 13). In 11:14, Jesus explains to his disciples what he meant by the euphemism and explicitly names Lazarus' death. The narrator describes the speech act by which Jesus informs the disciples about the truth of Lazarus' situation as speaking παρρησία ("then Jesus told them plainly").

Perhaps this "plain speech" here is only the decoding of a figurative expression by a non-figurative one. Two aspects of the text argue against assigning this function to παρρησία, however. First, Jesus uses a standard euphemism "fall asleep," so it is not even clear that he was trying to mask his meaning. Second, unlike other sections of the Fourth Gospel where misunderstanding, irony, and metaphor are intentional literary strategies to move characters to deepening levels of theological understanding (e.g., John 4),[39] here the misunderstanding is corrected as soon as Jesus realizes it has occurred.

The role of παρρησία in Hellenistic friendship conventions suggests another way of looking at the exchange between Jesus and his disciples in 11:11-15. It seems fair to ask if Jesus' direct speech to his disciples might be an act of friendship, through which Jesus informs the disciples of the hard truth of the death of their friend Lazarus and prepares them for the

---

[39] For a discussion of this aspect of John, See R. A. Culpepper, *Anatomy of the Fourth Gospel: A Study in Literary Design* (Philadelphia: Fortress, 1983); G. R. O'Day, *Revelation in the Fourth Gospel: Narrative Mode and Theological Claim* (Philadelphia: Fortress, 1986).

consequences of this death. The disciples need to face squarely Lazarus' death in order to begin to contemplate the significance of what is to come, and that is impossible unless they realize that Lazarus is dead, not merely ill and sleeping. Jesus himself links his "plain speaking" to the disciples' welfare ("For your sake I am glad I was not there, so that you may believe" v. 15). Jesus must speak frankly to the disciples about Lazarus's death in order to equip them for the role of disciple that the situation may demand of them (in this case, to see a revelation of God's glory in the raising of Lazarus and so come to believe, cf. 11:2 and 15). Jesus treats the disciples as equals by speaking plainly to them.

The importance of παρρησία as a mode of speaking and instruction in John can also be seen in 16:25-33. This passage, set at the end of the Farewell Discourse and immediately preceding the Farewell Prayer of John 17, contains Jesus' last words of instruction to his disciples. In v. 25, Jesus contrasts his present speaking to his disciples, which has been "in figures of speech" (ἐν παροιμίαις), with his eschatological teaching ("the hour is coming"), in which he "will tell you plainly (παρρησία) of the Father." The contrast between figurative and direct speech tends to shape the interpretation of these verses,[40] but again one wonders if Hellenistic friendship conventions suggest another context in which to read Jesus' words here, especially since the vocabulary of friendship (φιλέω) occurs twice in vv. 26-27. In those verses, Jesus links the effects of the eschatological teaching ("you will ask in my name") with the Father's love of the disciples (αὐτὸς γὰρ ὁ πατὴρ φιλεῖ ὑμᾶς) and the disciples' love of Jesus (ὑμεῖς ἐμὲ πεφιλήκατε).

Love and friendship are the goal of Jesus' "plain speaking." Jesus' speech is not simply intended to lead to fresh comprehension on the disciples' part. Instead, Jesus intends to lead them to trust the relationship of love and friendship that they have with God and Jesus and thus to speak to God on their own, without the intermediary of Jesus' speech on their behalf (v. 26). Jesus speaks plainly, with παρρησία, in order to point the disciples to a different way of being with God and one another. This is why in vv. 30-33 Jesus disputes the disciples' claim to comprehend his plain speaking and hence to believe (v. 29). Comprehension without enactment misses the point of speaking παρρησία. Plain speaking has its

---

[40] Interestingly, Schnackenburg, who noted the connection between παρρησία and friendship in connection with 15:15 (see n. 36), makes no connection between "speaking openly" and friendship here (*St. John*, 161-66).

effect when the disciples act on God's love of them and their love of Jesus.

The combination of plain speaking and love is also found in Jesus' words to the disciples about friendship in 15:15. Although the word παρρησία does not occur, the sense of plain speaking does. Jesus gives the following rationale for calling the disciples friends: "I do not call you servants any longer, because the servant does not know what the master is doing; but I have called you friends, because I have made known everything that I have heard from the Father." The disciples are Jesus' friends because he has spoken to them openly; he has made known to them everything (πάντα) that he has heard from the Father. As Schnackenburg has noted about 15:15, "In our present text, Jesus enables his disciples to participate in the intimacy and trust of the Father, by means of which they acquire that 'openness' (παρρησία) which is the privilege of a free man and a friend... ."[41]

In this verse, the two motifs of friendship, love and open speech, come together in Jesus' relationship with his disciples. They are his friends because he speaks plainly and openly to them and tells them everything about God (15:15; 16:25) and because he loves them and gives his life for them (13:1; 15:12-13). They will remain his friends if they keep his commandment and love one another as he has loved them (15:14, 17). They are empowered to keep his commandment because he has told them everything, and so they have their own new relationship with God who loves them (16:26-27).

The third context in Hellenistic friendship conventions in which παρρησία occurs is that of freedom of speech. This is related to the flattery/frank speech contrast, because a friend is someone who both in private and public always speaks openly and honestly, regardless of the cost. Two occurrences of παρρησία in John point to this context. At 7:25-26, the crowd notes, "Is not this the man whom they are trying to kill? And here he is, speaking openly (παρρησία), but they say nothing to him! Can it be that the authorities really know that this is the Messiah?" The crowd's words testify to Jesus' character as one who does not shirk from

---

[41] 110. Ambrose, in *De officiis ministrorum* 3.22.135, sees in John 15:15 one of the core practices of Christian friendship: "Let us reveal our bosom to [a friend], and let him reveal his to us. *Therefore,* he said, *I have called you friends, because all that I have heard from my Father, I have made known to you.* Therefore a friend hides nothing, if he is true: he pours forth his mind, just as the Lord Jesus poured forth the mysteries of his Father." See Konstan, "History of Christian Friendship," 106-10.

the exercise of free and frank speech. Despite the personal risk, Jesus speaks openly in the face of the authorities.

In the second occurrence, Jesus speaks to his own character and the open character of his ministry. In his trial before the high priest, in response to questions "about his disciples and his teaching" (18:19), Jesus answers, "I have spoken openly (παρρησία) to the world; I have always taught in synagogues and in the temple, where all the Jews come together. I have said nothing in secret" (18:20). In the light of Hellenistic friendship conventions, it is possible to read Jesus' words here as more than just the distinction between public and private teachings. Rather, they show also that Jesus embodies the traits of open and direct speech that are the hallmarks of friendship. At Jesus' trial, at the moment of greatest public exposure, Jesus describes his ministry as having been characterized by freedom of speech throughout its duration. Jesus has not held anything back in his self-revelation but has spoken with the freedom that marks a true friend. His open and honest words are more important than any risk to his person.

Here, too, in the exercise of free and frank speech, there is an important convergence between word and deed. As the incarnate Word, Jesus does not simply exercise freedom of speech; he lives freedom of action. Jesus' entire life and ministry is an exercise of παρρησία. For example, his ministry is marked by repeated journeys to Jerusalem (2:13; 5:1; 7:10; 10:22; 12:1), the official seat of those in religious and political power. Even when the personal risk is quite clearly known, Jesus does not hesitate to live his life in boldness and openness. In one of the initial acts of Jesus' ministry, Jesus visits the Jerusalem temple and announces with both word and deed the truth that shapes his work in the world (2:13-22). This act sets the tone for what is to follow and demonstrates the truth of Jesus' statement in 18:20, "I have spoken openly to the world." His trial before Pilate also embodies open and frank speech, because Jesus does not hesitate to speak the truth to this figure of power (see especially 18:33-38).

Conclusion

Hellenistic friendship conventions assist us in understanding further the portrait of Jesus that the Fourth Evangelist is creating with these bold words and actions. Such boldness resonates with what the Hellenistic philosophers taught about friendship. Jesus is a true friend not only because of his gift of his life but also because throughout his life he has spoken openly.

The two friendship traits that we have studied are connected: Jesus is willing to speak and act boldly throughout his life because he is willing to lay down his life. Jesus is the ultimate friend. Friendship in John is the enactment of the love of God that is incarnate in Jesus and that Jesus boldly makes available to the world.

4. THE USE OF "INTERNAL ANALEPSIS"
A NEW LOOK AT JOHN 5:36-37a

Martin ASIEDU-PEPRAH

It is my privilege to offer this essay to Prof. Francis J. Moloney, in fond appreciation of his inspiration to me, and also in acknowledgment of his intellectual versatility that saw him combine successfully the traditional historical-critical methods and the more recent narrative methods and approaches in his study of the New Testament.

Much has been written by NT scholars on the subject of "witness" and the variety of uses of that term in the Fourth Gospel.[1] The noun μαρτυρία occurs fourteen times in the Gospel, and the verb μαρτυρέω thirty-three times.[2] The high frequency of the usage of these two terms underscores their theological significance for the Fourth Gospel where "witness" has to do mainly with the identity and the soteriological significance of the person of Jesus. One particular instance of the use of the verb μαρτυρέω that has caught the attention of Johannine scholars is its perfect tense in 5:37a: καὶ ὁ πέμψας με πατὴρ ἐκεῖνος μεμαρτύρηκεν περὶ ἐμοῦ. While a number of scholars explain this text in reference to 1 John 5:9-10 and speak of the Father's direct, internal testimony within the hearts of believers,[3] others are of the opinion that the Father's testimony refers to the OT

---

[1] For an extensive bibliography on the theme of witness in the Fourth Gospel, see J. Beutler, *Martyria: Traditionsgeschichtliche Untersuchungen zum Zeugnisthema bei Johannes* (FTS 10; Frankfurt: Josef Knecht, 1972). See also J. M. Boice, *Witness and Revelation in the Gospel of John* (Grand Rapids: Zondervan, 1970); A. A. Trites, *The New Testament Concept of Witness* (SNTMS 31; Cambridge: Cambridge University Press, 1977). See also the extensive discussion in S. Pancaro, *The Law in the Fourth Gospel: The Torah and the Gospel. Moses and Jesus, Judaism and Christianity according to John* (NovTSup 42; Leiden: Brill, 1975), 208-31.

[2] See J. Beutler, "μαρτυρέω," *EDNT* 2 (1991): 389-91; see esp. 389.

[3] See J. H. Bernard, *A Critical and Exegetical Commentary on the Gospel according to St. John* (2 vols.; ICC; Edinburgh: T&T Clark, 1928), 1:250-51; R. E. Brown, *The Gospel According*

revelation at Sinai.[4] On his part, von Wahlde understands the testimony of the Father as relating to the word of the Father which he has entrusted to Jesus and which Jesus proclaims to the world.[5] The purpose of this essay is to draw attention to the fact that from the point of view of narrative-critical exegesis, John 5:37a, with the perfect μεμαρτύρηκεν, constitutes an "internal analepsis" and therefore the understanding of the nature of the Father's testimony in the verse should be sought for from within the Gospel narrative itself.[6]

The Fourth Gospel has been noted for its sustained use of juridical metaphor in its presentation of the identity of Jesus as well as his soteriological significance for the world.[7] It is within the framework of the Johannine juridical metaphor, which is best understood as a "juridical controversy," that the verb μαρτυρέω and its cognates are used as part of the legal terminology of the Gospel.[8] From the narrative-critical perspective, there are at least four instances in the Fourth Gospel (John 1:34; 3:26; 5:33; 5:37a) in which the perfect of μαρτυρεῖν is found in contexts where the narrator resorts to the literary technique of "internal analepsis." The position that I defend in this essay is that in all the four instances in which the narrator uses the technique of "internal analepsis," his/her aim is to

---

to John (2 vols.; AB 29-29A; New York: Doubleday, 1966, 1970), 1:227-28; C. K. Barrett, *The Gospel according to St John* (2d ed.; London: SPCK, 1978), 266-67.

[4] See Beutler, *Martyria*, 261-62; Pancaro, *Law*, 216-18; for a full discussion of Pancaro's view, see 216-26.

[5] U. C. von Wahlde, "The Witnesses to Jesus in John 5:31-40 and Belief in the Fourth Gospel," *CBQ* 43 (1981): 385-404; see esp. 390.

[6] According to G. Genette, an "analepsis" is "any evocation after the fact of an event that took place earlier than the point in the story where we are at any given moment" (*Narrative Discourse: An Essay in Method* [Ithaca: Cornell University Press, 1980], 40). When it evokes an event that occurred within the narrative itself, it is described as an "internal analepsis."

[7] T. Preiss is generally acknowledged as the first to have emphasized the importance of the Johannine juridical metaphor for a correct understanding of the theological thought of the Fourth Gospel. See T. Preiss, "La justification dans la pensée johannique," in *Hommage et reconnaissance.* (CTAP 2; Neuchâtel: Delachaux et Niestlé, 1946), 100-18.

[8] Trites, *New Testament*, 80, has rightly observed that the idea of witness in the Fourth Gospel needs "to be understood in terms of Old Testament legal language." On the understanding of the Johannine juridical metaphor as a bilateral "juridical controversy" as found in the OT, see M. Asiedu-Peprah, *Johannine Sabbath Conflicts As Juridical Controversy* (WUNT 2/132; Tübingen: Mohr Siebeck, 2001). On the literary genre of "juridical controversy," see P. Bovati, *Re-establishing Justice. Legal Terms, Concepts and Procedures in the Hebrew Bible* (JSOTSup 105; Sheffield: Sheffield Academic Press, 1994), 30-166. See also Asiedu-Peprah, *Johannine Sabbath Conflicts*, 16-24.

recall an earlier event in the narrative that has to do with "testimony." The use of the perfect tense of the verb μαρτυρεῖν in all four instances, no doubt, is intended to emphasize the fact that the testimony constitutes an established datum and therefore has an enduring effect.[9] It is also my guarded opinion that the understanding of John 5:37a as an "internal analepsis" sheds new light on the nature of the witness of the Father mentioned in the verse.

The essay will first of all examine the four instances in the Fourth Gospel in which the perfect of μαρτυρεῖν is found (1:34; 3:26; 5:33; 5:36-37a). The aim will be to examine each text within its context and to establish the reality of the literary technique of "internal analepsis" in each of them. It will then look at how the understanding of John 5:36-37a, as an "internal analepsis," sheds light on the nature of the Father's witness mentioned in v. 37a. A brief conclusion ends the essay.

"Internal Analepsis" in the Fourth Gospel

John 1:34

John 1:34 forms part of the literary unit of 1:19-34. The latter deals with a series of testimonies that John bore in Jesus' favor. V. 19 which may be considered as the introduction to the whole unit sets the tone by stating clearly the object of the unit: the appearance of John as a witness.[10] John's first testimony to Jesus takes place during his encounter with the envoys of "the Jews" (1:20-28). His testimony here is twofold. On the one hand, he declares openly (ὁμολόγειν) that he is not the Christ, or Elijah, or the Prophet (1:20-22), and on the other hand, he points to someone his interlocutors do not yet know and for whom he is a herald and a witness (1:26-27). The second testimony of John takes place the day after his encounter with the envoys of "the Jews" (1:29-34). Seeing Jesus coming toward him, John not only describes him as "the Lamb of God that takes

---

[9] See M.-J. Lagrange, *Évangile selon Saint Jean* (5th ed; EB; Paris: Gabalda, 1936), 151; Barrett, *John*, 264.

[10] The whole of the literary unit of 1:19-34 is enveloped in an *inclusio* by the noun μαρτυρία (v. 19) and the verb μαρτυρέω (v. 34). It is thus obvious that the dominant theme of the unit is that of "witness." On the use and function of *inclusio*, see W. G. E. Watson, *Classical Hebrew Poetry. A Guide to its Techniques* (JSOTSup 26; Sheffield: JSOT Press, 1984), 282-84.

away the sin of the world" (1:29), but also reminds his unnamed audience that Jesus is the person he was speaking about the previous day (see 1:30). And as if to establish the authenticity of his testimony, John speaks of an event at which he assisted, namely, the descent of the Spirit on Jesus. The use of the verb ὁράω in 1:32 is of particular significance here. In the Fourth Gospel, it is often used in contexts of revelation (see 1:18; 3:11; 3:32; 8:38, etc.).[11] The descent of the Spirit on Jesus (1:32) in the narrative past of the Gospel was a revelatory event at which John was privileged to assist. The purpose was to enable him identify and bear witness to Jesus as the Chosen One of God (1:33). Thus, it is on the strength of this revelatory event that John now bears witness to Jesus (κἀγὼ ἑώρακα καὶ μεμαρτύρηκα) in 1:34. That we are dealing here with an "internal analepsis" is obvious from the fact that 1:32-34 evokes an event that has already occurred in the narrative past of the Gospel. However, in this particular instance, the reference is to an event that has not been narrated to the reader. This kind of "internal analepsis" may be described as "completing analepsis."[12]

John 3:26

John 3:26 forms part of the larger unit of 3:22-36 which can be subdivided into three smaller units: 3:22-26 (baptismal ministry of both Jesus and the Baptist); 3:27-30 (last testimony of John to Jesus); and 3:31-36 (monologue by Jesus).[13] In the context of 3:22-36, v. 26 can be described as a "bridge-passage" in the sense that it concludes the point about the baptismal activity of both Jesus and John and at the same time leads to the discourse of the Baptist in v. 27ff. In terms of content, the verse focuses on the disciples of John. They draw their master's attention to the baptismal activity of Jesus and the success it is having and make reference to the testimony that John had borne Jesus beyond the Jordan. The testimony of

---

[11] See, for instance, F. J. Moloney, *The Johannine Son of Man* (2d ed.; BSR 14; Rome: LAS, 1978), 154-55. In the view of M. C. Tenney, John's dual testimony to Jesus in 1:29, 33 (namely, as the Lamb of God and as the one who baptises in the Spirit) highlights both Jesus' atoning ministry and his right to divine authority. See M. C. Tenney, "The Meaning of 'Witness' in John," *BSac* 132 (1975): 229-41; see esp. 230-31.

[12] See Genette, *Narrative Discourse*, 51.

[13] On the structure of John 3:22-36 as well as on the identity of the speaker in 3:31-36, see F. J. Moloney, *The Gospel of John* (SP 4; Collegeville: Liturgical Press, 1998), 104-7.

John being alluded to here was narrated to the reader in 1:24-28. Thus, 3:26 constitutes an "internal analepsis," and since it serves to recall an earlier portion of the narrative, it may rightly be described as a "repeating analepsis."[14] Once again, the narrator uses a perfect tense of the verb μαρτυρεῖν (μεμαρτύρηκας) to underscore the permanent nature of the testimony of the Baptist in Jesus' favor.

John 5:33

The immediate context of this verse is 5:31-40 where Jesus invokes a series of witnesses in his effort to convince "the Jews" of the truthfulness of his Christological claims. The invocation of these witnesses here is to be placed within the context of the ongoing juridical controversy between Jesus and "the Jews" in the Fourth Gospel. Within the framework of the two-party juridical controversy, the reliability of the witnesses to be adduced must be obvious to the opposing party.[15] It is for this reason that Jesus in 5:31-40 calls on witnesses whom "the Jews" have seen and heard, and whose reliability they acknowledge: John (vv. 33-35); the works of Jesus as testimony of the Father (vv. 36-38); and Scriptures (vv. 39-40).[16] In 5:33, Jesus reminds "the Jews" that they themselves had sent a delegation to enquire about John's person and activity and that John had borne witness "in favor of the truth" (μεμαρτύρηκεν τῇ ἀληθείᾳ). The latter refers to the eschatological revelation that Jesus brings as the only Son of the Father.

The testimony of John to which Jesus makes reference here is narrated in 1:19-28. Thus, 5:33 constitutes an "internal analepsis" serving to recall an earlier event in the narrative, and as was the case in the two previous instances (1:34 and 3:26), the event being recalled here has to do with

---

[14] See Genette, *Narrative Discourse*, 54; R. A. Culpepper, *Anatomy of the Fourth Gospel. A Study in Literary Design* (Philadelphia: Fortress, 1983), 57-58.

[15] On the invocation of witnesses in the two-party juridical controversy, see Asiedu-Peprah, *Johannine Sabbath Conflicts*, 97-100.

[16] Johannine scholars are divided over the number of witnesses in vv. 33-40. Some speak of a three-fold witness (Boice, *Witness and Revelation*, 75-77; J. Bernard, "Témoignage pour Jésus-Christ," *MSR* 36 [1979]: 3-55; see esp. 3; Moloney, *John*, 186), while others see a four-fold witness (Brown, *John* 1:227-28; Pancaro, *Law*, 210; Beutler, *Martyria*, 255; von Wahlde, "Witnesses to Jesus," 385-404; see esp. 386). The three-fold witness adopted in this study highlights the fact that the works accomplished by Jesus constitute the Father's testimony to Jesus in his ongoing ministry.

"testimony" and the perfect tense of the verb μαρτυρεῖν is employed to underscore its enduring effect.[17]

John 5:36-37a

John 5:36-37a forms part of the unit 5:36-38 which deals with the works of Jesus as testimony of the Father. In v. 36a, the Johannine Jesus states explicitly that he relies on τὴν μαρτυρίαν μείζω τοῦ Ἰωάννου. Even though the Greek construction is incorrect, the context suggests that the expression is to be understood in the sense that Jesus possesses a weightier testimony than the one given by John.[18] In 5:32, the reader was informed of an ἄλλος who bears witness (ὁ μαρτυρῶν) to Jesus and whom the reader had rightly identified with the Father.[19] The use of the present participle (μαρτυρῶν) here is meant to express God's timeless quality as the one who always bears witness to Jesus. The Father always speaks and acts through Jesus and, in so doing, bears witness continuously to Jesus' words and deeds.[20] As the Word made flesh and the only Son from the Father (1:14), Jesus comes from heaven and bears witness to what he has seen and heard (3:31, 32) and always acts in perfect unity with the Father (5:19). Thus, the Father is the only one who can truly bear witness to Jesus. The reader therefore understands the μαρτυρίαν in v. 36 as a reference to the testimony of the Father. In what then consists the testimony of the Father? The testimony of the Father is made manifest in τὰ ... ἔργα ἃ δέδωκέν μοι ὁ πατὴρ (v. 36a). The ἔργα here refers to Jesus' miracles that are part of the salvific work (ἔργον) that the Father has entrusted to him.[21] These works have been given to Jesus by the Father, and

---

[17] Understood in the sense indicated above, it becomes obvious that there is nothing unusual about the perfect tense in 5:33 as claimed by von Wahlde ("Witnesses to Jesus," 388).

[18] For the meaning given above, one would have expected μείζω ἢ τοῦ Ἰωάννου; see F. Blass, A. Debrunner, and W. Funk, *A Greek Grammar of the New Testament and Other Early Christian Literature* (Chicago: The University of Chicago Press, 1961), § 185.1.

[19] This view is generally recognised by Johannine scholars; see Beutler, *Martyria*, 257; J. Becker, *Das Evangelium des Johannes* (2 vols.; ÖTBK 4/1-2; Gütersloh: Gerd Mohn; Würzburg: Echter-Verlag, 1979, 1981), 1:252, and all the major commentaries on the Fourth Gospel.

[20] The present participle by itself does not express time but only the aspect of the verb. It should thus be understood here as expressing a timeless quality. See M. Zerwick, *Biblical Greek* (Roma: Editrice Pontificio Istituto Biblico, 1963), § 371.

[21] Against this view, Bultmann maintains that ἔργα "refers to the whole of Jesus' ac-

therefore constitute the work of the Father himself.[22] The use of the verb δίδωμι here is significant. The reader recalls that already in 3:16, the verb δίδωμι is used to indicate an action on the part of the Father that demonstrates his love for the world. In the giving of his only Son (μονογενής [1:14]) as a gift to the world, the Father offers the world the supreme proof of his love. Thus, the works that the Father has given (δέδωκεν) to Jesus to accomplish in the world (5:36a) should be understood as a manifestation of his love for humankind. These are the very works that Jesus is in the process of accomplishing (αὐτὰ τὰ ἔργα ἃ ποιῶ), and which places his credentials as the authentic envoy of the Father beyond doubt (5:36cβ). The accomplishment of miraculous deeds by an envoy of God as a means of persuading people to accept his message is well known in the Old Testament (see for instance Exod 4:1-17) and "the Jews" who are Jesus' opponents in the ongoing Sabbath controversy allude to it themselves in the confrontation with Jesus on 2:18. Thus, a miraculous deed constitutes the kind of testimony that Jesus' opponents would consider as reliable and valid in a bilateral juridical controversy. It is for this reason that Jesus appeals to the works he does in unity with his Father as an obvious witness capable of convincing his opponents of the truthfulness of his Christological claims.

If as argued above, the works accomplished by Jesus are the works of the Father himself (5:36), then it is quite understandable that Jesus should see in them the testimony of the Father on his behalf. This will in turn mean that 5:36 and 5:37 do not in actual fact constitute two different witnesses, the works and the Father, but one, namely, the Father's witness through the works.[23] The works accomplished by Jesus constitute the Fa-

---

tivity as the Revealer," and more precisely to "the κρίνειν and the ζωοποιεῖν " (*The Gospel of John. A Commentary* [Oxford: Basil Blackwell, 1971], 265). See also Becker, *Evangelium*, 1: 253-54. Most Johannine scholars agree, however, that a distinction needs to be made between the singular ἔργον which refers to the whole of Jesus' salvific mission, and the plural ἔργα which has to do with the many individual miracles and deeds which are all parts of Jesus' mission. See, for instance, Brown, *John*, 1:224; Barrett, *John*, 266; Beutler, *Martyria*, 259-60; Moloney, *John*, 187. See also W. Thüsing, *Die Erhöhung und Verherrlichung Jesu im* Johannesevangelium (NTAbh 21/1-2; Münster: Aschendorffsche Verlagsbuchhandlung, 1960), 58-59; Tenney, "The Meaning of 'Witness' in John," 233, who rightly observes that "the 'works' comprised [Jesus'] miracles or 'signs,' which illustrated the operation of divine power on every aspect of human life."

[22] See John 5:19 where the emphasis is clearly on the historical activity of the Son and its relation to the activity of the Father. The activities of Jesus are the activities of the father himself and they bear witness to the truthfulness of Jesus' Christological claims.

[23] See Boice, *Witness and Revelation*, 79.

ther's testimony to him in his ongoing ministry. The assertion in 5:37a should therefore be considered as the logical conclusion that Jesus draws from his statements in the preceding verse (v. 36). If the works which the Father has given him to accomplish, the very works he is in the process of carrying out, bear witness that the Father has sent him (v. 36), then it stands to reason that the Father has indeed borne witness to him in his ongoing ministry (v. 37a). In this sense, v. 37a (καὶ ὁ πέμψας με πατὴρ ἐκεῖνος μεμαρτύρηκεν περὶ ἐμοῦ) should be rendered as: "And so, the Father who sent me has himself borne witness to me." The καὶ which opens the verse is here understood as consecutive,[24] and the use of the perfect μεμαρτύρηκεν, as in the three previous instances (1:34; 3:26; 5:33), indicates that we are dealing here with an "internal analepsis."

The Testimony of the Father in John 5:36-37a

The understanding of 5:37a as "internal analepsis" as well as the use of the consecutive καὶ and the perfect μεμαρτύρηκεν, in my opinion, provide the key to the correct understanding of the nature of the witness mentioned in the verse. In effect, they point to the fact that the witness in question has to do with an earlier event (or events) in the narrative with an enduring effect. In other words, the witness that the Father has borne Jesus has to be sought for within the narrative past of the Gospel narrative.[25] The question that one could ask then is: "what event (or events)

---

[24] See J. Bligh, "Jesus in Jerusalem," *HeyJ* 4 (1963): 115-34; see esp. 132 n. 1. On the use of the "consecutive" καὶ, see Blass-Debrunner-Funk, *A Greek Grammar*, § 4422, 2; M. Zerwick, *Biblical Greek*, § 455γ. Many Johannine scholars consider the καὶ either as a simple conjunction ("and"), or as an adjunction ("also," "moreover"). The reference would then be to some new testimony. See Brown, *John*, 1:222; Beutler, *Martyria*, 260. Even though Schnackenburg considers the καὶ as epexegetic rather than consecutive, his understanding of v. 37a is virtually the same as the one proposed above. See R. Schnackenburg, *The Gospel according to St John* (3 vols.; HTC 4/1-3; London: Burns and Oates, 1980), 2: 123-124. von Wahlde claims that he finds Schnackenburg's explanation of the καὶ in v. 37a (as epexegetic) unconvincing, but he offers no reason to explain his stand ("Witnesses to Jesus," 386 n. 6).

[25] As mentioned in the beginning of this essay, a number of modern scholars explain v. 37a in reference to 1 John 5:9-10 and speak of the Father's internal witness within the hearts of believers (See for instance, Bernard, *John*, 1:250-51; Brown, *John*, 1:227-28; Barrett, *John*, 266-67). However, the fact that Jesus is here concerned with adducing concrete witnesses that "the Jews" have seen or heard makes this interpretation unlikely. Others are of the opinion that the testimony of the Father refers to the OT revelation at Sinai or the Torah described in general terms (see Beutler, *Martyria*, 261-62; Pancaro, *Law*, 216-

within the narrative would the "internal analepsis" with the perfect μεμαρτύρηκεν be referring to?"

There are several factors that need to be taken into consideration.
Firstly, there is the proximity of v. 37a to v. 36 in which Jesus speaks of
the works he does as a testimony of the Father. The works that Jesus accomplishes are his, but they are also the works of his Father. The basis for
the assertion is the perfect functional unity that exists between the Father
and the Son, and which enables the Son to act exactly as his Father does
(see 5:19)[26] The testimony that these works bear to Jesus in his ongoing
ministry is in fact the testimony of the Father himself (v. 36). The proximity of v. 37a (the testimony of the Father) to v. 36 (testimony of the
Father through the works of Jesus) indicates that the two verses are related in terms of their meaning. Secondly, the understanding of the intro-
ductory καί in v. 37a as "consecutive" means that v. 37a is best understood as the conclusion to Jesus' assertion in the preceding verse (v. 36).
The testimony of the Father (v. 37a) would then refer to the ἔργα mentioned in v. 36. Thirdly, there is also the fact that the ἔργα mentioned in v.
36 has to do with the many miraculous deeds of Jesus that constitute an
integral part of the salvific work (ἔργον) entrusted to him by his Father.
Since, these are the very works that Jesus is in the process of accomplish-

---

18. For a full discussion of Pancaro's view, see pp. 216-26). This position, in my opinion,
mistakenly assumes that the Ἰουδαῖοι who are Jesus' interlocutors in the present context
are the Jewish people, past and present. The term Ἰουδαῖοι has to be understood not by
reference to a historical world outside of the Fourth Gospel but within the narrative itself. In this latter sense, it refers to a group of people who have made up their minds
about Jesus and therefore reject his Christological claims. This group of people represents one side of the Christological debate that is ongoing within the narrative. See
Asiedu-Peprah, *Johannine Sabbath Conflicts*, 67-68 n. 67. Additionally, the fact that there is
an explicit reference to the witness of the Scriptures in 5:39 lessens the likelihood that
the witness in 5:37a is that of Scripture. See von Wahlde, "The Witnesses to Jesus," 387.
Von Wahlde himself is of the view that the witness of the Father in the present context
"is precisely the word of the Father which he has given to Jesus and which Jesus gives to
the world" ("The Witnesses to Jesus," 390). This position also lends itself to criticism.
Firstly, it does not take into consideration the exegetical import of the καί which opens
v. 37a (a consecutive καί, in my opinion) and therefore fails to see the link between v.
37a and the preceding verse (v. 36). Secondly, it does not give the perfect μεμαρτύρηκεν
the importance it deserves. Far from being insignificant, the perfect tense points to the
fact that we are dealing with an "internal analepsis" in v. 37a and therefore the testimony
in v. 37a has to do with an event or events within the narrative itself.

[26] On the interpretation of 5:19 in terms of perfect functional unity (which includes
unity of being) between the Father and the Son, see Asiedu-Peprah, *Johannine Sabbath
Conflicts*, 81-83, and n. 129.

ing, the logical conclusion that one may draw here is that the ἔργα has to do with the miraculous deeds of Jesus mentioned in the Gospel narrative up to the present point. Thus, in the light of these factors as well as of the general context of the ongoing juridical controversy in which Jesus is concerned with adducing concrete witnesses that his opponents have either seen or heard, one may conclude that the miraculous deeds already accomplished by Jesus should be considered as the events through which the Father has already borne witness (μεμαρτύρηκεν) to Jesus. In other words, what Jesus would be telling his opponents (vv. 36-37a) is that, the works he performs constitute the testimony of the Father, and those he has already performed (2:1-11; 4:46-54; 5:1-9a) show clearly that the Father has borne witness to him in his ongoing ministry. The effect of the perfect tense (μεμαρτύρηκεν) in v. 37a is to present the testimony of the Father "as an established datum."[27] The testimony that the God of Israel has himself borne Jesus through the ἔργα constitutes an enduring proof that lends credence to Jesus' Christological claims.[28]

In conclusion, the narrator of the Fourth Gospel resorts to the literary technique of "internal analepsis" each time he/she wants to recall an earlier portion or event of the narrative that deals with testimony relating to the identity and the soteriological significance of Jesus. And in each instance, the narrator employs the perfect tense of the verb μαρτυρέω to underscore the fact that the testimony in question constitutes an established fact and therefore possesses an enduring effect. In other words, the descent of the Spirit on Jesus as witnessed to by John (1:34), the witness of John to Jesus as recalled by the former's disciples (3:26), the witness of John as recalled by Jesus (5:33), and the witness of the Father as manifested in Jesus' works (5:36-37a) all constitute an enduring proof of the truthfulness of Jesus' Christological claims that he is the Christ, the Son of God, and that faith in his name leads to eternal life (cf. John 20:31). The understanding of 5:36-37a sheds an important light on the nature of the

---

[27] Barrett, *John*, 264.

[28] This explanation of μεμαρτύρηκεν as an internal analepsis referring to the works already accomplished by Jesus in the Gospel narrative was first noted by the present author in his book published two years ago. See Asiedu-Peprah, *Johannine Sabbath Conflicts*, 105-106. The view of Schnackenburg differs from the one proposed here because he maintains that the reference is to "everything which, in the Johannine view, can be perceived in the concrete: Jesus' works, his words..., and the Holy Scriptures" (*John*, 2:124). In my opinion, the words of Jesus cannot be included here because of the close link between v. 36 and v. 37a as well as the understanding of ἔργα as referring basically to the miraculous deeds of Jesus.

Father's witness in 5:37a. It points to the fact that the testimony of the Father has to do with Jesus' miraculous deeds that have already been accomplished in the Gospel narrative.

5. ANOINTING THE TEMPLE OF GOD
JOHN 12:1-8

Mary L. COLOE

Boundary crossing is hazardous. There is the risk of leaving behind the known and familiar to venture into alien territory. In taking this risk it is helpful to have a guide to follow, one who knows the path and can steer the new traveler in the right direction. Frank Moloney has been such a guide in my own academic work. As teacher, *Doktorvater*, colleague and especially friend, he has encouraged and enabled my own ventures into Johannine research, publishing and teaching. In this regard, Frank has transcended a further boundary, that of gender, and may rightly be called *midwife* to the birthing of many new scholars throughout his long years of doctoral supervision. The following chapter, to honor Frank's achievements, presents a woman who also dares to transcend gender boundaries when she acts as priest and prophet to anoint the new Temple of God.

Temple Background

In the Prologue to the Fourth Gospel, Jesus is introduced as the tabernacling presence of the divine λόγος (1:14). Cultic imagery, implied by the use of the term ἐσκήνωσεν, with its allusion to the Tabernacle, is then made explicit in chapter 2, in the first "public" action of Jesus when he drives the dealers and moneychangers from the Temple (2:13-22). Standing within the monumental edifice of the recently extended and renovated Temple, Jesus lays claim to this building, his Father's house (2:16), as a symbol of his own self-identity. Because of the intimacy between the λόγος and θεός (1:1), Jesus is the new locus of God's dwelling (1:14) and so he can rightly say, "Destroy this Temple, and in three days I will raise it up" (2:19); the narrator then adds, "He spoke of the Temple of his body" (2:21). In an earlier work I argued that this scene in John 2 is the hermeneutical key to understanding both Jesus' identity and mission in the Fourth Gospel.[1] It is up to the rest of the narrative to show how a Temple is destroyed by "the Jews" and raised by Jesus. If the text does not show this, then its claim to truthfulness (19:35) has no foundation.

The following chapters of *God Dwells with Us* demonstrated that the narrative does in fact support and carry out these programmatic words. Not only is the Temple a major Christological symbol, but this symbol is doubly transferred in its meaning:

  i. from a building to the person of Jesus (John 2; 4)
  ii. from the person of Jesus to the believing community (John 7; 14)[2]

At the cross the narrative reaches its conclusion when Jesus dies under the title, "the Nazarene" (19:19). Where other Gospels call this an *inscription* (Mark 15:25; Luke 23:38) or *charge* (Matt 27:37), the Fourth Gospel calls this a title – τίτλον (19:19) and it is a title reserved for the Passion account where it occurs twice in the Garden of Gethsemane (18:5, 7) and here on the cross. This unique Johannine title "the Nazarene" may be explained by the use of first century rabbinic exegetical methods which allow two passages using a similar term to be associated.[3] Isa 11:1 and Zech 12:6 can be associated through the similar term "branch."[4] The book of Zechariah is the only biblical text that names the builder of the new Temple; "Here is a man whose name is Branch, for he shall branch out from

---

[1] M. L. Coloe, *God Dwells with Us: Temple Symbolism in the Fourth Gospel* (Collegeville: Michael Glazier Liturgical Press, 2001), 65-84.

[2] This transformation from Jesus to the community begins in John 7:37-39 and continues in 14:2 using the Temple language of *My Father's House* (cf. 2:16). John 14 transforms the meaning of the phrase "My Father's House" into "My Father's Household" in the description of the many divine indwellings within the believers (14:10, 17, 23, 25). See Coloe, *God Dwells with Us*, chapters 6 and 8.

[3] This method, based on similar, not necessarily identical terms, is known as *kayotse bo bemaqom aher*. For further details of rabbinic exegesis see F. Manns, *L'Évangile de Jean à la lumière du Judaïsme* (SBFA 33; Jerusalem: Franciscan Printing Press, 1991) 307-19; also J. J. Scott Jr., *Jewish Backgrounds of the New Testament* (Grand Rapids: Baker Books, 1995) 127-33.

[4] For a more detailed discussion of these texts, see Coloe, *God Dwells*, 171-74. An article by H. P. Rüger makes a similar case for linking "Nazareth" with Isaiah 11:1 when examining the Synoptic usage in Matt 2:23; 13:54 and Mark 6:1. He makes no mention of the Johannine usage ("NAZAREQ/NAZARA NAZARHNOΣ/NAZΩRAIOΣ," *ZNW* 72 [1981]: 257-63).

this place and he shall build the temple of the Lord" (Zech 6:12). In the MT the word translated "Branch" in Zechariah (*Tzamah*) is not the same Hebrew word we find in Isaiah (*Netzer*), but by first century methods of exegesis it was possible to use these similar terms interchangeably and the evidence from Qumran shows that this interchange was happening.[5] Where in the synoptic usage, the term "Nazarene" would simply mean "Jesus from Nazareth," by the meticulous usage found in the Fourth Gospel this title establishes Jesus as "the Nazarene" – the Temple builder from Zechariah.[6] In the crucifixion, while "the Jews" destroy one Temple, the Temple of his body, Jesus is simultaneously raising another Temple just as he promised (2:21).

From the cross Jesus alters the relationship between his mother and the Beloved Disciple standing below (19:25b-27). In so doing, the disciple becomes son to the mother of Jesus; the disciple becomes brother/sister to Jesus, and child of the one Jesus calls Father.[7] This is the moment, through the gift of the Spirit, that discipleship becomes divine filiation in the Johannine perspective. Following this scene, when the Risen One appears to Mary Magdalene, he tells her, "Go to my brothers and sisters and say to them, I am ascending to my Father and *your* Father, to my God and your God" (20:17). The Hour of Jesus draws disciples into the Father's House, now properly termed the Father's Household.[8] Another way of saying this is that the new Temple/Household of God is the Johannine community in whom the Risen Christ dwells through the mediation of the Spirit.

The above paragraphs provide a sweeping overview of the arguments in my book where the community, as the living Household/House of God, is the new Temple raised up in the Hour. With this as background I now turn to John 12.

---

[5] 4Q161 (4QpIsa[a] line 18).

[6] In John 1:45, the only other place where Nazareth is mentioned, the text reads "Jesus son of Joseph from Nazareth," thus directly linking the locality with Joseph not Jesus.

[7] M. L. Coloe, "Raising the Johannine Temple (Jn 19:19-37)," *ABR* 48 (2000): 47-58, also *God Dwells*, 186-90.

[8] For a discussion of the use of this term "My Father's House" (14:2) see Coloe, *God Dwells*, 157-78.

John 12:1-8

In comparing the Johannine anointing with the scene, as it is found in the Synoptics, especially Mark and Matthew, there are four Johannine features:

  i. a time frame is given – "six days before the Passover" (12:1);
  ii. the unknown woman is named as Mary, sister to Martha and Lazarus from John 11 (12:3);
  iii. the Evangelist comments "the fragrance of the perfume fills the house" (12:3);
  iv. Judas is named and described as the one to criticize her action (12:4-6).

The rest of this paper will examine the significance of these Johannine features to discover what importance they have within the theological perspective of this Gospel as outlined above.

Six Days before Passover[9]

Naming such a specific time is not usual in the Fourth Gospel. Far more common is the general expression, "Now the Passover, the Feast of the Jews, was at hand"[10] (6:4; see also 7:2; 11:55). Scholars offer various interpretations for the naming of "six days." Barrett sees in this time frame and the perfume a reference to the *Habdalah* ceremony marking the end of the Sabbath on the Saturday night, with Passover beginning the following Friday evening.[11] Schneiders reckons the counting of days differently and places this meal on the Sunday evening and thus links it to the Eucharistic experience of the early Church.[12] Schnackenburg also suggests the Sunday but dismisses this time detail as having no "further meaning."[13] I agree with Barrett and Schneiders that the time detail, par-

---

[9] Both Holst and Fortna see this expression as part of the Johannine redaction of his source material; see R. Holst, "The one anointing of Jesus: another application of the form-critical method." *JBL* 95 (1976): 439; R. Fortna, *The Fourth Gospel and its Predecessor: From Narrative Source to Present Gospel* (SNTW; Edinburgh: T&T Clark, 1988), 144.

[10] ἦν δὲ ἐγγὺς τὸ πάσχα, ἡ ἑορτὴ τῶν Ἰουδαίων.

[11] C. K. Barrett, *The Gospel According to St John* (2d ed.; London: SPCK, 1978), 410-11.

[12] S. Schneiders, *Written That You May Believe: Encountering Jesus in the Fourth Gospel* (New York: Crossroad, 1999), 107.

[13] R. Schnackenburg, *The Gospel According to St John* (trans. K. Smyth et al.; 3 vols.;

ticularly the unusual way it is expressed, is significant. I suggest two possible backgrounds for this detail of time, one liturgical and one Christological, with each one building on and developing the other, as is so often the case in the Fourth Gospel.

Liturgical Background

In the reckoning of days I agree with Barrett that the meal at Bethany took place on the Saturday night at the conclusion to the Sabbath, six days before the Passover, which in the Fourth Gospel began on the Friday evening coinciding with the next Sabbath day (19:31). In this case the *Habdalah* ceremony provides a liturgical context for a scene involving a meal, sweet aromatic spices, and an anointing. According to Barrett, since both schools of Hillel and Shammai agree on the elements of meal, light and spices, it is likely that this service was happening at the time of Jesus.[14] The Talmud dates the *Habdalah* back to men of the Great Synagogue between the 6th and 4th Century BCE (Ber.33a) although the exact order and wording were not finalized until talmudic times.[15] The ceremony to conclude the Sabbath began as late as possible and it marked the separation of Sabbath from the rest of the week.[16] The *Habdalah* prayers made three distinctions, between the sacred and profane, between light and dark, and between Israel and other nations.[17] A special blessing was prayed over the spices since the close of Sabbath meant the departure of joy, and the departure of a second soul, which was present with the individual only while the Sabbath lasted. According to Millgram, the "sweet smelling spices symbolize the spiritual farewell 'feast' for the departing 'additional soul' which the Jew figuratively possesses on the Sabbath," while for Idelsohn

HTCNT; London: Burns & Oates, 1968-1982), 2: 366. Similarly R. Bultmann, *The Gospel of John: A Commentary* (trans. G. R. Beasley Murray et al.; Oxford: Blackwell, 1971), 414 n. 5; F. J. Moloney, *Signs and Shadows: Reading John 5-12* (Minneapolis: Fortress, 1996), 180 n. 4.

[14] Barrett notes there was controversy over the *order* of these elements but not the elements themselves (*John*, 411).

[15] A. E. Millgram, *Jewish Worship* (Philadelphia: Jewish Publication Society of America, 1971), 297.

[16] Rather than at sunset, the *Habdalah* service did not start until three small stars appeared in the sky together. S. Segal, *The Sabbath Book* (2d ed.; New York: Thomas Yoseloff, 1957), 127.

[17] A. Z. Idelsohn, *Jewish Liturgy and its Development* (New York: Schocken, 1932), 148.

the perfume of the spices was meant to invigorate the worshippers in this soul's absence.[18] Both of these aspects, farewell and encouragement, fit well in the context of the Gospel and may supply a liturgical background for the way in which the odor of the perfume is highlighted in this Gospel (12:3). These themes of farewell and encouragement will be made more explicit in the following chapters 13–17.

The *Habdalah* marked a movement from sacred *time* to ordinary *time* and within Judaism another way of demarcating the sacred from the secular was through a ritual of anointing. Holy objects, persons and spaces were set aside for God's service through anointing with special spices.

Then you shall take the anointing oil, and anoint the tabernacle and all that is in it, and consecrate it and all its furniture; and it shall become holy. You shall also anoint the altar of burnt offering and all its utensils, and consecrate the altar; and the altar shall be most holy. You shall also anoint the laver and its base, and consecrate it. Then you shall bring Aaron and his sons to the door of the tent of meeting, and shall wash them with water, and put upon Aaron the holy garments, and you shall anoint him and consecrate him, that he may serve me as priest (Exod 40:9-13).

While there was no specific anointing within the *Habdalah* ceremony, the odor of the spices and the blessings mark out in time what anointing does in space, namely, the separation between the sacred and profane. Whatever the historical meaning behind the woman's act of anointing Jesus, by placing this episode in a meal, possibly marking the close of Sabbath, where blessings are said to distinguish the sacred from the profane, this Gospel highlights the sacredness of Jesus' body. While the narrative does not describe the blessings and rituals to bring the Sabbath to a close, it would be presumed that a Jewish audience/readership would be familiar with these rituals, familiar also with the Johannine dating of Jesus' death on the eve of both Passover and the Sabbath, and so the naming of "six days before the Passover" for this community would be sufficient to evoke the liturgical context. This brings me to the second possible meaning behind the term "six days," namely a Christological meaning.

---

[18] Millgram, *Jewish Worship*, 300; Idelsohn, *Jewish Liturgy*, 149. For further on this additional soul see Segal, *Sabbath Book*, 184

Christological Background

The beginning of Jesus' public ministry was introduced by a specific reference to time, "On the third day, there was a marriage at Cana in Galilee" (2:1). Moloney argues that the time reference in this pericope is very significant and even a key to its understanding. The "three days" echoes the description of the "three days" of preparation before the manifestation of God's glory on Sinai (Exod 19).[19] As the public ministry draws to a close I believe the Evangelist again makes use of a specific time frame and the Exodus imagery to recapitulate his presentation of Jesus' identity and mission prior to the start of his Hour.

Exodus 35 introduces for a second time the instructions for building the tabernacle.

"Six days shall work be done, but on the seventh day you shall have a holy Sabbath of solemn rest to the LORD; whoever does any work on it shall be put to death; you shall kindle no fire in all your habitations on the Sabbath day." Moses said to all the congregation of the people of Israel, "This is the thing which the LORD has commanded. Take from among you an offering to the LORD; whoever is of a generous heart, let him bring the LORD's offering: gold, silver, and bronze; blue and purple and scarlet stuff and fine twined linen; goats' hair, tanned rams' skins, and goatskins; acacia wood, oil for the light, spices for the anointing oil and for the fragrant incense" (Exod 35:2-8).

The rest of the book of Exodus is taken up with these instructions and the building of the Tabernacle. All that has gone before, the plagues, the miracle at the Sea, the covenant, all lead to the culmination of the Exodus event in preparing a place so that God may have a dwelling with the people. By itself the mention of six days in 12:1 may have various other precedents, but the Johannine anointing episode links six days with an act of anointing and a "generous" amount of spices so that the house is filled with the odor of the perfume. It is when all three elements are taken together that the Exodus tabernacle background is suggested. If I am correct in making this Exodus link we have here a further example of the Jesus/tabernacle/Temple motif which this Gospel uses to emphasize both continuity with Israel's heritage while professing its fulfillment as promised in the Scriptures.

---

[19] F. J. Moloney, *John* (SP 4; Collegeville: Michael Glazier Liturgical Press, 1998), 66-70.

The Targums and the Anointing

The case for seeing the Christological significance of the anointing may be strengthened by considering the Targumic evidence, while noting the difficulty in dating these passages. In Exodus 40, Moses is told "you shall take the anointing oil and anoint the tabernacle ... you shall also anoint the altar of burnt offerings ... you shall also anoint the laver and its base" (40:9-11). Targum Pseudo-Jonathan, elaborating on the triple command *to anoint,* has the following:

Take anointing oil and anoint the tabernacle and consecrate it
  For the sake of the royal crown of the house of Judah and of the King Messiah.
You shall anoint the altar ...
  For the sake of the crown of the priesthood of Aaron and his sons and Elijah the High Priest.
You shall anoint the laver
  For the sake of Joshua your attendant, the head of the Sanhedrin of his people, by whom the land of Israel is to be divided, and (for the sake of) the Messiah, the son of Ephraim.[20]

The mention of the two crowns of royalty and priesthood and the name "Joshua" bears striking resemblance to the words of Zech 6:12, which I have already noted, indicate the one who will build the new Temple.

Take from them [the exiles Heldai, Tobijah and Jedaiah] silver and gold and make *crowns* and set [them] upon the head of *Joshua* the son of Jehozadak the high priest; and say to him, "Thus says the Lord of Hosts, 'Behold the man whose name is the Branch: for he shall branch out from this place, and he shall build the temple of the Lord. It is he who shall build the Temple of the Lord and he shall bear *royal* honor, and shall sit and rule upon his throne and shall be a *priest* upon his throne'" (Zech 6:10-13).[21]

Zechariah identifies Joshua, the Temple builder as one who can rightly wear the crowns of Kingship and Priesthood. Hanson notes that "In

---

[20] The Cairo Damascus Document speaks of dual Messiahs of Aaron and Israel CD 12:22-23; 13:20-22; CD 19:34-20:1; CD 14:18-19; CD 19:9-11. The antiquity of the idea of dual Messiahs is attested to by the fragments of the Damascus document found at Qumran.

[21] This is a confused text and where the Hebrew has plural "crowns," the Greek reads a singular "crown" and does not associate the role of King and Priest with only one person.

Greek 'Joshua' is of course indistinguishable from Jesus so an early Christian might well believe … that this passage concerned Jesus Christ."[22] In the Fourth Gospel these three roles will come together in the Hour of Jesus when, as the Royal Priest, he builds the new Temple of God.[23] It is possible that the Targum rendition of Exod 40:9-13 has developed as a midrash on Zech 6:10-13. The crowns of Kingship and Priesthood set upon the one to build the future temple, according to Zechariah, may have led to the triple elaboration of the Tabernacle's anointing in the Targum version. Even if the Targum were not pre-Christian, the Gospel of John and the Targum show signs of similar exegetical tendencies. Read in the light of these tendencies Mary's anointing not only identifies Jesus as the anointed Tabernacle/Temple of God, but also points ahead to his passion when he will be revealed as both King and Priest.

The House is Filled with the Fragrance of the Perfume

When the tabernacle has been built, Moses is instructed to take the specially prepared anointing oil and anoint it: "And you shall take the anointing oil, and shall anoint the tabernacle" (LXX Exod 40:9).[24] When Moses completes all the instructions of God, in words echoing back to Genesis (Gen 2:2), and picked up later in John (19:30), we read, "So Moses finished (συνετέλεσεν) the work" (Exod 40:33).[25] The final scene in Exodus is the tabernacle being filled with the presence of God's glory.

Then the cloud covered the tent of meeting, and the glory of the LORD filled the tabernacle. And Moses was not able to enter the tent of meeting, because the cloud abode upon it, and the glory of the LORD filled the tabernacle (Exod 40:34-35).

A similar expression is used when Solomon builds the Jerusalem Temple.

---

[22] Hanson relates the anointing passage to Haggai 2:6-9 where words are addressed to Zerubabel and Joshua; see A. T. Hanson, *The New Testament Interpretation of Scripture* (London: SPCK, 1980), 118-21.

[23] I have argued that the Passion account not only revealed Jesus as King but also as High Priest (Coloe, *God Dwells*, 201-6). See this place for further references to interpretations along similar lines.

[24] καὶ λήμψη τὸ ἔλαιον τοῦ χρίσματος καὶ χρίσεις τὴν σκηνὴν (LXX Exod 40:9).

[25] These three passages all use forms of the verb τελέω.

And when the priests came out of the holy place, a cloud filled the house of the Lord… for the glory of the LORD filled the house of the LORD (1Kings 8:10-11).

Prior to the giving of instructions for the tabernacle, God's glory is present on Mount Sinai for six days (Exod 24:16). On the seventh day the revelation begins. Echoes of the building of the Tabernacle and Temple pervade the episode in John 12. As "the hour" approaches God's glory, now to be seen in the flesh of Jesus (1:14), will be present with the disciples for six days, leading up to the full manifestation of his glory on the cross. As part of the preparation for this full manifestation, Mary repeats the actions of Moses. Just as Moses took specially prepared oil and anointed the tabernacle, Mary anoints Jesus, whose flesh is the tabernacle of God's presence. The wiping of the feet with Mary's hair also carries an allusion to Exodus. The Tabernacle was covered with curtains made from goats' hair (Exod 26:7), given by those of "generous heart" (Exod 35:6) and made by women whose hearts were moved with ability (Exod 35:26). Mary covers Jesus' feet with her own hair as she wipes away the perfumed oil poured out in generous abundance. The extended discourse we find in John 13–16, when Jesus instructs his disciples who will be formed into the new dwelling place of God (19:25-27),[26] has some parallel with the extended instructions given for the building of the Tabernacle (Exodus 25–31).[27]

In the building of the tabernacle the description of the spices used to make the anointing oil emphasize their purity and abundance. "Take the finest spices: of liquid myrrh five hundred shekel, and of sweet smelling cinnamon half as much, that is two hundred fifty and two hundred fifty of aromatic cane" (LXX Exod 30:23).[28] John 12 similarly emphasizes the purity of the ointment ("pure nard") the large amount and its expense (12:3, 5). Finally, the expression unique to the Fourth Gospel, "and the

---

[26] John 19:26-28 is the moment when Jesus' words in 2:19 are fulfilled when he draws disciples into his own experience of divine filiation through his words to his mother and Beloved Disciple. See Coloe, *God Dwells*, 185-90.

[27] Hanson also views this passage in John 12 as a reference to Jesus as the Temple but he sees v. 3 as an allusion to Haggai 2:6-9 where I place more emphasis on the Exodus account of the Tabernacle.

[28] καὶ σὺ λαβὲ ἡδύσματα τὸ ἄνθος σμύρνης ἐκλεκτῆς πεντακοσίους σίκλους καὶ κινναμώμου εὐώδους τὸ ἥμισυ τούτου διακοσίους πεντήκοντα καὶ καλάμου εὐώδους διακοσίους πεντήκοντα.

house was filled with the fragrance of the ointment"[29] recalls the description of God's glory filling the tabernacle (Exod 40:35) and particularly the
description of the Temple in Chronicles where "the house of the Lord
was filled with the cloud of glory."[30] These words also extend the anointing beyond the person of Jesus to include the entire house. The house and
its household are enveloped in the pervasive aroma of perfumed oils in
marked contrast with the pervasive odor of death feared when the tomb
of Lazarus was opened (11:39). In these various echoes of Exodus, the
scene of the anointing continues to allude to the Christological imagery of
tabernacle and Temple presented earlier in the Gospel (1:14; 2:19-21).

The Johannine additions to this anointing scene draw upon these cultic
images with great artistry and subtlety. As once God's glory was manifest
in the anointed Tabernacle and the Temple, this glory will now be manifested in the anointed body of Jesus given over to death. If the interpretation of the six days is also accurate in placing this meal on the night of
Sabbath when the *Habdalah* service occurred then a further liturgical
meaning enriches and supports the Christological approach taken above.

The Household of Bethany

There are a number of narrative reasons why this Gospel may have
linked this scene with that of the raising of Lazarus. The place Bethany
seems to be historically associated with both incidents.[31] If the Fourth
Evangelist already had a Passion Source where the anointing was part of
the overall passion narrative, then this incident, where an anointing is related to Jesus' burial, has strong theological ties with the Lazarus story of a
death, burial and resurrection. For narrative reasons the addition of the
names Lazarus, Martha and Mary provides a smooth progression from a
narrative of Jesus' miracles to a narrative of his passion.

Naming the woman as Mary, already introduced in 11:2, provides a
motive for her action that would otherwise be missing in the Johannine
account. In Mark the action becomes a messianic prophecy-in-action
when the woman anoints Jesus' head. Luke has Jesus interpret the woman's
action stemming from her loving gratitude for forgiveness. Neither of

---

[29] ἡ δὲ οἰκία ἐπληρώθη ἐκ τῆς ὀσμῆς τοῦ μύρου (John 12:3).
[30] καὶ ὁ οἶκος ἐνεπλήσθη νεφέλης δόξης κυρίου (LXX 2 Chr 5:13)
[31] See Holst's comments on Bethany ("One Anointing," 439).

these two motives applies to John. The woman anoints Jesus' feet and there is no suggestion of gratitude for the forgiveness of sin. Instead a motive is implied by this narrative's naming the woman as the sister of Lazarus "whom he had raised from the dead" (12:1). The explicit linking of these two scenes (11:2; 12:1) supplies the motive of love and gratitude for her brother's life.

The above are narrative reasons for linking this episode with the characters from the preceding chapter.[32] At a theological level, this scene is a proleptic experience of the post-Easter household of God. For the characters Lazarus, Martha and Mary, the anointing of a body in death and a resurrection are past events. They have moved through the trauma of death and burial to the joy of resurrection. In anointing Jesus' feet Mary anticipates the post-resurrection model of discipleship that Jesus will enact and command in the next chapter when he washes the feet of his disciples (13:1-11). The fact that they are a household is not incidental to the theology of the narrative. Martha, Mary and Lazarus are brother and sisters, imaging the post-Easter relationship between Jesus and his disciples whom he will call "brothers and sisters" and who will be children of his Father (John 20:17).

Judas' Objections

Where the Markan and Matthean accounts have an unnamed objector, the Fourth Gospel names Judas as the one who criticizes Mary's abundant generosity. As the one who holds the money-purse he claims first rights to her gift. "Why was this ointment not sold for three hundred denarii and given to the poor?" (12:5). Judas was introduced as the betrayer earlier in the Gospel (6:71). In chapter 12 the description of Judas is filled out by describing him as a thief (κλέπτης). In adding the term "thief" to the usual designation of Judas as the betrayer, the Evangelist associates Judas with the thieves and robbers who threaten the sheepfold seeking to kill and destroy (10:1, 7, 10).

If my arguments above are correct and the anointing is a proleptic image of the post-Easter community who form a new Temple/Household of God, what place does the figure of Judas hold for this community? Or

---

[32] There is also the need to resolve the unfulfilled statement of 11:2 that already had named Mary as "the one who anointed the Lord with her ointment."

in other words, who does the figure of Judas represent for the Johannine group? In chapter 10, the parable of the sheepfold is used within a juridical conflict between Jesus and the Pharisees/Jews. In this context, where Jesus identifies himself as the shepherd (10:2), the door (10:7, 9) and the good shepherd (10:11, 14), "the Jews" must therefore be represented by the terms, "thief and robber" (10:1, 8), "stranger" (10:5), and "hireling" (10:12, 13). By calling Judas a thief, he is associated with those among "the Jews" who oppose not only Jesus but also his disciples (9:34). In the words of F. Manns, "Judas becomes a model for 'the Jews'."[33] In narrative time the anointing shows the opposition and conflict between Mary and Ἰούδας and in the post-Easter community this conflict is continued between the members of the Johannine community and the Ἰουδαῖοι of the local Synagogue where followers of Jesus are no longer welcome (9:22; 12:42; 16:2). In dealing with the Fourth Gospel it is important to note that this association between Judas and "the Jews" is a narrative construct reflecting a very heated, possibly local, polemical situation at the end of the first century.

Conclusion

Whatever the exact action and meaning of the historical anointing, the Johannine account shows signs of careful redaction in line with the Fourth Evangelist's overall Christology of Jesus as the presence of God with us, perfecting Israel's former Tabernacle and Temple. Prior to the construction of the Tabernacle, six days are set aside leading to a holy Sabbath of solemn rest (Exod 35:2; cf. John 19:31). When the Tabernacle is completed, Moses is instructed to anoint it with specially prepared oils (Exod 30:22-38; 40:9) and the narrator's final comment is: "So Moses finished (συνετέλεσε LXX) the work" (Exod 40:33; cf. τετέλεσται John 19:30). The Tabernacle is then "filled with the glory of the Lord" (40:35). Six days before the final solemn Passover, when the Temple of Jesus' body will be destroyed and a new Temple raised up, Mary anoints Jesus' feet in preparation for this final transcending moment. Her actions reach beyond the historical Jesus to the post-Easter time when the community of disciples is the new house/hold of God. Mary's oils touch the body of Jesus and this Gospel adds that their perfume pervades the entire

[33] "Judas devient le type des Juifs (*Ioudas-Ioudaioi*)"; see Manns, *Jean*, 271.

house/hold. Not only is Jesus touched by her actions but also the future Temple, the household which will be raised up in Jesus' hour.

Boundary crossing is a hazardous movement. There is time for pause to move from what has been to what has not yet become. It is a liminal experience in time and space where for a moment right order seems suspended. Within Israel's rhythms of prayer and festivals one such boundary moment is ritualized every week in the passing of Sabbath and the beginning of a new week. Within the Gospel narrative, chapters 11–12 present in a highly symbolic narrative the transition from Jesus' public ministry to his private gathering of friends in his final movement to his Father. The scene of the anointing, in its familial intimacy and cultic allusions, honors this moment of transition and anticipates its final outcome when both Jesus and his "brothers and sisters" are revealed as the new Temple of God's dwelling.

6. MONOTHEISM AND DUALISM
RECONSIDERING PREDESTINATION IN JOHN 12:40

John PAINTER

In this chapter in honor of my friend and colleague Frank Moloney I have chosen to continue a struggle with a difficult Johannine problem. Does John teach that God predestined to unbelief and its consequences, the majority of Jews in Jesus' day, and is this view pre-eminently found in John 12:40?[1] Unqualified, divine predestination implies that there is no anterior cause lying behind the decree of God. The long prevailing view is that, John's use of the quotation of Isa 6:10 in 12:40 gives expression to a predestinarian view, attributing unbelief to the purpose and activity of God.[2] E. D. Freed is explicit. "Their unbelief is explained as predestined by God himself and fulfills what Isaiah had prophesied concerning Jesus."[3] To illuminate his discussion, C. K. Barrett calls attention to the appendix on predestination by R. Schnackenburg.[4] Schnackenburg's discussion is punctuated by references to "the decree of God" and consistently refers to predestination and divine determination.[5]

Nevertheless, Schnackenburg speaks of "the mystery of divine predetermination and human free will,"[6] recognizing that John sets the reality of

---

[1] "He has blinded their eyes and hardened their heart, lest they should see with their eyes and perceive with their heart, and turn for me to heal them."

[2] See C. A. Evans, *To See and Not Perceive: Isaiah 6:9-10 in Early Jewish and Christian Interpretation* (JSOTSup 64; Sheffield: JSOT Press, 1991), 130, 132-35.

[3] E. D. Freed, *Old Testament Quotations in the Gospel of John* (NovTSup 11; Leiden: Brill, 1965), 84-88, 122.

[4] C. K. Barrett, *The Gospel According to St John* (2d ed.; London: SPCK, 1978), 430. R. Schnackenburg, *The Gospel according to St John* (vol. 2; New York: The Seabury Press, 1980), 2:259-74. See also his commentary on 12:37-43 in *John*, 412-19.

[5] Schnackenburg, *John*, 2:273, 274, 414, 415.

[6] Schnackenburg, *John*, 2:417.

human decisions alongside God's predestination and maintains these un-reconciled, side by side.[7] He speaks of the puzzle, "the mystery of the di-vine decree" that it "does not remove the obscurity of human guilt."[8] He insists that the Evangelist makes "no effort to produce a theological syn-thesis."[9] Barrett probably agrees and says, "The divine predestination works through human moral choices, for which men are morally responsible."[10] Such language lends support for the notion that the decree and action of God stands behind apparently free human moral choices. Maarten Menken asserts that God "is the determining force behind" the working of the devil in human beings.[11] Is God also, according to Menken, the determining force behind apparently free moral choices?[12]

With regard to John 12:40 Schnackenburg says, "The Evangelist has altered the wording of the Isaiah passage" so that "the action of God is more strongly emphasized."[13] He concludes that v. 41 leaves little doubt that "God was responsible for the blinding and hardening, and Jesus, God's representative, could have brought healing. ...Jesus is not destined to heal these people ... God has also deprived these people of the possi-bility of salvation and healing through his Son," and "the Johannine form is one of the sharpest in that it attributes the blinding and the hardening to God directly and without disguise."[14]

By placing human freedom and responsibility alongside predestination, Schnackenburg may have modified the meaning of both categories, "the Evangelist does not envisage absolute reprobation of individuals,"[15] "he does not want the blinding and hardening by God to be taken as a decree by which men are struck as by fate. ... God's general decision to harden,

---

[7] Schnackenburg, *John*, 2:265, 270, 271.

[8] Schnackenburg, *John*, 2:274 and see 263-64, 273.

[9] Schnackenburg, *John*, 2:270.

[10] Barrett, *John*, 431.

[11] M. J. J. Menken, *Old Testament Quotations in the Fourth Gospel* (Kampen: Pharos, 1996), 109.

[12] Menken says that he does not go into "the relation between divine determination and human freedom; ... I only refer to the fact that for the Evangelist determination does not apparently cancel freedom" (*Old Testament Quotations*, 122).

[13] Schnackenburg, *John*, 2:271. Barrett quotes Hoskyns to the effect that the changes to the quotation of Isaiah 6:10 in John 12:40 "are best explained by the intention of the writer of the gospel to emphasize the judgement as the action of God" (*John*, 431). See also E. C. Hoskyns, *The Fourth Gospel* (ed. F. N. Davey; 2d ed.; London: Faber & Faber, 1947), 429.

[14] Schnackenburg, *John*, 2:415, 416.

[15] Schnackenburg, *John*, 2:273.

as expressed in Scripture, does not affect individual human beings in such a way that they cannot escape from the circle of darkness."[16] The name of Judas is not written in the prophecy of betrayal. We learn this only in the event of betrayal.[17] Judas was not trapped in his fate, and John knows nothing of an ordinance of God dividing people in advance into two classes, chosen and rejected.[18] Schnackenburg argues that, for John, the hard of heart are the Pharisaic and rabbinical ruling groups of his day, whose "hardness of heart is the culmination of all Jewish rejection of God."[19] Reference to the hardening as "the culmination of all Jewish rejection of God" implies that it is a consequence of persistent rejection. This is better seen as judgment than predestination.[20] Isaiah's commission to be the instrument of the judgment of God is in response to faithless Judah (Isa 1:1-23). Obduracy is the fruit of faithlessness and is the judgment of God.

In John the signs offer the opportunity for outsiders to become insiders. For those who remain outside in unbelief, the signs become instruments of judgment. The status of outsiders remains for those who believe on the basis of the signs, but refuse to confess openly (12:42-43). Either they progress to open confession or the signs become instruments of judgment.[21]

Schnackenburg discusses 8:43-44 in relation to the possible role of the devil in 12:40.[22] He rightly asserts that John does not teach that people derive from separate fixed origins, God and the devil. He wrongly treats the dualistic material as an example of determinism.[23] He argues that 12:40 makes no reference to the devil and that, where "God's opponent" is mentioned (8:44; 12:31), he is not an active agent.[24] His argument regarding 12:40 is circular because he assumes the unidentified "he" of 12:40 does not refer to the devil. He also overlooks the relevance of the aggres-

---

[16] Schnackenburg, *John*, 2:417.

[17] Schnackenburg, *John*, 2:273.

[18] Schnackenburg, *John*, 2:264.

[19] Schnackenburg, *John*, 2:274.

[20] See Barrett's quotation of Hoskyns in note 3 above.

[21] See J. Beutler, "Faith and Confession: The Purpose of John" in *Word, Theology, and Community in John*, 19-31 (ed. J. Painter, R. A. Culpepper, and F. F. Segovia; St. Louis: Chalice Press, 2002), 20-21, 23-24.

[22] Schnackenburg, *John*, 2:263.

[23] Menken also sees divine determination behind the devil (*Old Testament Quotations*, 109).

[24] Schnackenburg, *John*, 2:416.

sively active role of the power of darkness (evil) in John. This certainly does not remove human freedom and responsibility. Rather it is the ground for exhorting the readers to walk in the light lest the darkness overwhelm them, 12:35-36, 46. This context calls for close examination for clues to the interpretation of 12:40.

The case argued in this chapter can now be outlined. The Evangelist identifies the power of darkness as the force that blinded people and prevented them from believing (12:40). The blindness was made possible in those with an inclination or attraction to the values of the darkness (3:19-21; 12:6). Support for this reading of John 12:40 is found in: i) The relation of the Evangelist's worldview to Qumran; ii) The case of Judas; iii) The form of the quotation; iv) The context in which the quotation is found; v) Comparative New Testament evidence, and; vi) Patristic interpretation.

John 12:36b-43 and the Johannine Worldview

Commentators have not seriously considered the possibility that John portrays the power of darkness as the cause of unbelief in response to the signs of Jesus. If the Prince of this world corresponds to the Angel of darkness, Spirit of darkness (Spirit of falsehood) of Qumran, the aggressive role of the darkness in John takes on added meaning and force. In the Qumran texts, the Spirit of falsehood not only leads astray all the sons of darkness, but also is active amongst the sons of light (1 QS 3.17-18, 20-23). So also in John, it is not only the Jews who are led astray by the devil. Judas, one of the twelve, became a devil (6:64, 70-71), who would betray Jesus when the devil enters him (John 13:2, 27).

There is a strongly dualistic perspective in the Fourth Gospel as well as the Qumran Texts.[25] Contrary to common interpretation, this dualism is not deterministic, because it places all people between light and darkness, between God and the devil. In this deadly conflict, humanity is called to choose.

Menken, following Schnackenburg, defends the deterministic inter-

---

[25] For a fuller treatment see my forthcoming essay, "Monotheism and Dualism: John and Qumran," in *The Christology and Theology of the Fourth Gospel* (ed. G. Van Belle; Leuven: Peeters, 2004). See also J. Painter, *The Quest for the Messiah: The History, Literature, and Theology of the Johannine Community* (2d ed.; Nashville: Abingdon, 1993), 35-52.

pretation of dualism and makes three points against identifying the devil as the cause of the blinding and hardening in John 12:40.[26]

i. "[T]he substitution of God by the devil is too much at variance with the obvious meaning of Isaiah's text." But John has radically altered the quotation of 6:10 to signal a change in the reference to blinding and hardening. Menken also depends on these changes for his reading.

ii. "The parallels John 8:43-44; 6:70-71; 13:2 (cf. also 1 John 2:11; 2 Cor 4:4) say only that the devil is working in human beings, but they say nothing of the determining force behind him." They say nothing because they have nothing to say. Menken's assumption that the decree of God stands behind the activity of the Spirit of Falsehood in 1 QS 3.13–4.26 fails to take account of the incompatibility and bitter struggle between truth and falsehood (4.17). Of the Spirits of Light and Darkness 1 QS (3.25–4.1) says, "He [God] loves the one and everlastingly delights in its works for ever; but the counsel of the other he loathes and for ever hates its ways." In John, the power of darkness is not the other face of the light and the devil is not the mask of God. Certainly in 1 QS God has appointed the two Spirits of Truth and Falsehood in which all people are to walk (3.18, 25-26; 4.16-17). Human life is lived between truth and falsehood, light and darkness. To love [choose] the one or to hate [reject] the other is to live and choose between them (John 3:19-21). This is one side. The other is that the struggle between Truth and Falsehood is fierce, that God loves the one and hates the other.

iii. "God … causes morally wrong human decisions … not only in John … but also several times in the OT and elsewhere." Are all such incidents examples of predestination rather than judgment? We need only be concerned with the references in John. Menken refers to "a negative determination to unbelief by God … in 6:64-65; 9:39; 10:26. In 6:64-65 Jesus confronts unbelief and betrayal and explains, "No one is able to come to me unless it is given to him from (of) the Father." At the end of chapter 9, after giving sight to the blind man, Jesus says, "For judgment I have come into this world, that those who do not see may see and that those who do see may become blind" (9:39). In the shepherd discourse, Jesus says to a gathering of antagonistic Jews, "You do not believe because you are not my sheep" (10:26). If this is the best support Menken can find in John, then his case is weak.

First, there is nothing in John akin to the negative determination of

---

[26] Menken, *Old Testament Quotations*, 109-111.

12:40 where, *if God's decree of predestination is involved*, God's action is the active root cause of unbelief. The judgment of John 9:39 needs to be understood in the context of John 9 and 3:19-21. The once blind man is an example of the *judgment* (3:19; 9:39) through which the blind come to see, not only physically but also spiritually in growing faith, culminating in confession in the face of intimidation (9:33-34).[27] The Pharisees become increasingly blind in their dealing with the man. They claimed to be the custodians of the truth of God. Being spiritually blind they claimed to see (9:41) and consequently remained blind. The judgment is the coming of the light into the world (3:19-21, see 9:5). The response of coming to the light or rejecting it separates belief from unbelief. The language of blindness, developed symbolically in John 9, has influenced John's shaping of the quotation in 12:40. The action of 12:40 is judgment in response to human action, not predestination, the fundamental underlying cause of it all. For John, the cause is the darkness, 1:5; 12:35-36, 46.

In 10:26 Jesus addresses another aggressive audience. From their demeanor Jesus concludes that they do not believe. This is the evidence that they are not his sheep. There is no suggestion of a precisely fixed group of a certain number. Nor is there any indication that God has prevented any from being his sheep. Jesus does not say, "You cannot believe because you are not my sheep" but, "you do not believe ..." If they believed (obeyed his voice), they would be his sheep!

John 6:64-65, addressed to the disciples, shows that Jesus is not taken by surprise by defection and betrayal. The falling away of disciples is a greater scandal than general unbelief. But it is treated in the same way. "No one is able to come to me unless it is given to him from (of) the Father." Menken does not mention 6:44, which is addressed to the Jews, "No one is able to come to me unless the Father who sent me draws (ἑλκύσῃ) him." Neither 6:44 nor 6:64-65 says God acts negatively to prevent coming. They say that God's giving, or drawing, is essential for coming to Jesus. They do not say that all such inevitably come. In John 12:31-32 Jesus says, "if I am lifted up, I will draw (ἑλκύσω) all people to myself." This theme is elaborated with the context of 12:40 below. It is a good example of the coordinated (not conflicting) roles of the Father and the Son in John. The Father draws through the uplifting of the Son.[28]

---

[27] See Beutler, "Faith and Confession," 24-25; Painter, "John 9 and the Interpretation of the Fourth Gospel," *JSNT* 28 (1986): 31-61.

[28] Contrary to Schnackenburg, *John*, 2:415 and Menken, *Old Testament Quotations*, 120.

If 12:40 is read as the action of God, there is no case for understanding it as the implementation of the decree of God from all eternity. John nowhere uses predestination terminology. His language refers to the judgment of God. This is supported by the links with Isaiah 6; John 9 and 3:19-21.[29] But the changes to the quoted text from Isa in 12:40; the surrounding context of 12:31-50; and the worldview of John all press an alternative interpretation. The judgment is effected by the power of darkness from which Jesus came to save the world, 12:47. Choosing the darkness rather than the light involves consignment to the darkness and all that brings. This is the judgment.

The distinctive Johannine worldview, first enunciated in the Prologue, supports the interpretation of Isaiah 6:9-10 in John 12:40. If the darkness assaults the light (1:5), the light is not overwhelmed (οὐ κατέλαβεν). The Gospel story tells of a new assault on the darkness by the light (3:19-21). Jesus is the light of the world, 8:12; 9:5. Those who follow him are released from the power of darkness. Nicodemus comes to Jesus by night (3:2), out of the darkness into the light. Jesus challenges the crowd to walk in the light to avoid being overwhelmed (καταλάβῃ) by the darkness, to believe in the light and become sons of light (12:35, 36, 46). At the end of Jesus' ministry, when Judas, intent on betraying Jesus, leaves the supper, the narrator tells us, "and it was night" (13:30).

The Case of Judas

Schnackenburg recognizes the relevance of Judas to this discussion. The loss of Judas, like the unbelief of the people in 12:37-40, is the subject of a Scripture fulfillment formula.[30] From the first mention, Judas is the one who betrayed Jesus, being one of the twelve (6:64, 70-71).[31] The nar-

---

[29] For such consequential judgement see also Rom 1:24, 26, 28.

[30] Schnackenburg, *John*, 2:273, 416.

[31] See also 12:4-6; 13:2, 18, 21-30 (especially 26-30); 14:22; 17:12 (but not by name); 18:2-3, 5. In the New Testament there are twenty two references to Judas, the betrayer, twenty in the Gospels (concentrated in John) and two in Acts. In the Synoptic lists of the disciples this Judas is always last and identified as the one who betrayed Jesus. Reference to Judas as one of the twelve (or one of the disciples) and the betrayer is normal in John (6:70-71; 12:4; 17:12). The initial naming identifies him as Judas, son of Simon Iscariot. This form of the name is also used in 13:2, 26. The name Judas Iscariot is used in 12:4 and is supported by 14:22. John always uses the Hellenistic declinable form of Iscariot. Only in the act of betrayal is reference to Judas as a disciple lacking as is Iscariot. There,

rator says Jesus knew from the beginning who did not believe and who would betray him (6:64). Jesus then elaborates, "Have I not chosen you twelve? And one of you is a devil." The narrator explains retrospectively, "He spoke of Judas son of Simon Iscariot; for he, [being] one of the twelve, was about to betray him." (6:70-71). The paradox of Judas runs throughout John's portrayal of him. The scandal that one of the twelve should betray Jesus is not masked but accentuated. His characterization as a devil does not diminish his responsibility. He is culpable and responsible.[32] Culpability and connection with the devil are continuing themes in the story of Judas.

At the anointing in Bethany (12:1-8) there is no mention of the devil. The narrator reveals that Judas' protest about the "waste" was a deception. Rather he was a thief, who coveted the money for himself (12:4-6). A moral flaw in his character is the source from which the scandalous act of betrayal flows. Inclination to the values of the world of darkness led him to be overwhelmed.

During the final supper the narrator reveals that the devil had already put into the heart of Judas to betray Jesus (13:2). The reference implies a recent decision. Nothing suggests predestination by God. The source of this motivation is the devil. Judas remains present for the footwashing. Jesus washes his feet also.[33] Jesus' words, "you are not all clean," challenge Judas (13:10-11). As in 6:64, we are told that Jesus knew who would betray him. But there is no suggestion that Jesus chose Judas *to betray him*, or that such knowledge makes Jesus the author of Judas' act. Judas was not trapped by his destiny, as the retrospective stance of the narrative implies. Only when Judas had betrayed Jesus was his role as betrayer fixed forever.

---

in the course of four verses, Judas is twice identified as "the one who betrayed Jesus" (18:2, 5). As Jesus gave himself up, the narrator notes dramatically, "And Judas who betrayed him was standing there with them" (18:5).

[32] Schnackenburg says, "Even of Judas Iscariot it may be true that it is not he personally, not he by name, who falls under the decree of God. Scripture says merely, 'He who ate my bread has lifted his heel against me' (13:18). The fact that this disloyal table companion was that man was learnt by experience, though the Evangelist does say of him in retrospect that the devil put the idea of treachery into his heart (13:2). The interpretation of the unbelief of the Jews and Judas's betrayal retains its obscurity, but it is at least clear that the Evangelist does not envisage absolute reprobation of individuals" (*John*, 2:273; see also 263, 274).

[33] My argument at this point is in agreement with F. J. Moloney, "A Sacramental Reading of John 13.1-38," *CBQ* 53/2 (1991): 237-56 and chapter 5 "The Fourth Gospel" in his *A Body Broken for a Broken People: Eucharist in the New Testament* (2d. ed.; Peabody: Hendrickson, 1997), 113-50.

That Jesus washed Judas' feet challenges the appearance of determinism that retrospectivity brings. At the same time, the scandal of the act of betrayal is accentuated. Its impact is reduced by appealing to its prediction in Scripture (13:18). Ps 41:9 is the Scripture fulfilled by Judas' betrayal. Jesus knows in advance and Scripture foretells the betrayal of Judas. Ps 41:9, like other fulfillment texts, is recognized as prophecy only after the event it predicts. Whether this can be the Scripture fulfilled according to 17:12 is far from clear. In 17:12 the scandalous nature of the loss of Judas is noted. The scandal is reduced because it was foreseen and predicted in Scripture. But that is not to say that it was caused by God. John has gone to great lengths to set in opposition the reality of Judas as chosen, and Judas the devil who betrays Jesus. His betrayal of Jesus exemplifies 1 QS 3.21-23 where the Angel of darkness also leads astray the sons of righteousness.

At the supper Jesus explicitly passes the morsel only to Judas. This is the signal that Jesus knew who would betray him and identifies Judas (13:26). It is also the gift of the morsel to Judas, the opportunity for Judas to turn aside from the path of betrayal. But Judas betrayed Jesus. The gift of the morsel marks the moment from which there is no return. At this time Satan enters him. "Then taking the morsel he went out immediately, and it was night" (13:30). The force of this symbolism is overpowering. Judas leaves the light of the world and is overwhelmed by the darkness (12:35).

After reference to the fulfillment of Scripture in the betrayal of Judas, and the loss of the son of ἀπωλείας from the number of the disciples (17:12), Judas is mentioned only at the arrest of Jesus. He is described as the one who betrayed Jesus. Again there is reference to Jesus not losing any of those given to him (see 6:39; 17:12; 18:9). Here (18:9) there is no exception clause as there is in 17:12. Jesus, in giving himself up, ensures that none of his disciples is lost (18:8; cf. 17:11-19).

That God determined the betrayal by Judas is nowhere suggested. Knowledge and prediction imply that God is prepared and ready to bring his good purpose into being out of evil intent. Even one chosen by Jesus, can be lost. Jesus' prayer for the disciples reinforces awareness of the jeopardy in which the disciples live (17:14, 17).

John's treatment of Judas is remarkably similar to his treatment of the unbelief of the people in 12:36b-43. In both cases there is Scripture fulfillment and the indication of external negative influence. In the case of Judas that influence is named the devil, Satan. In John 12:40 the influence is the third person singular "he." Alongside this sinister influence is the culpability of Judas as a thief and of those "who loved the glory of men more than the glory of God" (12:43 and see 12:35-36, 46 and 3:19-21, "who love the darkness rather than the light")!

John 12:38, 40 and Quotation Formulae

In John there are seventeen uses of Scripture quotation formulae (1:23; 2:17; 6:31, 45; 7:38, 42; 10:34; 12:14-15, 38, 39-41; 13:18; 15:25; 17:12; 19:24, 28, 36, 37) and one identifiable quotation (by the crowd) without quotation formula (12:13). The only book mentioned by name is the prophet Isaiah (1:23; 12:38, 39, 41).[34] Frequently, in John 1–12, quotations of Scripture (or what has been written, γεγραμμένον ἐστίν, 2:17; 6:31, 45; 10:34; 12:14) are used to establish controversial positions such as the role of John the Baptist as witness to Jesus and the messiahship of Jesus. References to the Scripture (ἡ γραφή) in 7:38, 42; 13:18; 17:12; 19:24, 28, 36, 37) overlap chapters 1–12 and 13–21.

In John 12:38-40 two texts from Isaiah are specifically introduced and identified. From 12:38 John uses the fulfillment formula, "that the Scripture may be fulfilled," or some variation (ἵνα πληρωθῇ) 12:38; 13:18; 15:25; 17:12; 19:24, 36-37; ἵνα τελειωθῇ, 19:28).[35] The fulfillment formula most clearly demonstrates the apologetic intention and exemplifies the *pesher* method widely known in the Qumran Texts. What is spoken of in Scripture is seen to be fulfilled in current events.

Those events most damaging to the Evangelist's purpose are shown to be fulfillments of Scripture. The three most troublesome events are the betrayal of Jesus by Judas, the unbelief of the Jews, and the rejection and crucifixion of Jesus. All nine quotations from John 12:38 are *specifically* presented as Scriptures fulfilled in the events narrated.[36] The unbelief of the Jews constitutes the primary scandal, but the betrayal by Judas brings

---

[34] In 12:38, 40, it is the narrator who quotes Isa 53:1 and 6:10 while in 1:23 John (the Baptist) quotes Isa 40:3, though these are the words of the narrator in the Synoptics.

[35] The reference in 12:38 is unique in John. The fulfillment formula is applied to "the word of the prophet Isaiah … that he spoke." Most commonly references are to "what is written" (15:25), or to the Scripture (13:18; 17:12; 19:24, 28, 36).

[36] The cluster of fulfillment formulae from 12:38 on might indicate the use of *testimonia* such as was suggested by R. Harris, *Testimonia* (2 vols.; Cambridge: Cambridge University Press, 1916-1920).

the scandal into the very heart of Jesus' chosen disciples. The fulfillment formulae assure the reader that these events were foreseen and their destructive force neutralized. In Jesus, God is able to bring good out of evil.

John 12:36b-43 in Context

This paragraph (12:36b-43) forms part of the conclusion to Jesus' public ministry. The coming of the Greeks in 12:20 marks the arrival of the hour for the glorification of the Son of Man (12:23). It is marked by two sets of sayings introduced by "Now!"

The first of these (12:27) echoes the Gethsemane scene from Mark, but lacks the trauma of the crisis faced by Jesus in Mark's account. The second "Now!" (12:31-33) announces the hour has come for the judgment of the world and the exorcism of the Prince of this world, "Now is the judgment of this world, now shall the ruler of this world be cast out; and I, if I am lifted up from the earth, will draw (ἑλκύσω) all people to myself." The verb ἑλκύειν is rarely used in the NT (8 times) and of these 5 are in John, 6:44; 12:32; 18:10; 21:6, 11. Only 6:44 is relevant to 12:32. There Jesus says, "No one can come to me except the Father who sent me draw him." In 12:32 Jesus says, "If I am lifted up, I will draw all people to myself." Jeremiah 31:3 [LXX 38:3] may illuminate these texts. It reads εἵλκυσά σε εἰς οἰκτίρημα.[37] This fits well the idea of John 12:32 that the uplifted Jesus reveals the love of God, which draws all people to him. In unified and coordinated action, the Father draws all people through the uplifting of the Son. The uplifting features the cross, as 12:33 explains. It is also the means by which Jesus is exalted to his former glory (17:5).

With the announcement of his impending death, Jesus warns the crowd that the light is with them for only a little while (12:35a cf. 9:4-5). The scene concludes with Jesus' appeal to his hearers (12:35b-36a): i) "Walk as you have light that the darkness may not overwhelm you." ii) "As you have light, believe in the light, that you may be sons of light."[38] The rejection of Jesus is implied, "he went out and hid himself from them" (12:36b).

The narrator then sets out to explain why, *in spite of* the many signs, the

---

[37] "...therefore with loving kindness have I drawn thee."
[38] Compare "Sons of light." See 1 QS 1.9; 2.16; 3.13, 14, 25; 1 QM 1.1, 3, 9, 11, 13.

crowd failed to believe in Jesus (12:37-43). The paradox is stressed. The use of the imperfect ἐπίστευον (12:37) makes the failure to believe less than definitive. But if the signs failed to produce belief, what would? If the Evangelist's account of the signs was intended to produce belief (20:30-31), the signs themselves ought to lead to belief (10:37-38). Why did they fail?

John asserts that unbelief fulfills the word of the prophet Isaiah (12:38a).[39] What follows is a composite quotation of Isa 53:1 and Isa 6:10, separated by John's explanation and introduction to the second quotation (12:39). The quotation is followed by an outline of the context for what Isaiah said (12:41). In 12:38a, 39 and 41 John reiterates that the quotations are what Isaiah said. The first quotation agrees exactly with the LXX but the Evangelist has radically modified the second, except for the last three words.

Although Jesus' withdrawal signals failure (12:36b), and the Evangelist explains the failure in a summary conclusion (12:37-43), this is followed by a new discourse by Jesus (12:44-50). Jesus' renewed appeal for his hearers to believe in him continues the theme of the liberating power of the light. Having appealed to his relationship to the Father, he says, "I have come into the world as light, that every one who believes in me may not remain in the darkness" (12:46). The significance of the surrounding context for the interpretation of John 12:40 is not adequately recognized. The reference to the casting out of the Prince of this world, the place of darkness (v. 31), is followed by appeals to walk in the light (v. 35), believe in the light (v. 36b), and become children of light (36c), to avoid being overwhelmed by the darkness (v. 35). The quotation in 12:40 is about being overwhelmed by the darkness, which is like blindness (12:35b). Though this looks like failure, and the Evangelist's summary suggests failure, Jesus' new phase of discourse appeals for belief in him (the light) to escape from the darkness (12:44-46). This hardly fits the interpretation of 12:40 as terminal blindness consequent on the divine decree. Nor does the use of the imperfect ἐπίστευον in 12:37 suggest definitive and final unbelief. The Gospel traces the story of Nicodemus, one of the fearful rulers, who moves towards open confession in 19:38-42.

---

[39] Compare the appeal to the fulfillment of Scripture to explain the loss of Judas (17:12).

The Text of the quotations within editorial formulae

Although he had done so many signs in their presence they were not believing in him (ἐπίστευον εἰς αὐτόν) that the word of the prophet Isaiah may be fulfilled which he spoke (εἶπεν), "Lord, who has believed our report? And to whom is the arm of the Lord revealed?" For this reason they were not able to believe, because again Isaiah said (εἶπεν), "He has blinded their eyes and hardened their heart, lest they see with their eyes and perceive with their heart and turn, and I will heal them (καὶ ἰάσομαι αὐτούς)." Isaiah said (εἶπεν) these things because (ὅτι) he saw *his* glory (τὴν δόξαν αὐτοῦ) and he spoke of *him* (ἐλάλησεν περὶ αὐτοῦ). Nevertheless, even many of the rulers believed in *him* (ἐπίστευσαν εἰς αὐτόν).

The text of Scripture used by John has been examined carefully in the major commentaries and in the monographs by E. D. Freed, Craig Evans and Maarten Menken.[40] The quotation of Isa 53:1 in 12:38 is identical in wording with the LXX. The opening word (Κύριε) has no basis in the Hebrew text, confirming that John drew on the LXX. Determining whether the Hebrew or LXX provided the quotation of Isa 6:10 in John 12:40 is more complex. John agrees with no known form of the text of Isaiah, differing quite radically from the Hebrew, the LXX (except for the last three words), the Targums, and other quotations of this text in the New Testament. The agreement of the last three words (καὶ ἰάσομαι αὐτούς) with the LXX, and the identification of the quotation in 12:38 with the text of the LXX, suggest that, in 12:40, John has modified the text of the LXX to suit his own purpose and context. Menken has shown there is evidence of the use of the Hebrew, influenced by the LXX and modified by John.[41] Either way, the changes at the beginning are John's.

John's interpretation of Isaiah

The narrator reports what Isaiah *said* to explain why the mass of people did not believe in spite of the many signs done by Jesus. Over and over he refers to what Isaiah said, 12:38, 39, 41. Elsewhere quotation formulae using "said" or "say" are found only in 1:23; 7:38, 42; 19:37. In the last

---

[40] Freed, *Old Testament Quotations*, 82-130; Evans, *To See and Not Perceive*, esp. 129-135; Menken, *Old Testament Quotations*, 99-122.
[41] Menken, *Old Testament Quotations*, 121.

three, reference is to what "Scripture" says or said, meaning what is written. But 1:23, like 12:38, 39, 41 might identify Isaiah as the speaker within the text. That Isaiah is the speaker in Isa 53:1 is plausible. Does John assert that Isaiah is the speaker in 12:40? The rarity of the idiom in the scripture quotation formulae makes this difficult to decide. But the use of "Scripture says" (or said) suggests a looser interpretation allowing that, in what Isaiah *wrote*, the Lord is the speaker.

John 12:38

It is sometimes argued that the "report" is to be understood as the teaching of Jesus and that "the arm of the Lord" refers to the divine action in the signs of Jesus.[42] Appeal to the words of Jesus makes little sense at this point. They constitute a more serious stumbling block for belief than the signs (or *works* as Jesus refers to them, 10:38). Only the signs of Jesus are indirectly referred to as "the arm of the Lord" in John 12:37-38.

This quotation raises the question, "and to whom is the arm of the Lord revealed?" The narrator alludes to the signs as evidence of the saving acts of God. Failure to perceive them as such is the basis of unbelief (see 6:26). The question "Who has believed?" presupposes unbelief. But how could they fail to believe when Jesus had done so many signs before their very eyes? Those who did not see God's saving action in Jesus' signs could not believe. Why did they not see it? The quotation of Isa 53:1 takes us thus far. John's full answer takes us through 12:39-43.

John 12:39-43

The narrator turns specifically to the question of why the crowd *could not* believe (12:39). The opening διὰ τοῦτο could refer back to 12:38 or to what follows. The following ὅτι identifies the cause of unbelief in the saying from Isa in 12:40. The argument moves from "did not believe" (12:37), to "could not believe" (12:39), and 12:40 explains why not. John's changes to the opening of this quotation initially obscure the identification with Isaiah 6:10. Line by line this becomes clearer, and the narrator eventually tells us that Isaiah said these things *because* he saw his glory and he spoke of him, thus identifying Isa 6:10.

---

[42] Thus C. K. Barrett, *John*, 431; Freed, *Old Testament Quotations*, 84-85.

In Isa 6:9-10, the Lord (אֲדֹנָי or ὁ κύριος in the LXX) is the speaker who commissions Isaiah to his task using verbs in the imperative mood. John 12:40 abbreviates the text and uses third person, perfect and aorist, indicative active verbs. In the last line John retains the first person singular future indicative of the LXX. It probably read the Hebrew passive as an indirect identification of the Lord as the one who would heal. This is made explicit in the LXX. But John has set the third person verbs against the final first person verb. Two opposed agents are in view.

Maarten Menken acknowledges the contribution of Rudolf Schnackenburg and builds on his contribution.[43] They argue that in 12:40 John has adapted Isa 6:10 to fit the context of the Gospel and express the view that Isaiah saw the glory of the pre-incarnate Jesus, who speaks and is the subject of the final clause, "and I will heal them."[44] According to Schnackenburg, Menken, and the vast majority of interpreters, the third person verbs at the beginning refer to God. Schnackenburg and Menken identify the pre-incarnate Jesus as the speaker, "he [God] has blinded their eyes and hardened their heart, lest …I [Jesus] heal them." Menken, in agreement with Schnackenburg, concludes, "The negative determination by God cannot end in healing by Jesus."[45] Like Schnackenburg,[46] he argues that the attribution of distinctive roles to God and to Jesus is characteristically Johannine. "God is presented as the one who determines salvation, and Jesus as the one who realizes salvation."[47] But this is some distance from God blinding and hardening the people lest Jesus heal them. The latter is quite un-Johannine, constituting a serious objection to their view. In John, Jesus and the Father are one (10:30; 17:11, 21-23); as the Father works so does the Son (5:17, 19); he speaks only the words of the Father (3:34; 12:49-50); the Father draws (6:44) by means of the uplifted Son (12:32).

Menken largely restates Schnackenburg's position in a systematic, comprehensive, clear, and concise fashion. He makes one major contribu-

---

[43] Menken, *Old Testament Quotations*, 100-1. He refers to Schnackenburg's "Joh 12:39-41. Zur christologischen Schriftauslegung des vierten Evangelisten," in *Neues Testament und Geschichte: Historisches Geschehen und Deutung im Neuen Testament* (FS für O. Cullmann; ed. H. Baltensweiler - B. Reicke; Zürich: Theologischer Verlag; Tübingen: Mohr 1972), 167-77; Schnackenburg, *John*, 2:259-74, 412-19.

[44] "Pre-incarnate" is my term; "pre-existent" fails to indicate the point of reference.

[45] Menken, *Old Testament Quotations*, 119-20.

[46] Schnackenburg, *John*, 2:415.

[47] Menken, *Old Testament Quotations*, 120.

tion. Schnackenburg gives no textual explanation for the way 12:40 distinguishes God from the pre-incarnate Jesus in Isa 6:10.[48] Menken sets out a way to do this.

In Hebrew, the Lord commands the prophet to deafen, blind, and harden the people lest they see, hear, and understand, and turn and be healed. The Lord is the speaker (the voice of the Lord [קוֹל אֲדֹנָי, τῆς φωνῆς κυρίου in the LXX] 6:8). Menken argues that, according to John, Isaiah saw the glory of the pre-incarnate Jesus, who addresses the prophet in Isa 6:9-10.[49] The pre-incarnate Jesus says, "He has blinded their eyes and hardened their hearts lest … I would heal them."

But Isa 6:10 (Hebrew or LXX) does not distinguish two agents! Menken uses the LXX of Isa 6:12 to explain how the pre-incarnate Jesus speaks in the first person, and of God in the third person in John 12:40. In Isaiah, Menken notes the variation of use of אֲדֹנָי (6:1, 8, 11) and יהוה (6:3, 5, 12). But this does not distinguish God from Jesus. The one Isaiah saw (6:1) is אֲדֹנָי but Isaiah says he has seen יהוה צְבָאוֹת (6:5). He notes that all references using אֲדֹנָי or יהוה in Isa 6:1-11 are translated by κύριος. But in 6:12 יהוה is translated by ὁ θεός. Menken suggests that this is the basis for John to distinguish God, as the agent of blinding and hardening, from the pre-incarnate Jesus who would heal. The pre-incarnate Jesus is the speaker in 6:10 (John 12:40). As speaker he refers to God as "he" who has blinded and hardened the people.

Menken's neat solution has its problems. John identifies the glory of the pre-incarnate Jesus with Isaiah's vision. The reader would know that the prophet was commissioned by the Lord to be the instrument of judgment on the people. If they read ὁ θεός in 6:12, they also know that it is τῆς φωνῆς κυρίου (6:8) that commissioned the prophet to the task of deafening, blinding, and hardening the people. The use of ὁ θεός in 6:12 is hardly a clear reference to an alternative ultimate source of blindness

---

[48] According to Schnackenburg, the Evangelist says in his commentary on Isa 6:10, "the prophet spoke in this way because he saw [Christ's] glory" (*John*, 2:273). Also, "God was responsible for the blinding and hardening, and Jesus, God's representative, could have brought healing. … Jesus is not destined to heal these people" (*John*, 2:415).

[49] While the Hebrew and LXX say that Isaiah saw the Lord, John 12:41 says "he saw his glory and spoke concerning him." John 12:42 interprets this to mean Jesus' glory, probably his pre-incarnate glory (17:5), not that he foresaw the glory revealed in the signs (2:11). Compare the tradition found in the Targum to Isa 6:1, 5. There Isaiah says he saw "the glory of God," and "the glory of the *shekinah* of the King of the ages" (מלך עלמיא יקר שכינה).

and hardness. More seriously, the opposition this creates between Jesus and God is intolerable in John.

John accepts the "I" (in 12:40) as the voice of the Lord (Isa 6:8), which he identifies as the pre-incarnate Jesus (12:41) Yes! But why should we think that God is the one who blinds and hardens? The only reason for doing this is the meaning of the unmodified text of Isaiah where the Lord commands Isaiah to blind and harden where otherwise the Lord would heal. Commentators regularly treat the quotation as if the alterations made no difference. Menken recognizes that John changes Isaiah's meaning. But he attempts to retain God's role although John has identified that with the pre-incarnate Jesus. The result is that God is set against Jesus, and the signs, which were to bring belief and life (20:30-31), are predetermined by God to bring blindness, hardness of heart, and consequent unbelief. This makes no sense of God's will to save or the unity of will and action of the Father and the Son.

In Isaiah the prophet describes the judgment of God on a faithless people. There is no reference to the hidden decree of God that stands behind and causes faithlessness. In the prophetic message, faithlessness has its condemnation. In John, the agent of blinding and hardening could be God, but nothing explicitly indicates this. The changes John makes are not necessary if he wished to maintain the blinding and hardening as the action of God. All that needed to be done was to identify Isaiah's vision with the glory of the pre-incarnate Jesus, as he does in 12:41-42. The pre-incarnate Jesus then is the means by which God's judgment is effected. Menken's understanding of the changes set Father and Son in an intolerable tension.

John's changes suggest an interpretation that is not possible with an unmodified text. Clues are provided by the immediate context of 12:36b-43; and by the question implied by 12:37, which the quotations from Isaiah (John 12:38, 40) are made to answer. The quotations are given to explain why the people did not believe *in spite of the signs*. In Isaiah 6, God commanded the prophet's action in response to the faithlessness of the people. It is God's judgment on their faithlessness. In the surrounding context of the quotation in John, Jesus also expresses the disastrous consequences of faithlessness (12:35-36, 46), but in a language and idiom different from Isaiah. Jesus stresses the blinding effect of walking in the darkness in words that have a direct bearing on the meaning of 12:40. That idiom gives expression to the antithetical language of light and darkness that dominates the Gospel. This language, and the worldview it implies, calls attention to the relationship of John's antithetical language to the language of the Qumran texts, and the role of the devil in John.

Comparative New Testament Evidence

Language introduced or excluded by the Evangelist is a clue to the origin of the obduracy. The use of τυφλός in John 9 may have suggested the use of the verb τετύφλωκεν in John 12:40. Blindness was generally considered to be incurable.[50] According to John, God's purpose in creation is not for eyes to be blind, an issue that almost surfaces in John 9:2. Rather, in John, it is God who makes the blind to see (John 9 and see Isa 35:4-6).

The notion of blinding is sinister. The rare use of τυφλόω in the LXX, where it is used only three times, suggests that we need to account for the introduction of the term at this point in John. This impression is confirmed by the New Testament where the verb is used only three times, in John 12:40; 2 Cor 4:4; and 1 John 2:11. These uses are mutually clarifying. According to Paul in 2 Cor 4:4, the god of this world has blinded the minds (ἐτύφλωσεν τὰ νοήματα)[51] of the unbelievers, to keep them from seeing the light of the Gospel of the glory of Christ, the image of God. Paul addresses the problem of unbelief and concludes that the fault lies neither with the Gospel, nor with those who preach it, but with Satan who has blinded those who, as a consequence, are unable to believe.

1 John 2:11 says, "The one hating his brother is in the darkness and walks in the darkness and does not know where he goes (compare John 12:35b), because the darkness blinded his eyes (ἡ σκοτία ἐτύφλωσεν τοὺς ὀφθαλμοὺς αὐτοῦ)." In John and 1 John it is eyes that are blinded, and both use the idiom of "walking in the darkness." 1 John and 2 Corinthians use the aorist tense while the Gospel uses the perfect tense. But in these instances aorist and perfect tenses are not sharply distinct and the notion of blinded eyes rather than minds is more a difference of idiom than meaning, because physical blindness is not the point. In the Gospel this is confirmed by the way, in the quotation of Isa 6:10, blinded eyes are in parallel with hardened heart and the failure to see with eyes with the failure to perceive [νοήσωσιν] with heart. John is not far from the notion

---

[50] Schrage, *TDNT* VIII: 271, 273.
[51] In 2 Cor 4:4 it is τὰ νοήματα that are blinded while in John 12:40 the hardened heart is not able to perceive (νοήσωσιν).

of the blinding of the minds [νοήματα], though his use of heart rather than mind reveals a more Semitic train of thought.[52] What is clear is that God is not the agent of blinding in either 2 Corinthians or 1 John. In 2 Corinthians the agent is the god of this world and in 1 John the agent is the darkness.[53] In John the emphasis falls on the blinding, and is clarified by the description of the hardening of the heart, which destroys the perceiving heart. What we are talking of here is a spiritual blindness of which eye and heart have become symbols.[54]

The Support of Origen and Cyril of Alexandria

The understanding of the devil as the agent of blinding and hardening in John 12:40 has the support of Origen[55] and Cyril of Alexandria.[56] Given that Greek was their language, and they were not dualists, their reading of John 12:40 must carry considerable weight. Since Augustine emphasized the sovereignty of God, the idea of predestination has dominated the interpretation of this verse. But the interpretation of Origen and Cyril has the support of a contextual reading and is consistent with a reading of the dualistic sections of the Qumran Texts. That John has the power of darkness in mind in 12:40 is also suggested by the relationship of John 12 to the Gethsemane account in Luke. There, in response to the act of betrayal by Judas and the actual arrest, Jesus says, "but this is your hour, and the power of darkness" (Luke 22:53). John 12:27 echoes the Synoptic Gethsemane prayer and, in what follows in John 12:31-46 Jesus speaks of his conflict with the prince of this world and the conflict of the light with the darkness.

---

[52] See *TDNT* IV: 950.

[53] Compare here Eph 6:12; Col 1:13; 1 John 5:19; Luke 8:12; and from Qumran 1 QM 13.1–14.9; 1 QS 3.13-26, especially 3.20-24.

[54] In the LXX ἐπαχύνθη is used to signify the hardening of the heart of the people. John uses ἐπώρωσεν. The terms seem to be interchangeable, *TDNT* V:1023.

[55] Fragment XCII (*Die Griechischen Christlichen Schriftsteller der ersten drei Jahrhunderte*, 554ff.); W. Bauer, *Das Johannesevangelium, erklärt* (HNT 6; Tübingen: J. C. B. Mohr [Paul Siebeck], 1933), 165; J. Blank, *Krisis: Untersuchungen zur johanneischen Christologie und Eschatologie* (Freiburg: Lambertus, 1964), 304-5; M. Wiles, *The Spiritual Gospel: The Interpretation of the Fourth Gospel in the Early Church* (Cambridge: Cambridge University Press, 1960), 109.

[56] See *PG* 74, 96-97.

Conclusion

If Jesus' activity was aimed at calling forth belief, what prevented belief? In Isa 6:10 the Lord is the speaker. John 12:41-42 identifies the pre-incarnate Jesus as speaker. Schnackenburg and Menken argue that this reading sets the Father in opposition to the Son in a quite un-Johannine way and the changes made by the Evangelist are responsible for the conflict. No changes to the Isaiah text were necessary to identify the pre-incarnate Jesus as the agent in the vision experienced by the prophet. Jesus and his signs would then be the instruments of the Father's judgment on faithlessness. John's changes to the text of Isa 6:10 at the beginning of 12:40 introduce conflict between the one who blinds and Jesus who would heal.

Clues from a comparative study of the dualistic language of John and Qumran, the use of this language in the surrounding context, evidence of the New Testament motif of "blinding," and patristic interpretation in Origen and Cyril of Alexandria, suggest an alternative interpretation.

The Gospel presupposes the reality of the power of darkness. It is because of the pervasive power of darkness in the world created by the λόγος that the λόγος became flesh. The "incarnation" by itself did not overcome the power of darkness. Consequently Jesus' ministry is portrayed as an assault on the power of darkness, 3:19-21; 8:12; 9:5, 39-41; 12:35-36a, 46. His ministry is portrayed as a struggle leading up to a decisive assault, 12:31-33.[57] In the struggle, the signs of Jesus play an important role. But 12:36b-43 informs the reader that the signs failed to be decisive. How could this be? The Evangelist's answer is that the people were unable to believe because the prince of this world, the power of darkness, had blinded their eyes and hardened their heart. Nevertheless, Jesus' ministry of signs was significant and "even of the rulers many believed," though imperfectly (12:42-43). The values of these believers were corrupted by the darkness, 1 John 2:11. They loved the glory of man rather than the glory of God, 12:43. They were unwilling to confess their faith openly. The concluding summary (12:36b-43) serves to reinforce the critical nature of the lifting up of Jesus as the judgment of the world and of the prince of this world. What is more, immediately following the announcement of failure, Jesus renews his appeal calling on his hearers to

---

[57] See Painter, *Quest*, 124-28; "Theology and Eschatology in the Prologue of John," *SJT* 46 (1992): 27-42.

believe (12:44-50), and the Gospel tells the continuing story of one of the rulers (Nicodemus, 19:38-42) struggling towards an open confession of faith.

Read in this way 12:40 does not concern predestination to unbelief by God. Rather it warns of the consequences of walking in the darkness. Those who walk in the darkness will be overwhelmed by it. This is the judgment. It is a moral consequence for those who reject the light. Those who choose the darkness find themselves overwhelmed by it.

In spite of John's understanding of Jesus' triumph over the prince of this world and the world of darkness (12:31; 16:33), the finished Gospel recognizes that the power of darkness continues to confront the believers in the world, even after the death and resurrection of Jesus. The Farewell discourses look to the Paraclete/Spirit of truth to continue the judgment of the world (see 16:4b-11). Jesus prays that the disciples, left in the world, will be kept from the corrupting power of darkness by the power of the name and word of God (John 17:9-19), so that the possibility of belief may remain open for the world (17:21-26). Nothing here suggests a neatly determined situation. Rather John has created an understanding of the world in which choice of the light or the darkness, in small as well as large matters, shapes our "destiny."

7. THE COVENANT MOTIF:
A KEY TO THE INTERPRETATION OF JOHN 15–16

Rekha M. CHENNATTU

Although the word covenant (διαθήκη) never appears in the Gospel of John, covenant motifs run like an underground stream throughout the whole text.[1] A reading of chapters 15–16 in light of the covenant paradigm transcends the boundaries of the Gospels and brings us into the current discussion of the relationship between the Old and New Testaments. It is my privilege and honor to offer this interpretation of John 15–16 as a tribute to my Guru, *Doktorvater*, colleague, and friend, Francis J. Moloney, who transcends many boundaries in his unswerving pursuit of truth, while unraveling the meaning and significance of the biblical texts. A committed scholar, excellent teacher, and an exceptionally warm and caring person, Frank Moloney proclaims God's Word in response to many challenges of contemporary society.

Covenant in the Old Testament

The biblical metaphor of covenant defines the distinctive relationship between Yahweh and the people of Israel.[2] Scholars agree that the idea of covenant in the OT is not univocal; a great variety of formularies for

---

[1] See R. M. Chennattu, *Johannine Discipleship as a Covenant Relationship* (Peabody: Hendrickson Publishers, 2005), forthcoming.

[2] See D. J. McCarthy, *Old Testament Covenant: A Survey of Current Opinions* (GPT; Oxford: Basil Blackwell, 1972), 1-9; D. N. Freedman, "Divine Commitment and Human Obligation," *Int* 18 (1964): 419; E. W. Nicholson, *God and His People: Covenant and Theology in the Old Testament* (Oxford: Clarendon Press, 1986), viii; S. L. McKenzie, *Covenant* (UBT; St. Louis: Chalice Press, 2000), 4-9.

making and renewing covenants with Yahweh as well as with human partners was known and practiced in ancient Israel.[3] Thus, "a true appreciation of covenant in all its richness must recognize the variety within the covenant traditions themselves."[4] Within that variety, however, some elements remain constant.

The challenge to accept Yahweh and to abandon other gods constituted a climactic moment in ceremonies of covenant-making/renewal in the OT (e.g., Exodus 24; Joshua 24). All the OT covenant stipulations had the same function, namely, a call to a decision to accept an exclusive relationship with Yahweh (e.g., Exodus 23; Deuteronomy 26–27). The exhortation to keep God's commandments was normally part of the speeches before the making/renewal of the covenant (e.g., Deut 30:16; Exod 34:11; Josh 24:14-15). Similarly, public consent was an integral element of the OT covenant ceremonies. Before the covenant-making in Exodus 24 and the covenant-renewal in Joshua 24, the people of Israel repeatedly confessed their acceptance of Yahweh. The public declaration of their commitment to Yahweh was usually followed by the covenant-making/ renewal ritual, as in Exod 24:8 and Josh 24:25-28.

Immediately after making the Sinai covenant (Exodus 24), Yahweh promised to dwell among the people of Israel and asked them to make a tabernacle for him (Exod 25:8). The indwelling presence of Yahweh with the people of Israel, symbolized by the tabernacle, was a sign of their covenant status.[5] If Israel was faithful to the covenant stipulations laid out in the law, God would dwell in their midst (Exod 29:45-46; cf. Num 14:14; Lev 26:11-12; Deut 12:11).[6] The covenant between Yahweh and Israel was based therefore on choices: God's choice of Israel, and Israel's choice of God. The choice of Israel underscored a free decision to be obedient and faithful to God.

Furthermore, knowledge of God was always implied in Israel's covenant relationship with Yahweh (cf. Exod 29:45-46; Jer 4:22; 9:24; Isa 1:3; 11:2; Hos 2:20; 4:1, 6; 5:4; 6:6). Hosea speaks of knowledge of God when

---

[3] See K. Baltzer, *The Covenant Formulary in Old Testament, Jewish, and Early Christian Writings* (trans. D. E. Green; Philadelphia: Fortress, 1971), 19-93. See also the pioneering works of G. E. Mendenhall, *Law and Covenant in Israel and the Ancient Near East* (Pittsburgh: The Biblical Colloquium, 1955).

[4] McCarthy, *Old Testament Covenant*, 89.

[5] See R. E. Clements, *God and Temple: The Idea of the Divine Presence in Ancient Israel* (Oxford/Philadelphia: Fortress, 1965).

[6] McKenzie, *Covenant*, 50-51.

he declares: "There is no faithfulness or covenantal love, and no knowledge of God in the land" (Hos 4:1b).[7] "For I desire covenantal love and not sacrifice, the knowledge of God rather than burnt offerings" (Hos 6:6).[8] In 4:1b, lack of faithfulness (אֱמֶת) and covenantal love (חֶסֶד) is equated with the lack of knowledge of God (דַּעַת אֱלֹהִים). In 6:6, covenantal love (חֶסֶד) parallels knowledge of God (דַּעַת אֱלֹהִים), and sacrifice (זֶבַח) parallels burnt offerings (עֹלוֹת). From these parallels it can be seen that knowledge of God implies a profound experience of God's loyalty and covenantal love for Israel as God's covenant partner. As a result of this experience one is obliged to keep the commandments and to deal with fellow Israelites as one would deal with a covenant partner.[9] Lack of this knowledge is understood as a failure to live up to the covenant relationship. For example, the oracles against the people of Judah point out their lack of knowledge as a moral failure (Isa 1:3; see also Jer 4:22; 5:4; 22:15-16; Hos 4:6). In sum, the most important elements of an OT covenant relationship include:

- A call to love God and keep God's commandments;
- A public declaration of the community's total commitment to Yahweh;
- The promise of God's indwelling or abiding presence;
- Motifs of election and knowledge of God.

John 15–16

Johannine scholars differ in their views of the internal structure of chapters 15–16. Moloney regards 15:1–16:3 as the second discourse[10]; Segovia considers John 15:18–16:4a the second discourse[11]; Tolmie and Carson maintain that John 15:1–16:33 is the second phase of the farewell dis-

---

[7] אֵין־אֱמֶת וְאֵין־חֶסֶד וְאֵין־דַּעַת אֱלֹהִים בָּאָרֶץ:

[8] כִּי חֶסֶד חָפַצְתִּי וְלֹא־זָבַח וְדַעַת אֱלֹהִים מֵעֹלוֹת:

[9] See R. de Menezes, *Voices from Beyond: Theology of the Prophetical Books* (Mumbai: St. Paul's, 2003), 110-13.

[10] F. J. Moloney, *Glory not Dishonor: Reading John 13–21* (Minneapolis: Fortress, 1998), 55-76; see also Y. Simoens, *La gloire d'aimer: Structures stylistiques et interprétatives dans le Discours de la Cène (Jn 13–17)* (AnBib 90; Rome: Biblical Institute Press, 1981), 152-58.

[11] F. F. Segovia, *The Farewell of the Word: The Johannine Call to Abide* (Minneapolis: Fortress, 1991), 169-212.

course;[12] while others place a break either at 15:25 or at 15:27.[13] The present study agrees with Tolmie and Carson in regarding John 15:1–16:33 as a single unit. However, it differs from them inasmuch as it employs the covenant motifs as a hermeneutical key to interpret the structure and meaning of the discourse. The instructions in chapters 15–16 are united by the overarching theme of discipleship and its obligations. Within this larger unit, the following smaller subdivisions can be discerned.

- A call to discipleship (15:1-17)
- Jesus' warnings to the disciples (15:18–16:24)
- The disciples' profession of faith (16:25-33)

John 15:1-17 is a self-contained unit consisting of the metaphor of the vine and the branches. This metaphor defines discipleship in terms of an abiding relationship with Jesus and the mission of the disciples in terms of bearing fruit and glorifying the Father. Verse 18 signals a new section by changing the focus from "the internal affairs of the community" to "the external affairs of the community in the world."[14] The theme of "the disciples vs. the world" is introduced and the cost of discipleship is developed in 15:18–16:24. Jesus' warning of the consequences of discipleship holds this long section together as a single unit (15:18–16:24).[15] The change of time from future (16:23-24) to the present "hour" ($\ddot{\omega}\rho\alpha$, 16:25a) of Jesus indicates a new beginning in v. 25. The imminence of the hour is characterized by having Jesus stop speaking in symbols and figures (16:25b). This is confirmed by the announcement of the disciples, "Now you are speaking plainly, not in any figure" (16:29). The unit begins with Jesus' announcement of the hour ($\ddot{\omega}\rho\alpha$), the affirmation of the disciples'

---

[12] D. F. Tolmie, *Jesus' Farewell to the Disciples: John 13:1–17:26 in Narratological Perspective* (BibIntS 12; Leiden: Brill, 1995), 30-31; D. A. Carson, *The Gospel According to John* (Grand Rapids: Eerdmans, 1991), 510-50.

[13] For those who see a break at John 15:25, see E. C. Hoskyns, *The Fourth Gospel* (ed. F. N. Davey; London: Faber & Faber, 1947), 479-87; L. Morris, *The Gospel According to John* (NICNT; Grand Rapids: Eerdmans, 1992), 677-82; and for those who see a break at John 15:27, see C. K. Barrett, *The Gospel According to St. John: An Introduction with Commentary and Notes on the Greek Text* (2d ed.; Philadelphia: Westminster, 1978), 478-83; E. Haenchen, *John* (2 vols.; trans. R. W. Funk; Hermeneia; Philadelphia: Fortress, 1984), 2:133-42.

[14] Segovia, *Farewell of the Word*, 125-27.

[15] These warnings are a normal part of covenant-renewal procedures (e.g., Josh 24:16-20). The warnings have also been recognized as part of the farewell genre; see Moloney, *Glory not Dishonor*, 67 n. 35.

belief, the affirmation of God's love for the disciples and Jesus' self-revelation in terms of his origin and destiny (16:25-28). This is followed by the disciples' profession of faith (16:29-30) and Jesus' response (16:31-33) that reconfirms the disciples' belief and the imminent presence of the hour (ὥρα).

The Call to Discipleship (15:1-17)

Four elements of an OT covenant relationship can be identified in the discipleship discourse of John 15:1-17: (i) a call to abide in Jesus and in his love; (ii) a call to glorify the Father through bearing much fruit; (iii) a call to keep the commandment to love one another; and (iv) a call to the status of being the chosen people of God.

Abiding in Jesus/God

The verb "to abide" (μένω) is very significant in the covenantal language of the OT (LXX). After a detailed study of the use of the verb μένω in the LXX, Malatesta contends that "the combination of μένειν and its cognates with the Covenant, the commandments, and with Yahweh himself connotes *a relationship of fidelity to and communion with Yahweh*, and that such expressions prepare the Johannine use of the verb."[16] The covenant relationship between Yahweh and Israel demands that the latter abide in obedience to the Law (LXX Deut 27:26) or abide in Yahweh (LXX Isa 30:18).

The verb μένω is charged with persuasive theological significance in the Gospel. The Evangelist used μένω for the first time in the context of Jesus' baptism to reveal the divine origin and identity of Jesus as the one in whom the Spirit abides (1:31-34).[17] The abiding of the Spirit in Jesus is the sign of his identity as the incarnate Word of God (1:14), who baptizes

---

[16] E. Malatesta, *Interiority and Covenant: A Study of* εἶναι ἐν *and* μένειν ἐν *in the First Letter of Saint John* (AnBib 69; Rome: Biblical Institute Press, 1978), 60. The italics are mine.

[17] Both the OT use of μένω (God's abiding presence) and κατασκηνόω (God's indwelling presence) are important for the understanding of the Johannine use of μένω. See the discussions in F. Hauck, "μένω," *TDNT*, 4:574-76; J. Heise, *Bleiben: Menein in den Johanneischen Schriften* (Tübingen: J. C. B. Mohr [Paul Siebeck], 1967), 22-28; D. Lee, *Flesh and Glory: Symbolism, Gender and Theology in the Gospel of John* (New York: Crossroad, 2002), 88-89.

with the Holy Spirit (1:33) and who is in continual relationship with God (1:1-2, 18). The second occurrence of μένω is during the dialogue between Jesus and the disciples in 1:38: ῥαββί, ... ποῦ μένεις;[18] Throughout the Gospel, Jesus will reveal the full answer to this question, viz., the intimacy shared between Jesus and the Father (e.g., 5:19-20; 14:2, 23; 15:9-10).

By inviting the disciples to abide in Jesus and in his words (cf. 4:40; 6:27, 56; 8:31-32) and by making this an integral part of the process of becoming a disciple (1:35-51; 4:4-42), the Evangelist presents discipleship in terms of an everlasting covenant relationship. As the narrative unfolds, after revealing his identity as the bread of life (6:48), Jesus makes two claims, that those who eat this bread abide in him (6:56) and that they will live forever (6:58).[19] Abiding in Jesus therefore enables the disciples to share the new life of God that transcends death.[20] Abiding in the word of Jesus becomes the hallmark of Johannine discipleship: "If you abide (μείνητε) in my word, you will truly be my disciples" (8:31).

The Evangelist develops the abiding motif further in John 15:1-17 by the metaphor of the vine and the branches and teases out the intimate and binding covenant relationship between Jesus and his disciples. Jesus is presented as the true vine and the Father as the vinedresser who cares for the well-being of the vine and tends its branches, the disciples (vv. 1-2). According to the prophetic traditions, Yahweh is the gardener and Israel is God's fruitful vine with many branches (Ezek 19:10; see also Ps 80:8-16 [LXX Ps 79:9-17]). Israel is also described as a choice vine (Jer 2:21) and God's vineyard (Isa 5:1-7; 27:2-6).[21] The Johannine account proves very faithful to Jewish traditions concerning Yahweh when it ascribes to the

---

[18] The dialogue between Jesus and the disciples can be interpreted either literally (Where do you stay?) or symbolically (Where do you abide?). The confession of faith in v. 41 ("We have found the Messiah") suggests the symbolic meaning of their query in v. 38 ("Where do you abide?"), since the object of their seeing is not Jesus' home or village but the revelation of Jesus' identity as the Messiah. For the symbolic reading of v. 38, see also X. Léon-Dufour, *Lecture de l'Évangile selon Jean* (4 vols.; Paris: Seuil, 1988-96), 1:189; R. M. Chennattu, "On Becoming Disciples (John 1:35-51): Insights from the Fourth Gospel," *Sal* 63 (2001): 477-80.

[19] In the OT, the early use of the symbol of bread is later reinterpreted in the prophetic tradition as the Torah (see Amos 8:11-12).

[20] For the Johannine discipleship in terms of an abiding relationship, see C. L. Winbery, "Abiding in Christ: The Concept of Discipleship in John," *TE* 38 (1988): 104-20. Lee compares the abiding relationship between Jesus and his disciples with that of Sophia and her followers (*Flesh and Glory*, 90-91). See also M. Scott, *Sophia and the Johannine Jesus* (JSNTSup 71; Sheffield: JSOT Press, 1992), 157-59.

[21] For the rabbinic use of the vine to describe Israel, see *Lev. R.* 36.2. See also Str-B, 2:563-64.

Father the role of vinegrower (γεωργός),[22] but it reinterprets the identity and designation of God's vine and vineyard. Many commentators have recognized a replacement theme here, namely, *Jesus the true vine* replaces Israel.[23] But the text says something more by deliberately repeating and developing the metaphor of the vine and the branches: "I am the vine and you are the branches" (v. 5). The disciples of Jesus are presented as the branches of the true vine. *Jesus together with his disciples* now stands for the new Israel, the faithful and fruitful vine of God. The organic oneness of the branches with the vine and with one another wonderfully communicates the mutual indwelling of Jesus and his disciples. The image of the vine and branches becomes a powerful symbol of the community of the disciples in covenant relationship with Jesus. Just as there can be no branches without the vine, one cannot talk about the vine and its fruitfulness without its branches. The mutuality and binding force of the covenant relationship between Jesus and the disciples are thus forcefully underlined. The community of the disciples, designated in the metaphor as the fruitful branches (vv. 3-5) abiding in Jesus, is now the new vineyard of Yahweh.[24] A certain commitment and way of life are expected from the disciples called to manifest God's life of love and to reveal God's creative presence (v. 8). The disciples' abiding covenant relationship with Jesus is further explored in terms of their fruitfulness or mission.

Glorifying the Father

An abiding relationship between Jesus and his disciples leads to bearing much fruit (καρπὸν πολύν, vv. 5, 8). There is no other way to prove

---

[22] The idea of God as the γεωργός of the cosmos and all that it contains was also familiar to Hellenistic readers; see C. H. Dodd, *The Interpretation of the Fourth Gospel* (Cambridge: Cambridge University Press, 1953), 411.

[23] For example, "Jesus has replaced Israel as the faithful and fruitful vine of God" (Segovia, *Farewell of the Word*, 136), or "The striking feature of the symbolism of the vine in John 15 is that it ceases to represent Israel and takes on Christological significance" (R. A. Culpepper, *The Gospel and Letters of John* [IBT; Nashville: Abingdon, 1998], 214). See also A. Jaubert, "L'image de la vigne (Jean 15)," in F. Christ, ed., *Oikonomia: Heilsgeschichte als Thema der Theologie: Oscar Cullmann zum 65.Geburtstag gewidmet* (Hamburg: H. Reich, 1967), 93-96. While the commentators focus mainly on the revelation of Jesus' identity, the metaphor of the vine and branches serves to unravel the mystery of Johannine discipleship.

[24] For a discussion on abiding as a symbol of community and friendship, see Lee, *Flesh and Glory*, 88-109, esp. 105-9.

themselves to be or to become (γίνομαι) disciples of Jesus except by bearing much fruit, and this is also the only way the Father will be glorified by or in them (v. 8; cf. 1:12). Abiding in Jesus and bearing fruit (v. 5) signify an intrinsic communion with God in which one shares the life of God. Only thus is one truly a disciple. The mission that flows from this new identity and existence as "branches" of Jesus "the vine" is therefore a manifestation of their new life (cf. γεννηθῇ ἄνωθεν, 3:3, 5). As the vine and its fruits are so intimately connected, with fruits reflecting the quality of the vine, so also the "being" of the disciples and their fruits/actions are inseparable. Johannine discipleship transcends the dichotomy that is traditionally attributed to one's being and one's doing, since one's deeds are manifestations of one's true being as it was manifested in Jesus' life.[25]

The metaphor of the vine and the branches indicates that Johannine Christology lies at the heart of Johannine discipleship. The disciples are called to be the fruitful branches of the vine and the model for their fruitfulness is Jesus' own committed life that springs from his abiding relationship with the Father. This short section (vv. 1-17) brings together many aspects of Jesus' mission, which is described elsewhere in the Gospel as Jesus' way of glorifying the Father (cf. 17:4). Jesus has shared the love of the Father with his disciples (vv. 9, 12); Jesus has been faithful in observing the commandments of the Father (v. 10); Jesus has spoken the words of the Father and made known to the disciples all that he heard his Father speaking to him (vv. 3, 11, 15). The disciples are called to the same mission, to glorify the Father, to make God's ongoing revelation present in and through their life and fruit-bearing ministry.[26]

Keeping the Commandments (15:9-17)

Keeping the commandments is an indispensable condition for abiding in Jesus' love (v. 10) and for being friends of Jesus (v. 14). The command to abide in Jesus' love is preceded by a conditional clause, "if you keep (τηρήσητε) my commandments (τὰς ἐντολάς μου)" (v. 10), and the call to be Jesus' friends is followed by a similar conditional clause, "if you do

---

[25] See R. M. Chennattu, "The *Svadharma* of Jesus: An Indian Reading of John 5:1-18," in *Seeking New Horizons: Festschrift in Honour of M. Amaladoss, S.J.* (ed. L. Fernando; Delhi: VEWS & ISPCK, 2002), 317-35, esp. 324-29.

[26] See R. M. Chennattu, "Women in the Mission of the Church: An Interpretation of John 4," *VJTR* 65 (2001): 760-73; repr. in *SedB* 34 (2002): 39-45.

(ποιῆτε) what I command (ἐντέλλομαι) you" (v. 14). Viewed from the perspective of these conditional clauses, how do we interpret the abiding relationship and the friendship that Jesus is proposing to his disciples?[27] According to the Johannine Jesus, if the disciples want to abide in his love and if they want to remain as his friends, then they must keep the commandments.[28] By using these conditional clauses and the stipulation to keep the commandments, the Evangelist parallels the abiding relationship and friendship between Jesus and his disciples with the OT covenant relationship between Yahweh and Israel. One needs to obey God's voice and keep God's covenant commandments in order to be God's vine (cf. Jer 2:21; 3:13) and God's treasured possession (Exod 19:5; see also Josh 7:11; 24:25). Similarly, the disciples are expected to keep the commandments in order to establish and maintain their friendship with Jesus and their covenant status in the community.

Being the Chosen People of God (15:16)

The metaphor of the vine and the branches, symbolizing the community of Jesus' disciples, alludes to the concept of God's chosen people.[29] Jesus' words "I chose (ἐξελεξάμην) you and appointed (ἔθηκα) you" (v. 16) remind the readers of the OT election of the people of Israel. The concept of election is linked to the theology of covenant relationship in terms of both divine promises and human commitments. A similar process is going on in the unfolding metaphor of the vine and branches. Jesus now claims that he has chosen the disciples (15:16)[30] and, in their turn, the

---

[27] On the basis of v. 15, Lee suggests that "Jesus uses the language of personal friendship, overturning servile models of relationship" (*Flesh and Glory*, 103). S. van Tilborg interprets Jesus' friendship with his disciples as a way of extending the household (οἶκος) of his heavenly Father. The greater and more influential the οἶκος is, the more numerous are the friends (*Imaginative Love in John* [BibIntS 2; Leiden: Brill, 1993], 148-50).

[28] For the echoes of the OT covenant commandments (of Deuteronomy) in John's Gospel, see M. J. O'Connell, "The Concept of Commandment in the Old Testament," *TS* 21 (1960): 351-403. Brown argues for an implicit reference to a covenant theme in the new commandments of John 13:34; 15:12, 17 (*John*, 2:557). See also J. W. Pryor, *John: Evangelist of the Covenant People: The Narrative & Themes of the Fourth Gospel* (London: Darton, Longman and Todd, 1992), 157-80.

[29] R. Schnackenburg, *The Church in the New Testament* (New York: Herder and Herder, 1966), 109. See also Dodd, *Interpretation*, 410-12.

[30] The disciples of Jesus as the "chosen people" of God is attested throughout the NT books (e.g., Mark 13:20; Matt 24:31; Luke 18:7; Rom 8:33; 1 Thess 1:4; Eph 1:4; 2 Tim 2:10; Titus 1:1; 2 John 1:1; Rev 17:14).

disciples have received this vocation as a gift from God (see 3:27). As the election motif elicits the necessity for Israel to choose God and keep his commandments, the disciples are called to abide in Jesus' love and keep the covenant commandments. This is a choice that they must make. Just as the failure in living up to the expectations of the OT covenant led Israel to exile (e.g., 2 Kings 23:26-27; Isa 5:11-13; Lam 4:42; Amos 7:17), the failure to abide in Jesus and bear fruit will lead the disciples to isolation and destruction (John 15:6).

The discipleship discourse in John 15:1-17 echoes a number of key elements associated with Israel's covenant relationship with God. As Israel of old entered into a covenant with Yahweh, so the disciples are chosen and called to remain in faithful relationship with Jesus and to live by his commands. In union with Jesus, and with each other, they are the new vineyard of Yahweh.

Jesus' Warning to the Disciples (15:18–16:24)

Following the discourse on discipleship, developed through the metaphor of the vine and the branches, the next section of the discourse (15:18–16:24) elaborates further on discipleship by examining its consequences. There are two major subunits focusing on the reactions of the unbelieving world in general (15:18-27) and then on the reactions of the Jewish world in particular (16:2-24). In the center of these two units, 16:1 states the purpose of Jesus' warnings to the disciples: to prevent their falling into apostasy.[31] Both units, describing the opposition of the world and the opposition of the synagogue, have a threefold structure: persecution (15:18-20; 16:2), the reason for this persecution (15:21-25; 16:3), and the assurance of help from the Paraclete (15:26-27; 16:4-24). The overall structure of 15:18–16:24 can be summarized as follows.

a	Persecution:	the world will hate you (15:18-20)
b	Reason:	no knowledge of God (15:21-25)
c	Assurance:	the gift of the Paraclete (15:26-27)
d	Purpose	to prevent apostasy (16:1)
a¹	Persecution:	they will expel you from the synagogues (16:2)
b¹	Reason:	no knowledge of God (16:3)
c¹	Assurance:	the gift of the Paraclete (16:4-24)

---

[31] I use the hard expression "apostasy" to continue the OT theme associated with Israel's betrayal of the covenant relationship with God.

Persecution (a): The World Will Hate You (15:18-20)

The disciples have to face many consequences of their faith in Jesus. Jesus warns that the world (ὁ κόσμος) will hate the disciples because they belong to the chosen community of God (15:18-22).[32] The negative consequence of discipleship is described first in terms of hatred (μισέω) by the world (15:18-19) which is the same response of the world to Jesus' revelation (3:20; 7:7). The response of the world to both Jesus and his disciples is examined further in terms of persecution (διώκω, 15:20a) and keeping or not keeping the word of Jesus (τηρέω, 15:20b). As Jesus experienced persecution during his ministry, the disciple will suffer likewise.[33] The abiding relationship of the disciples with Jesus constitutes a community of love that stands out over against the world, which hates Jesus and does not keep his word. Jesus prepares his disciples to meet the challenges of discipleship and to remain as a visible communitarian sign of God's ongoing revelation in human history.

Reason (b): No Knowledge of God (15:21-25)

The references to hatred and persecution by the world are followed by the reason for the hatred and persecution described in terms of the world's lack of knowledge of God: οὐκ οἴδασιν τὸν πέμψαντά με (15:21; cf. Ισραηλ δέ με οὐκ ἔγνω, Isa 1:3). In the OT the lack of knowledge of God signaled a rupture in the covenant relationship between Yahweh and Israel (Isa 1:3-4). This ignorance and the consequential unbelief were often referred to by the symbol of darkness in John's Gospel. The world that does not know God, does not have the light of life and lives in dark-

---

[32] The term ὁ κόσμος refers to the unbelievers who rejected the Father and Jesus. ὁ κόσμος is used in the Gospel with three different meanings: (1) the universe (e.g., 11:9; 17:5, 24; 21:25); (2) humanity (e.g., 3:16; 6:14; 8:26); (3) all those who rejected the revelation of God in Jesus (e.g., 7:7; 14:17; 15:18; 12:31). For the different uses and meanings of ὁ κόσμος in John's Gospel, see Brown, *John*, 1:508-9; F. J. Moloney, *Belief in the Word: Reading John 1-4* (Minneapolis: Fortress, 1993), 37.

[33] For the dialectical relationship between the consequences of the mission of Jesus and that of the disciples, see B. Lindars, "The Persecution of Christians in John 15:18-16:4a," in *Suffering and Martyrdom in the New Testament: Studies Presented to G. M. Styler by the Cambridge New Testament Seminar* (ed. W. Horbury and B. McNeil; Cambridge: Cambridge University Press, 1981), 48-69, esp. 59-62.

ness.[34] Jesus' claim, if "the world" had known the Father, they would have recognized the presence of God in Jesus, challenges his opponents' claim to fidelity to the covenant relationship with Yahweh (cf. Exod 29:45-46; Jer 9:24; Isa 11:2).

Assurance (c): The Gift of the Paraclete (15:26-27)

The reassuring words of Jesus consist of a threefold statement about the gift of the Paraclete and a statement about the role of the disciples as witnesses (15:26-27). Jesus first promises that he will send the Paraclete to the disciples (v. 26a), and then reveals the divine origin of the Paraclete by explicitly mentioning that the Paraclete proceeds from the Father (v. 26b). Since the origin of Jesus is intimately connected to his mission, one needs to interpret the origin of the Paraclete not in terms of ontological "procession" from the Father, but in terms of the Paraclete's mission in the world.[35] Just as the works of Jesus were to reveal the love and glory of the Father, the works of the Paraclete are to bear witness to Jesus in the world (v. 26c). Jesus also reminds the disciples, as future recipients of the Paraclete, of their work to bear witness to him (15:27). Jesus was sent into the world to make God known (17:6, 26); Jesus now promises to send the Paraclete to the disciples that they in turn may continue to make visible God's presence and unconditional love in the time following Jesus' departure (cf. 17:18).

Purpose (d): To Prevent Apostasy (16:1)

At the center of these two units describing the opposition the disciples will meet from the world and the synagogue, 16:1 explains why the disciples are forewarned of this opposition: in order to keep them from giving up their faith (σκανδαλίζω, 16:1). The verb σκανδαλίζω is used twice in John's Gospel (6:61; 16:1) and on both occasions it has the meaning of

---

[34] As C. R. Koester has pointed out, darkness in the Fourth Gospel symbolizes (1) "the powers that oppose God"; (2) "the lethal estrangement from God"; (3) human "ignorance and unbelief" (*Symbolism in the Fourth Gospel: Meaning, Mystery, Community* [2d ed.; Minneapolis: Fortress, 2003], 143-44).
[35] Carson, *John*, 528-29.

causing someone to sin or to give up one's faith.[36] The real danger that Jesus envisages for his disciples is not the possibility of persecution per se but the possibility that they may give up their belief in the revelation of God in Jesus.[37] The act of forewarning found here follows the OT covenant pattern. Before the renewal of the Sinai covenant, a similar concern about forsaking Yahweh was expressed in the warnings of Joshua and in his commands "to put away other gods" (cf. 24:16, 23). Just as in the case of the OT covenant-renewals, the real concern of Jesus' warning lies in the danger of the disciples' apostatizing by denying the revelation of God in Jesus.

Persecution (a¹): They Will Expel You from the Synagogues (16:2)

The second unit moves from discussing the opposition the disciples will meet from a disbelieving world to the opposition they will meet from "the Jews."[38] Jesus forewarns that the Jewish community ("they") will expel the disciples from the synagogues (16:2a) because of their faith in Jesus as the one sent by God.[39] The fear of being put out of the synagogue (ἀποσυνάγωγος) mentioned elsewhere in the Gospel (9:22; 12:42) reflects not only the experience of the characters in the story but also the experience of subsequent generations of disciples.[40] The expulsion from the

---

[36] For a detailed discussion of the meaning of σκανδαλίζω, see also K. Müller, *Anstoss und Gericht: Eine Studie zum Jüdischen Hintergrund des paulinischen Skandalon-Begriffs* (SANT 19; München: Kösel-Verlag, 1969), 46-67. The verb is used in later Christian writings with a specific reference to those who have stumbled from the faith or apostates; see *Did.* 16.5; Herm. *Vis.* 4.1.3; Herm. *Mand.* 8.10.

[37] Barrett, *John*, 483-84; R. Schnackenburg, *The Gospel According to St. John* (3 vols.; trans. C. Hastings; London: Burns & Oates/New York: Herder and Herder, 1968-82), 3:121.

[38] The expression "the Jews" refers to the characters in the story who are ignorant of Jesus' identity and origin and thus reject the revelation of God in Jesus. For a detailed discussion of the use of the expression "the Jews" in John's Gospel, see F. J. Moloney, "'The Jews' in the Fourth Gospel: Another Perspective," *Pacifica* 15 (2002): 16-36.

[39] I maintain the distinction that the designation "they" in 15:20-25 is a reference to "the world," to unbelieving humanity in general that includes "the Jews"; but "they" in 16:2 is an exclusive reference to the Jewish community because of its explicit reference to the excommunication from the synagogue (ἀποσυνάγωγος).

[40] R. E. Brown suggests that "crypto-Christians" believed in Jesus but did not acknowledge their faith publicly since they were afraid of being expelled from the synagogue (*The Community of the Beloved Disciple: The Life, Loves, Hates of an Individual Church in New Testament Times* [New York: Paulist, 1979], 71-73).

synagogue implies a definitive breaking of the bond between the Jewish community and the disciples, and it reflects the experience of the Johannine community.[41] Jesus also forewarns that those who put the disciples to death will think that they are offering a "spiritual service" or "worship" (λατρείαν προσφέρειν) to God (16:2b).[42] Lindars claims that 16:2b "comprises John's most serious warning to his readers. It is a real fear that a violent persecution is about to begin; … [and] this action will be carried out with a genuinely religious motive."[43] By placing this alarming possibility before the disciples and readers, the Johannine Jesus encourages them to endure it within the framework of Jesus' own suffering and sacrifice (17:17-19). The presence of irony is very clear: on the one hand, the persecutors mistakenly think that they are offering a service to God; on the other, the martyrdom of disciples is a true offering to God.

Reason (b¹): No Knowledge of God (16:3)

The reference to the expulsion from the synagogue is followed by the reason for this exclusion: the lack of knowledge of God (οὐκ ἔγνωσαν τὸν πατέρα οὐδὲ ἐμέ, 16:3).[44] Despite their claims to the contrary, Jesus has earlier accused "the Jews" of their lack of knowledge and communion with God: "You have never heard his voice or seen his form; … you do

---

[41] Schnackenburg, *John*, 3:121; Moloney, *Glory not Dishonor*, 72. J. L. Martyn has argued that the twelfth benediction of the *Birkat ha-Mînîm* of the *Tefillah* (Eighteen Benedictions) was reformulated to include Christians among the *mînîm*, in order to recognize and expel the Jewish Christians from the synagogues (*History and Theology in the Fourth Gospel* [3d ed.; Louisville: Westminster John Knox, 2003], 46-66). There is very little support today to make the link between the expulsion (ἀποσυνάγωγος) in John's Gospel and the *Birkat ha-Mînîm*; see P. W. van der Horst, "The Birkat ha-minim in Recent Research," *ExpTim* 105 (1993-94): 363-68. For a modified view that the sages at Jamnia were aware of the messianic claims of Christians who were thus identified among the *mînîm* whom they sought to exclude from the synagogue, see W. D. Davies, "Reflection on Aspects of the Jewish Background of the Gospel of John," in R. A. Culpepper and C. C. Black (eds.), *Exploring the Fourth Gospel: In Honor of D. Moody Smith* (Louisville: Westminster/John Knox, 1996), 43-64, esp. 49-52.

[42] Paul's pre-Christian persecution of the church was understood by him as a service to God. A similar conviction among the first-century Jewish community is reflected in rabbinic writings. For example, "… if a man sheds the blood of the wicked it is as though he had offered a sacrifice," *Num. Rab.* 21.3. See also *m. Sanh.* 9.6.

[43] Lindars, "Persecution of Christians," 65.

[44] Jesus' accusation repeats the words of Yahweh verbatim; see Ισραηλ δέ με οὐκ ἔγνω, Isa 1:3.

not believe him whom he has sent" (5:37-38); "You do not know him [God]" (7:28; see also 8:27, 55). Their lack of knowledge of God implies that they are in darkness and that they do not share the light of life (cf. 1:4-5).[45] As Carson pointed out, "These people enjoyed far less antecedent knowledge of God than they claimed."[46] This is a serious accusation against the Jewish characters in the story, since lack of knowledge of God is interpreted by the prophetic tradition as a failure to live up to the covenant relationship (Isa 1:3-4). In contrast to the experience of the world and "the Jews," Jesus promised the disciples that they would know Jesus (cf. 10:14),[47] the Father (14:7), and the Spirit of truth (14:17), enabling them to love Jesus and believe in the revelation of God he embodied (16:27, 30).

Assurance (c′): The Gift of the Paraclete (16:4-24)

The negative consequences of discipleship are followed by the comforting promise of Jesus that he will send the Paraclete who will accompany the disciples, empower them to meet the challenges of persecutions, and help them remain faithful to their abiding covenant relationship with God (16:4-24). In this passage, the gift of the Paraclete is seen from the perspective of what the Spirit accomplishes, namely, making the indwelling presence of the covenant God visible for the disciples.

Jesus' discourse first introduces the inseparable link between his departure and the arrival of the Paraclete (16:4-7); the discourse then focuses on the juridical role of the Paraclete (16:8-11). In the Psalms, Yahweh has been depicted as the judge of the world: "God has taken his place in the divine council; in the midst of the gods he holds judgment" (Ps 82:1). Jesus argues elsewhere in the Gospel that the Father has given him the authority to judge (5:22, 27; cf. 3:19; 5:27; 8:26; 9:39; 12:31); Jesus now passes this authority on to the Paraclete.

The judging activity of the Paraclete is described by ἐλέγχω (16:8). The verb ἐλέγχω has an extensive semantic range, but it can be translated as either to "bring to light" (cf. 3:20) or to "prove guilty" (cf. 8:46). The English verb that is closest to the Greek ἐλέγχω is "expose," since it has

---

[45] Koester, *Symbolism*, 144.

[46] Carson, *John*, 526.

[47] For a detailed discussion, see R. M. Chennattu, "The Good Shepherd (Jn 10): A Political Perspective," *JPJRS* 1 (1998): 93-105, esp. 98-101.

the same double meaning as ἐλέγχω: "to make visible" and "hold up to reprobation."[48] The Paraclete will expose the world concerning sin, righteousness, and judgment (16:8). First, the world's sin is that it does not recognize the presence of God in Jesus or believe in Jesus as the incarnation of God (16:9). Second, the truth regarding righteousness is revealed in Jesus' departure to the Father through his death and resurrection (16:10). Jesus' departure is the vindication and ratification of his life by the Father.[49] Third, "the ruler of this world" (16:11; cf. 12:31) is defeated by God's vindication of Jesus, which in turn exposes God's judgment on the world (16:11).

The Paraclete's role as guide (16:13) is a further example of how the Paraclete continues the works of the covenant God and Jesus. Jesus reassures the disciples that the Paraclete will guide (ὁδηγήσει) them into the truth. The verb ὁδηγέω recalls God's leading the people of Israel in the desert (Exod 15:13, 17; Num 24:8; Deut 1:33).[50] The same notion is recognized in the language of the Psalms, where "guide me in your truth" refers to the covenant relationship and its obligations (Pss 25:5, 9; 143:10). The role ascribed to the covenant God in the OT, viz., guiding the people to truth and life, is assumed by Jesus when he is presented as the way, the truth, and the life (14:6), and the same task is now entrusted to the Paraclete: "He will guide you into the truth" (16:13).

Truth (ἀλήθεια) is a theologically charged word in John's Gospel. The prologue first speaks of Jesus as the one filled with grace and truth (1:14) and then claims that grace and truth (ἡ χάρις καὶ ἡ ἀλήθεια) came from Jesus Christ (1:17). In Jewish thinking, חֶסֶד וֶאֱמֶת (χάρις and ἀλήθεια) are attributes of God revealed in the Torah;[51] they (חֶסֶד וֶאֱמֶת) are the qualities of Yahweh, as the covenant God and covenanted partner with Israel, abounding in steadfast love and faithfulness (Exod 34:6). In the Prologue, the Evangelist uses ἡ χάρις καὶ ἡ ἀλήθεια to announce the revelation of the same covenant God that has come through Jesus Christ (cf. 1:17). Moreover, truth (ἀλήθεια) in John's Gospel is often closely associated and

---

[48] Hoskyns, *Fourth Gospel*, 484.

[49] Hoskyns describes Jesus' departure as "God's imprimatur upon the righteousness manifested in the life and death of His Son" (*Fourth Gospel*, 485).

[50] Hoskyns, *Fourth Gospel*, 485-86.

[51] See *Midr. Ps.* 25.10, "All the paths of the Lord are mercy and truth. By *mercy* [חֶסֶד] is meant deeds of loving kindness, and by *truth* [אֱמֶת] is meant the law of the Lord. For to whom shall the paths of the Lord be given? Unto such as keep his covenant and his testimonies."

identified with the Spirit: τὸ πνεῦμα τῆς ἀληθείας, "the Spirit of Truth" (14:17; 15:26; 16:13). Like Jesus the incarnate Word, the Paraclete will reveal the life of God (15:26). Viewed from this perspective, the task of the Paraclete in 16:13 is to guide the disciples into truth (ἀλήθεια) which is the revelation of a new covenant relationship with God. In sum, the Paraclete's role is to expose the world's wrong and to guide disciples into the truth of God's revelation in Jesus.

The Disciples' Profession of Faith (16:25-33)

This final section of the discourse begins with Jesus' proclamation of the coming "hour" when the ultimate revelation of God will take place on the cross (16:25). The event of the hour has the power to change the relationship between the Father and the disciples (cf. 16:26-27). This new and transformed covenant relationship of love between the Father and the disciples is possible because the disciples, unlike "the Jews" in the narratives, have loved Jesus and believed in his divine origin (16:27). The intimacy that Jesus shares with God will also be granted to the disciples who love and believe in him.

Israel's identity resides in her single-minded commitment to Yahweh expressed in a pledge to be obedient to the covenant laws and to serve only Yahweh (Josh 24:21, 24; Exod 24:3, 7).[52] In a similar way, the Johannine disciples express their total commitment to Jesus in 16:30: "Now we know that you know all things and do not need to have anyone question you; by this we believe that you came from God."

From the beginning of the Johannine story in the prologue (1:1-5, 18), the motif of Jesus' origin from God has been a primary concern (1:51; 3:13; 6:33, 38, 41, 42, 50, 51, 58; 7:28; 8:14, 42; 13:3).[53] This motif has also been the key issue that emerged during the Christological debates in chapters 5–10 and divided the characters in the narrative (1:46; 7:25-31, 40-44; 8:42, 48-59). In the revelation that precedes the profession of the disciples' faith, Jesus' reassuring words affirm two things: i) the disciples have loved Jesus (16:27b); ii) they have believed that he came from God

---

[52] See the comment on Josh 24:24 in T. C. Butler, *Joshua* (WBC 7; Waco: Word Books, 1983), 276.

[53] See W. R. G. Loader, "The Central Structure of Johannine Theology," *NTS* 30 (1984): 188-99.

(16:27c). The disciple's solemn profession of faith is echoed by Jesus' affirmation of their response to him: i) they know Jesus (16:30a); (ii) they believe that Jesus has come from God (30:16b). The disciples thus acknowledge Jesus' divine origin, his knowledge of God, and his authority to reveal the Father (cf. 16:25).[54] The emphatic use of "now" (νῦν) and the repeated expressions "we know" (οἴδαμεν) and "we believe" (πιστεύομεν) point to the oath that generally precedes covenant-making (cf. Exod 24:3, 7; Josh 24:21, 24). This solemn profession as a group is something that the disciples have not done before. This profession of faith by the disciples and its confirmation by Jesus bring his mission to closure, allowing him to announce that he has accomplished the work that God gave him (17:4).

Conclusion

There are many parallels between OT covenant relationship and Johannine discipleship. Abiding in God's love and keeping God's commandments are the hallmark of both OT covenant relationship and Johannine discipleship. Knowledge of God, covenant obligations, and warnings to avoid apostasy are other common motifs. Just as Yahweh promised his indwelling presence among the people of Israel (Exod 29:45-46; Lev 26:11-12), so also Jesus promises the abiding presence and ongoing guidance of God in and through the gift of the Paraclete (14: 15-17, 21, 23; 15:26-27; 16:12-15). Finally, as the people of Israel professed their absolute commitment to Yahweh during the covenant ceremonies (Exod 24:3, 7; Josh 24:21, 24), so also the disciples, as one body, pledge their faith in Jesus as the only authentic revealer of God (16:29-30).

By the careful arrangement and modification of the farewell discourses, the Fourth Evangelist presents discipleship as a covenant relationship paralleling the theological framework of OT covenant motifs. However, there is one major difference. OT covenant theology restricted the relationship to Yahweh and the descendants of Israel; Johannine discipleship is char-

---

[54] Brown, *John*, 2:725-26. Some scholars suggest here the reflections of the Johannine community's experience of rubbing shoulders with other religions and propose a comparison between Jesus, the true revealer, and other "revealers" from the Greek worlds; see H. N. Bream, "No Need to Be Asked Questions: A Study of John 16:30," in *Search the Scriptures: New Testament Studies in Honor of Raymond T. Stamm* (ed. J. M. Myers, O. Reimherr, and H. N. Bream; GTS 3; Leiden: Brill, 1969), 49-74.

acterized by a universal appeal that includes Jews (cf. chapters 1-3), Samaritans (cf. chapter 4), and Gentiles (cf. 4:46-54; 7:35; 11:52; 12:20, 32). The Johannine notion of discipleship thus transcends all ethnic and religious boundaries in its invitation to all to become "children of God" (1:12-13). The Johannine discipleship as a covenant relationship implies an ever-deeper experience of God's abiding love, and it calls for a commitment to collaborate with God's creative and life-giving works or actions (τὰ ἔργα τοῦ θεοῦ).[55] In other words, the disciples are called to the same mission of Jesus, to "glorify" the Father, to make the ongoing revelation of God's creative life of love visible in and through their fruit-bearing ministry in contemporary society.

---

[55] For a discussion of the "works of God," see Chennattu, "*Svadharma* of Jesus," 325-29.

8. "HE GAVE UP THE SPIRIT": A READER'S REFLECTION ON JOHN 19:30b

Robert KYSAR

Francis J. Moloney argues that the narrator of the Fourth Gospel reports that Jesus "handed over *the Spirit*" to the core of the new church gathered at the foot of the cross. He insists that παρέδωκεν τὸ πνεῦμα should be translated "handed over *the* Spirit" and not "gave up *his* spirit." Moreover, the crucifixion is Jesus' "glorification" which is the occasion of the outpouring of the Spirit spoken of in John 7:39.[1] Moloney once again transgresses the normative reading of the passage established by the majority of commentators. For good reason, the expression at 19:30b (παρέδωκεν τὸ πνεῦμα) is most often translated "(he) gave up *his* spirit" (RSV and NRSV) and is understood in many commentaries to refer to Jesus' surrender of his life (cf. possible parallels in Matt 27:50b; Mark 15:37b; Luke 23:46b).[2]

This brief essay is both an experiment in interpretation and, in another sense, in New Testament theology.[3] I want to explore the possibilities of the ambiguity in this passage's use of τὸ πνεῦμα.[4] What happens when

---

[1] F. J. Moloney, *The Gospel of John* (SP 4; Collegeville: Liturgical Press, 1998), 504-5, 508-9. Cf. R. E. Brown, *The Gospel According to John* (AB 29-29A; 2 vols.; Garden City: Doubleday, 1966, 1970), 2:931 and *The Death of the Messiah: From Gethsemane to the Grave. A Commentary on the Passion Narratives of the Four Gospels* (ABRL; 2 vols.; New York: Doubleday, 1994), 2:1082-83.

[2] Unless indicated otherwise, all English translations are from the New Revised Standard Version.

[3] This paper was originally written for and read in an abbreviated form in the Johannine Literature Section, at the SBL Annual Meeting, 1998 and later a version was presented to the Emory University Graduate School New Testament Colloquy.

[4] I use "ambiguity" in the sense of polyvalence and not the simpler experience of two possible meanings, one of which is correct and the other wrong, and between which the

one takes the phrase to refer to *both* Jesus' human spirit *and* the divine Spirit/Paraclete? What are the theological implications of such a reading? However, it is necessary first to have before us at least a sampling of the commentators' views of its meaning.

The Commentators

Without excessive over generalization and for our purposes here, we can summarize the views of contemporary commentators in four relatively distinct but sometimes overlapping categories.

In *the first category* are those who maintain (sometimes without argument) that πνεῦμα in verse 30b refers to Jesus' own spirit or life. Schnackenburg, Bernard, and Beasley-Murray are among representatives of this view, which is probably the most widely endorsed reading of the passage.[5] The most common argument is simply that the bestowal of the Spirit is found in 20:22 and therefore cannot be in view here. As Barrett writes, "There is no room for an earlier giving of the Spirit."[6] Often commentators see in "handed over the spirit" a paraphrase of Luke 23:6.[7] Other arguments for

reader must choose. In this sense, I disagree with P. Ricoeur's distinction between ambiguity and metaphor (*The Rule of Metaphor: Multi-disciplinary Studies of the Creation of Meaning* [Toronto/Buffalo/London: University of Toronto Press, 1977], 91).

[5] R. Schnackenburg, *The Gospel According to St. John* (3 vols.; New York: Crossroads, 1968-82), 3:285; cf. 3:461 n.70; J. H. Bernard, *A Critical and Exegetical Commentary on the Gospel According to St. John* (ICC; 2 vols.; Edinburgh: T&T Clark, 1928), 2:641-42; and G. R. Beasley-Murray, *John* (WBC 36; Waco: Word, 1987), 353. Others who hold similar views include: A. Schlatter, *Der Evangelist Johannes: Ein Commentar zum Vierten Evangelium* (Stuttgart: Calwer, 1960), 352; A. Plummer, *The Gospel According to St. John* (TC; Grand Rapids: Baker, 1981), 332; K. Grayston, *The Gospel of John* (NC; Philadelphia: Trinity International, 1990), 163; J. R. Michaels, *John* (GNC; New York: Harper and Row, 1983), 321; and J. Marsh, *Saint John* (PGC; Baltimore: Pelican, 1968), 618-19. Cf. B. M. Newman and E. A. Nida, *A Translator's Handbook on the Gospel of John* (HT; London/New York/Stuttgart: United Bible Societies, 1980), 593.

[6] C. K. Barrett, *The Gospel According to St. John* (2d ed.; Philadelphia: Westminster, 1978), 554. Cf. R. Kysar, *John* (ACNT; Minneapolis: Augsburg, 1986), 290. Several suggest that this handing over of Jesus' human spirit *prepares* for the giving of the Holy Spirit. E.g., G. H. C. MacGregor, *The Gospel of John* (MNTC; New York/London: Harper and Brothers, nd), 349 and R. H. Lightfoot, *St. John's Gospel: A Commentary* (Oxford: Clarendon, 1956), 319.

[7] Barrett, *Gospel*, 554; F. F. Bruce, *The Gospel of John* (Grand Rapids: Eerdmans, 1983), 374 (who sees it too as fashioned from Ps 31:5); J. N. Sanders and B. A. Mastin, *The Gospel According to St. John* (BNTC; London: Black, 1968), 410. J. H. Bernard believes there is a deliberate translation of the Hebrew of Isa 53:12 (*A Critical and Exegetical Commentary on the Gospel According to St. John* [ICC; 2 vols.; Edinburgh: T&T Clark, 1928], 2: 641).

the word's reference to the human spirit include: The flow of the argument in chapter 20;[8] the absence of an indirect object to whom the spirit is given (such as the disciples);[9] and the fact that Jesus' glorification (which he says must occur before the giving of the Holy Spirit) includes his resurrection as well as his death.[10]

The second category comprises those who, like Moloney, mount an argument that in this case τὸ πνεῦμα refers to the Holy Spirit or Paraclete. Hoskyns and Davey seem to have been influential in the formation of this view. Their argument links the narrator's words with the previous episode in which Jesus has spoken to his mother and the Beloved Disciple. Jesus bows his head *toward them* and bestows the divine Spirit on them. Verse 30 fulfills 7:37-39 when it is read in the light of the blood and water flowing from Jesus' side. The association with 1 John 5:8 "seems to make this interpretation not only possible, but necessary."[11] Brown follows Hoskyns and Davey, proposing that Jesus' mother represents the church and the Beloved Disciple, the Christians. However, with his characteristic caution he writes that, if such an interpretation is "plausible, … this symbolic reference is evocative and *proleptic* … [but] the actual giving of the Spirit does not come now but in xx 22 after the resurrection."[12] For Brown there is an implicit distinction between the giving of the Holy Spirit to the representatives of the new community in Christ at the foot of the cross and the "disciples" in 20:19-23. Moloney is more definite: "The words of the narrator are not a euphemism for death. … Jesus hands over, entrusts, *the Spirit* to his new family gathered at the foot of the cross (vv. 24-27)."[13]

---

[8] D. A. Carson, *The Gospel According to John* (Grand Rapids: Eerdmans, 1991), 621.

[9] B. Lindars believes the only possible implicit indirect object is God (*The Gospel of John* [NCB; London: Oliphants, 1972], 582-83).

[10] G. R. O'Day, "The Gospel of John: Introduction, Commentary, and Reflections," *The New Interpreter's Bible* (12 vols.; Nashville: Abingdon, 1995), IX: 833. For a summary of the interpretations of the ancient Christian commentators, see M. Edwards, *John* (BBC; Oxford: Blackwell, 2004), 184-85.

[11] E. C. Hoskyns, *The Fourth Gospel* (ed. F. N. Davey; London: Faber, 1940), 532.

[12] Brown, *John*, 2: 931. Brown nuances his interpretation more carefully in *The Death of the Messiah*. There he writes, "the Evangelist rethought the tradition of Jesus' breathing his last and equated πνεῦμα with the Holy Spirit." However, he stills says such an interpretation is only "plausible" (2:1082-83). Cf. G. D. Bampfylde, "John XIX,28: A Case for a New Translation," *NovT* 11 (1969): 247-60.

[13] Moloney, *John*, 505. Cf. T. L. Brodie, *The Gospel According to John: A Literary and Theological Commentary* (New York/Oxford: Oxford University Press, 1993), 551. B. J. Malina and R. L. Rohrbaugh say, "The spirit breathed out by the exalted Jesus along with this newly open fountain, with water spurting from Jesus' side, relates to birth from wa-

In *the third category* of commentators are those who are uncertain – who recognize the possibility of both Jesus' own spirit and the divine Spirit as the reference of πνεῦμα without settling for one or the other. Ellis, for instance, calls it "possible but dubious" that πνεῦμα in this passage refers to the Holy Spirit.[14] However, Dodd most honestly represents the dilemma of determining the meaning of this phrase. He acknowledges that it is probable that πνεῦμα is the "breath-soul" but possible too that "the Evangelist intended to suggest a secondary meaning."[15] Later he writes,

Whether the unusual phrase παρέδωκε τὸ πνεῦμα … is to be understood in the sense that Jesus in dying bequeathed the Holy Spirit to the world He was leaving, or whether it simply means that He surrendered the spirit (or vital principle) to God who gave it (cf. Eccl. xii.7), *I do not feel able to decide.*[16]

He assumes that the divine Spirit is "released" in Jesus' death but that it must still be given to the disciples by the risen Lord.[17]

The final category is comprised of others who have hinted or even asserted that there may be a double meaning inherent in this use of πνεῦμα. Sloyan concludes that the word probably does not refer to the Holy Spirit, but adds, "knowing [the Fourth Evangelist] for the incurable player on words that he is – especially the word πνεῦμα (cf. 3:8) – we would be unwise to say that he surely did not have the double meaning in mind."[18] McPolin is more certain of it. He contends that the verse is a "theological picture" in which Jesus hands over his spirit in a double sense. "Jesus dies and through his death communicates the Holy Spirit."[19] Add these

ter and spirit referred to in 3:5" (*Social-Science Commentary on the Gospel of John* [Minneapolis: Fortress, 1998], 275). Cf. J. M. Ford, *Redeemer–Friend and Mother* (Minneapolis: Fortress, 1997), 195, 275-76.

[14] P. F. Ellis, *The Genius of John: A Composition-Critical Commentary on the Fourth Gospel* (Collegeville: Liturgical Press, 1984), 273.

[15] C. H. Dodd, *The Interpretation of the Fourth Gospel* (Cambridge: Cambridge University Press, 1963), 223.

[16] Dodd, *Interpretation*, 428 (italics mine).

[17] Dodd, *Interpretation*, 442.

[18] G. Sloyan, *John* (IBC; Atlanta: John Knox, 1988), 212.

[19] J. McPolin, *John* (NTM 6; Wilmington: Michael Glazier, 1979), 249. G. M. Burge also reads the passage as conveying "a characteristically Johannine double meaning." However, he writes, "The Spirit is not actually given [in 19:30b] (cf. 20:22), but in a symbolic, proleptic fashion – at the shifting of the eras when the moment of sacrifice comes – the movement of God toward humanity is the Spirit" (*The Anointed Community: The Holy Spirit in the Johannine Tradition* [Grand Rapids: Eerdmans, 1987], 134-35).

authors, Keener,[20] Smith[21] and Ashton to the list of those who find Johannine double entendre in this verse. The latter writes, "[having read 19:30] the reader will not stop at the obvious meaning but is sure to see an allusion to the gift of the Spirit."[22]

A Reader's Response

There is, then, ample reason to read the expression as *both* a reference to Jesus' death *and* as a bestowal of the divine Spirit/Paraclete. The careful reader will naturally sense an ambiguity or double meaning in the narrator's words.[23]

On the one hand, taking πνεῦμα in verse 30b as a reference to Jesus' own spirit perfectly fits the crucifixion scene, indicating the death of the crucified. Obviously, the narrative context dictates the translation "his spirit." Moreover, the reader recognizes here another of several occasions on which the narrator speaks of Jesus' spirit (cf. 11:33; 13:21). Along with many of the commentators, the reader might sense that 19:30b suggests Jesus sovereignly determines his own demise by freely handing over his spirit. The narration of Jesus' bestowal of the divine Spirit is unquestionably found in 20:22. Furthermore, 19:30b is similar to Matthew 27:50b (ὁ δὲ Ἰησοῦς πάλιν κράξας φωνῇ μεγάλῃ ἀφῆκεν τὸ πνεῦμα, "And Jesus cried again with a loud voice and yielded up his spirit"). This has suggested to some a traditional expression for Jesus' death which the Fourth Evangelist has adapted.[24] There can be little doubt that the expression invites the reader to imagine Jesus' death on the cross.

On the other hand, the clause also suggests passing on the divine Spirit. Without knowledge of comparable expressions in the crucifixion scenes in other Gospels, would the reader immediately identify the reference to Jesus' spirit? From the reader's perspective (i.e., from a reader response approach), there are several reasons why the reference of πνεῦμα remains ambiguous.

---

[20] C. S. Keener, *The Gospel of John: A Commentary* (2 vols.; Peabody: Hendrickson, 2003), 2:1140.

[21] D. M. Smith, *John* (ANTC; Nashville: Abingdon, 1999), 361-62.

[22] J. Ashton, *Understanding the Fourth Gospel* (Oxford: Clarendon, 1991), 424.

[23] R. A. Culpepper lists the clause, παρέδωκεν τὸ πνεῦμα, among those passages in which the text suggests "double or multiple meanings" (*The Anatomy of the Fourth Gospel: A Study in Literary Design* [Minneapolis: Fortress, 1983], 165).

[24] See Brown, *Death of the Messiah*, 2:1082-83.

First, unprivileged by the later narrative of the risen Christ's bestowal of the Spirit in chapter 20, readers have no reason at this point in the story to exclude the possibility that πνεῦμα refers to the divine Spirit. On a number of occasions the text refers to the divine Spirit or the Paraclete with the simple expression τὸ πνεῦμα. As a matter of fact, the expression is used more often of the divine Spirit than of Jesus' human spirit.[25] The promise of the Paraclete also uses the expression with the modifiers, "of truth" and "holy."[26]

Second, we have been led to believe that the Paraclete's coming coincides with Jesus' departure and that Jesus himself will send the Paraclete (16:7). Readers have been encouraged to anticipate Jesus' sending of the Spirit/Paraclete (14:15-17, 25-26; 15:26-27; 16:7-11, 13-15) and have no reason to expect the later narrative of the risen Christ's bestowal of that gift (20:22). The text invites readers to look forward to the fulfillment of the promise of the Paraclete on the occasion of Jesus' death. The linking of 19:30b with the blood and water from Jesus' side surely echoes 7:37-39, as many have observed, and simply enhances the possibilities of reading πνεῦμα as the divine Spirit.

Therefore, the precise reference remains ambiguous and uncertain. Such an ambiguous reference is very much in character with a great deal of the language of the Gospel of John. It is not necessary here to establish that polyvalence is one of the persistent features of Johannine language. The use of double entendre in such words as ἄνωθεν and ὑψόω in chapter 3 is sufficient to remind us that the Evangelist is an "incurable player on words," as Sloyan so aptly expresses it.[27] The frequent enticement of the meaning of words and phrases is one of the common experiences in reading the Fourth Gospel.[28] Moreover, we cannot say simply that John uses

[25] The expression, τὸ πνεῦμα, is used of the divine Spirit in John 3:6, 8, and 34; 6:63; and 7:39.

[26] The expression τὸ πνεῦμα is found used of the Paraclete in 14:17; 15:26; and 16:13 with the modifier "of truth" (τῆς ἀληθείας) and with τὸ ἅγιον at 14:26. John 20:22 reads simply πνεῦμα ἅγιον.

[27] Sloyan, *John*, 212.

[28] Cf. R. Kysar, "Johannine Metaphor–Meaning and Function: A Literary Case Study of John 10:1-18," *Semeia 53: The Fourth Gospel From a Literary Perspective* (eds. R. A. Culpepper and F. F. Segovia; Atlanta: Scholars, 1991), 81-112; "The Making of Metaphor: Another Reading of John 3:1-15," in *"What is John?" Readers and Readings of the Fourth Gospel* (ed. F. F. Segovia; SBLSymS 3; Atlanta: Scholars, 1996), 21-42; and "The Dismantling of Decisional Faith: A Reading of John 6:25-71," in *Critical Readings of John 6* (ed. R. A. Culpepper, BibIntS 22; Leiden/New York/Köln: Brill, 1997), 161-82. I also find intriguing N. R. Peterson's discussion of Jesus' language in the Fourth Gospel, *The Gospel of*

ordinary language but gives it a new and extraordinary reference, for we do not always know what the "ordinary sense" is. The text takes pleasure in puzzling the reader, suggesting several possible meanings at once without clear conclusion.[29] The incident of ambiguity in 19:30b, within the framework of the habitual polyvalence of the Gospel's language as a whole, does not, or should not, necessarily surprise us.

However, what would it mean if the text suggests that on two different occasions Jesus bestows the Spirit/Paraclete, once as the crucified and once as the risen Christ? Such duplication seems both unnecessary, confusing, and even fallacious. On a purely literary basis, the only precedent for such a repetition in the Gospel of John is found in the discourses of chapters 14–16. There we find a number of themes repeated several times with some variations. Cases in point are the repetition of the promise of the Paraclete (14:15-17, 25-26; 15:26-27; 16:7-11, 13-15) and the promise of answered prayer (14:13-14; 15:7, 16; 16:23-24, 26). Still, those are examples of repetition in *the words of Jesus* – another of the features of the style of this Gospel. The bestowal of the Spirit is *an act*! For the replication of the same act, there appears to be no precedent in this Gospel. What theological importance would such a repetition in 19:30b and 20:22 have?

Theological reflections

In a sense, an ambiguous reading of 19:30b is profoundly theological in the context of Johannine thought. However, I find it theologically unsatisfactory to resolve this ambiguity by means of arguing that Jesus bestows the divine Spirit on two different groups at two different times – that is, to say that at 19:30b the divine Spirit is given to a limited circle of those at the foot of the cross and at 20:22 to the disciples. The ambiguity is more pervasive than that. I remain convinced that μαθητής (used in 20:19) is a broad term in the Fourth Gospel that identifies any believer (cf. e.g., 6:60-67, where the "disciples" and the "twelve" are clearly distinguished).[30] Still,

---

John and the Sociology of Light: Language and Characterization in the Fourth Gospel (Valley Forge: Trinity International, 1993).

[29] Anderson argues that the Christology of the Fourth Gospel entails the dialectical thinking of the Evangelist, a claim for what I would call the ambiguity of Johannine Christology. See P. N. Anderson, *The Christology of the Fourth Gospel* (WUNT 2/78; Tübingen: Mohr, 1996; and Valley Forge: Trinity International, 1997).

[30] Cf. Culpepper, *Anatomy*, 115 and more recently the provocative essay by S. M.

there are theologically significant and slightly different meanings to the possibility of two bestowals of the Spirit in the Gospel narrative. Read as a giving of the Spirit/Paraclete, 19:30b suggests that the new family of God (cf. 1:12) – formed around the foot of the cross and represented in the new association of Jesus' mother and the Beloved Disciple[31] – is empowered with the presence of the divine.[32] The empowered "disciples" on whom Jesus breathes the Spirit in 20:22 are given peace and a mission (20:21) as well as authority (20:23) through that Paraclete.

Nor is it satisfactory to speak of some sort of "proleptic" bestowal of the Spirit here while the actual event is recorded in 20:22. Theologically such an idea is vague. What, after all, would a "proleptic" handing over of the Spirit mean? Experientially, the reader has no way of distinguishing a proleptic from an actual bestowal.[33] As a consequence of the double meaning of τὸ πνεῦμα, the community of faith is founded on both the cross and the presence of its risen Lord. Both bestowals of the Spirit are upon and for the sake of the church.

The "handing over" of the Spirit/Paraclete by the dying Jesus knits Johannine pneumatology into the fabric of its crucifixion Christology. Such a christological pneumatology seems to be a dominant theme in the Gospel as a whole. Even the testimony of the Baptizer alerts the reader that Christ is the one "who baptizes with the Holy Spirit" (1:33). In the farewell discourses, Jesus specifically links his departure with the sending of the Paraclete: "if I go (away), I will send [the Paraclete] to you" (16:7). The crucifixion and resurrection seem to be prerequisites for the bestowal of the Spirit/Paraclete. If we take his departure to mean his death, Jesus' handing over the Spirit as his last human act weds the gift of the Paraclete with the crucifixion and with his earthly ministry. The dying Christ, as well as the risen Christ, bestows the Spirit, since his death is his glorification.

The hint that the divine Spirit is bestowed by the dying Jesus teases us with a possible meaning of the cross in the Fourth Gospel. Clearly the Johannine theology of the cross is distinctive in the Gospels, indeed, I be-

---

Schneiders, "'Because of the Woman's Testimony …': Reexamining the Issue of Authorship of the Fourth Gospel," *NTS* 44 (1998): 513-35.

[31] Culpepper, "The Pivot of John's Prologue," *NTS* 27 (1980): 1-31.

[32] Cf. Moloney, *John*, 504-5. Ford suggests that while the two bestowals seem "inconsistent," 20:22 "nicely complements the feminine creative activities of John 19 with creation" – God's breathing the spirit in to Adam (*Redeemer*, 275-76).

[33] This in spite of Brown's (see note 12) and Burge's (see note 19) interpretations.

lieve, in the whole of the New Testament.[34] I do not claim to solve the problem of that question, but only to make a suggestion. Might it be that the death of Jesus is saving, at least in part, because it is his death that unleashes the divine Spirit/Paraclete into the world? I think there is more involved than that.[35] Yet a pneumatic soteriology rooted in Jesus' death may be a part of the puzzle too long ignored.

Such a pneumatic soteriology might illumine the meaning of the association of Jesus' death with the slaying of the Passover lambs. The "exodus" occasioned by Jesus' death is accomplished through the divine presence in the Paraclete. The Paraclete leads the new community out into new life, even as Jesus promised such a Paraclete would lead believers to "all truth" (16:13). Hence, Jesus' death is a new exodus, if you will, in the sense that the Spirit now begins her work in the community of faith – a saving and freeing work.

Much as 19:30b binds the gift of the divine Spirit to the death of Jesus, the narrative of the risen Christ's breathing the Holy Spirit on to the disciples in 20:22 equally weds the bestowal of the Paraclete with Christ's resurrection. Consequently, the coming of the Spirit is tied to both the crucifixion and the resurrection. As the crucifixion and resurrection are blended in Johannine thought, so too is the bestowal of the Spirit associated with both the dying and risen Christ. If the dying Jesus hands over the divine Spirit and the risen Christ breathes it on to the disciples, christologically the earthly incarnate Jesus and the exalted, risen Lord are one. The Gospel suggests that both the cross and the resurrection are occasions for the giving of the Spirit. Certainly Bultmann is right in saying that the Johannine Jesus does not "need" his resurrection to give life to others, and indeed his resurrection, rather than being the occasion which exalts Jesus to his redemptive role, is little more than another σημεῖον.[36] Agreeing with Bultmann, Ashton claims the resurrection appearances in the Fourth Gospel are "superfluous."[37] So, Jesus' bestowal of the Spirit from the cross is not out of character for his portrayal in this Gospel. Brown is helpful when he suggests that the Fourth Evangelist conceives of Jesus'

---

[34] Cf. the provocative work of Ford, *Redeemer*; Spirit is part of her conception of salvation as friendship.

[35] R. Kysar, *John, the Maverick Gospel* (rev. ed.; Louisville: Westminster John Knox, 1993), 49-54.

[36] Cf. for instance, R. Bultmann, *The Gospel of John: A Commentary* (Oxford: Blackwell, 1971), 634.

[37] Ashton, *Fourth Gospel*, 425.

"hour" as the crucifixion, resurrection and ascension.[38] If each of these is not conceived as air-tight compartments separate from the others and they are all part of Jesus' glorification (e.g., 17:1), his gift of the Spirit may be appropriate both from the cross and in the resurrection appearance.

Another theological suggestion implied in the possibility that πνεῦμα at 19:30b hints at both the divine Spirit and human spirit is the relationship between the two. On the basis of the Gospel text, one might conclude that the Spirit/Paraclete is synonymous with Jesus' spirit. Scholars have often argued that the Paraclete is Jesus' *alter ego*.[39] The Baptizer's testimony that the Spirit descended on Jesus (1:32-33) might then be understood as the divine bestowal of Jesus' own spirit, his own person. We have all puzzled over the enigmatic promise that Jesus will come to the disciples again (e.g., 14:3, 18, 28; 16:22). Does it refer to an eschatological parousia, the resurrection appearances, or the coming of the Spirit/Paraclete? If, in handing over his own spirit Jesus is handing over the divine Spirit, might the coming of the Spirit/Paraclete be the coming of Jesus' own person?[40] If so, the promise in 14:18-19 then takes on new meaning: "I will not leave you desolate; I will come to you. Yet a little while, and the world will see me no more, but you will see me." Jesus' own self comes to the disciples in the form of the Spirit/Paraclete. In this connection it is interesting to remember that 1 John 2:1-2 uses παράκλητος to speak of Jesus himself in his heavenly function: "we have an *advocate* with the Father, Jesus Christ the righteous."[41]

---

[38] Brown, *John*, 2:1013-15. Brown suggests that the Evangelist fits "a theology of resurrection/ascension that by definition has no dimensions in time and space into a narrative that is necessarily sequential" (*John*, 2:1014). We might also add to that the crucifixion. Because of the collapse of crucifixion and resurrection into one event, I find unconvincing the argument that πνεῦμα at 19:30b cannot refer to the Holy Spirit because Jesus' departure or glorification is not completed in his death.

[39] For example, Brown, *John*, 2: 644-47, 1135-43.

[40] Interestingly Pokorný tries to argue that Christ's resurrection and the Christians experience of the Holy Spirit were originally "two dimensions of the same event." See P. Pokorný, *The Genesis of Christology: Foundations for a Theology of the New Testament* (trans. M. Lefébure; Edinburgh: T&T Clark, 1987), 113-14, 149. Such an argument is intriguing but most speculative, and we must finally admit that the relationship between the Easter and Pentecost experiences lies beyond the reach of our historical ambitions.

[41] MacGregor claims we find in 19:30b "John's characteristic idea that at Jesus' death his spirit was set free from the limitations of the body that it might be bestowed upon the Church" (*John*, 349). While such an interpretation imposes a body-spirit dualism on the Johannine text, MacGregor does seem to assume that Jesus' spirit is synonymous with the divine Spirit.

Perhaps this identification of Jesus' "human spirit" with the Spirit/Paraclete enlightens just a bit one of the most intriguing features of the resurrection stories in John. The risen Christ bestows the Spirit but continues to appear to the disciples. The Gospel ends with the risen Christ popping up in unexpected places and times.[42] Is it the case that the Fourth Gospel makes no real distinction of kind between Jesus' spirit and the divine Spirit?[43] While strict Trinitarians would wish for more clarity than this, the Gospel's text allows us little in the way of orderly theological construal of the second and third persons of the Trinity.[44]

In summary, reading τὸ πνεῦμα at 19:30b as ambiguous impacts a number of important theological themes in this Gospel, including its view of the church, the Spirit, Christ, and the cross.

Conclusion

An appreciation of the ambiguity of John 19:30b is rich with theological suggestions, albeit a none too systematic and orderly theological construction. However, allow me to remind you that I am not arguing that πνεῦμα is *clearly* a reference to the divine Spirit/Paraclete but only that it is ambiguous in its reference. Without pretending to penetrate the intention

---

[42] If we argue for the ambiguity of πνεῦμα in John 19:30b, we are obliged, it seems to me, to consider the same possibility for the expression in Matt. 27:50b, although such an argument is beyond the scope of both this paper and its author. It is interesting, however, to note that the First Gospel nowhere narrates the bestowal of the Holy Spirit, and readers of Matthew are left with the promise of 28:20, "I am with you always." Is the identification of Jesus himself with the Spirit, which we find implicit in the ambiguity in the Johannine passage, suggested by the conclusion of Matthew?

[43] Brown's attempts to distinguish the risen Christ and the presence of the Paraclete are, I fear, unsuccessful and may reflect an overly Trinitarian reading of chapter 20 (*John*, 2: 1013-15, 1139-40).

[44] A related point is the significance of the use here of the verb παραδίδωμι. Matthew uses the verb "yielded up" (ἀφῆκεν–27:50b) and John "handed over" (παρέδωκεν). Παραδίδωμι occurs in a number of passages in the passion story (12:4; 13:2, 11, 21; 18:2, 5, 30, 35, 36; 19:11, 16; 21:20), in each case used in reference to another person or group of people and with a sense of betrayal and/or treachery. Ironically the verb is now used of Jesus and with a sense of gracious giving. The one who has been handed over to execution now hands over the Spirit to believers. The gift of the Spirit stands in sharp contrast with the treachery of humans and is an act of self-giving love. Jesus transforms the tragedy of the cross into an occasion for the eschatological fulfillment of the divinely promised Spirit (cf. 15:13). Bultmann is wrong in claiming that it "would be over subtle" to say that παραδίδωμι means voluntary death (*John*, 675). The Johannine polyvalence is coupled with Johannine irony in 19:30b.

of the author, we may say that the text (or, if you prefer, the implied author) hints that the expression refers to both Jesus' human spirit and the divine Spirit/Paraclete. *Perhaps we ought not rush forth quickly to resolve this equivocation but to allow it to work in our imaginations and our constructions of meaning from exposure to this text.*

Another of the reasons for this paper is to explore how New Testament theology might be done within a strictly synchronic reading of the text without recourse to the history behind the text. What I have tried to do is to demonstrate the rich possibilities of exploring the theological implications of the text as it confronts us – even as it confronts us with puzzling ambiguity. New Testament theology has traditionally piggybacked on the historical critical enterprise, with the result that one could not construct theological meaning without first constructing a historical context for a given passage or book. My goal here has been simply to demonstrate that a purely literary reading of a text can, at times at least, yield interesting theological reflections without elaborate reconstruction of the history behind the text. If this experimental reading of John 19:30b is at least partially successful, then this method of doing New Testament theology might be a possible new direction for the discipline.

9. "BLESSED ARE THOSE WHO HAVE NOT SEEN": JOHN 20:29

Raymond F. COLLINS

In the vast amount of literature on the Fourth Gospel, to which Francis Moloney has contributed substantially not only quantitatively but also qualitatively, little attention has been paid to its beatitudes, John 13:17 and 20:29. In the course of the past eighty-five years, more than three quarters of a century, only a pair of articles have been written which focus specifically on the beatitude with which the body of the Gospel narrative comes to its close, as it had been composed by the Evangelist himself.[1]

Virtually all scholars agree that John 21 is the addition of a later redactor.[2] The immediately preceding verses, John 20:30-31, are a literary epilogue to the Evangelist's own work.[3] This epilogue was written by the Evangelist himself, whom the redactor of the final chapter imitated in composing John 21:25. The pair of verses in the epilogue constitute a kind of metatext in which the Evangelist comments on the composition and purpose of his narrative. Thus, the conclusion of the narrative itself is John 20:29b, "Blessed are those who have not seen and yet have come to believe."[4] Since early in the twentieth century only Benedetto Prete and Ron Cameron have devoted any particular study to this concluding beatitude.[5]

---

[1] See the extensive bibliographies compiled by E. Malatesta (*St. John's Gospel: 1920-1965* [AnBib 32; Rome: Pontifical Biblical Institute, 1997]) and G. van Belle (*Johannine Bibliography: 1966-1985. A Cumulative Bibliography on the Fourth Gospel* [BETL 82; Louvain: University Press - Peeters, 1988]) as well as the survey of current publications in *NTA*.

[2] See, for example, the editor's introduction, written by F. J. Moloney, to R. E. Brown, *An Introduction to the Gospel of John* (ABRL; New York: Doubleday, 2003), 5.

[3] Thus, even Lagrange. See M.-J. Lagrange, *Évangile selon Saint Jean* (EB; Paris: Gabalda, 1936), 519.

[4] In this essay, New Testament texts are cited according to the NRSV.

[5] B. Prete, "Beati coloro che non vedono e credono (Giov. 20, 29)," *BeO* 9 (1967):

Every commentary on the Fourth Gospel necessarily discusses the meaning of John 20:29b, but few draw attention to the Evangelist's compositional redaction in which he composed these words as the finale of his story. Still fewer commentators draw attention to the Evangelist's choice of the literary form of a beatitude as the final expression of his literary endeavor. Richard Cassidy once described its words as "a majestic comment on Thomas' confession."[6]

This lack of concentrated attention on the significance of John 20:29b is especially remarkable when consideration is paid to its narrative function and its literary form. It is, moreover, the final utterance of Jesus in the body of the Fourth Gospel whose principal theme might well be summarized under the rubric "Jesus the Revealer." On all three counts, literary form, narrative ending, and final word of Jesus, John 20:29b deserves more attention than it has hitherto received.

The Beatitude

A clue as to the literary form of the logion is its initial word, μακάριοι ("blessed"). This adjective occurs only one other time in the Gospel (John 13:17), but the following arthrous and conjoined participles, ἰδόντες and πιστεύσαντες, "those who have seen" and "those who have believed" respectively, echo the words of Jesus' question in John 20:29a: "Because you have seen me, you have believed."[7] John 20:29b reprises these two verbs

97-114. Prete begins his article with an exposition of the positions taken apropos of the verse by M.-É. Boismard in "Saint Luc et la rédaction du quatrième évangile (Jn. IV 46-54)," *RB* 69 (1962): 185-211 and by R. Schnackenburg in "Zur Traditionsgeschichte von Joh. 4,46-54," *BZ* 8 (1964): 58-88. Each of these earlier studies relates the beatitude of John 20:29 to the logion of John 4:48.

R. Cameron, "Seeing is Not Believing: The History of a Beatitude in the Jesus Tradition," *Forum* 4 (1988): 47-57. As the subtitle suggests, this is a study in the *wirkungsgeschichte* of a tradition. Cameron opines that the beatitude assures continuity with the past and provides those who were not eyewitnesses that they can be blessed with faith.

[6] R. J. Cassidy, *John's Gospel in New Perspective: Christology and the Realities of Roman Power* (Maryknoll: Orbis, 1992), 71.

[7] C. K. Barrett explains why it is better to take the words of the Evangelist's Greek text – which lacks punctuation in the ancient majuscule manuscripts – as a declarative sentence. See C. K. Barrett, *The Gospel According to John* (2d ed.; London: SPCK; Philadelphia: Westminster, 1978), 573; cf. R. E. Brown, *The Gospel According to John* (AB 29-29A; 2 vols.; Garden City: Doubleday, 1966, 1970), 2:1027; F. J. Moloney, *The Gospel of John* (SP 4; Collegeville: Liturgical Press, 1998), 29. The ecumenical German version, the *Einheitsübersetzung*, the KJV, JB, NJB, NIV, NEB, and REB interpret the logion as a declarative

in the same sequence in which they appear in the Greek text. Not only is the use of the pair of verbs the literary echo of the language of Jesus' initial commentary on the state of Thomas' faith, the verbs themselves are among the most common vocabulary of the Fourth Gospel.[8] The logion employs some of the Evangelist's favorite words. On the other hand, μακάριοι, the first word of the logion, is virtually foreign to the Evangelist's customary usage.

The absence of a principal verb from John 20:29b provides another clue as to its literary form. Ellipsis is a common feature of the exclamations found in classical Greek and Hellenistic literature.[9] The presence of both of these clues, the presence of μακάριοι and the absence of a principal verb, in John 20:29b permit the logion to be characterized as a particular form of exclamation. It is a beatitude, the only true beatitude in the Fourth Gospel.

A beatitude is essentially an expression of praise or congratulations. Our contemporaries readily make statements such as, "How happy you must be ..." or "How lucky are those who ... ." English uses the adjectives "happy," "lucky," or "fortunate" in uttering such praise or congratulations. Only the deeply religious would say "blessed" in making such statements, imparting to the adjective significant theological content.[10] The Greek beatitude makes use of the adjective μακάριος.[11] This Greek word is typically translated "happy" or "prosperous." It was used in much the same way as the corresponding English-language adjectives are used. In Greek as in English, the reason why a person or group of people is considered to be happy or fortunate is mentioned in the beatitude itself.

---

sentence. The NRSV, however, interprets John 20:29a as if it were a rhetorical question, "Have you believed (πεπίστευκας) because you have seen (ἑώρακάς) me?" So, too, did many minuscule manuscripts and the RSV, as well as the revised NT of the NAB and some modern commentators.

[8] The verb πιστεύω is used ninety-six times in the body of the Fourth Gospel and twice in the Evangelist's own epilogue (John 20:30-31). The verb does not, however, appear in the epilogue appended to the Evangelist's work by the redactor (John 21). The verb ὁράω appears thirty times in the body of the Gospel. As πιστεύω, it does not appear in the redactor's epilogue. In the body of the Gospel the pair of verbs appear together in John 6:36 and 11:40; cf. John 1:50; 3:36; 4:48; 6:30; 19:35; 20:8, 25.

[9] Thus, BDF, 127.

[10] A dictionary commonly used in the United States, *Webster's New Intercollegiate Dictionary*, thus offers as the first definitions of "bless:" 1) to hallow or consecrate by religious rite or word; 2) to hallow with the sign of the cross; 3) to invoke divine care for; 4a) Praise, glorify (~his holy name); 4b) to speak gratefully of (~ed him for his kindness).

[11] The term "beatitude" used to designate sayings that have this literary form derives from *beatus*, the Latin equivalent of the Greek μακάριος.

As expressions of praise or congratulations, beatitudes typically are one-liners, isolated sentences. The beatitude is essentially an oral form rather than a literary form. A series of beatitudes such as found in Matthew's Sermon on the Mount (Matt 5:3-11) and Luke's Sermon on the Plain (Luke 6:20-22) are a literary creation, small anthologies of beatitudes.[12] Utterances such as that spoken by the woman in the crowd, "Blessed is the womb that bore you and the breasts that nursed you" (Luke 11:27) represent the oral form of the beatitude more typically than does the well-known Matthean collection known as "The Eight Beatitudes." Phrased in Jewish idiom,[13] the woman's words are words of praise for Jesus' mother. Our contemporaries might say something like "How happy your mother must be!" or, directed to the mother herself, "How happy you must be to have a son/daughter like that!" Other one-liners found in Luke's Gospel are Jesus' response to the woman, "Blessed rather are those who hear the word of God and obey it!" (Luke 11:28) and the exclamation of an anonymous diner who said, "Blessed is anyone who will eat bread in the kingdom of God" (Luke 14:15).

The beatitude is a very old literary form. The oldest literary attestation of the form is found in the *Homeric Hymn to Demeter* 480-483: "Happy is he among men upon earth who has seen these mysteries!" Later use of the form is well attested in Egyptian, Greek, both classical and Hellenistic, and Jewish literature. Beatitudes are also well attested in the Hebrew Scriptures. Generally these scriptural beatitudes are expressed in the form of *Reden*, affirmations, rather than in the form of *Anreden*, formulas of direct address. All but four of the Hebrew Scriptures' forty-five beatitudes are in the third person,[14] typically in a generic third person singular, using the formula, אַשְׁרֵי־הָאִישׁ אֲשֶׁר ("blessed is the man who"). The majority of these beatitudes are to be found in the Wisdom literature,[15] particularly in the Psalms and the Book of Proverbs.[16]

---

[12] Similarly, *2 Enoch* 42:6-14; 4Q525.

[13] See J. A. Fitzmyer, *The Gospel According to Luke* (AB 28, 28A; Garden City: Doubleday, 1981, 1985], 2:928) who notes the use of synecdoche and the strong possibility that Luke was influenced by Gen 49:25c in the composition of the beatitude.

[14] Only four of the biblical beatitudes are in the second person (Deut 33:29; Ps 128:2; Qoh 10:17; Isa 32:20).

[15] H. D. Betz identifies the wisdom beatitude as one of the four types of beatitudes, the secular, religious, and ironic being the other types ("The Beatitudes of the Sermon on the Mount," in *Essays in the Sermon on the Mount* [trans. L. L. Welborn; Philadelphia: Fortress, 1985], 17-36, esp. 25. See also B. Gladigow, "Der Makarismus des Weisen," *Hermes* 95 (1967), 404-33.

[16] Ps 1:1; 2:12; 32:1, 2; 33:12; 34:9; 40:5; 41:2; 65:5; 84:5, 6, 13; 89:16; 94:12; 106:3;

Immersed in the tradition of the Jewish Scriptures as his narrative was, it is likely that the Evangelist was inspired by the scriptures' use of beatitudes when he composed the words "Blessed are those who have not seen and yet have come to believe," putting them into the form of a beatitude as the finale to his narrative about Jesus.[17] Apart from its first word, the vocabulary of the beatitude is properly the Evangelist's own. Apparently he has composed the beatitude *ad hoc*.

John 13:17

The Evangelist previously employed the first word of his beatitude, μακάριοι, "blessed," in John 13:17, "If you know these things, you are blessed (μακάριοί ἐστε) if you do them." Moloney has described this utterance as "a beautifully balanced Greek sentence."[18] The words form an *inclusio* with the knowing and doing of Jesus in John 13:1-5,[19] thereby identifying the Evangelist's portrayal of Jesus washing the feet of his disciples as a discrete literary unit and setting it apart from the rest of his narrative.

The picturesque but striking scene portrays Jesus as one whose knowledge led to action. He knew that his hour had come (John 13:1), that the Father had given all things into his hands (John 13:3), and that he had come from God and was going to God (John 13:3). Consequently he washed the disciples' feet. This example was part of his gift,[20] a legacy of the departing Jesus to those whom he was about to leave behind.[21] This gift was not only a precious memory; it was also an example for the disciples to follow.[22] The scene focuses on Jesus and his disciples. Jesus'

112:1; 119:1, 2; 127:5; 128:1, 2; 137:8, 9; 144:15 [2x]; 146:5 – twenty-six altogether. The Book of Proverbs contains eight beatitudes (3:13; 8:32, 34; 14:21; 16:20; 20:7; 28:14; 29:18).

[17] Schnackenburg has suggested – implausibly, in my judgment – that the Evangelist inherited the form from the synoptic tradition. See R. Schnackenburg, *The Gospel according to St John* (3 vols.; New York: Crossroad, 1968-82), 3:25.

[18] See Moloney, *John*, 376.

[19] Inclusion is a notable characteristic of Johannine style. See Brown, *John*, 1:cxxxv, reprised in Brown-Moloney, *Introduction*, 287.

[20] Note the use of ἔδωκα in John 13:15.

[21] See John 13:1, 3.

[22] H. Weiss identifies this as being one of the two examples of what he calls "Example Christology" in the New Testament. See H. Weiss, "Foot Washing in the Johannine Community," *NovT* 21 (1979): 298-325, esp. 323.

knowledge flowed into action as he washed the disciples' feet. His was the action of a servant; his disciples were similarly to serve one another (John 13:14-15).

The Narrative

A story is a tale that is told. A narrative is a collection of episodes sequentially arranged so that the episodes flow from and into one another.[23] In this way a narrative plot is developed. The episodes are not only "told" in the sense that they are set out one after the other and can then be counted; they interlock with one another so that the sequence of episodes constitutes the unfolding of a story.

As literary critics constantly remind us, an episode is meaningful in and of itself, but its full meaning is unfolded within the context of the narrative to which it belongs. Thus it is with the Johannine story of Jesus' washing the feet of his disciples. It is a beautiful and significant scene in and of itself but its full meaning is revealed only when the episode is considered within the entire Johannine Gospel. Accordingly, the logion of John 13:17, "If you know these things, you are blessed if you do them," must be considered as the peroration to the mini-discourse of John 13:12-17 but it must also be considered within the context of the entire Johannine narrative.[24]

Several commentators on John 13:17 have noted that Jesus' words are in the form of a beatitude.[25] Thus, Bultmann rendered the verse: "Blessed

---

[23] The primary meaning of "tell" is to count or enumerate. This meaning is apparent in the Irish description of the pious person telling their beads, that is, praying the Rosary. More commonly, the basic meaning of the verb is reflected in the use of "teller" to identify someone who counts money in a bank; "untold" to describe, sufferings, for example, as too many to count; and "all told" meaning when they are all counted up, as in "all told, there are four canonical Gospels."

[24] An intermediate level of consideration would be an examination of the verse within the context of the Farewell Discourse(s), John 12-17. The length and purpose of the present essay preclude such an examination.

[25] Thus, Brown, Bultmann, Lindars, Schnackenburg, and J. Zumstein, "Le lavement des pieds (Jean 13,1-20): Un exemple de la conception johannique du pouvoir," *RTP* (2000): 345-60, esp. 351. Brown calls the logion a macarism, while Schnackenburg identifies it as a "blessing" which he distinguishes from a saying having the form of a macarism. See Brown, *John*, 2:570; R. Bultmann, *The Gospel of John* (trans. G. R. Beasley-Murray; Oxford: Basil Blackwell, 1971), 476; B. Lindars, *The Gospel of John* (NCB; London: Oliphants, 1972); Schnackenburg, *John*, 3:25. Weiss also identifies the logion as a be-

is he who acts in accordance with what he has seen and heard."[26] In this paraphrased form the logion is one for which parallels are attested in Hellenistic literature.[27] In the way in which the Evangelist has actually composed it, however, the logion of John 13:17 is not a beatitude in the strict sense. The utterance is in the form of a double conditional sentence rather than in the form of an exclamation. Nonetheless, since the form and function of the literary genre of the beatitude has developed considerably during the course of its usage in Greek and Hellenistic literature, the term "beatitude" might well be used of the logion. Its literary form is fittingly described as a "borderline beatitude."[28]

The Micro Context

As the peroration of the mini-discourse of John 13:12-17, this borderline beatitude recapitulates the basic ideas of the narrative unit. Blessedness, happiness accrues to those present provided that two conditions are fulfilled: [29] 1) that they know these things, that is, that they grasp the significance of them; and 2) do them, that is, act accordingly. On the narrative level and within the framework of the footwashing itself, the demonstrative ταῦτα ("these things") points to what the disciples have seen and heard.[30] They have seen Jesus washing their feet; they have been exhorted to do likewise, they are to wash one another's feet (John 13:14).[31]

---

atitude, with which he sees a Synoptic parallel in Luke 11:28. See Weiss, "Foot Washing," 316.

[26] Bultmann, *John*, 476.

[27] So Hesiod, "Prosperous and happy is the one who knowing all these things does them," (*Works and Days*, 826-27) and Seneca, "He is not happy who only knows them, but he who does them" (*Epistulae morales*, 75.7). See also, Musonius: "Virtue is a skill which is not only able to perceive but is also concerned with action" ("On Training," see C. Wachsmuth and O. Hense [eds.], *Joannis Stobaei Anthologium* [5 vols.; Berlin: Weidmann, 1974; reprint of the 1884-1912 ed.] 3.29.78.3-5).

[28] The expression comes from H. D. Betz, *The Sermon on the Mount including the Sermon on the Plain (Matthew 5:3-7:27 and Luke 6:20-49)* (Hermeneia; Minneapolis: Augsburg, 1995), 103.

[29] Note the verbs in the second person plural, οἴδατε and ποιῆτε.

[30] Apropos John 13:15, Demke speaks of an experience which creates the obligation to be expressed in later conduct ("die zum Weiterwirken verplichtet;" see C. Demke, "Das Evangelium der Dialoge: Hermeneutische und methodologische Beobachtungen zur Interpretation des Johannesevangeliums," *ZTK* 97 (2000): 164-82, esp. 177; similarly, Zumstein who speaks of behavior whose concrete form is to be reinvented in every new situation (see "Le lavement," 356).

[31] Thus, though dating prior to the advent of narrative criticism in Johannine studies,

At the episodic level, albeit with due attention paid to the fact that the Fourth Gospel is replete with symbolism and that much of it must be read on both a narrative and a symbolic plane, one might, as Moloney has done, read the exhortation implicit in the borderline beatitude as an exhortation to live out the implications of one's baptism. Moloney writes: "The blessedness of the Johannine believer flows from the living out, the "doing" of all that is implied by entering into discipleship through baptism."[32]

If the narrative of the footwashing is to be read at the symbolic level with reference to baptism,[33] – and even if it is not![34] – one must ask if μακάριοι has only the meaning that it has in the beatitudes of Greek literature, that is, "happy" or "fortunate." Does the term have a Johannine meaning, as do so many other terms used by the Evangelist? The question is all the more legitimate insofar as the saying of John 13:7 is not a beatitude in the narrow sense of the term.

Barrett, Brown, Sanders. See Barrett, *John*, 444; Brown, *John*, 2:570; J. N. Sanders, *The Gospel According to St John* (ed. and completed by B. A. Mastin; BNTC; London: Adam and Charles Black, 1968). See also Weiss, "Foot Washing," 300.

Lagrange capitalized on the plural form of the verbs to note that this was but one example among many. See Lagrange, *Jean*, 256. Haenchen has taken a moralistic approach, interpreting John 13:17 as a "warning against pride and perhaps also an aversion to suffering." See E. Haenchen, *John* (2 vols.; trans. R. W. Funk; Hermeneia; Philadelphia: Fortress, 1984), 2:103.

It is curious to note that several commentators offer no comment on the verse, among them, R. H. Lightfoot (*St. John's Gospel* [Oxford: Oxford University Press, 1957]), S. Schulz (*Das Evangelium nach Johannes* [NTD 4; 13th ed.; Göttingen: Vandenhoeck & Ruprecht, 1975]), H. Strathmann (*Das Evangelium nach Johannes* [NTD 4; 11th ed.; Göttingen: Vandenhoeck & Ruprecht, 1968), and H. van der Bussche (*Jean: Commentaire de l'Évangile Spirituel* [BibVC; Bruges: Desclée de Brouwer, 1976]). Without commenting on John 13:17, van der Bussche observes that Jesus' example was one of Christian charity, rather than footwashing *per se* (*Jean*, 381). Brown discerns in what Jesus did an act of humility (*John*, 2:570), as did C. H. Dodd (*The Interpretation of the Fourth Gospel* [Cambridge: Cambridge University Press, 1953], 401).

[32] Moloney, *John*, 379; see also Weiss, "Foot Washing," 320. Brown, with allusion to Luke 22:19, has suggested that there might possibly be a reference to the Eucharist (*John*, 2:570).

[33] For which Moloney makes a plea in "A Sacramental Reading of John 13:1-38," *CBQ* 53 (1991): 237-56, holding that baptism is a sub-theme of the account of the footwashing. Demke judiciously observes that the present form of the text of the narrative account of the footwashing includes two explanations, a symbolic-christological or sacramental explanation in John 13:6-10, and a exemplary-ethical explanation in vv. 12-17. See Demke, "Evangelium der Dialoge," 172; cf. Zumstein, "Le lavement," 350-51.

[34] Koester expresses reservations with regard to seeing the foot-washing as a symbol for baptism. See C. R. Koester, *Symbolism in the Fourth Gospel: Meaning, Mystery, Community* (2d. ed.; Minneapolis: Fortress, 2003), 133-34.

Reading the borderline beatitude as the summarizing peroration of the mini-discourse that follows the footwashing itself and with reference to John 13:1-5 with which it forms an *inclusio*, it would seem that the blessedness to which Jesus refers in John 13:17 is that which Jesus will enjoy when he goes to the Father (John 13:1, 3). The disciples are to do what they have seen Jesus doing; they will be blessed insofar as they, too, will go to the Father. Just a few verses later in the narrative, the departing Jesus announces to his disciples: "If I go and prepare a place for you, I will come again and will take you to myself, so that where I am, there you may be also" (John 14:3). If the disciples see and do what Jesus has done, they will enjoy the beatitude that Jesus is to enjoy.

The Macro Context

Should there be a symbolic reference to baptism in John 13:1-17 as well as in the borderline beatitude with which it concludes, the reference is to a world that lies beyond the narrative. This is the world of the Johannine community and its baptismal practice. A reference to such a world lies beyond the scope of the narrative itself.

On the other hand, the footwashing episode is embedded within a longer narrative of which it forms an integral part. Accordingly, the beatitude must be seen not only as the peroration to Jesus' post-footwashing discourse, it must also be seen within the context of the entire Fourth Gospel. When the borderline beatitude is read with the entire narrative as its frame of reference, the discerning reader notices immediately that the action words of the two conditional clauses are among the Evangelist's lexical favorites.

The Fourth Evangelist uses the verb "to know" (οἶδα) more frequently than do the other three Evangelists combined. He uses the verb to denote not so much knowledge that is being acquired as it connotes the possession of knowledge, sometimes by means of intuitive insight.[35] Appearing in the peroration of the mini-discourse following the washing of the feet, the connotation of "knowing" in John 13:17 hearkens back to Jesus' own

---

[35] See, especially, I. de la Potterie, "Οἶδα et γινώσκω: Les deux modes de la connaissance dans le quatrième Évangile," *Bib* 40 (1959): 709-25, 722. In this study de la Potterie does not specifically address the meaning of οἶδατε in John 13:17, even though he extensively treats the knowledge of the disciples of Jesus in the second part of his article (717-25).

self-knowledge (John 13:1, 3) and the disciples' lack thereof at the time of the footwashing (John 13:7). "These things" that the disciples did not know but would come to know with insight are who Jesus was and what it was that he did.

Having that insight, they will indeed be blessed – with, however, a proviso. They will be blessed on the condition that they act accordingly. Jesus, the Johannine exegete par excellence,[36] provides an appropriate commentary on his own borderline beatitude: "Very truly, I tell you, the one who believes in me will also do (ποιήσει) the works that I do and, in fact, will do (ποιήσει) greater works than these (τούτων), because I am going to the Father" (John 14:12). The reader of the Fourth Gospel surely recognizes in Jesus' words the language of the beatitude and a reference to the episode of the footwashing with the ensuing mini-discourse. The things that the disciples are to do are not only washing one another's feet as Jesus washed their feet; they are also to do the works that Jesus does, and even greater works than these.

These broader implications of the borderline beatitude of John 13:17 are confirmed when due attention is paid to its place within the Johannine narrative. Following the magisterial work of Raymond Brown, it has become commonplace for commentators on the Fourth Gospel to designate John 1-12 as "the Book of Signs" and John 13-20 as the "Book of Glory." The episode of the foot-washing with its mini-discourse (John 13:1-17) is the opening scene of the Book of Glory. This inaugural scene consists of a short narrative followed by a short discourse. The Book of Glory begins in earnest with the Evangelist's long rendition of Jesus' farewell discourse(s).

The footwashing scene, with the words that immediately follow, is the hinge that joins the narrative of the Book of Signs (John 1:19-12:50) with the lengthy discourse (John 13:18-17:26) with which the Book of Glory begins. As a hinge, the footwashing scene is a transitional unit that looks back to what has transpired and forward to what is yet to come. A transition is generally resumptive of what precedes and anticipates what follows.

The charge that Jesus gives to the disciples in the mini-discourse of John 13:12-17 anticipates the multi-faceted reflection on the succession in ministry that is contained in the farewell discourse(s).[37] Looking back, it

---

[36] See John 1:18.
[37] See, for example, John 13:34; 15:12.

refers not only to the scene that has just been narrated; it also looks back upon the narrative that has preceded, the narrative of the many things that Jesus has done.

John 20:29

In the Johannine narrative the borderline beatitude of John 13:17 functions directly as the peroration to the mini-discourse that follows the footwashing scene, but it has a broader function within the narrative as a whole. Something similar must be said apropos the beatitude of John 20:29. In narrow focus the beatitude serves as the conclusion to the scene of the risen Jesus appearing to the disciples, Thomas being present (John 20:26-29). In broader focus, Jesus' logion is the conclusion to the entire Johannine narrative.

The Beatitude

In form, John 20:29 is a beatitude in the strict sense of the term. It begins with the customary μακάριος. As is the case with so many exclamations, it lacks a principal verb. The absence of the verb εἰμί, "to be," characterizes the logion as having a character other than that of the declarative sentence. According to this beatitude – the only pure beatitude in the Fourth Gospel – those who are blessed are "those who have not seen and yet have come to believe." The generic participles (οἱ μὴ ἰδόντες καὶ πιστεύσαντες), joined by καί and qualified by a single article, function as the generic singular of the typical gnomic saying, or the אַשְׁרֵי־הָאִישׁ אֲשֶׁר ("blessed is the man who") of the biblical tradition. It is not a single individual but an entire class of people that is envisioned.

The rhetorical force of the beatitude is strengthened by its double contrast. The beatitude speaks of those who do not see and those who believe. Its formulation is characterized by what the Greeks called *antithesis*, the rhetorical device of contrast used for the sake of emphasis. The rhetorical contrast is even more striking in the five words of the Evangelist's Greek text than it is in the eleven words of the NRSV translation of the beatitude. The terseness of the Evangelist's words provides a sharp focus for the contrast.

In the immediate narrative context within which it is located, the beatitude is characterized by contrast in yet another way. The beatitude is the second part of a two-part logion in which Jesus replies to Thomas: "Because you have seen me, you have believed. Blessed are those who have not seen and yet have come to believe" (John 20:29). In this two part utterance, the second logion stands in sharp contrast with the first.

The Micro Context

The two-part utterance must be seen within the narrative for which it serves as a conclusion. The Evangelist provides narrative preparation for the episode of Thomas and the risen Jesus (John 20:26-29) in the disciples' report to Thomas about their experience of the risen Jesus (John 20:19-25). The pair of scenes describing the appearance of the risen Jesus (John 20:19-23, 26-29) form a diptych whose hinge is the description of the meeting between Thomas and the other disciples (John 20:24-25). Thomas dismisses their report, saying: "Unless I see the mark of the nails in his hands, and put my finger in the mark of the nails and my hand in his side, I will not believe" (John 20:25). This dismissive remark has forever earned Thomas the reputation of being the doubting Thomas.

The scene of Jesus appearing to the disciples with Thomas present (John 20:26-29) is basically a doublet of the scene of Jesus appearing to the disciples without the presence of Thomas (John 20:19-23). New Testament narratives of the appearances of the risen Jesus have as their central motif either the mission of the disciples or the recognition of Jesus. The Evangelist's twin narratives treat each of these themes from a perspective that is particular to the Fourth Evangelist, first the mission of the disciples in John 20:19-23, then the recognition of Jesus in John 20:26-29. The Evangelist's use of the hands and side motif in John 20:25, 27 harkens back to the scene of the soldier piercing Jesus' side (John 19:34). The episode of the soldier piercing Jesus' side prepares for the recognition motif in John 20:24-29, providing the reader with another example of the Evangelist's skillful narrative style.

In keeping with the Evangelist's theological interests, the depiction of the recognition of Jesus in John 20:24-29 recedes into the background as the Evangelist exploits the recognition in order to speak about doubt and faith. The appearance of Jesus to the disciples with Thomas present is a show and tell scene. Jesus shows the doubtful member of the Twelve his crucified and raised body, the pierced side assuring its continuity. He tells

Thomas: "Do not doubt but believe" (John 20:27c).[38] Thomas' confession of faith, "My Lord and my God," (John 20:28) constitutes his recognition response. Thereupon Jesus can say to Thomas: "Because you have seen me, you have believed" (John 20:29a). Thomas' doubt has been overcome because he has seen. Jesus then offers his initial comment on Thomas' faith: "Because you have seen me, you have believed."

From a narrative point of view what has happened is that Thomas' dismissive retort has set off a chain of events in which three statements are made about seeing and believing. Thomas' initial statement was: "Unless I see ..., I will not believe" (ἐὰν μὴ ἴδω ..., οὐ μὴ πιστεύσω, John 20:25). Then Jesus says: "Because you have seen me, you have believed" (ὅτι ἑώρακάς με πεπίστευκας, John 20:29a). Jesus then concludes his remarks by saying: "Blessed are those who have not seen and yet have come to believe" (μακάριοι οἱ μὴ ἰδόντες καὶ πιστεύσαντες, John 20:29b). When the three sayings are compared with one another, the progression among them with regard to faith is apparent: 1) without sight,[39] no faith (John 20:25); 2) sight with faith (John 20:29a); 3) without sight, faith (John 20:29b).

Jesus' dialogue with Thomas, both the series of imperatives in John 20:27 and the clearly interpretive comment of 20:29a, are in the second person singular. On the level of the Johannine narrative, Jesus speaks directly to and about Thomas, one of the Twelve (John 20:24). He is the one of the Twelve who entertained doubts as to the resurrection of Jesus. On the level of the Evangelist's compositional redaction, however, there is more to this scene than first meets the eye.

Compositional Redaction

The Evangelist has identified Thomas as "one of the Twelve" (John 20:24). In the Fourth Gospel the only other person meriting this appellation is the one who was going to betray Jesus, namely, Judas Iscariot (John 6:71). In the entire Johannine narrative only two individuals are specifi-

---

[38] The Greek text of John 20:27c employs an apparent contrast: μὴ γίνου ἄπιστος ἀλλὰ πιστός. The double negative of the first imperative clause functions as a positive. In effect, Jesus twice tells Thomas to become a believer.

[39] Readers of the text in English translation may overlook the fact that the negative condition, rendered "unless" in English, is a two word phrase in Greek, ἐὰν μή, literally, "if not."

cally identified as being "one of the Twelve:"[40] the betrayer and the doubter, hardly praiseworthy roles to be played by members of the company of Twelve.

In fact, unlike the Synoptists for whom "the Twelve" is an important figure in their respective characterizations of the disciples,[41] the Twelve play a relatively insignificant role in the Fourth Gospel.[42] Apart from the identification of Thomas as one of the Twelve in John 20:24, only one pericope in the Fourth Gospel deals more or less explicitly with the Twelve. That passage is John 6:66-71. The episode begins with Jesus querying the Twelve about their possible defection and ends with the metaphorical description of one of them as a devil,[43] one who is then identified as Judas Iscariot, "one of the Twelve." This negative portrayal of the Twelve is consistent with the Evangelist's redactional perspective: "These named disciples do not seem to embody the fullness of Christian perception, as may be seen when the named disciples in general and Simon Peter in particular are compared with the Beloved Disciple."[44]

The discerning reader who compares the Johannine narrative with the stories about Jesus told by the three Synoptists will surely note that the figure of the doubting Thomas does not make an appearance in these earlier Gospels. In the Synoptic narratives, "Thomas" is simply a name appearing on a list of the members of the group of Twelve.[45]

The reader of these stories will also observe that the longer stories, the Gospels according to Matthew and Luke, make mention of the doubt of Jesus' disciples after Jesus' resurrection from the dead. Matthew says that when Jesus appeared to the Twelve disciples, now eleven in number, they worshipped "but some doubted" (οἱ δὲ ἐδίστασαν, Matt 28:17). Luke

---

[40] The nomenclature is proper to the Fourth Gospel.

[41] See R. F. Collins, "The Twelve," *ABD* 6:670-671; "The Twelve: Another Perspective," in *These Things Have Been Written: Studies on the Fourth Gospel* (LTMP 2; Louvain: Peeters, 1990; Grand Rapids: Eerdmans, 1991), 68-86, esp. 69-78; *The Many Faces of the Church: A Study in New Testament Ecclesiology* (CNT; Crossroad: New York, 1993), 95-96, 105-108, 124-25. The essay was originally published as "'The Twelve': Another Perspective: John 6,67-71," *MelT* 90 (1989): 95-109.

[42] See Collins, *These Things Have Been Written*, 78-86.

[43] The description of Judas as a devil is a bit more than mere metaphor. The Fourth Gospel presents Judas as an agent of the devil (John 13:20).

[44] R. E. Brown, *The Community of the Beloved Disciple: The Life, Loves, and Hates of an Individual Church in New Testament Times* (New York: Paulist, 1979), 84. The quotation is taken from a part of the book in which Brown describes what he calls "Apostolic Christians" (pp. 81-88).

[45] Matt 10:3; Mark 3:18; Luke 6:15; cf. Acts 1:13.

deals with the disciples and their disbelief in a different fashion. He tells his readers that the apostles dismissed the women's proclamation of the Easter message as "an idle tale" (ὡσεὶ λῆρος) and that they "did not believe them" (ἠπίστουν αὐταῖς,[46] Luke 24:11). Later, when Jesus appeared to "the eleven and their companions,"[47] Luke recounts that "they were disbelieving (ἀπιστούντων) and still wondering" (Luke 24:41).

The Evangelist Mark does not mention the disciples' lack of post-resurrection faith. Indeed, apart from the small group of three faithful women, the disciples had disappeared from Mark's story by the time that Jesus is crucified. In the so-called canonical ending of Mark (Mark 16:9-20) an unknown editor has appended to Mark's story about Jesus a brief anthology of narratives describing the appearances of Jesus after the resurrection. This editor was careful to note that when Jesus appeared to the Twelve, now eleven in number, "he upbraided them for their lack of faith (τὴν ἀπιστίαν αὐτῶν) ... because they had not believed (οὐκ ἐπίστευσαν) those who saw him after he had risen" (Mark 16:14).

The Fourth Evangelist does not deal with the disciples' lack of faith after the resurrection in such general fashion, as did the Synoptists and Mark's editor. The Fourth Evangelist dealt with the disciples' doubt in specific fashion. He chose Thomas to represent the disciples' doubt,[48] thereby firmly establishing Thomas' reputation in Christian folklore as the "doubting Thomas." The Fourth Evangelist's characterization of Thomas is a caricature. Thomas serves as a foil, made to bear the burden of the disciples' doubt. He is a representative figure whose portrayal by the Evangelist graphically illustrates the doubt of the Twelve Apostles.[49]

---

[46] The verb ἀπιστέω ("not believe") is cognate with the adjective πιστός used of Thomas in John 20:27. English translations of words belonging to the negative word group sometimes speak of doubt, sometimes of disbelief or unbelief.

[47] See Luke 24:33.

[48] See Collins, "Representative Figures," in *These Things Have Been Written*, 1-45. For Thomas, see pp. 35-37. The essay was originally published as "The Representative Figures of the Fourth Gospel," *DRev* 94 (1976): 26-46, 118-32. In contrast, Bultmann held that "the doubt of Thomas is representative of the common attitude of men who cannot believe without seeing miracles" (*John*, 696). Culpepper has observed that Thomas' doubt is "given representative value for all future skeptics" (R. A. Culpepper, *Anatomy of the Fourth Gospel: A Study in Literary Design* [FF; Philadelphia: Fortress, 1983], 119).

[49] With the exception of John 13:16, the Evangelist resolutely avoids the use of the word ἀπόστολος.

The Macro Context

Only when the reader appreciates the Evangelist's characterization of Thomas can he or she appreciate the full import of the Gospel's final beatitude (John 20:29b). Formulaically uttered by the risen Jesus, the beatitude is a kind of blessing whose narrative function is similar to the Great Commission of the Gospel according to Matthew (Matt 28:18-20). Both the beatitude and the Great Commission extend the narrative time of the Evangelist's story beyond the story itself.

The faith commended in the beatitude is belief without the benefit of physical sight. This is faith in the full Johannine sense of the term. Such faith is based neither on an immediate experience of the risen Jesus nor on the visual experience of the risen tomb. This faith is unlike that of the Evangelist's Thomas who wanted to see the risen body in its similarity with the crucified body before he would believe. It is a faith unlike that of the Evangelist's Simon Peter who, in an experience that contrasts with that of the Beloved Disciple who saw the empty tomb and believed (John 20:8),[50] saw the empty tomb and seems not to have believed (John 20:6-7).[51]

In the final spoken words of the Johannine story about Jesus, the Revealer pronounces as blessed those who have faith without the benefit of sight. In ordinary parlance the word "blessed" simply means happy or fortunate. Placed on the lips of Jesus the adjective μακάριοι must admit of the connotations that it had in John 13:17, where it is implied that to be blessed is to anticipate going to the Father. The believers whom Jesus proclaims as blessed can and should anticipate going to the Father; they are believers who have eternal life, as the Evangelist himself comments in his own epilogue to the story (John 20:31).[52]

In regard to the promise inherent in the beatitude it is important to note that, although it is difficult to identify the primary characteristics of a beatitude in terms of its form and function, Betz, after extensive study of biblical and extra-biblical beatitudes, was able to reach only four summa-

---

[50] The Evangelist uses the verb θεωρέω to describe Peter's "sight." Often in the Fourth Gospel, this verb is used to describe seeing that is merely physical, without any significant perception accruing therefrom. At most this type of sight leads to the acceptance of Jesus as a wonder worker (2:23; 4:19; 6:2; cf. 6:19). In comparison, the Evangelist uses the verb ὁράω to describe the Beloved Disciple's "sight." This is the sight that leads to belief, as the Evangelist states apropos the Beloved Disciple in John 20:8.

[51] Note the use of a verb in the singular ἐπίστευσεν ("he believed") in John 20:8.

[52] See 3:36; 6:47; 11:25; 20:31.

rizing conclusions. One of them is: "The future orientation [of a beatitude] is eschatological as well as this-worldly."[53] Betz has said this apropos the biblical beatitudes in general; it is certainly apropos to the beatitude in John 20:29b. This beatitude speaks of eternal beatitude.

In contrast with Thomas and Peter, those who are blessed in Jesus' solemn and final utterance of the Fourth Gospel are members of the Johannine Community in the first instance. The Beloved Disciple gave witness so that they might believe (John 19:35); they know that his testimony is true, as the author of the great epilogue has commented (John 21:24).

A beatitude phrased in the third person has, however, a gnomic character. Such beatitudes are imbued with general import. Many of them have a hortatory purpose,[54] as do the beatitudes found in Ps 32:2 and Matthew's Sermon on the Mount (5:3-12). Implicitly, beatitudes encourage those who listen to them to embrace a way of life. Jesus' borderline beatitude (John 13:17) urges the disciples to do what they have seen Jesus do. The beatitude that serves as the finale of the Fourth Gospel likewise has a hortatory purpose. It urges those who have not seen to believe.[55]

Those who read the Fourth Gospel today are among those who have not seen. Its concluding beatitude encourages these readers to believe. Readers of the Johannine narrative believe because of the word that has been witnessed to them,[56] the witness of the Beloved Disciple to which the Fourth Gospel bears witness. These readers are people who are and who will be blessed, notwithstanding their lack of sight. These are those to whom the final beatitude is ultimately addressed. Those upon whom the Revealer imparts a final blessing are none other than those who faithfully read the Fourth Gospel today.[57] Ultimately the import of the great

---

[53] Betz, *Sermon on the Mount*, 93.

[54] Betz' fourth conclusion is that beatitudes are "connected with ethics and morality" (*Sermon on the Mount*, 93).

[55] See also U. Schnelle, *Antidocetic Christology in the Gospel of John: An Investigation of the Place of the Fourth Gospel in the Johannine School* (Minneapolis: Fortress, 1992), 71.

[56] See J. Painter, *John: Witness & Theologian* (London: SPCK, 1975), 105.

[57] In reaching this conclusion, I strongly disagree with Bultmann who asked "Does the blessing extol those born later?," answering his own question with "That can hardly be possible" (*John*, 696). For a view similar to mine, see Prete who describes the beatitude as "a more universal consideration which is valid for all time" ("Beati coloro," 111-12). Similarly, Schnelle who comments: "In this macarism John states something that from that point on applies to later generations in distinction from the eyewitnesses" (*Antidocetic Christology*, 14). Moreover, if Culpepper's claim is valid that Thomas' doubt has representative value for all future doubters (*Anatomy of the Fourth Gospel*, 119), *a fortiori*, the beatitude has value for all future believers.

beatitude of the Fourth Gospel can be summarized in these words of Udo Schnelle: "The aim is to induce faith in the readers or hearers of the Gospel; they are no longer eyewitnesses (20:29), and yet they are to be included in the saving event that stretches from the incarnation to the glorification of Christ."[58]

---

[58] Schnelle, *Antidocetic Christology*, 71.

10. THE USE OF VERBAL VARIETY IN THE FOURTH GOSPEL

Francis T. GIGNAC

It is a great privilege for me to contribute to this Festschrift in honor of Francis J. Moloney on the occasion of his 65th birthday. He is recognized as the world's foremost Johannine scholar. It is my hope that this analysis of some Johannine vocabulary will serve as a tribute to him and as a token of my great esteem for him as a scholar, teacher, and administrator for whom students' interests are always paramount.

As is well known, the author of the Gospel according to John tends to use words in complementary distribution, reflecting on the linguistic level the duality familiar to us on the thought level, e.g., the contrasts between light and darkness, joy and grief. Several adjectives are so used. As pointed out by the late George D. Kilpatrick, the Dean Ireland's Professor of Exegesis of Holy Scripture at our mutual alma mater, the University of Oxford, some adjectives are used always and only attributively, others always and only predicatively.[1] For instance, καλός is found in the attributive position at 2:10[bis] and at 10:11[bis], 14, 32, 33, while ἀγαθός is found in the predicative position at 1:46; 7:12; and (substantively as an object) in 5:29.

Similarly, ἀληθινός is used always and only attributively, ἀληθής always and only predicatively. Thus, ἀληθινός is found used attributively at 1:9; 4:23; 6:32; 15:1; and 17:3, and ἀληθής is found used predicatively at 3:33; 4:18; 5:31, 32; 7:18; 8:13, 14, 17, 26; 10:41; and 21:24. But there are five passages in our editions that do not conform to this usage.

Our texts at 4:37 have ἀληθινός used predicatively: ἐν γὰρ τούτῳ ὁ λόγος ἐστὶν ἀληθινός. But there are variant readings. ἀληθής is the easier

---

[1] G. D. Kilpatrick, "Some Notes on Johannine Usage," *BT* 11:4 (1960): 1-5.

reading but it occurs only in a few cursives. But ὁ ἀληθινός is found in
𝔓⁶⁶ ℵ A C³ D Θ *f* ¹³ and 𝔐. At 6:55, ἀληθής is read attributively twice,
modifying βρῶσις and πόσις. But the adverb ἀληθῶς is found in both
places in 𝔓⁶⁶* (D) Θ 0250 𝔐 lat sy, and ἀληθής is found in the first occurrence and the adverb ἀληθῶς in the second in ℵ² *f* ¹³ *pc.*

At 7:28 our texts have ἀλλ' ἔστιν ἀληθινὸς ὁ πέμψας με, but ἀληθής
is found in 𝔓⁶⁶ ℵ 544 *pc.* At 8:16 we have ἡ κρίσις ἡ ἐμὴ ἀληθινή ἐστιν,
but ἀληθής is read in 𝔓⁶⁶ ℵ Θ Ψ 0250 *f* ¹·¹³ 𝔐. Finally, at 19:35 our texts
have καὶ ἀληθινὴ αὐτοῦ ἐστιν ἡ μαρτυρία, but ἀληθής is found in ℵ
124 Chrys. The anomalous readings in our editions are probably the result
of scribes failing to perceive the stylistic pattern of this author.

This suggests strongly that these pairs of adjectives do not differ in
meaning in this Gospel but that they are simply used in complementary
distribution. Consequently, I would not see a specific meaning such as
"noble" or "model" in ὁ ποιμὴν ὁ καλός in 10:11[2] or "the only real" in
τὸ φῶς τὸ ἀληθινόν in 1:9.[3]

πέμπω - ἀποστέλλω

Verbs are similarly so used in this Gospel. Many commentators see a
distinction in meaning between πέμπω and ἀποστέλλω.[4] But it has long
been known that these two verbs are used suppletively by this author.[5]

---

[2] *Pace* R. E. Brown, *The Gospel According to John* (AB 29-29A; 2 vols.; Garden City:
Doubleday, 1966, 1970), 1:384, 386, 395-98.

[3] Brown, *John*, 1:499-501.

[4] So B. F. Westcott, *The Gospel according to Saint John* (London: John Murray, 1887;
repr. Grand Rapids: Eerdmans, 1954), 294, 298 (ἀπ. = despatch, envoy, conveying notions of commission, delegated authority; π. = only the immediate relation of the sender
to the sent); quoted also by G. Beasley-Murray, *John* (WBC 36; Waco: Word Books,
1987), 379-80; K. H. Rengstorf, "ἀποστέλλω (πέμπω), ἐξαποστέλλω, ἀπόστολος,
ψευδαπόστολος, ἀποστολή," *TDNT* 1:398-447, esp. 405 (ἀπ. = Jesus grounding his
authority in God's; π. = the participation of God in Jesus' work); C. R. Mercer,
"ΑΠΟΣΤΕΛΛΕΙΝ and ΠΕΜΠΕΙΝ in John," *NTS* 36 (1990): 619-24 (ἀπ. = God as
sender + commission; π. = God identified in terms of his act of sending); J. Seynaeve,
"Verbes ἀποστέλλω et πέμπω dans le vocabulaire théologique de saint Jean," in
L'Évangile de Jean: Source, rédaction, théologie (ed. M. de Jonge; Gembloux: Duculot, 1977),
385-89 (ἀπ. = l'envoi; π. = la tâche); M. Waldstein, "Die Sendung Jesu und der Jünger im
Johannesevangelium," *IkaZ "Communio"* 19:3 (1990): 203-21 (all sendings are functions of
the one sending of Jesus).

[5] This was demonstrated by C. C. Tarelli in "Johannine Synonyms," *JTS* 1/47 (1946):
175, and cited by Kilpatrick, "Some Notes," 4.

Thus, πέμπω is used in the present indicative (20:21), future indicative (13:20; 14:26; 15:26; 16:7), and aorist participle (26 times, always with the article); ἀποστέλλω is used in the aorist indicative (21 times) and in the perfect system (10 times including variants). A clear parallel is found in 5:36-37, where ὁ πατήρ με ἀπέσταλκεν is followed immediately by ὁ πέμψας με πατήρ. No distinction in meaning should therefore be made, for instance, in the two sendings at 20:21: καθὼς ἀπέσταλκέν με ὁ πατήρ, κἀγὼ πέμπω ὑμᾶς.[6]

ἀγαπάω - φιλέω

One pair of verbs whose meaning in John has been discussed extensively is ἀγαπάω and φιλέω.[7] ἀγαπάω is used thirty-seven times in John: of God's love for the world (3:16), of people's preference for darkness

---

[6] So C. K. Barrett, *The Gospel According to St. John: An Introduction with Commentary and Notes on the Greek Text* (2d ed.; Philadelphia: Westminster, 1978), 569 ("the two verbs seem to be used synonymously in this Gospel"); N. Turner, *A Grammar of New Testament Greek. Vol. 4: Style* (Edinburgh: Clark, 1976), 76 ("a needless synonym" listed under Pointless Variety in Style); A. J. Köstenberger, "The Two Johannine Verbs for Sending: A Study of John's Use of Words with Reference to General Linguistic Theory," in *Linguistics in the New Testament: Critical Junctures* (ed. S. E. Porter and D. A. Carson; JSNTSup 168; Sheffield: Sheffield Press, 1999), 125-43, esp. 142 (stylistic variation "may function in John's use of 'sending' verbs as a supplementary [but not necessarily primary or ultimately determinate] factor").

[7] See esp. R. Bultmann, *The Gospel of John: A Commentary* (trans. G. R. Beasley-Murray et al.; Oxford: Blackwell; Philadelphia: Westminster, 1971) 253 n. 2 ("same meaning"), 711 n. 5 ("the exchange of ἀγαπᾶν and φιλεῖν cannot be significant"); R. Schnackenburg, *The Gospel According to St John* (3 vols.; New York: Crossroad, 1982) 3:362-63 ("used synonymously"); D. A. Carson, *The Gospel According to John* (Leicester: Inter-Varsity; Grand Rapids: Eerdmans, 1991), 648 ("nothing should be made of the change"); 648 n. 1 ("this is an instance of John's penchant for minor stylistic variations"); J. Barr, "Words for Love in Biblical Greek," in *The Glory of Christ in the New Testament: Studies in Christology in Memory of George Bradford Caird* (ed. L. D. Hurst and N. T. Wright; Oxford; Clarendon, 1987), 3-18; J. P. Louw and E. A. Nida, *Greek-English Lexicon of the New Testament Based on Semantic Domains* (New York: United Bible Societies, 1988), § 25.43; F. J. Moloney, *The Gospel of John* (SP 4; Collegeville: Liturgical Press, 1998), 559 ("the Johannine practice of using synonymous verbs for stylistic variety"); but, seeing different meanings in them, C. Spicq, *Agape dans le Nouveau Testament: Analyse des textes* (3 vols.; Paris: Gabalda, 1958-59), esp. 3:125-218; K. L. McKay, "Style and Significance in the Language of John 21:15-17," *NovT* 27 (1985): 319-33 ("variation of forms ... gently significant"); A. G. Brock, "The Significance of φιλέω and φίλος in the Tradition of Jesus Sayings and in the Early Christian Communities," *HTS* 90 (1997): 393-409, esp. 405-8 (φιλέω vocabulary comes from the tradition of certain communities).

over light (3:19) and the authorities' preference of human praise over the glory of God (12:43), of the Father's love for the son (3:35; 10:17; 15:9; 17:23, 24, 26), of the love for Jesus the Jews should have had (8:42), of Jesus' love for Martha, Mary, and Lazarus (11:5), of Jesus' love for his own (13:1), of Jesus' love for the Beloved Disciple (13:23; 19:26; 21:7, 20), of the new commandment and its model of Jesus' love (13:34; 15:12, 17), of the disciples' love for Jesus (14:15, 21, 24, 28) and the love of them by Jesus and/or the Father (14:21, 23; 15:9; 17:23), of Jesus' love for the Father (14:31), and twice in the final dialogue with Simon Peter (21:15, 16). φιλέω occurs twelve times: of the Father's love for the Son (5:20), of Jesus' love for Lazarus (11:3, 36), of loving one's life (12:25), of the world loving its own (15:19), of the Father loving the disciples because they loved Jesus (16:27), of Jesus' love for the Beloved Disciple (20:2), and five times in the final dialogue between Jesus and Simon Peter (21:15-17).

The parallel usages are the following. (1) The Father's love for the Son. ἀγαπάω is used in 3:35; 10:17; 15:9; 17:23, 24, 26, e.g., ὁ πατὴρ ἀγαπᾷ τὸν υἱόν (3:35); φιλέω is used in the parallel expression ὁ γὰρ πατὴρ φιλεῖ τὸν υἱόν (5:20). (2) Jesus' love for Martha, Mary, and Lazarus. This is expressed by ἠγάπα in 11:5, but his sisters tell Jesus ὃν φιλεῖς ἀσθενεῖ in 11:3 and the Jews say ἴδε πῶς ἐφίλει αὐτόν in 11:36. (3) Jesus' vs. the world's love for his own. In 13:1 Jesus is described as loving his own with ἀγαπήσας ... ἠγάπησεν. In 15:19 it is said that the world would love (ἐφίλει) its own (but cf. 15:9-13a where the words for love are related to ἀγαπάω while in 13b-15 they are related to φιλέω). (4) The Father's love for the disciples because they loved Jesus is expressed by forms of ἀγαπάω in 14:21, 23 and 17:23 but with forms of φιλέω in 16:27. (5) Jesus' love for the Beloved Disciple is expressed by ἠγάπα in 13:23; 19:26; 21:7, 20 and by ἐφίλει in 20:2. (6) In the final dialogue with Simon Peter ἀγαπᾷς is used twice, φιλῶ and φιλεῖς are used a total of five times.

With the possible exception of (3) above, where a contrast might be drawn between the love of Jesus for his own and that of the world, and (6) which will be discussed further, the two verbs seem to be used interchangeably with no distinction in meaning.

In the final dialogue with Simon Peter in chap. 21, there is a remarkable variety of synonyms in vv. 15-17. Besides the two words for love, there are two verbs for feed or tend (βόσκω and ποιμαίνω), two nouns for sheep (ἀρνία and πρόβατα), and two verbs for know (οἶδα and γινώσκω[8]).

---

[8] For discussion of a possible aspectual difference between these two verbs, see esp.

A difference in meaning does not seem to be warranted. James Barr's trenchant conclusion is worth quoting in full:

> To say this is not to say that the two verbs are completely 'synonymous'. The total possible range of φιλεῖν within biblical Greek is not identical with that of ἀγαπᾶν. There is a difference of stylistic level, of associations, and of nuances. But within any one individual passage these differences do not amount to a distinction of real theological reference: they do not specify a difference in the kind of love referred to.[9]

τρώγω - ἐσθίω

The verb τρώγω is sometimes thought to be used in contrast to ἐσθίω, with its suppletive aorist based on the stem φαγ-.[10] The aorist ἔφαγον is found fifteen times (4:31, 32, 33; 6:5, 23, 26, 31[*bis*], 49, 50, 51, 52, 53, 58; 18:28); τρώγω is found five times, always in the present (6:54, 56, 57, 58; 13:18). In the last reference, Ps 40(41):10 LXX reads ὁ ἐσθίων ἄρτους μου. This appears in John as ὁ τρώγων μου τὸν ἄρτον. The present ἐσθίω is never found in this Gospel. This suggests that τρώγω serves as the present of the verb "eat" in John.

ἐσθίω tends to be used in classical Greek of human beings eating (cf. German *essen*), but also in a metaphorical sense, whereas τρώγω tends to mean "gnaw," "nibble," "munch," and is used in early Greek of animals eating (cf. German *fressen*). But already in Herodotus it is used of human beings eating vegetables or fruit, extended to include other foods in Attic, and it became the normal word for "eat." In Modern Greek, the present of the verb "eat" is τρώγω, the aorist ἔφαγα. Therefore, it seems unjustified to see in the switch from φαγ- to τρώγω in vv. 54-58 of the Bread of Life discourse in John 6 any emphasis on the reality of the eucharistic elements.[11]

I. de la Potterie, "Οἶδα et γινώσκω: Les deux modes de la connaissance dans le quatrième évangile," *Bib* 40 (1959): 709-25; Brown, *John*, 1:513-15; K. L. McKay, "On the Perfect and Other Aspects in New Testament Greek," *NovT* 23 (1981): 289-329.

[9] Barr, "Words for Love," 15.

[10] Moloney, *John*, 224, 381, argues strongly for a distinction of meaning between ἐσθίω and τρώγω because of the eucharistic background of the passages in which τρώγω occurs.

[11] *Pace* BDAG, s.v., "J[ohn] uses it to offset any tendencies to 'spiritualize' the concept so that nothing physical remains in it, in what many hold to be the language of the

ὁράω - θεωρέω

Another set of verbs sometimes contrasted in meaning is ὁράω and θεωρέω. ὁράω never occurs in the present system in John but only in the suppletive future ὄψομαι (10 times), the perfect active ἑώρακα (20 times), and the aorist active εἶδον (36 times). In the future it is used of seeing Jesus/the Lord (16:16, 17, 19), of Jesus seeing his disciples again (16:22), of Jesus promising his first disciples that they will see (1:39; cf. 1:50, 51), of not seeing life (3:36), of seeing the glory of God (11:40), and of looking upon the one whom they have pierced (19:37, citing Zech 12:10). In the perfect it is used of seeing God/the Father (1:18; 5:37; 6:46[bis]; 14:7, 9[bis]), of seeing Jesus/the Lord (6:36; 9:37; 15:24; 20:18, 25, 29), of people seeing all Jesus had done (4:45), of what Jesus has seen from the Father (8:38), and of seeing Abraham (8:57). In addition, it is paired with forms of μαρτυρέω in 1:34; 3:11, 32; 19:35. In the aorist it is used thirty-six times in various senses: of seeing the Spirit (1:33), of seeing where Jesus was staying (1:39, 46), of Jesus seeing Nathanael coming toward him (1:47) and under the fig tree (1:48, 50), of not seeing the kingdom of God (3:3), of Samaritans seeing Jesus (4:29), of seeing signs (4:48; 6:14, 26, 30), of Jesus seeing the paralytic (5:6), of the crowd realizing that Jesus had not embarked (6:22, 24), of seeing that no prophet arises from Galilee (7:52), of Abraham rejoicing to see Jesus' day (8:56), of Jesus seeing a young blind man (9:1), of the Jews seeing Mary get up and leave (11:31), of Mary meeting Jesus (11:32), of Jesus seeing Mary and the Jews weeping (11:33), of the Jews inviting Jesus to see where they laid Lazarus (11:34), of the crowd coming to see Lazarus (12:9), of Greeks wanting to see Jesus (12:21), of not seeing with one's eyes (12:40, citing Isa 6:10), of Isaiah seeing God's glory (12:41), of a slave seeing Jesus in the garden (18:26), of the chief priests and guards seeing Jesus (19:6), of Jesus seeing his mother and the Beloved Disciple (19:26), of the soldiers seeing that Jesus was already dead (19:33), of the Beloved Disciple seeing and believing (20:8), of the disciples seeing the risen Lord (20:20), of Thomas seeing Jesus' hands (20:25, 27), of those who have not seen and have believed (20:29), and of Peter seeing the Beloved Disciple (21:21).

Lord's Supper." Similarly, C. Spicq, "ΤΡΩΓΕΙΝ: Est-il synonyme de ΦΑΓΕΙΝ et d'ΕΣΘΙΕΙΝ dans le Nouveau Testament?" *NTS* 26 (1979-80): 414-19 (a crescendo in the three feedings in chap. 6: barley loaves, manna, Eucharist; a nuance of savoring, appreciating the food; an insistence on the realism of the eating).

Forms of θεωρέω occur twenty-four times, always in the present system, including the imperfect ἐθεώρων [*v.l.* ἑώρων] (6:2), except for the aorist subjunctive θεωρήσῃ [*v.l.* future θεωρήσει] (8:51), and the future θεωρήσουσιν used for the aorist subjunctive [*v.ll.* θεωρήσωσιν, θεωροῦσιν] (7:3). It is used of people seeing the signs or works of Jesus (2:23; 6:2; 7:3), of the Samaritan woman perceiving that Jesus was a prophet (4:19), of the disciples seeing Jesus walking upon the water (6:19), of seeing the Son and believing in him (6:40) or the Son of Man ascending (6:62), of seeing death (8:51), of seeing the young man born blind when he was a beggar (9:8), of a hired hand seeing a wolf coming (10:12), of the Pharisees seeing that they were not prevailing (12:19), of seeing Jesus and the one who sent him (12:45[*bis*]), of the world not seeing the Spirit (14:17), of the world not seeing Jesus but his disciples seeing him (14:19[*bis*]; 16:10, 16, 17, 19), of the disciples seeing Jesus' glory (17:24), of Peter and the Beloved Disciple seeing the burial cloths (20:6), of Mary of Magdala seeing the two angels (20:12) and Jesus standing there (20:14).

The closest parallel usages are the following. (1) People seeing the signs or works of Jesus, expressed by forms of θεωρέω in 2:23; 6:2; and 7:3, by forms of the aorist εἶδον in 4:48; 6:14, 26, 30, and by ἑωρακότες in 4:45; in 6:2 ἑώρων is also found in 𝔓⁶⁶* ℵ *f*¹ 𝔐. (2) Seeing Jesus and believing in him, expressed by ἑωράκατέ [με] καὶ οὐ πιστεύετε in 6:36 and by πᾶς ὁ θεωρῶν τὸν υἱὸν καὶ πιστεύων εἰς αὐτόν in 6:40, as well as by εἶδεν in 20:8 and ἰδόντες in 20:29. (3) Not seeing the kingdom of God: ἰδεῖν (3:3), not seeing life: ὄψεται 3:36, not seeing death: θεωρήσῃ 8:51. (4) Seeing Jesus before his departure: μικρὸν καὶ οὐκέτι θεωρεῖτέ με, καὶ πάλιν μικρὸν καὶ ὄψεσθέ με (16:16, sim. 17, 19). (5) Seeing the glory of God: ὄψῃ τὴν δόξαν τοῦ θεοῦ (11:40) and ὅτι εἶδεν τὴν δόξαν αὐτοῦ (12:41), or of Jesus: ἵνα θεωρῶσιν τὴν δόξαν τὴν ἐμήν (17:24). Again, a clear distinction in meaning does not seem justified. These two verbs, ὁράω and θεωρέω, seem to be used synonymously in John.

βλέπω - θεάομαι

Two other verbs for seeing are used in John, βλέπω and θεάομαι. βλέπω occurs seventeen times, only in the present system: the present indicative eleven times (1:29; 9:15, 19, 21, 25, 41; 11:9; 20:1, 5; 21:9, 20), the imperfect indicative once (13:22), the present subjunctive twice (5:19, 39), and the present participle three times (9:7, 39[*bis*]). The compound ἀναβλέπω is also found four times, used in an ingressive sense (9:11, 15, 18[*bis*]). θεάομαι is found six times, five times in the aorist middle (1:14, 38; 4:35; 6:5; 11:45) and once in the perfect middle (1:32). This distribution suggests that βλέπω and θεωρέω have replaced ὁράω in the present system.[12] θεάομαι is used in two passages in which the idea of contemplation is possible (1:14, 32), but this meaning seems unlikely for the other four (1:38; 4:35; 6:5; 11:45).

γνωρίζω - φανερόω

Another pair of verbs in John is γνωρίζω and φανερόω. γνωρίζω is found in 15:15: ὑμᾶς δὲ εἴρηκα φίλους, ὅτι πάντα ἃ ἤκουσα παρὰ τοῦ πατρός μου ἐγνώρισα ὑμῖν, and in 17:26: καὶ ἐγνώρισα αὐτοῖς τὸ ὄνομά σου καὶ γνωρίσω. φανερόω is found nine times: of Jesus being made known to Israel (1:31), of Jesus revealing his glory (2:11), of one's works being clearly seen (3:21), of Jesus being told by his brothers to manifest himself to the world (7:4), that the works of God might be made visible (9:3), of Jesus revealing God's name (17:6), and in the epilogue three times of Jesus revealing himself again (21:1[*bis*], 14).

Both uses of γνωρίζω are roughly parallel to ἐφανέρωσά σου τὸ ὄνομα τοῖς ἀνθρώποις of 17:6. There does not seem to be any distinction in meaning.[13]

---

[12] ὁράω is relatively rare in Hellenistic Greek, restricted mainly to the imperatives ὅρα and ὁρᾶτε (McKay, "On the Perfect," 326-27). See also C. C. Tarelli, "Johannine Synonyms," 175-76; W. Michaelis, "ὁράω, κτλ.," *TWNT* 5:315-82, esp. 345 (θεωρέω = present of ὁράω); F. Thordarson, "ὁρῶ- βλέπω- θεωρῶ: Some Semantic Remarks," *SO* 46 (1971): 108-31 (Modern Greek βλέπω present, εἶδα aorist; dialectically θωρῶ, εἶδα in Crete, Rhodes, Cyprus, Chios, S. Italy, etc.); L. A. Sánchez Navarro, "Acerca de' ΟΡΑΩ en Jn," *EstBib* 55:2 (1997): 263-66 (θεωρέω serves as the present of ὁράω). But G. L. Phillips, "Faith and Vision in the Fourth Gospel," in *Studies in the Fourth Gospel* (ed. F. L. Cross; London: Mowbray, 1957), 83-96 (following E. A. Abbott, *Johannine Vocabulary* [London: A. & C. Black, 1905], §§ 1597-1611), finds a progressively higher form of insight in βλέπω, θεωρέω, ὁράω (εἶδον), and θεάομαι. Similarly, S. E. Farrell, "Seeing the Father (Jn 6:46, 14:9)," *ScEs* 44 (1992): 1-24, 159-83, 307-29, finds seven levels of seeing expressed variously by ὁράω, βλέπω, θεάομαι, θεωρέω, εἶδον, ὄψομαι, and ἑώρακα, respectively.

[13] *Pace* M. N. A. Bockmuehl, "Das Verb φανερόω im Neuen Testament: Versuch einer Neuauswertung," *BZ* 32:1 (1988): 87-99, who sees a strong Christological and soteriological function (incarnation, work, lordship, resurrection, and parousia of Jesus) in φανερόω. R. Bultmann ("φαίνω, κτλ.," *TWNT* 9:1-10, esp. 3-6) and P.-G. Müller ("φανερόω," *EWNT* 3:988-91) see φανερόω as synonymous with γνωρίζω.

κλαίω - δακρύω

Another pair of verbs in John is κλαίω and δακρύω. κλαίω, classical "cry," "wail," "lament," "howl," which comes to mean "weep for," "lament," "mourn," "bewail," occurs eight times in John: of Mary supposedly going to the tomb of Lazarus to weep there (11:31), of Jesus seeing her and the Jews weeping (11:33), of the disciples weeping after Jesus' departure (16:20), and four times of Mary of Magdala weeping at Jesus' tomb (20:11[*bis*], 13, 15). δακρύω, "shed tears," "weep," is used only once: of Jesus weeping for Lazarus (11:35). It is not impossible here that δακρύω is used to distinguish Jesus' tears from the ritual mourning of Mary and the Jews.[14]

ἀναβαίνω - πορεύομαι - ὑπάγω

Finally, there are three verbs used for "going away" in John: ἀναβαίνω, πορεύομαι, and ὑπάγω. ἀναβαίνω is used sixteen times, πορεύομαι seventeen times, and ὑπάγω thirty-two times.

ἀναβαίνω is used in the quotation of Gen 28:12 of the angels of God ascending (1:51), of Jesus and others going up to Jerusalem (2:13; 5:1; 7:8[*bis*], 10[*bis*]; 11:55; 12:20) or to the temple area (7:14), of someone climbing over a wall (10:1), of Simon Peter boarding a boat (21:11), of anyone going up to heaven (3:13), of the Son of Man ascending (6:62), of the risen Jesus ascending to the Father (20:17[*bis*]).

πορεύομαι is used of a man leaving (4:50[*bis*]), of Jesus' departure (7:35[*bis*]), of people going home (7:53), of Jesus going to the Mount of Olives (8:1) and leaving the temple area (8:59), of Jesus bidding a woman go (8:11), of a shepherd walking (10:4), of Jesus going to awaken Lazarus (11:11), of Jesus going to prepare a place for his disciples (14:2, 3), of Jesus going to the Father (14:12, 28; 16:7, 28), of Jesus bidding Mary of Magdala to go to his brothers (20:17).

ὑπάγω is used of where the wind goes (3:8), of Jesus bidding the woman to go call her husband (4:16), of a boat arriving at shore (6:21), of disciples leaving Jesus (6:67), of Jesus going to Judea (7:3; 11:8), of Jesus going to the one who sent him/God (7:33; 13:3; 16:5[*bis*], 10, 17), of Jesus

[14] So F. J. Moloney, "Can Everyone Be Wrong? A Reading of John 11:1–12:8," *NTS* 49 (2003): 519.

knowing where he is going (8:14[*bis*]), of Jesus going away (8:21[*bis*], 22; 13:33, 36[*bis*]; 14:4, 5, 28), of the young man told to go wash in Siloam (9:7, 11), of Mary going to the tomb (11:31), of Jesus commanding to let Lazarus go (11:44), of Jews turning to Jesus (12:11), of one not knowing where one is going (12:35), of the disciples going and bearing fruit (15:16), of letting the disciples go (18:8), of Simon Peter going fishing (21:3).

The parallel usages are the following. (1) Both πορεύομαι and ὑπάγω are used of people going in the normal sense: πορεύομαι, e.g., of a man leaving (4:50[*bis*]), of people going home (7:53), of Jesus going to the Mount of Olives (8:1) and leaving the temple area (8:59), of Jesus bidding a woman go (8:11), of a shepherd walking (10:4), of Jesus going to awaken Lazarus (11:11), of Jesus bidding Mary of Magdala to go to his brothers (20:17); ὑπάγω, e.g., of Jesus bidding the woman to go call her husband (4:16), of Jesus going to Judea (7:3; 11:8), of the young man told to go wash in Siloam (9:7, 11), of Mary going to the tomb (11:31), of one not knowing where one is going (12:35), of Simon Peter going fishing (21:3). (2) Both πορεύομαι and ὑπάγω are used of Jesus going away or to God/the Father/the one who sent him: πορεύομαι of Jesus' departure (7:35[*bis*]), of Jesus going to prepare a place for his disciples (14:2, 3), of Jesus going to the Father (14:12, 28; 16:7, 28); ὑπάγω, e.g., of Jesus going to the one who sent him/God (7:33; 13:3; 16:5[*bis*], 10, 17), of Jesus knowing where he is going (8:14[*bis*]), of Jesus going away (8:21[*bis*], 22; 13:33, 36[*bis*]; 14:4, 5, 28). Thus, there seems to be no difference in meaning between these two verbs.

ἀναβαίνω is used not only in a more restrictive sense of Jesus and others going up to Jerusalem (2:13; 5:1; 7:8[*bis*], 10[*bis*]; 11:55; 12:20) or to the temple area (7:14), of someone climbing over a wall (10:1), of Simon Peter boarding a boat (21:11), but also of the angels of God ascending (1:51), of anyone going up to heaven (3:13), of the Son of Man ascending (6:62), and of the risen Jesus ascending to the Father (20:17[*bis*]). In these last four usages, it seems to be used synonymously with πορεύομαι and ὑπάγω, so any distinction of meaning among these three verbs in John does not seem to be justified.

This brief analysis of Johannine vocabulary suggests strongly that the author uses various verbs synonymously and often in complementary distribution, as he does adjectives. I hope that this linguistic study will contribute to a clearer understanding and appreciation of the author's message–the goal of all exegesis.

11. TRANSCENDING MESSIANIC EXPECTATIONS: MARK AND JOHN

Frank J. MATERA

Christian faith proclaims that Jesus of Nazareth was the promised Messiah, the fulfillment of Israel's messianic hope. This confession of faith, however, should not be understood naively as if Jesus fulfilled clearly defined messianic categories. Contemporary scholarship insists that messiahship was not a univocal category against which Jesus, or anyone else, could be measured.[1] It would be more accurate to say that the first Christians defined the concept of messiahship in light of the salvation they experienced in Jesus. In doing so, they transcended messianic boundaries.

In keeping with the theme of this volume, this essay will explore how the Gospels of Mark and John transcend messianic boundaries in their presentations of Jesus. The choice of these writings is appropriate since the one whom this volume honors has written outstanding commentaries on each of these Gospels in which he has paid careful attention to their narrative lines.[2] Since the manner in which Mark and John present Jesus as the Messiah is best understood in light of the stories they tell, this essay will focus on their narratives in order to see how each transcends messianic boundaries. It concludes by noting several ways in which these Gospels converge in summoning others to transcend messianic boundaries.

---

[1] For an overview of messianic expectations, see J. J. Collins, *The Scepter and the Star: The Messiahs of the Dead Sea Scrolls and Other Ancient Literature* (ABRL; New York: Doubleday, 1995); J. Neusner, W. S. Green, E. Frerichs (eds.), *Judaism and their Messiahs at the Turn of the Christian Era* (Cambridge: Cambridge University Press, 1987); H.-J. Fabry and K. Scholtissek, *Der Messias* (NEchtB 5; Würzburg, Echter, 2002).

[2] F. J. Moloney, *The Gospel of John* (SP 4; Collegeville: The Liturgical Press, 1998); *The Gospel of Mark: A Commentary* (Peabody: Hendrickson, 2002).

The Gospel of Mark: How Does One Recognize the Messiah?

Narratives are subversive. Even if one is familiar with the events that underlie the story, the manner in which the narrator "plots" them determines what and how readers will hear the story. Moloney writes: "*Whatever the first readers knew of the life-story of Jesus of Nazareth was subverted by the Markan story.*"[3] This statement is insightful because, however familiar the first readers were with the events of Jesus' life, the Markan Evangelist confronted them with a story they had not heard, a story intended to subvert and transcend their understanding of Jesus' messiahship.

The Markan Story

The Markan Gospel begins with a prologue (1:1-13) in which the narrator presents the reader with important information about the identity of Jesus and his relationship to God, information to which the characters in the narrative are not privy. For example, the prologue informs the reader that Jesus is the Christ, the Son of God (1:1; 11), the stronger one (1:7), the Spirit-anointed Son of God (1:10), the one more powerful than Satan (1:12-13).

The first part of the Gospel (1:14–8:30) presents Jesus as the herald of the kingdom of God who inaugurates and proclaims the kingdom by his mighty deeds. Although many respond positively to his call to repent and believe in God's good news of the in-breaking kingdom, others do not.[4] Mark plots his story so that Jesus' ministry raises the question of his identity: "Who then is this whom even wind and sea obey?" (Mark 4:41); "Where did this man get all of this?" (Mark 6:2).[5] At the end of part one, however, Peter correctly identifies Jesus when, in contrast to a series of false opinions (see 8:28 which echoes 6:14-16), he confesses, "You are the Messiah" (8:30).

In the second part of the narrative (8:31–15:47) it becomes apparent

---

[3] Moloney, *Mark*, 16.

[4] E.g., Jesus' first disciples embrace his proclamation of the kingdom by leaving their livelihood to follow him (1:16-20), whereas the religious leaders challenge his authority (2:1–3:6).

[5] Scriptural quotations are taken from the New American Bible. On these questions about Jesus' identity, see J. D. Kingsbury, *The Christology of Mark's Gospel* (Philadelphia: Fortress, 1983), 71-89.

that even though Peter's confession is formally correct (Jesus is the Messiah), Peter *and even the readers of the narrative* need to transcend this messianic confession which has not taken into account the necessity for the Messiah to be rejected, to suffer, to die, and to rise from the dead.[6] As Jesus makes his way to Jerusalem (8:31–10:52), therefore, he teaches his disciples that his messianic destiny is the way of the Son of Man who must suffer, die, and rise from the dead (8:31; 9:31; 10:33-34).[7]

Although Jesus clearly teaches his disciples that he must suffer and die, they do not comprehend why (8:32; 9:32) since they do not understand the mystery of the Son of Man who came not to be served but to serve and give his life as a ransom for many (10:45); nor can they fathom what Jesus means by rising from the dead (9:10).

When Jesus enters Jerusalem those who accompany him welcome him as the royal, Davidic Messiah, expecting the restoration of David's kingdom (11:9-10), even though Jesus has proclaimed the in-breaking kingdom of God rather than the kingdom of David. To counter these misdirected messianic expectations, Jesus challenges the scribal claim that the Messiah is the son of David (12:35-37), raising the question, if he is not David's son, whose son is he?[8] But the desire to identify Jesus as the Davidic Messiah persists, and this is how the religious authorities understand Jesus' claim. When Jesus stands before the Sanhedrin and is accused of threatening to destroy the temple and replace it with a temple not made by human beings (14:58), the high priest asks, "Are you the Messiah, the son of the Blessed One?" And Jesus responds, "I am" (14:62).[9] On the basis of his response and his claim that he will be enthroned at God's right hand as the vindicated Son of Man (14:62), Jesus is condemned,

---

[6] The narrator has already told his readers *the truth* that Jesus is the Messiah, the Son of God, but he has not yet told them *the whole truth*: the destiny of Jesus as the Son of Man to suffer, die, and rise from the dead. This is why even the readers of the narrative must transcend Peter's confession that Jesus is the Messiah. On this literary technique of withholding the whole truth, see M. Sternberg, *The Poetics of Biblical Narrative: Ideological Literature and the Drama of Reading* (Bloomington: Indiana University Press, 1987), 230-63.

[7] The background for Jesus' destiny as the Son of Man is Daniel 7. Just as the one like a son of man received "dominion, glory, and kingship" (Dan 7:14) after a period of intense persecution and suffering (Dan 7:25-27), so Jesus will be vindicated by God after his passion and death.

[8] On the basis of Ps. 110:1, Jesus argues that the Messiah cannot be David's son since David (the speaker of the Psalm) addresses the Messiah as his Lord.

[9] On the basis of the temple charge the high priest asks Jesus if he is the Messiah, suggesting that the high priest believes that the one who claims to build God's eschatological temple also claims to be the Messiah.

handed over to Pilate, crucified as a messianic pretender, "the King of the Jews" (15:26), and mocked as the Messiah, the King of Israel, who saved others but cannot save himself (15:31-32).

After Jesus dies the centurion, seeing *how* Jesus dies, proclaims, "Truly this man was the Son of God!" (15:39). From the point of view of the Markan narrator, this is the climactic confession of Jesus' identity since it echoes how God identified Jesus at the baptism and transfiguration (1:11; 9:7). The only human character within the narrative, then, to identify Jesus as God's son does so *after* Jesus has died and *before* there is any report of his resurrection.[10]

This Gospel which begins with a prologue that Moloney entitles, "The beginning," concludes with an epilogue (16:1-8) that he aptly names, "A new beginning,"[11] for instead of narrating an appearance of the Risen Lord, the Markan story challenges its readers to return to Galilee where they will see the crucified one who has been raised from the dead. Jesus, the Shepherd Messiah, the crucified Christ, has gone before them as he promised (16:7; see also 14:28).

The Plot of the Markan Story

The plot of Mark's story is a plot of conflict: conflict between the kingdom of God and the rule of Satan; conflict between Jesus and the religious leaders over the question of authority; conflict between Jesus and his disciples who refuse to accept that the Messiah must suffer and die.[12] Although the conflict between the rule of God and the rule of Satan is the conflict that underlies all conflicts – so that those who oppose Jesus unwittingly align themselves with Satan – it is through the conflicts between Jesus and the religious authorities on the one hand, and between Jesus and his disciples on the other, that the Markan narrator shows what it means to transcend messianic boundaries.

In the view of the religious authorities, Jesus must be put to death because he has usurped God's authority (ἐξουσία). Mark signals this conflict

---

[10] Demons identify Jesus as the Son of God (3:11; 5:7) because they are other-worldly beings. But no human character within the narrative identifies Jesus as the Son of God before Jesus dies.

[11] Moloney, *Mark*, 21.

[12] On the plot of Mark's Gospel, see J. D. Kingsbury, *Conflict in Mark: Jesus, Authorities, Disciples* (Minneapolis: Fortress, 1989).

of authority early in the narrative when he notes, "The people were as-tonished at his teaching, for he taught them as one having 'authority' (ἐξουσία) and not as the scribes" (1:22). Because he claims such ἐξουσία the Pharisees and Herodians plot to destroy him (3:6). When Jesus arrives in Jerusalem and takes possession of the temple, the chief priests, the scribes, and the elders ask him by what ἐξουσία he does these things (11:28). Since the religious leaders decline to answer Jesus' question about the origin of John's baptism, he refuses to justify the authority with which he acts. Instead he tells the parable of the wicked tenants (12:1-12) which functions as a story within the Gospel story and answers the question by means of an allegory. Jesus is the "beloved son" (12:6) whom the vineyard owner (God) has sent with his authority, and the religious leaders are those who killed the servants and will soon kill the beloved son (12:1-12). In the conflict stories that follow, Jesus shows his authoritative under-standing of God's will (12:13-17), God's power (12:18-27), God's law (12:28-34), and the Messiah's origin (12:35-37). Nevertheless, the religious leaders conspire to put him to death because they view him as a false claimant to messiahship who usurps God's ἐξουσία and makes himself the Messiah.

The conflict between Jesus and his disciples is of a different sort. Un-like the religious leaders, they believe Jesus is the Messiah, even though they do not understand what this means. But whereas Jesus presents him-self as the Son of Man who must be rejected, suffer, die, and rise from the dead, the disciples are concerned about rank and privilege (9:34; 10:35-41). They cannot comprehend why Jesus must suffer and die (9:32). They think of messiahship in terms of restoring David's kingdom (11:9-10).

Jesus was put to death as a messianic pretender, "the king of the Jews" (15:26), thereby calling into question his authority to act as the herald of the kingdom of God. In what sense then can he be called the Messiah? Given the apparent failure of the kingdom of God to come in power, in what sense did he complete his mission as God's Messiah? In response to these questions, the Markan Evangelist plots his story in a way that sub-verts and transcends any messianic category that views Jesus as the Da-vidic Messiah. Mark is not denying that Jesus was a royal figure, God's Messiah and Israel's Shepherd king. Nor is he denying that Jesus' ministry inaugurated a kingdom. But in every instance, he summons readers to transcend their messianic expectations. He insists that the Messiah must be defined in terms of Jesus rather than Jesus in terms of any messianic category. Therefore, he presents Jesus' messiahship in light of a scandalous death on the cross. Understood from this vantage point, the Messiah is the crucified Son of God, the one whose destiny is the destiny of the rejected Son of Man who will return as the glorious Son of Man to gather the elect (13:26-27). Understood from this perspective, the Messiah is the king of Israel who once fed God's scattered people in the wilderness (6:34-44) and now goes before his disciples to Galilee where he will gather his scattered flock (16:7).[13] Understood from this perspective, the Messiah is the Spirit-anointed Son of God (1:11) who trusts in God by refusing to come down from the cross and save himself (15:29-30). The crucified Messiah will return as the glorious Son of Man, and when he does, God's kingdom will come in power for all to see.

The Gospel of John: Where Does the Messiah Come From?

The Gospel of John begins with a prologue (1:1-18) in which the Evangelist provides the reader with privileged information about the origin and identity of Jesus. Before the narrative begins, then, the reader knows that Jesus is the incarnate Word of God (1:14). The reader also knows where Jesus comes from (πόθεν) as well as who sent him (ἀπο-στέλλω, πέμπω) into the world: he comes from God, his Father, who sent him into the world.[14] This information is crucial to John's understanding of Jesus' messiahship, and unless the characters within the narrative come to believe that Jesus is the one whom God sent they will not understand what it means to confess that he is the Messiah. Through the story he tells, therefore, the Fourth Evangelist summons readers to transcend their understanding of messiahship.

---

[13] Mark portrays Jesus as Israel's Shepherd king in the feeding of the 5000 when he writes, "When he disembarked and saw the vast crowd, his heart was moved with pity for them, for they were like sheep without a shepherd; and he began to teach them many things" (Mark 6:34). This description recalls Ezekiel 34 which portrays God as a shepherd seeking his scattered sheep (Ezek 34:11) and appointing one shepherd, his servant David, over them (Ezek 34:23). Mark's use of προάγω in 14:28 and 16:7 also portrays Jesus as a shepherd, "going before" his disciples.

[14] The Evangelist employs πόθεν several times in texts that deal with Jesus' origin (John 7:27, 28; 8:14; 9:29, 30; 19:9). The verbs ἀποστέλλω and πέμπω occur throughout the Gospel to indicate that God sent Jesus into the world. For ἀποστέλλω, see John 3:17, 34; 5:36, 38; 6:29, 57; 7:29; 8:42; 10:36; 11:42; 17:3, 8, 18, 21, 23, 25; 20:21. For πέμπω, see John 4:34; 5:23, 24, 30, 37; 6:38, 39, 44; 7:16, 18, 28, 33; 8:16, 18, 26, 29; 9:4; 12:44, 45, 49; 13:16, 20; 14:24, 26; 15:21; 16:5, 7; 20:21.

The Johannine Story

In the first part of the narrative (1:19–12:50), the Son whom God has sent into the world reveals his glory to the world through a series of signs, only to be rejected by the world (12:37). This part of the story consists of four movements: the witness of John and the appearance of Jesus (1:19-51); the period that begins at Cana with the revelation of Jesus' glory and concludes at Cana with a further revelation of Jesus' glory (2:1–4:54); the presence of Jesus at four Jewish feasts at which he transcends the meaning of these feasts (5:1–10:14); and the arrival of the hour when the Father glorifies Jesus (11:1–12:50).

The question of messiahship plays a central role in the first movement (1:19-51) with John the Baptist emphatically denying that he is the Messiah (1:20) and implicitly identifying Jesus as the Messiah by calling him the Lamb of God who takes away the sin of the world (1:29),[15] the one upon whom the Spirit descended and remained (1:32), the Son of God (1:34).[16] John acknowledges that he did not recognize who Jesus was when he first appeared, foreshadowing the theme of the Messiah's unknown origins (see 7:28), but he now recognizes that Jesus ranks ahead of him and existed before him (1:30). On the next day he identifies Jesus as the Lamb of God to two of his disciples (1:35-37). On the basis of John's witness, they follow Jesus. One of them, Andrew, tells his brother Peter they have found the Messiah (1:41),[17] thereby indicating that John identified Jesus as the Messiah when he called him the Lamb of God. On the next day, Jesus calls Philip, and he tells Nathaniel that Jesus is the one to whom the law and the prophets testify (1:46). When Jesus tells Nathaniel that he saw him under a fig tree before Nathaniel spoke to him, Nathaniel effusively confesses that Jesus is the Son of God, the King of Israel (1:49). Although these titles are formally correct, Jesus intimates that Nathaniel and the other disciples must transcend their messianic expectations if they are to understand who he is. They must believe in him, the Son of Man, as the point of communication between heaven and earth (1:51).[18]

---

[15] Although the meaning of "the Lamb of God" is disputed, the phrase suggests that Jesus' death is expiatory precisely because he is God's lamb.

[16] Some witnesses read "the chosen one of God," and a few "the chosen Son of God." There is strong textual support, however, for "the Son of God."

[17] In describing Jesus as the Messiah, Andrew uses Μεσσίας, a Greek transcription of the Hebrew, found only one other time in the New Testament, John 4:25.

[18] In 1:51, the Evangelist alludes to the account of Jacob's dream in Gen 28:10-15, in which Jacob sees a stairway "reaching to the heavens; and God's messengers were going

Having presented Jesus as the Messiah, God's Lamb who takes away the sin of the world, and as the Son of Man, in the second movement (2:1–4:54) the Evangelist describes a number of responses to Jesus who reveals his glory to the world. Although all of these responses contribute to the overall portrait of the Messiah the narrative presents, two are especially important.

In the first (3:22-35), John's disciples complain that Jesus is baptizing and that everyone is coming to him. In response, John reaffirms that he is not the Messiah (3:28-30). The Johannine narrator then provides a comment (3:31-36) which echoes important information from the prologue: the one whom John the Baptist has correctly identified as the Messiah is from above, the Son whom the Father sent into the world.

In the second episode (4:4-42), Jesus encounters a Samaritan woman who says of the Messiah, "when he comes, he will tell us *everything*" (4:25). When Jesus tells her *something* of her past life, she wonders if he might be the Messiah (4:29). The woman's understanding of the Messiah is too narrow to comprehend who Jesus is. The citizens of the Samaritan town, however, come closer to the mark when they exclaim, "we know that this is truly the savior of the world" (4:42).

In the third movement (5:1–10:14), the question of Jesus' messiahship plays a prominent role. After feeding the five thousand in the wilderness, Jesus perceives that the crowd has not understood the deeper significance of the sign he has performed: that he is the bread that has come down from heaven. Therefore he withdraws from the crowd lest it attempt to make him its messianic king (6:15). Jesus, of course, is the King of Israel, as Nathaniel confessed (1:49), and he will be crucified as the King of the Jews (19:19), but his kingdom is not of this world (18:36), and any notion of messiahship that contradicts this must be transcended.

When Jesus is in Jerusalem for the Feast of Tabernacles, some wonder if the religious leaders have accepted him as the Messiah. In an ironic statement, some affirm, "But we know where he is from (πόθεν). When the Messiah comes, no one will know where he is from (πόθεν)" (7:27). In response, Jesus ironically raises the question about his origin that underlies the narrative: "You know me and also know where I am from (πόθεν)?[19]

---

up and down on it" (Gen 28:12). Just as that stairway was the point of communication between heaven and earth, so the Son of Man will be the point of communication between heaven and earth.

[19] The New American Bible construes these words as a declarative sentence, but the context suggests that Jesus' statement is an ironic question.

Yet I did not come on my own, but the one who sent me, whom you do not know, is true" (7:28). The people are correct insofar as they affirm the hidden origin of the Messiah. Not even the Baptist recognized Jesus when he appeared (1:26), but they do not know that Jesus comes from God and was sent by God.

The question of Jesus' origin arises again when some in the crowd think that he is the Messiah (7:40-44). But others object that he is not qualified to be the Messiah since he is not of David's stock and does not come from Bethlehem. Because he is a Galilean, they think they know Jesus' origin. Unable to transcend their notions of Davidic messiahship, they do not believe that he is the Messiah, the Son whom the Father sent into world.

The third movement comes to a climax during the Feast of Dedication when, in an episode that echoes the trial scenes of the Synoptic Gospels, "the Jews" ask Jesus, "How long are you going to keep us in suspense? If you are the Messiah, tell us plainly" (10:24).[20] By identifying himself as the Good Shepherd who lays down his life for his sheep (10:11-18), Jesus has already revealed that he is Israel's Shepherd Messiah. But because they are not his sheep, they have not believed in him (10:25). By affirming his oneness with the Father (10:30), however, Jesus answers their question: he is the Messiah. This affirmation of oneness with the Father results in "the Jews" accusing Jesus of blasphemy by making himself God (10:33). Jesus, of course, has not claimed that he is God but that he is *one* with God because he is the one whom the Father "has consecrated (ἡγίασεν) and sent into the world" (10:36).[21] If "the Jews" were Jesus' sheep, they would transcend their messianic expectations and recognize that the Messiah is the one whom God consecrates and sends into the world.

In the fourth movement (11:1–12:50), Jesus raises Lazarus from the dead. In the midst of this narrative, Martha, the sister of Lazarus, affirms that she has always believed that Jesus is "the Messiah, the Son of God, the one who is coming into the world" (11:27), a response that Moloney shrewdly notes does not correspond to Jesus' question in 11:25-26, sug-

---

[20] As in the Synoptic trial scene, the major issue revolves around Jesus' messiahship (John 10:24; see Mark 14:61) which leads to an accusation of blasphemy (John 10:33; see Mark 14:64) because Jesus affirms that he is the Son of God (John 10:33, 36; see Mark 14:62). The words, "the Jews," have been placed in quotation marks to indicate that in the Fourth Gospel "the Jews" designates the opponents of the Johannine community, those who do not believe that Jesus comes from God.

[21] See also Peter's confession of Jesus as ὁ ἅγιος τοῦ θεοῦ in 6:69.

gesting that even though Martha's confession is formally correct, she has not comprehended that Jesus has power over death *now* as well as on the last day when the dead will be raised.[22] Even Martha must transcend her messianic understanding of Jesus.

The raising of Lazarus sets in motion the Sanhedrin's plan to put Jesus to death (11:45-53). When Jesus learns that the Gentiles wish to see him, he knows that the hour has come for his glorification (12:20-23). Because the hour is at hand, he tells "the Jews" that when he is "lifted up from the earth" he will draw everyone to himself (12:32). Aware that he is speaking of his death, the crowd objects to his messiahship. If he is the Messiah, how can he speak of himself – the Son of Man – as being put to death since the law says that "the Messiah remains forever" (12:34).[23] As has happened throughout the first part of the Gospel, the characters of the narrative have measured Jesus against their expectations for the Messiah rather than their expectations for the Messiah against the revelation that Jesus brings from the Father.

In the Book of Glory, the second half of the story (13:1–20:31), the Father glorifies Jesus, and Jesus glorifies the Father by being lifted up on the cross. Although there are fewer references to messiahship in this part of the Gospel, the reader already knows that Jesus is the Son, the one whom the Father has sent into the world. This part of the narrative has three movements: Jesus' farewell discourses (13:1–17:26); the Passion Narrative (18:1–19:42); and the Resurrection narratives (20:1–21:25).[24]

In the first movement (13:1–17:26), Jesus says farewell to his disciples and explains that his death will be his return to the Father from whom he came (16:28). In doing so, Jesus provides his disciples with privileged information for understanding his identity and the significance of his imminent death. If the disciples believe that he comes from the Father, then they will know who he is. If they believe that his death is a return to the Father, then they will understand that his death is a moment of glorifica-

---

[22] Moloney, *John*, 327-28; "Can Everyone be Wrong? A Reading of John 11.1–12.8," *NTS* 49 (2003): 505-27.

[23] The scriptural text intended here is problematic. If the crowd has in view LXX Ps 88:37, that David's line will remain forever, then it may be assuming that the Messiah will not die. See F. J. Moloney, *The Johannine Son of Man* (2d ed.; BSR14; Rome: LAS, 1978), 182-84.

[24] Chapter 21 is the end of the canonical text, but most commentators assume that it was added by a later redactor and treat it as an appendix that functions as a further ending.

tion rather than humiliation and defeat. Although the question of messiahship is never raised in the farewell discourse, what Jesus says about
himself contributes to the way in which the Evangelist defines Jesus' messiahship.

In the second movement (18:1–19:42), Jesus is brought to Pilate as a
messianic pretender, the King of the Jews. The Johannine narrator, however, does not describe Jesus' crucifixion as a moment of humiliation or
abandonment since Jesus has already defined his death in terms of glorification and return to the Father. Rather, the Evangelist presents Jesus as
reigning from the cross. The Messiah's death is his glorification, and the
inscription of the charge against him – written in Hebrew, Latin, and
Greek – proclaims his kingship to the entire world.

The third movement (20:1–21:25) provides Jesus' disciples with an opportunity to come to faith. For, even though they professed their faith in
him before he died (16:30), they have not yet experienced his resurrection.
Accordingly, the Risen Lord appears to them to bring them to the fullness
of faith.

The Meaning of the Johannine Story

At the end of the story, the Johannine narrator explains why he has
written: "that you may believe that Jesus is the Messiah, the Son of God,
and through this belief you may have life in his name" (20:31). In retrospect, it becomes apparent that the narrator has told his story so that believers will grow in faith that Jesus is the Messiah, the Son of God. This
faith, however, requires that believers must transcend their messianic
categories. Jesus is not the Davidic messiah, nor is he a royal figure whose
kingdom belongs to this world. He is the Messiah because he is the incarnate Word of God. He is the Messiah because he came from God and has
returned to the Father who sent him into the world. He is the Messiah because he takes away the sin of the world. He is the Messiah because he is
the bread that has come down from heaven, the resurrection and the life.
Given the unique nature of his messiahship, those who confess him as
Messiah must transcend their understanding of what it means to be the
Messiah.

Transcending Boundaries: Convergence and Divergence

Although Mark and John plot their stories differently, there are a number of points at which their narratives converge. The final part of this essay highlights these points of convergence as well as those ways in which these narratives diverge from each other in their presentation of Jesus as the Messiah.

The Need to Transcend Messianic Expectations

Both Evangelists affirm that Jesus is the Messiah. This is apparent from the opening words of Mark's Gospel ("The beginning of the gospel of *Jesus Christ* the Son of God ...", 1:1) and the closing words of John's Gospel ("But these are written that you may believe that *Jesus is the Messiah, the Son of God* ...", 20:31).[25] In telling their stories, however, each Evangelist subverts messianic expectations and challenges those who hear or read the story to transcend their understanding of messiahship if they wish to comprehend the significance of Jesus. For example, Mark plots his narrative to show that even though Peter's confession is formally correct ("You are the Messiah," 8:29), Peter *and the readers of this Gospel* must go beyond this confession and embrace Jesus' teaching that "the Son of man must suffer greatly and be rejected by the elders, the chief priests, and the scribes, and be killed, and rise after three days" (Mark 8:31; see also 9:31; 10:33-34). The Johannine narrative makes a similar point when, early in the story, Andrew identifies Jesus as the Messiah (John 1:41) and Nathaniel calls him the Son of God, the King of Israel (John 1:49). Although these titles are formally correct, the characters in the narrative *and the readers of the Gospel* must go beyond their understanding of these titles and believe in Jesus as the Son of Man who is the point of communication between heaven and earth (John 1:51) if they are to understand the significance of his messiahship. Even Martha, who confesses that Jesus is "the Messiah, the Son of God, the one who is coming into the world" (John 11:26), must transcend her confession and see in Jesus the one who is the resurrection and the life (John 11:25) *now* as well as on the last day, if she is to understand what it means to call Jesus the Messiah.

---

[25] The opening of Mark's Gospel does not employ Χριστός in an explicitly titular sense; the titular uses of Χριστός in 8:29; 14:61; 15:32 indicate that Mark has not reduced Χριστός to a part of Jesus' name.

The Need to Transcend Davidic Expectations

Unlike the Gospels of Matthew and Luke, which highlight Jesus' Davidic lineage (Matt 1:1; Luke 1:32), Mark and John do not portray Jesus as a royal descendant of David, born in Bethlehem. It is true that, in the Markan narrative, Bartimaeus addresses Jesus as the Son of David (Mark 10:47, 48) and that the Markan narrator presents Bartimaeus as a model of faith in contrast to Jesus' disciples who cannot "see" (that is, understand) his messianic destiny (Mark 10:52).[26] Moreover, when Jesus enters Jerusalem many acclaim him as the one who will restore David's kingdom, suggesting that he is the Davidic Messiah. But Jesus' criticism of the scribal claim that "the Messiah is the son of David" (Mark 12:35) indicates that the category of Davidic messiahship must be transcended since even David calls the Messiah his Lord. The sonship of the Messiah, therefore, must be rooted elsewhere (Mark 12:37). As for the Fourth Evangelist, he is not at all disturbed by objections that Jesus is not of David's stock and was not born in Bethlehem (John 7:40-44) since he views the Messiah's origin in an entirely new light. It is not the one who comes from Bethlehem who is the Messiah but the one who comes from God.

The Need to Transcend Royal Expectations

Both Evangelists agree that Jesus is a royal figure and that it is formally correct to identify him as the King of the Jews, the King of Israel. But they are also aware that the language of kingship can be misunderstood, even if the king is the ideal and righteous leader who obeys God's law, as portrayed in the *Psalms of Solomon*.[27] Thus when Jesus senses that the crowd would make him king, he withdraws (John 6:15), and when Pilate asks Jesus if he is a king, his answer is evasive since Pilate and Jesus understand kingship differently (Mark 15:2; John 18:34). Both Gospels argue that Jesus' messianic kingship can only be understood in light of the cross.

---

[26] Mark employs two stories of blind men (8:14-26 and 10:46-52) to bracket a section in which he portrays the growing incomprehension of the disciples concerning Jesus' messianic destiny (8:26-10:45), thereby drawing a contrast between the blind who see because Jesus has opened their eyes and the seeing disciples who are blind because they cannot understand Jesus' destiny as the Son of Man.

[27] See *Psalms of Solomon*, 17 and 18, which portray the Messiah as a thoroughly righteous king who drives the wicked from Jerusalem. This Messiah king is an example of a national messiah who effects Israel's national restoration.

Therefore, although they report the political charge brought against Jesus by the characters of the narrative – that Jesus is a messianic pretender, the King of the Jews – they interpret it in a way that the characters within the narrative do not.

For Mark and John, Jesus is Israel's king who reigns from the cross because his death is redemptive (Mark 10:45; John 12:32). However, whereas Mark emphasizes the abandonment that Jesus experienced at death (Mark 15:34) and the paradoxical nature of his kingship, John focuses on Jesus' crucifixion as the moment when the Father glorifies his royal Son because the Son has completed the work the Father sent him to do (John 19:30; see 4:34). In this way, John transcends Mark's presentation of Jesus' kingship, suggesting that when the Son of Man is lifted up he already reigns from the cross.

The Need to Transcend Israel's Shepherd King

The royal Messiah is Israel's Shepherd King, the one who cares for God's people. It is not surprising then that Mark and John develop this messianic motif, first in their accounts of Jesus feeding the crowd in the wilderness and then in relationship to Jesus' death and resurrection. Mark portrays Jesus as a shepherd caring for the people because "his heart was moved with pity for them, for they were like sheep without a shepherd" (Mark 6:34). Therefore, Jesus first feeds God's people by teaching them, presumably about the kingdom of God (Mark 6:34). In the Johannine narrative, Jesus feeds the crowd (John 6:1-15) and *then* explains the significance of the sign he has performed. He is the bread that comes down from heaven for the life of the world (John 6:26-59).

Both Evangelists relate the theme of Jesus the Shepherd Messiah to Jesus' death. In the Markan Gospel, Jesus tells his disciples that the Shepherd will be struck down, but once he has been raised he will go before (προάγω) them to Galilee. At the empty tomb the young man instructs the women to tell Jesus' disciples that the crucified one has been raised and goes before (προάγω) them to Galilee (Mark 16:7). The Johannine Gospel develops the shepherd motif further: Jesus the Good Shepherd freely lays down his life for the sheep (John 10:11, 15, 17, 18) and dies, not only for Israel, but for all the scattered children of God (John 11:52). In the Gospel appendix, the Risen Shepherd instructs Peter to feed his lambs and feed his sheep (John 21:15-19).

The Need to Transcend Appearances

Both Gospels agree that there is something hidden about Jesus' identity that is not apparent until after his death and resurrection; in some sense Jesus is a hidden Messiah. For example, in the Gospel of Mark, people think that Jesus is John the Baptist or Elijah returned to life, or that he is a prophet like the prophets of old (Mark 6:14-16). Moreover, even though Peter confesses that Jesus is the Messiah (Mark 8:27-30), the disciples cannot comprehend why the Messiah must suffer and rise from the dead (Mark 9:31-31). In the Fourth Gospel, John the Baptist acknowledges that he did not recognize the Messiah when he appeared (John 1:33), showing that there is an ironic sense in which the Jerusalemites are correct, though they do not understand the whole truth when they say, "When the Messiah comes, no one will know where he is from" (John 7:27).

It is only the death and resurrection that dispels the secrecy surrounding Jesus' messiahship. In the Markan narrative, therefore, the centurion correctly confesses that the one crucified as a messianic pretender was truly the Son of God (Mark 15:39). If the disciples go to Galilee, they will see that the risen one is the crucified Messiah, the one who will return as the vindicated Son of Man. In the Gospel of John, the appearances of the Risen Lord provide his disciples with an opportunity to confess that he truly came from the Father, that his death was the moment of his glorification when he laid down his life for the sheep, and that he is returning to his Father to send the Paraclete and prepare a place for them.

The Need to Transcend Time

In different ways, both Evangelists agree that one must transcend the present in order to transcend messianic boundaries. In the Johannine narrative, for example, one cannot understand who the Messiah is apart from the Prologue that identifies Jesus as the incarnate Word of God, the Word which existed with God in the beginning. If the characters within the narrative do not know where the Messiah comes from, it is because they do not believe that he is one with God, and comes from God, who sent him into the world. For John, then, the question of messiahship is intimately connected with the question of origins. The essential question is where does Jesus come from (πόθεν)? Faith in Jesus as the Messiah must transcend the present and believe that he is the incarnate Word who comes from God to reveal the Father to the world.

In contrast to the Fourth Gospel, the Markan narrative challenges readers to transcend the present and look to the future when the crucified one will return as the glorious Son of Man. Then, when the Son of Man returns in his Father's glory (Mark 8:38) to gather the elect (Mark 13:27), all will see that Jesus, the Son of Man, is the enthroned Messiah, the Son of the Blessed One (Mark 14:62).

The Continuing Need to Transcend Messianic Expectations

Believers must not deceive themselves by supposing they can transcend messianic boundaries once and for all, even when they understand Jesus' messiahship in terms of pre-existence, death, resurrection, and parousia. Since the Messiah has not returned, and since the final resurrection of the dead has not occurred, the process of transcending messianic boundaries is ongoing. Only when the Son of Man returns (Mark 13:26) and the dead hear the voice of the Son of God (John 5:25) will believers know what it means to confess that Jesus is the Messiah. In the meantime, they must transcend boundaries, as does the one to whom this essay is dedicated.

12. PAUL AND MARK BEFORE THE CROSS: COMMON ECHOES OF THE DAY OF ATONEMENT RITUAL

Brendan BYRNE

Towards the close of his recent full-scale commentary on Mark's Gospel Francis Moloney comments: "There is something profoundly Pauline in what Mark is trying to do as he takes away all initiative from human beings and places it with God."[1] That comment is made in connection with the events at the empty tomb (16:1-8) and specifically the women's sharing in the fear and flight of the male disciples (v. 8). In this present study, contributed in honor of one who has been a close friend, colleague and immense source of support for over thirty years, I should like to extend that description "profoundly Pauline" to an earlier moment in the Markan narrative: the climactic description of Jesus' death upon the cross (15:37-39).

The congruence between the theologies of Mark and Paul has, of course, long been a matter of note.[2] What I propose to do in this paper is to bring together Mark's description of Jesus' death (15:37-39) and Paul's allusion to God's putting forth Christ as ἱλαστήριον in Rom 3:25 against the background of the two Pentateuchal texts (Exodus 25–26 and Leviticus 16) where the furnishing of the Most Holy Place ("Holy of Holies")

---

[1] F. J. Moloney, *The Gospel of Mark: A Commentary* (Peabody: Hendrickson, 2002), 351.

[2] And of controversy: see most recently, J. Marcus, "Mark - Interpreter of Paul," *NTS* 46 (2000): 473-87, who, particularly in relation to Christ's death, challenges the widely influential view of M. Werner (*Der Einfluss paulinischer Theologie im Markusevangelium: eine Studie zur neutestamentlichen Theologie* (BZNW 1; Giessen: Töpelmann, 1923) playing down any Pauline influence upon Mark. Moloney notes, without further comment other than indicating references, that "Parallels are often drawn between the Pauline and Markan presentation of the cross" (*Mark*, 330-31 n. 285).

and the Day of Atonement ritual are in view. That the Pauline passage makes allusion to the latter ritual is widely, though by no means universally, agreed. My thesis is that the curious order of events as told by Mark in describing Jesus' death and its aftermath – specifically the Evangelist's telling of the rending of the Temple curtain (v. 38) *between* the description of Jesus' expiry (v. 37) and the response of the centurion (v. 38) – is best accounted for in the light of the influence of a similar tradition. In short, reading Mark 15:37-39 in the light of the Pentateuchal passages and the Pauline allusion stirs up rich intertextual resonances that greatly illuminate what the Evangelist is attempting to convey by interposing the note about the rending of the Temple curtain at precisely this point. To be more specific, I shall argue that Mark intends the reader to understand the rending of the Temple as a signal that the shedding of Jesus' blood in death represents the divine enactment of a climactic and definitive Day of Atonement, expiating the sins not simply of Israel but of the entire world – or at least of all who, in the steps of the Roman centurion, view what took place on Calvary with the eyes of faith. Acknowledging the crucified One to be in truth God's Son brings subsequent believers under the scope of a divine act that at one stroke has rendered void and obsolete the Temple ritual and made available on a universal scale, prefigured in the person of the Gentile centurion, its expiatory function. In this way, to my mind, the Markan portrayal of Jesus' death offers a narrative presentation of a central Pauline tenet: the justification of the ungodly through faith in God's action in Christ.

Mark 15:37-39

Let us turn our attention to Mark's description of Jesus' death and its immediate aftermath, keeping an eye upon the other two Synoptic accounts (Matt 27:50-54; Luke 23:44-47). Following the description of the mockery of Jesus upon the cross, all three Evangelists approach the moment of Jesus' expiry with the notice about darkness coming upon the land from the sixth to the ninth hour (Mark 15:33; Matt 27:45; Luke 23:44). Mark, (also Matthew [27:46]), describes how at the ninth hour Jesus uttered a cry of dereliction using the opening words of Psalm 22 (v. 34). Then, following the curious interlude about waiting for Elijah (vv. 35-37), comes the actual moment of death:

Then Jesus gave a loud cry and breathed his last (ἐξέπνευσεν).

And the curtain of the temple was torn in two, from top to bottom (καὶ τὸ καταπέτασμα τοῦ ναοῦ ἐσχίσθη εἰς δύο ἀπ᾽ ἄνωθεν ἕως κάτω).

Now when the centurion, who stood facing him, (ὁ παρεστηκὼς ἐξ ἐναντίας αὐτοῦ) saw that in this way he breathed his last (ὅτι οὕτως ἐξέπνευσεν εἶπεν), he said, "Truly this man was God's Son!" (ἀληθῶς οὗτος ὁ ἄνθρωπος υἱὸς θεοῦ ἦν) (15:37-39).

The peculiarity of this sequence in Mark – notably the interposition of the indication about the rending of the Temple curtain (v. 38) between the description of Jesus' death and what would appear to be the centurion's reaction to the mode (cf. οὕτως) of the death – is striking. The earliest known reader of Mark, namely Matthew, found at least two things odd. He clearly felt constrained to "improve" the "wait for Elijah" episode by dividing the two reactions to Jesus' cry between one bystander who runs to get a sponge and reed, and another who says, "Wait, ..." (27:47-48); he postpones the indication of the curtain's tearing until after the centurion's reaction and then makes it the first of a series of apocalyptic events (earth-quake; splitting of rocks; opening of tombs and appearances of the dead) that seem to presage the resurrection (27:51-53). Luke, for reasons that are clear from the way he has handled Elijah earlier in his narrative (1:17; 4:25-26; 9:8, 19, 30, 33), omits the Elijah reference entirely and, in respect of the tearing of the curtain goes in the opposite direction to Matthew, placing it before the description of Jesus' death and his single loud cry (23:45-46). Both Matthew and Luke, then, seem to have found the sequence of events in Mark anomalous and sought each in his own way to construct a better sense.

Mark, I suspect, would have been in no slight measure irritated by both attempts to improve on his narrative. The sequence, as he tells it, is firmly clamped together by the fact that it is the *manner* of Jesus' death that prompts the centurion's response, the phrase οὕτως ἐξέπνευσεν in v. 39 catching up the ἐξέπνευσεν of v. 37. But what is the narrative attempting to convey to the reader by the interposed information concerning the Temple curtain?

Some have argued that Mark interposes the detail about the rending of the curtain because it is principally the sight of this phenomenon that evokes the response of the centurion in v. 39. That is, they find a genu-inely causal link between the events told across vv. 38-39.[3] Such an inter-

---

[3] See especially, H. M. Jackson, "The Death of Jesus in Mark and the Miracle from

pretation, involving a seeing on the part of the centurion that is thoroughly physical, requires that the curtain he sees be the outer curtain of the Temple, the one giving entrance from the outer court to the Holy Place, not the inner curtain dividing off the innermost recess of the Holy Place, namely the Most Holy Place.[4] But it is difficult to see how what the centurion "saw" in Jesus' manner of dying ("seeing that in this way he breathed his last" [v. 39c]) could embrace so remote a circumstance as the rending of the curtain in the Temple some considerable distance away. The suggestion is rendered more difficult still by the notice that the centurion stood facing Jesus.[5] He can hardly be "seeing" both Jesus' expiration *and* a dramatic event occurring in the Temple at the same time.[6] Such an approach ties everything down far too physically. We do not have a narrative that purports to be realistic in the sense of claiming that anyone on Golgotha was aware of what was happening in the Temple. The centurion responds to the manner of Jesus' death as it took place immediately before him – notably to the fact that, in a manner totally unprecedented in a death by crucifixion, a loud cry preceded it.[7] There is something awe-inspiringly different about *this* death by crucifixion.

The interposed information concerning the Temple curtain (v. 38) is, then, provided not to *explain* why the centurion reacted as he did but, as I shall argue, *to pave the way* for it. It is information for the reader that Mark introduces at this point in order to bestow upon the centurion's confession the full theological and symbolic freight the Evangelist wishes it to bear. And in this connection, I maintain, it is the rending of the inner rather than the outer curtain that is far more appropriately in view.[8] For a

the Cross," *NTS* 33 (1987): 16-37; S. Motyer, "The Rending of the Veil: a Markan Pentecost?" *NTS* 33 (1987): 155-57; R. H. Gundry, *Mark: A Commentary on His Apology for the Cross* (Grand Rapids: Eerdmans, 1993), 950-51.

[4] For a discussion of the evidence concerning the curtains in the Herodian Temple, see R. E. Brown, *The Death of the Messiah: From Gethsemane to the Grave: A Commentary on the Passion Narratives in the Four Gospels* (2 vols.; ABRL; New York: Doubleday, 1994), 2:1109-13. Brown's own ultimate view is that, as far as the Markan narrative is concerned, it is neither possible nor valuable to determine which curtain is in view.

[5] The possessive pronoun in the phrase ἐξ ἐναντίας αὐτοῦ could refer to the Temple. However, the immediately following phrase referring once more to Jesus' expiry ties the reference much more naturally to Jesus himself.

[6] Cf. C. C. Black, "Christ Crucified in Paul and Mark: Reflections on an Intracanonical Conversation," in E. H. Lovering and J. L. Sumney (eds.), *Theology and Ethics in Paul and His Interpreters: Essays in Honor of Victor Paul Furnish* (Nashville: Abingdon, 1996), 184-207, see 197-98 n. 48.

[7] Moloney, *Mark*, 330.

[8] Cf. C. Schneider: "From all accounts the outer curtain has no true cultic significance

specific *theological* purpose the narrative is informing the reader that in the instant between Jesus' expiry and the centurion's reaction, the curtain screening off the Most Holy Place was torn.

In 1989 Timothy J. Geddert could summarize no less than thirty-five different interpretations of Mark 15:38 in the scholarly literature.[9] Clifton Black has since added another,[10] and here am I proposing to add one more. Needless to say, I cannot here review and refute all rival interpretations. I shall simply propose my own by way of positive exposition. My procedure, as already indicated, will be to return to Mark's description of Jesus' death, following consideration of two other biblical *loci* that in my view shed crucial light upon it: first, the Greek (LXX) description of the construction of the Tabernacle of Meeting in Exodus 25–26 and the prescriptions concerning the High Priest's functions on the Day of Atonement in Leviticus 16; secondly, Paul's allusion to this ritual in Rom 3:21-26. In this way I hope to draw out the full range of symbolism I believe to be operative in the Markan account, specifically in the notice concerning the Temple curtain.

Exodus 25–26 and Leviticus 16

Exodus 25 follows upon the people's acceptance of the covenant ordinances and Moses' sprinkling upon them the "blood of the covenant" (24:7-8). It prescribes the making of the Tent of Meeting and its furnishing. Vv. 10-16 describe the manufacture of the ark of the covenant, vv. 17-22 the making, out of pure gold, of the ἱλαστήριον ἐπίθεμα which is over it as a cover. The culminating statement in v. 22 is particularly noteworthy: "There I will meet with you, and from above the ἱλαστήριον, from between the two cherubim that are on the ark of the covenant, I will deliver to you all my commands for the Israelites."[11]

---

at all. It simply replaces the doors when they are opened by day" ("καταπέτασμα," *TDNT* 3:628-30, see 629); cf. also Moloney, *Mark*, 329.

[9] T. J. Geddert, *Watchwords: Mark 13 in Markan Eschatology* (JSNTSup 26; Sheffield: JSOT Press, 1989), 141-43.

[10] "Christ Crucified in Paul and Mark" (n. 6 above). See further, H. L. Chronis, "The Torn Veil: Cultus and Christology in Mark 15:37-39," *JBL* 101 (1982): 97-114; Motyer, "Rending of the Veil," 155-57; H. W. Jackson, "The Death of Jesus in Mark and the Miracle from the Cross," *NTS* 33 (1987): 16-37; also the most thorough discussion of R. H. Gundry in his commentary *Mark: A Commentary on His Apology for the Cross* (Grand Rapids: Eerdmans, 1993), 949-51, 972-75.

[11] The difficulty in finding an accurate single-word translation of ἱλαστήριον

The commands for the furnishing of the Tabernacle continue in the following chapter (26) with the prescription concerning the curtain, καταπέτασμα, in vv. 31-35:

You shall make a curtain of blue, purple, and crimson yarns, and of fine twisted linen; … You shall hang the curtain under the clasps, and bring the ark of the covenant in there, within the curtain; and the curtain shall separate for you the holy place from the most holy place. You shall put the ἱλαστήριον on the ark of the covenant in the most holy place.

The curtain then serves to screen "the most holy place" ("holy of holies"), where the ark and the ἱλαστήριον are, from the "holy place." The LXX in fact has a somewhat variant reading in v. 34: where the Hebrew has "you shall put the ἱλαστήριον on the ark of the covenant in the most holy place," the LXX reads "You shall *cover* (or "screen") with the curtain (κατακαλύψεις τῷ καταπετάσματι) the ark of the covenant in the most holy place." Thus the LXX draws particular attention to the "screening" function of the curtain in regard to the most holy place.

Leviticus 16 describes the ritual for the Day of Atonement. Following instructions about Aaron's dress and the scapegoat offering (vv. 4-10), vv. 11-16 prescribe the rituals that he is to perform *inside* the curtain, making atonement for himself and his house and for the sanctuary:

Aaron shall present the bull as a sin offering (περὶ τῆς ἁμαρτίας) for himself, and shall make atonement for himself and for his house; he shall slaughter the bull as a sin offering (περὶ τῆς ἁμαρτίας) for himself.

He shall take a censer full of coals of fire from the altar before the LORD, and two handfuls of crushed sweet incense, and he shall bring it inside the curtain and put the incense on the fire before the LORD, that the cloud of the incense may cover the ἱλαστήριον that is upon the covenant, or he will die.

He shall take some of the blood of the bull, and sprinkle it with his finger on the front of the ἱλαστήριον, and before the ἱλαστήριον he shall sprinkle the blood with his finger seven times.

He shall slaughter the goat of the sin offering that is for the people (τὸν χίμαρον τὸν περὶ τῆς ἁμαρτίας τὸν περὶ τοῦ λαου) and bring its blood inside the curtain (ἐσώτερον τοῦ καταπετάσματος), and do with its blood as he did with the blood of the bull, sprinkling it upon the ἱλαστήριον and before the ἱλαστήριον.

("expiatory [cover]"; "mercy seat") leads me, for the purposes of this study, to simply retain the Greek word in all references.

Thus he shall make atonement for the sanctuary, because of the uncleannesses of the people of Israel, and because of their transgressions, all their sins;
and so he shall do for the tent of meeting, which remains with them in the midst
of their uncleannesses (Lev 16:11-16).

The sequence concludes with a universalizing summary relating the ritual not simply to the purification of the sanctuary but to the sinfulness of
the people as a whole: "... to make atonement for the people of Israel
once in the year for all their sins" (v. 34).

What is prescribed in v. 15 is particularly interesting. Here, within the
scope of one comparatively short sentence, in connection with the Day of
Atonement, we have references (1) to the high priest's ("Aaron") entering
behind the curtain, (2) to his sprinkling blood upon the ἱλαστήριον, the
blood of a bull which (3) is "for a sin-offering," translated in Greek as
περὶ τῆς ἁμαρτίας. This Greek phrase regularly occurs in the LXX to
render a comment explaining the purpose or effect of rituals (slaughter of
sacrificial animals and sprinkling of their blood) prescribed for the expiation of sin and purification from the cultic impurity it has brought about.
Sometimes the phrase denotes the precise sacrifice known as a "sin-
offering" (e.g., Lev 9:2; 14:31; Ps (LXX) 39:7).[12] It appears in a metaphorical sense in the Fourth Servant Song (Isa 53:10), immediately before the
twofold reference to the Servant's making righteous (v. 11) or bearing (v.
12) the sins of "many" (cf. Mark 10:45; 14:24). Most significantly for our
purposes, Paul employs the phrase with reference to the soteriological
function of the death of Christ in Rom 8:3-4:

For what the law could not do, in that it was weak because of the flesh, God
(has done): sending his Son in the likeness of flesh dominated by sin and as a sin-
offering (περὶ τῆς ἁμαρτίας), he condemned sin in the flesh, in order that the
righteous requirement of the law might be fulfilled in us, who walk now, not according to the flesh, but according to the Spirit.

In the face of the impotence of the law to deal with sin and so avert
the "condemnation" that justly hangs over human beings (cf. 8:1), Paul
points to the Christ-event as involving a condemnation of sin itself (8:3)
and the divine enablement, through the Spirit, of a righteous pattern of
living that opens up the way to eternal life (8:4-11). All this was achieved
through a profound entrance on the part of the Son into the sinful human

---

[12] See G. A. Anderson, "Sacrifice and Sacrificial Offerings (OT)," *ABD* 5:879-80.

condition, an entrance which culminated in his death functioning as a "sin-offering" (περὶ τῆς ἀμαρτίας).[13] This Pauline soteriological statement in Romans 8 builds upon and develops the more sustained presentation of Christ's death in sacrificial imagery appearing earlier in the letter, in 3:24-25. To this let us now turn.

Rom 3:24-25

Here we are, of course, plunging headlong into one of the most theologically dense and most controversial passages of Romans. Within the scope of this present paper I have to assume a number of interpretative positions justified more fully elsewhere.[14] It is necessary, though, to set the more precisely soteriological statements within the wider context of the passage as a whole:

But now, apart from law, the righteousness of God stands revealed, although the law and the prophets bear witness to it, the righteousness of God through faith in Jesus Christ for all who believe. For there is no distinction – for all have sinned and lack the glory of God. They are being justified as a gift by his grace through the redemption that has come about in Christ Jesus. God put him forward as a means of expiation (ὃν προέθετο ὁ θεὸς ἱλαστήριον), (operative) through faith, in (the shedding of) his blood (διὰ [τῆς] πίστεως ἐν τῷ αὐτοῦ αἵματι). This was to display God's righteousness because of the passing over of sins formerly committed in the (time of) God's patience; it was (also) to display God's righteousness at the present time: that God himself is righteous and justifies the one who has faith in Jesus (Rom 3:21-26).

Paul is here at a cardinal point of his exposition of the Gospel in Romans.[15] From the start (1:16-17) he has maintained that the salvific summons of the Gospel is inclusive rather than exclusive in regard to the nations of the world (Gentiles). It is central to this inclusive vision that human beings appropriate eschatological justification through faith in God's gracious action in Christ rather than through doing the "works of the (Jewish) law," through which, Paul has just maintained, "shall no human being be justified before (God)" (3:20). Since this negative view of the law's working clearly appears to put in question God's faithfulness to Is-

---

[13] See further, B. Byrne, *Romans* (SP 6; Collegeville: Liturgical Press, 1996), 243.
[14] See Byrne, *Romans*, 122-35.
[15] R. B. Hays, "Psalm 143 and the Logic of Romans 3," *JBL* 99 (1980): 107-15.

rael, to whom the Torah was given as a path to life, Paul has to defend the proposition that such a view does not threaten God's righteousness. The negative implication of the Gospel, namely that "all" – Jews as well as Gentiles – "have sinned" (3:23a; 5:12d; cf. 1:18–3:20 as a whole), may appear to suggest that God has failed Israel – an impious suggestion which Paul allows to surface in 3:1-8. The response comes in 3:21, where, moving away from the consideration of universal human failure, Paul triumphantly points to the Christ-event as the eschatological demonstration of God's righteousness on a universal scale. In Christ, God has shown righteousness – saving faithfulness – not just for Israel, but, as Creator, for the entire world. Moreover, at one and the same time, in the face of universal human unrighteousness, God communicates to human beings, through the vehicle of faith in the Christ event, participation in the divine righteousness.[16] Through faith (in contrast with "works of the law") they are "made righteous" ("justified") and so set upon the path to salvation (Romans 5–8).

This, to my mind, is the major assertion of the long and complex sequence cited above. The more specifically soteriological statements appearing in vv. 24-25a, despite the attention they have attracted in the Christian tradition, are not there for their own sake as a principal point of instruction. They have a subsidiary function, serving to explain how the death of Christ operated as the instrument of the divine righteousness to bring about the effects (demonstration of God's righteousness and justification of believers) that are the principal assertion.

Along with many other interpreters, I would argue that the reference to Christ in v. 25 as ἱλαστήριον put forward by God shows that Paul, most likely reflecting an earlier tradition (with which he trusts the Roman community, not founded by him, to be familiar), is alluding to the Day of Atonement ritual.[17] In the Christ-event God was doing, on a universal scale and in a climactic and final way, what God did each year for Israel: graciously and unilaterally effecting renewal of the covenant relationship by wiping away the yearly accumulation of sins and offences on the part of the people. The focal point of this divine expiation was, as we have seen, the once-yearly ritual when the high priest entered the Holy of Ho-

---

[16] For this "bi-polar" sense of "God's righteousness" in Paul, see Byrne, *Romans*, 60, 123-24; also B. Byrne, "Interpreting Romans Theologically in a Post-'New Perspective' Perspective," *HTR* 94 (2001): 227-41, esp. 233-38.

[17] For thorough discussion and further literature, see D. Moo, *The Epistle to the Romans* (NICNT; Grand Rapids; Cambridge (UK): Eerdmans, 1996), 231-36.

lies to *enact* through the sprinkling of the blood of the slain goat upon the ἱλαστήριον the divine expiation and covenant renewal (Lev 16:34). It is important to appreciate that at this moment the high priest did not act as representative of the people before God; he acted on behalf of God, *enacting* in a tangible, physical way the invisible cleansing that was being unilaterally and graciously bestowed upon the people.

Beyond the term ἱλαστήριον, further support for the view that an allusion to the Day of Atonement ritual is operative at this point in Romans is the verb Paul uses in respect to the divine action: "God put him forward" (ὃν προέθετο ὁ θεός). Though the verb is open to alternative meanings, most suitable here is the sense "put forward publicly," "… out in the open."[18] Paul presumably speaks of the divine action in this way because he wants to draw a contrast between *this* operation of the Day of Atonement ritual and all others that had gone before. In them the action took place in the innermost recesses of the Temple, hidden from the view of all save that of the high priest. But this last and climactic expiation took place in the most public way imaginable, the place of public execution, the very antithesis of the Temple and its holiness. In this thoroughly God-less place God was "justifying the ungodly" (Rom 4:5), making "him who knew no sin into sin" that "we (believers) might become in him the righteousness of God" (2 Cor 5:21).

A final hint of the "Day of Atonement" association is the phrase "in his blood" (ἐν τῷ αὐτοῦ αἵματι) standing in apposition to ἱλαστήριον following the somewhat awkward but characteristically Pauline insertion "through faith." God works the expiatory effect not through the high priest's sprinkling of the blood of the goat of the sin offering but through the sprinkling of Christ's blood in death. Or, to put it the other way round and perhaps more conformably to the way the association originally ran: the sprinkling of Christ's blood in death effects, on an eschatological and universal (Gentiles as well as Jews) scale, what the sprinkling of animal blood enacted in the former rite: expiation, covenant renewal, justification (cf. Rom 5:9: δικαιωθέντες νῦν ἐν τῷ αἵματι). For Paul, of course, this is not an automatic, purely objective event: it is those who appropriate it through faith who are beneficiaries of the divine action.

[18] The verb προτιθέναι in the middle voice in Greek can mean either "propose to oneself," "purpose" or "put forward publicly," "display." The former meaning brings out the sense of divine initiative and long-standing purpose behind the death of Christ. The latter is easier from a syntactical point of view and accords well with the aspect of "revelation" (v. 21) and "display" (vv. 25b-26) in the wider context.

Mark 15:37-39 Again

Let us, in fact, return now to the Markan description of Jesus' death and specifically to the interposed notice about the rending of the Temple curtain. Amid the plethora of interpretations on offer, how are we to understand the rending of the curtain following the death of Jesus? Almost everyone is agreed that we have to do with a divine event, indicated by the passive construction. Francis Moloney, noting that the death of Jesus marks the turning point of the ages, comments simply and aptly that in the tearing apart of the curtain "God enters the story."[19] Moloney further draws attention to the fact that the tearing apart (ἐσχίσθη) of the curtain following Jesus' death corresponds to the tearing apart (σχιζομένους) of the heavens at the beginning of the story immediately following Jesus' baptism at the hands of John (1:10).[20] I would press this observation further by pointing out how in both cases, at the beginning and end of the narrative, the rending signals a divine response to the humble association of Jesus with sinful humankind: submission to baptism along with the repentant mass that approached John at the Jordan; being crucified along with two bandits in fulfillment of the deeper "baptism" with which he "had to be baptized" (10:38d). In the first instance the rending of the heavens was followed by the Father's assurance, "You are my Son, the Beloved; with you I am well pleased" (1:11), an assurance repeated for the benefit of three privileged disciples at the transfiguration (9:7b) just after Jesus had for the first time made clear to his disciples the fact that the fulfillment of his messianic mission would involve rejection, suffering and death (8:31). In the final instance of rending (15:38), there is no accompanying divine voice acknowledging Jesus as "beloved Son." In startling paradox the acknowledgment comes from the opposite direction entirely. It stems from human lips, the stained human lips of the centurion who has supervised the execution.

In acknowledging the crucified One to be "in truth the Son of God,"[21] the Gentile centurion gives utterance to the foundational tenet of the Christian Gospel (Mark 1:1; cf. Rom 1:1-4; Gal 1:16; cf. John 20:31; 1 John 5:5, 10, 13). By so doing he has enabled the "transaction" taking

---

[19] Moloney, *Mark*, 328.

[20] Moloney, *Mark*, 328.

[21] Despite its anarthrous form, the centurion's confession is to be understood in this full christological sense; see the extensive discussion in Brown, *Death of the Messiah* 2:11466-52; also Moloney, *Mark*, 330 n. 282.

place at this moment on Calvary to model perfectly, in narrative form, Paul's sense (Rom 3:24-26) of God's justification of the "ungodly" (= the Gentile) through faith (Rom 4:5). He is the paradigmatic recipient through faith of God's saving outreach to the nations of the world, amongst whom the readers of Mark's Gospel are clearly to be numbered.

What of the Temple itself? As Francis Moloney points out, the rending of the curtain has both positive and negative aspects.[22] Positively, it paves the way for the centurion and those who follow him in his confession of faith to receive the saving blessings flowing from Christ's obedience unto death (cf. Phil 2:8). Negatively, it signals an end to the mode of expiation in force hitherto: the sacrificial system of the Jerusalem Temple. The rending of the curtain presages the destruction of the Temple, which will occur, as Jesus has himself foretold (13:1-2), a generation later in 70 CE, an event of which Mark's readers are likely to have been keenly aware.[23] But long before this physical destruction, the expiatory system conducted in the Temple had been replaced and rendered void by God's action on Calvary. In his earlier cleansing action in the Temple (11:15-17), Jesus justified what he was doing by appeal to Scripture: "My house shall be called a house of prayer for all the nations" (v. 17, citing Isa 56:7). Viewed retrospectively from Calvary, that action gains full prophetic force: Jesus' obedient death is bringing about a new "house of prayer for all the nations" (Gentiles). Ironically, the charges laid against him at his trial before the Council – the claim that he would destroy "this temple made with hands, and in three days build another not made with hands" (14:58) – contained a kernel of truth: his death has brought about a "house of faith" where believers of all nations have unrestricted access to the reconciling presence of God.[24] Those who respond to the preaching of the Gospel in faith and who participate in the eucharistic rite instituted on the night before he died bring themselves under the scope of the culminating Day of Atonement worked by God on Calvary. Though Jesus' blood has been "sprinkled" once and for all, its saving effects linger on for those who consume the broken bread and drink the cup, which "is the blood of the covenant, poured out for many" (Mark 14:22-24).[25]

---

[22] Moloney, *Mark*, 329 n. 279; Moloney makes this point against Brown's wholly negative interpretation of the rending – as a divine judgment upon the Temple and those who administer it (cf. *Death of the Messiah* 2:1099-1106, 1113-18).

[23] Cf. Moloney, *Mark*, 13-14.

[24] Cf. Chronis, "The Torn Veil," *JBL* 101 (1982): 97-114, esp. 107-14.

[25] I am of course aware that Mark, along with Matthew (26:26-29) and in contrast to

This last reference, in the eucharistic narrative, to "blood poured out for many" (14:24), along with Jesus' earlier pronouncement that the Son of Man had come "not to be served but to serve and give his life as a ransom for many" (10:45), puts beyond doubt the Evangelist's adherence to the belief that Jesus' death had the vicarious expiatory effect foretold in Isaiah's depiction of the Servant (Isa 53:10, 12). This is clearly an area where Mark and Paul both draw upon and reflect a very early Christian tradition that found meaning in Christ's death in this way (besides Rom 3:24, cf. 4:25; 5:9; 1 Cor 5:7; 11:25; 15:3).[26] If my analysis of the rending of the Temple curtain is correct, then I would argue that the expression of this truth is not confined in Mark's Gospel to the two references in 10:45 and 14:24,[27] but finds dramatic, narrative expression in the climactic description of Jesus' death.

While Matthew and Luke may have missed the point of what their forerunner Evangelist was attempting to do, Paul, I suspect would have nodded his head in total agreement. The Gentile centurion who comes to faith before the cross, finding himself drawn into an overwhelming outreach of God's reconciling grace, models the Gentile believer justified by faith apart from the works of the law. Mark's description of Jesus' death, particularly the interposition of the detail about the Temple curtain, gives perfect narrative expression to the truth standing at the heart of Paul's mission to bring about "an obedience of faith from all the nations" (Rom 1:5b).

Luke (22:19-20) and Paul (1 Cor 11:23-25), has no *anamnesis* command concerning the Eucharist. However, the Markan narrative clearly presupposes the eucharistic practice of the Christian community (cf. Moloney, *Mark*, 287-88) and implicitly functions aetiologically in its regard.

[26] Cf. Marcus, "Mark–Interpreter of Paul," 484-85.

[27] So Black, "Christ Crucified in Paul and in Mark," 199-200 n. 55.

13. TELLING STORIES OF HEALING IN A BROKEN WORLD

Elaine M. WAINWRIGHT

In Gerd Theissen's creative study *The Shadow of the Galilean*, in which his central character Andreas, a Roman official, tracks Jesus but always arrives in the wake of his shadow, Theissen tells a story of Miriam and Hannah. Miriam is the daughter of the house who is very ill and her mother Hannah tells her stories of Jesus' healings of others, even young girls like herself. After Andreas has listened to a number of these stories and seen their effect on the very ill Miriam he exclaims: "I believe that if she had run out of stories I myself would have added some and invented some."[1] Why would Theissen, who has sought to imaginatively reconstruct the telling of stories of Jesus' healing even during his life-time and ministry, have had Andreas say these words? One answer may be found in a recognition of the power of stories as articulated by Mair who says:

> Stories inform life. They hold us together and keep us apart. We inhabit the great stories of our culture. We live through stories. We are *lived* by the stories of our race and people."[2]

Each Easter Christians live anew into the great story of their Christian culture, the story of life being more powerful than death, the story of the entry of divinity into the very heart of humanity and its foundational experience of suffering and death. And in recent years they have done this at

[1] G. Theissen, *The Shadow of the Galilean. The Quest of the Historical Jesus in Narrative Form.* (trans. J. Bowden; Philadelphia: Fortress; London: SCM, 1987), 99.

[2] M. Mair, "Psychology as Storytelling," *IJPCP* 1 (1988): 127, quoted in J. Freedman and G. Combs, *Narrative Therapy: The Social Construction of Preferred Realities* (New York: W. W. Norton, 1996), 32.

a time when our world seems broken, when the forces and powers that are death-dealing seem greater than those that are life giving and life transforming.[3] If Freedman and Combs are right, and I believe they are, this great story that has just been told is informing lives anew. It is holding communities together. It may also, on both a local and global level, be driving people apart if different great stories or grand narratives are being used in a way that is death-dealing – a key characteristic, even if not made explicit, in our present great global conflict. Many Christians are, however, seeking to live into this story of life in the relationships and events of their daily lives and in the ways in which they are with and among others, especially those most vulnerable. But the Christian story is also much greater than each of us with a power that comes from incarnation, from divinity caught up into the life of humanity. For Christians, therefore, the intimate connection between this belief and experience and their great story means that they are "lived" by their Gospel story.

It is against this backdrop that I wish to explore the telling of particular stories, namely stories of healing, stories of transformation. My focus will be the healing stories, which are a key characteristic of the Gospel of Mark. I will be concerned with the telling of these stories by a community of believers in Jesus in the second half of the first century. Given the urgency of current world events, I want to ask how such stories of healing can function in dialogue with contemporary stories to transform hearts and lives, religious and social imagination and Christian praxis.

Setting the Global Context

As I both prepared and revised this paper, I realized how difficult it is for us to hear stories of healing in the present conflict in Iraq.[4] During the invasion, we were bombarded, as it were, with stories of bombardment, of advances of troops, of coalition victories, of the liberation of a people from journalists "embedded" in the war machine. Robert Fisk, on the other hand, brought us stories of suffering on the streets and in the hospitals of Baghdad: a story of Saida Jaffar, a two year old girl, swaddled in

---

[3] This paper was first written during the Easter season of 2003 and revised for this publication at the same time in 2004.

[4] There are many aspects of our broken world that I could have focused on in this paper, but the invasion and subjection of Iraq by "coalition" forces is the one which has touched our minds and hearts most recently in a profound way and continues to do so.

bandages, a tube into her nose, another into her stomach. All he could see of her was her forehead, two small eyes and a chin; or three-year-old Mohamed Amaid, his face, stomach, hands and feet all tied tightly in bandages. We are left to imagine the hospital staff working with primitive equipment, poor medical supplies and amidst an ongoing war to care for these children, to mend their badly damaged bodies. How much more, however, will be needed to mend their more badly damaged lives and the lives of their family, friends, neighbors, indeed all the people of Iraq.[5]

I was reminded of Theissen's account of Hannah telling the stories to Miriam when I read the following story, again from Robert Fisk:

Heartbreaking is the only word to describe 10-year-old Maryam Nasr and her five-year-old sister Hoda. Maryam has a patch over her right eye where a piece of bomblet embedded itself. She also had wounds to the stomach and thighs. I didn't realise that Hoda, standing by her sister's bed, was wounded until her mother carefully lifted the little girl's scarf and long hair to show a deep puncture in the right side of her head, just above her ear, congealed blood sticking to her hair but the wound still gently bleeding. Their mother described how she had been inside her home and heard an explosion and found her daughters lying in their own blood near the door. The little girls alternately smiled and hid when I took their pictures.[6]

I wondered what stories of healing this mother was telling Maryam and Hoda. And yet this is where the stories of healing and of hope will be found – in the lives of mothers and fathers, brothers, sisters and friends, as well as health care professionals like Dr. Harith and the other doctors at al-Nasiriya general hospital. These were the doctors who not only saved but also protected the life of American Private Jessica Lynch, only to be savagely victimized by her supposed saviors, an American battalion. These stories are being lived now among the people of Iraq and it will take time for them to emerge as stories, and by then, as is already happening, the West will have lost interest. Carol Guzy a photographic journalist says, however, that the images she and others produce, like the stories Robert Fisk tells, are a voice for the voiceless who carry the stories; she speaks

[5] http://news.independent.co.uk/world/fisk/story.jsp?story=392161. Accessed 20 April, 2003.

[6] http://bt.premium-link.net/$59122$1879596656$/story.jsp?cb_content_name= Robert+Fisk%3A+Wailing+children%2C+the+wounded%2C+the+dead%3A+victims+of +the+day+cluster+bombs+rained+on+Babylon%3Cbr%2F%3E%0ARef+-+393458& story=393458&host=3&dir=668. Accessed 20 April, 2003.

Elaine M. Wainwright*

with feeling of the glimmer of hope and the amazing examples of compassion, like that of Dr. Harith and others at al-Nasiriyah hospital, that she sees in the most desperate of situations.[7]

The members of the Markan community were like the people of contemporary Iraq, a community affected by war and socio-political upheaval. We do not know the exact date of the initial compilation of this Gospel nor its location with anything beyond informed speculation. It is commonly held, however, that the Gospel was compiled either just prior to or subsequent to the Jewish War, i.e., sometime between the mid-sixties to mid-seventies of the Common Era.[8] If its location was Rome, the Gospel was being shaped shortly after the death of Peter, and during the tumultuous period of the reign of Nero and beyond, with its persecution of the followers of Jesus. If it was the Syro-Palestinian region then the people were experiencing the Roman War, which afflicted the area prior to and subsequent to 70 CE. Such may be reflected in the vivid language of Mark 13 when he speaks of there not being left even "one stone upon another" in the temple of Jerusalem (Mark 13:2); or of "wars and rumors of war" (13:7) or nation rising against nation, and kingdom against kingdom" (13:8). This is reflected in the literature that describes the events of this era and it echoes in our own consciousness as we contemplate our world today. It is the healing stories of this first century community which I seek to read in a world of the twenty-first century in which "wars and rumors of war" and all their aftermath abound.

Given that one of the more recent focal points of the extensive research career of Francis Moloney has been the Gospel of Mark, it seemed appropriate to offer for this Festschrift in his honor, a paper that explores Markan stories of healing. Also, given his long career in Australia during which time he brought the biblical text to life in the hearts and lives of myriads of Australian people through public lectures, I have chosen to offer for this volume a revised public lecture, to honor this aspect of Frank's contribution to biblical studies.[9]

---

[7] www.museum.og/newstories/interviews/mp3/journalists/bio.asp?ID=10. Accessed 20 April, 2003. Such stories are as relevant one year later when the conflict continues and healing is hidden under violence and ongoing conflict and fighting.

[8] For a recent discussion of the likely dating and location of this Gospel see F. J. Moloney, *The Gospel of Mark: A Commentary* (Peabody: Hendrickson, 2002), 11-15.

[9] This lecture was delivered as the 2003 *Pompellier Lecture* in Auckland in May, 2003 and I wish to thank the Catholic Institute of Theology for the invitation to present this lecture. The chapter still carries some of the elements of oral presentation.

Mark's Stories of Healing in a Broken World

The Gospel of Mark is a finely woven story, almost like a drama in two acts, which tells the unfolding story of Jesus *Christos,* son of God.[10] Although an initial written copy of this story may have been made in the late sixties or early seventies of the first century, the culture that received it was an oral culture. Most people therefore would have heard the story orally for a long time into the future beyond its being written.[11] Attentiveness to repeated words and phrases, placement of stories, frames around narratives and other such devices would have all been techniques to convey meaning for *listeners* rather than *readers.* And so the basic frame of the Gospel is an important key to understanding the way this Gospel portrays Jesus.

The Healing Stories within the Gospel's Framework

I am not going to grapple here with what that first century community might have understood by the titles it was giving to Jesus. Rather, I want to demonstrate where the stories of healing are placed and how they function to give meaning to the Jesus whose story is being told.

The beginning of the Gospel of *Jesus Christos, Son of God* (Mark 1:1)

> 1:21-28 – *Man with unclean spirit*
> 1:29-31 Heals Simon's mother-in-law
> > 1:32-34 Healing of many and casting out of demons - (summary)
> > 1:39 Exorcisms – (summary)
> 1:40-45 Leper cleansed
> 2:1-12 Paralytic

[10] Mark 1:1 has the first occurrence of the phrase *Jesus Christos* and a textually variant "son of God" at the end of the opening verse. The first half of the Gospel which focuses on the healing ministry of Jesus culminates in the proclamation of Jesus as the *Christos* (Mark 8:29). The second part of the drama, which turns toward Jesus' suffering in Jerusalem, reaches its high point when the centurion says of the dying Jesus, "Truly this one was son of God" (15:39).

[11] It is estimated that no more than between 5 – 10% of people could read at that time. According to E. Struthers Malbon, "Most people in the ancient world couldn't read; maybe 10 percent, give or take, were literate. Perhaps a higher percentage of Jews were readers because reading the Scriptures was important. The world was not for readers; the world was for hearers." See E. S. Malbon, *Hearing Mark: A Listeners' Guide* (Harrisburg: Trinity Press, 2002), 5.

2:15-17 Those who are well/sick (summary)
3:1-6 Man with withered hand
    3:10-12 Many healings and exorcisms (summary)
        3:20-27 – *Jesus and Beelzebul*
        5:1-20 – *Gerasene Demoniac*
5:21-43 Jairus' daughter and Woman with Haemorrhage
      6:1-5 – Nazareth – couldn't do any mighty works
      6:7-13 – Mission of the Twelve (commission and summary)
      6:53-57 – Healing of Sick in Gennesaret (summary)
7:24-30 Syrophoenician Woman's daughter is healed
7:31-37 Deaf and Dumb man healed
8:22-26 Healing of Blind man of Bethsaida

You are the Christ (8:29)

9:14-29 Healing of the Epileptic Boy
      9:38-41 – Doing mighty works in Jesus' name (summary)
10:46-52 Healing of blind Bartimeus
14:3-9 The woman who pours healing ointment over Jesus

Truly this one was son of God (15:39)

There are three types of narratives of healing:
• the casting out of demons,
• the healing of physical illness or disability;
• the summary, a number of which punctuate the narrative as a whole and bring together references to the casting out of demons and healing of bodies.

Up to chapter 10 of the narrative, except for chapter 4 whose focus is on Jesus' teaching in parables, there is a healing text in every chapter. Given this detail and the absence of much significant teaching material until chapters 11–13, it is clear that the Markan story of Jesus *shows* him emphatically as healer, and the proclamation of the Gospel provides its listeners with many stories of healing.[12]

In light of this general overview, I turn now to examine more specifi-

---

[12] The language of narrative study speaks of both "telling" and "showing" in relation to characterization. See M.A. Powell, *What is Narrative Criticism* (GBS; Minneapolis: Fortress, 1990), 52-53.

cally some of these stories of healing in order to determine how they may have functioned for their first century recipients in the Markan community. This will provide a stepping-stone that will enable us to return to the question of how these and other stories of healing might function for us today in our broken world.

In order to illustrate, my focus will be the first two stories of healing in Mark's Gospel. They are, in fact, the opening stories in Mark's account of Jesus' unfolding ministry. That ministry is narrated as beginning with the summary of the Gospel:

Jesus came into Galilee, preaching the Gospel of God, and saying,
The καιρός *(opportune time) has been/is fulfilled and the* βασιλεία/*empire of God has come/is near; repent, and believe in the Gospel* (Mark 1:14b-15)

This summary is followed by two stories in which four fishermen are called from their family and occupation to begin the formation of a new fictive kinship group around Jesus (1:16-20), to be participants with Jesus in the inauguration of the opportune time of God and the empire of God, which offers an alternate vision to the empire of Rome. The first four healing stories are the first demonstrations of what this alternate *basileia*, this alternate vision and social organization, might mean.

Before engaging with the Markan healing stories, it is important to note that there are other places in the Hellenistic world where one could find collections of healing stories. In the Hippocratic texts, one finds in *The Epidemics* many stories of healings and failures to heal in the field of emerging "professional" medicine.[13] On the stelea of the Epidaurian temple of Asklepios, renovated toward the end of the fourth century BCE, there are over 70 stories of healing effected by Asklepios, the god of healing for those who visited his sanctuary.[14] Judaism, however, does not seem to have a tradition of collections of stories of healing, although there are healing stories scattered amid the later Rabbinic material and a few stories of healings by prophetic figures in the Hebrew Scriptures.[15] Recipi-

---

[13] Contemporary studies of healing in the ancient world, especially those undertaken from a cultural anthropological perspective, explain the health care system of the time as functioning in three realms: the professional, the popular and the folk. See J. J. Pilch, *Healing in the New Testament: Insights from Medical and Mediterranean Anthropology* (Minneapolis: Fortress, 2000), 94-103.

[14] See L. R. LiDonnici, *The Epidaurian Miracle Inscriptions: Text, Translation and Commentary* (TT 36; GRRS 11; Atlanta: Scholars, 1995).

[15] Eg. 1Kgs 17:17-24; 2Kgs 4:32-37; 5:1-14.

ents of the Gospel story may well have been familiar with the tradition of recounting stories of healings associated with Asklepios as there were healing shrines of various sizes scattered throughout the Roman empire, including Syria and Palestine.[16] Recounting stories of healing is, therefore, a feature of the world in which the Gospel of Mark was shaped. Our search is to try to understand the function of this telling of such stories. I want to emphasize here that I am not seeking to establish the historicity or otherwise of the healings of Jesus or of Asklepios or the Hippocratic medics. My focus is on the telling of the stories and their effects on listeners.

Looking at the brief collection of healing stories, which begins Mark's story of Jesus' ministry in chapter 1, we find that the three different types of stories are included: casting out of demons/unclean spirits (1:21-28), healings of bodily ailments (1:29-31; 40-45), and summaries (1:32-34; 39). In two healings (1:40-45; 2:1-12) and one casting out of a demon (1:21-28), the recipients are male but the opening story of bodily healing is of a woman, Simon's mother-in-law (1:29-31).

An Unclean Spirit is Driven Out (1:21-28)

The story of the driving out of an unclean spirit is an extraordinary opening to the Markan healing stories because the way the story is told makes it very clear that it is not a simple recounting of an historical memory. The very framing of the story in verses 22 and 27 with the references to Jesus' teaching and his ἐξουσία, or authority as it is often translated, or freedom as Anne Dawson describes it,[17] points to the meaning-making function of the story. Indeed, this aspect of the Markan story strongly suggests the approach to interpreting the Gospel healing stories that is informed by cultural anthropology. This approach John Pilch calls "the hermeneutic" or "meaning-making" approach.[18] We shall see this approach combined with an analysis of the narratives of the healing stories as we proceed.

---

[16] A. Duprez, *Jésus et les Dieux Guérisseurs à propos de Jean V* (CahRB 12; Paris: Gabalda, 1968), 68.

[17] A. Dawson, *Freedom as Liberating Power: A Socio-political Reading of the ἐξουσία Texts in the Gospel of Mark* (NTOA 44; Göttingen: Vandenhoeck & Ruprecht, 2000), 127-29.

[18] J. J. Pilch, "Understanding Biblical Healing and Selecting an Appropriate Model," *BTB* 18 (1988): 60-66.

In the story of Jesus' casting out of the unclean spirit from the man in the synagogue, the setting is clearly significant. The place is Capernaum (v. 21), a Jewish town on the north-west corner of the Sea of Galilee, which was the setting for the previous stories of the calling of Peter, Andrew, James and John into the new fictive kinship or discipleship group Jesus was establishing. A further delineation of the setting is that it is in the synagogue (v. 21), the Jewish holy place where the community gathered for its ritual re-telling of its sacred story and the renewal of its relationship with God in prayer. The temporal setting further emphasizes this sacredness: it is the Sabbath (v. 21), the day specifically designated as holy, the time for the ritual activities of the synagogue. It is here that Jesus is presented as teaching. I think Anne Dawson's insight about the ἐξουσία of Jesus being understood as freedom rather than authority is a significant one. It makes good sense in this context because the scribes were, in fact, the authorized teachers and they had ἐξουσία understood as *authority* or official authorization. Jesus, however, is characterized in a way that differs from the scribes. He freely interprets God's *basileia* in a different way to what people had come to expect. He does this in the synagogue, the Jewish place of teaching. His ἐξουσία as freedom and as authority is presented as a challenge to that of the scribes, a deviance, but this deviance was affirmed or authorized through the narrative of his baptism which has already indicated, to the hearers of the story, that he is beloved of God (1:11).

It is in this context, that the listener is introduced to another who is out of place or deviant, in relation to the story's time and location, both of which are sacred or holy, according to the Jewish symbolic world of holy and unholy, clean and unclean. Neither the holy place nor the holy time is able to render this man clean. Indeed it was within this system that he is named as possessed of an unclean spirit. The words of the unclean spirit clearly indicate that there is a contest here articulated as questions: "What have you to do with us? Have you come to destroy us" (v. 24)? Both questions are challenges in an *agonistic* or challenge/riposte society where honor or status and power were always at risk. Before Jesus or the community can expel the deviant one, who represents a threat to the holy order of their space and time, the unclean spirit speaks in the language of challenge, naming Jesus as the Holy One of God (v. 24). In using this title, the unclean spirit recognizes Jesus in the way he has already been presented in the narrative (1:11).

To name Jesus thus is an attempt by the unclean spirit to protect itself from a power that is greater. Having been named as the Holy One of

God, Jesus is then seen as exercising the power of a holy one of God, when, with a great show of power, the demon is cast out of the man. The restoration and transformation, which is of God and a manifestation of God's *basileia*, has come near, indeed, has come into the very midst of the people. It is the true Holy One of God, not a designated sacred space or sacred time, which is able to heal or restore. The restoration, is of time and of space. And it is this that the closing frame calls a new teaching with *exousia*, freedom and authority, which is contrasted with that of the scribes in the story-telling.

The telling of this story of healing is framed, therefore, so that it points to its function, not just at the level of a story of transformation of an individual.[19] Rather, the story has hermeneutic or meaning-making potential in relation to the community as community. In this regard, the cultural anthropological insight of Mary Douglas is significant. She says that:

[t]he human body is a model which can stand for any bounded system. Its boundaries can represent any boundaries which are threatened or precarious. The body is a complex structure. The functions of its different parts and their relations afford a source of symbols for other complex structures.[20]

In this story, it is the entire body of the man that ought to be holy because of the holy place, the synagogue, and holy time, the Sabbath, but this body is inhabited by the unclean spirit. Narratively and culturally, the man functions as representative of an entire community that is deviant, in terms of what is named clean or holy, in the very place and at the very time when it considers itself most holy. The unclean may have been expressive of, or be giving meaning to, anxiety around the eroding of time-honored Jewish traditions as the emerging Christian community moved away from its Jewish roots. It may also have been understood as a manifestation of the new community's internal disintegration because of outside threats such as persecution.[21]

Telling this story of Jesus' healing of the man with an unclean spirit may have shaped the imagination of the Markan community to believe in

---

[19] The individual aspect of healing could be the topic of another study, just as it was the focus of Theissen's reconstructed story with which this paper opened.

[20] M. Douglas, *Purity and Danger* (New York: Frederick A. Praeger, 1966), 115.

[21] Current social scientific theory also suggests that possession by an evil or unclean spirit can be the result of colonial domination, an experience of many in the first century who were under the power of Rome. See E. van Eck and A. G. van Aarde, "Sickness and Healing in Mark: A Social Scientific Interpretation," *Neot* 27 (1993): 37-39.

the healing/transformative power of Jesus in their midst in a way that restored community holiness or *basileia* fidelity. It may also have empowered them to become a community of healing, a restored/transformed community in a deviant world marked by religious tension, wars and rumors of war, challenge and threat from within and without. The telling of the story names and transforms the social and religious imagination of its hearers. It makes meaning and it can empower to transformative or healing action, the healing being of the community.

Van Eck and van Aarde, two south African second testament scholars summarize such an approach in terms of first century understandings of health.

> In the first century Mediterranean world health was perceived as but one example of good fortune, and sickness as but one example of a wide range of misfortunes. Sickness was a state of being which … could range from anxiety, illness, feelings of inferiority, grief and fear of death, up to concern for the social order. As such, sickness became a human experience when it became meaningful. And sickness became meaningful when worrisome or biological signs were given socially recognizable meanings, that is, when a person with such behavior or signs was labeled unclean (or ill in some way), and therefore unfit to be part of the holy community. This … might lead the ill person to seek healing, the elimination of evil agents, a sense of access to power, the enhancement of status, increase of prosperity, attention from posterity or even the transformation of the social order. From this it is therefore clear that in the first-century Mediterranean world, illness referred to a social and personal perception of certain disvalued states, all of which were regarded as but one example of a wide range of misfortunes.[22]

One of the elements in this story that is significant for us today is that of *naming*. The spirit is named as "unclean" by a community that constructs its world according to values it believes to be of God. To name as "unclean" is an exercise of ἐξουσία, of authority or of power. So too is naming as "holy" an exercise of power. Naming is, therefore, always perspectival and associated with power and hence requires great care and careful discernment. The way we name in the stories we tell, whether they be our grand narratives or the more immediate interpretations of contemporary events and people, has a powerful effect. It can be destructive or it can be transformative; it can be contrary to the divine desire for humanity,

---

[22] van Eck and van Aarde, "Sickness and Healing," 39.

which the Gospel names as the *basileia of God*, or it can bring to birth or fruition this transformative desire. The way we name in our stories, will in turn shape our praxis.

I am reminded here of the story told by Richard Lloyd Parry from al-Nasiriyah "So who really did save Private Jessica?" To answer this question, one must tell the story of Dr. Harith, a 24-year-old junior resident at the hospital, caught up in the process of saving a human life at great risk to himself and others. What a challenging exercise it would be for a local Christian community to bring this contemporary story and the first Markan healing story into dialogue as part of a theological process, reflecting on the community's own naming of clean and unclean, their marginalizing of any "other," their failing to be the community of healing and transformation that the Gospel both challenges and invites us to.

A Woman with Fever is Raised Up (1:29-31)

The second story in this opening of Mark's Gospel is of a healing of physical illness – Simon's mother-in-law is lying sick with a fever. In this story, as in the previous one, setting is clearly significant. There is a repetition of the previous story's setting, namely the synagogue (v. 29). In this story, however, the setting is the "house" and it seems to be contrasted with the synagogue of the previous story. Jesus and the small fictive kinship or discipleship group leave the synagogue and enter a house but it is not just any house but that of Simon and Andrew (v. 29), two of the four initially called into the new kinship group associated with the *basileia* ministry of Jesus. For the community of reception of Mark's Gospel, the house was not only the actual place of their gathering as community, but also a microcosm or symbol of the growing *basileia* movement. This may have been particularly so when the house was associated with Simon who by this time, *circa* 70 CE, is considered symbolic leader of the new fictive kinship of believers in Jesus and his *basileia* vision.

But this house is not completely whole. There is sickness here. The woman with the fever is lying sick in bed and hence the household is not functioning. Van Eck and van Aarde draw an interesting conclusion regarding this aspect of the story saying:

> Simon's mother-in-law was healed in a house, not in the synagogue or the temple. And just as important, Simon's mother-in-law, after she had been healed,

immediately started to serve the household again. Jesus therefore not only healed someone to be able to serve the household again, but also made the household itself whole.[23]

Such an interpretation indicates that they have accepted the gender construction of the first century Mediterranean world, with its public/private division, as a given rather than a construction of the social imagination which was constantly being negotiated. Careful attention to the language of the text shows that this story is more than a story of the healing of an individual woman or of the social body, the household, to its former gendered status. Jesus, an outsider to the household, reaches out across the socio-cultural gender divide and takes the hand of the woman with the fever, symbolically crossing or breaking through such a construction. In taking her hand in his he breaches the boundary and crosses the limits so that bodily boundaries touch, demonstrating that other gendered relationships are possible. Then in the language of the text, the woman is lifted or raised up (ἤγειρεν 1:31) just as Jesus is raised up in the concluding story of the Gospel (ἠγέρθη 16:6). Language associated with her is also associated with Jesus. This is equally so for the language of service (διηκόνει v. 31). Van Eck and van Aarde say of this "she immediately started to serve the household again,"[24] seeing her service as simply household service and a woman's cultural place. Listening again to this language in the Markan text, we note that it is language used of Jesus in 10:45, Jesus came "not to be served but to serve."[25] It is also a descriptor of the women who accompany Jesus from Galilee to the foot of the cross (15:41).[26] These women followed (ἠκολούθουν) Jesus, as did Simon and Andrew, James and John, and they were serving (διηκόνουν) him just as Simon's healed mother-in-law was serving the household. The imperfect tense of these two verbs as they refer to women indicates that their serving was ongoing, not confined to a particular moment or a particular household. According to the Australian scholar John Collins, the verb διακονέω also has much more a sense of an ambassadorial function, speaking and acting on behalf of another.[27] It functions, therefore, to include women among the discipleship, or new fictive kinship, group with men.

---

[23] van Eck and van Aarde, "Sickness and Healing," 45.

[24] van Eck and van Aarde, "Sickness and Healing," 45.

[25] ὁ υἱὸς τοῦ ἀνθρώπου οὐκ ἦλθεν διακονηθῆναι ἀλλὰ διακονῆσαι

[26] αἳ ὅτε ἦν ἐν τῇ Γαλιλαίᾳ ἠκολούθουν αὐτῷ καὶ διηκόνουν αὐτῷ,

[27] J. N. Collins, *Diakonia: Reinterpreting the Ancient Sources* (Oxford: Oxford University Press, 1990).

Again narrative and cultural codes work together in this story where illness is given social meaning and the gendered body represents the gendered space of the household. The *basileia* ministry of Jesus, the holy one of God, continues to be transformative. The restored body of the woman with the fever, who was named initially in terms of a physical illness which was also rendering the household dysfunctional, is now named with the language associated with Jesus. She has been lifted up and she is engaged in *diakonia* in the restored household. As Michael Trainor says in his recent study of Mark, "the Christian household becomes the place of healing, where an alternative model of social equality and freedom is evident."[28] Telling such a story shapes the religious imagination of its hearers. To imagine something different is the first stage in our actually bringing it into being. The Christian household can therefore, become a place of healing, an alternative model of social equality and freedom, because the imagination of that community is healed and shaped toward a *basileia* vision of God's desire for the human community by the stories of Jesus, the holy one of God who is healer.

Summaries (1:32-34)

The summary of 1:32-34 reiterates and further emphasizes the effect of the previous two stories. Jesus is healer not only of human bodies possessed by unclean spirits or disabled by illness, but also of religious and socio-cultural contexts. The *basileia* of God was not only near at hand in the ministry of the actual Jesus of Nazareth, it is near at hand in the later telling of the story. The *basileia* of God is at hand when the followers of Jesus tell the story of his ministry of healing and transformation in order to shape communities who live the *basileia* vision: God's transformative dream that the human community lives in justice and right ordered relationships with one another and with the resources of their community. It is this ongoing power of the *basileia* that the summary seems to emphasize.

Again, Michael Trainor's analysis of the household in Mark's Gospel provides us with a key insight into this summary. He has noted that the reference to the crowd around the door as it has often been understood (v. 33), may in fact be evoking the gathering of the crowd within the large

---

[28] M. Trainor, *The Quest for Home: The Household in Mark's Community* (Collegeville: Liturgical Press, 2001), 94.

household or *domus* which may have been the typical place in which urban households gathered, the homes of the wealthier members of the community.[29] The Markan picture of the crowds gathering πρὸς τὴν θύραν, or toward the door may indicate that this household is overflowing because it is one in which *all* who are sick or possessed with demons are healed.[30] It is a community that will need to be constantly transformed as it faces new situations, which are named in terms of sickness or possession, if it is going to continue to manifest the *basileia* of God.

Within the opening stories of the Markan Gospel, listeners encounter the two types of illnesses that characterize the health care system as it was understood: possession and physical ailment. Stories of healing tell of the transformative power of Jesus in relation to individuals and in summary and as such they give new meaning to communities struggling with disintegration in their immediate communities and in society generally. John Pilch summarizes this when he says,

> Jesus and all the people of his culture dealt with sickness as illness and not as disease (understood as a biomedical condition). Mark's taxonomy clusters illnesses, not diseases. Jesus and all healers of that period could only perceive illnesses, not diseases. Since illness concerns the socio-cultural meaning of a sickness experience, it makes good sense to view a teacher as a healer. Notice in each healing instance the almost total disregard of symptoms… Instead there is constant concern for meaning. The context of Jesus' healing activity is frequently during this teaching activity – in the synagogue for example. He is engaged in identifying meaning in life.[31]

Re-telling Stories of Healing in a Broken World

The claim of this paper has been that the *telling* of the healing stories of Jesus within the Markan community functioned to shape a new religious and socio-cultural imagination that would lead in its turn to a transformation of the socio-religious and cultural order of society. This transformation was named as the *basileia* of God, understood as God's desire for the human community, articulated by the Hebrew prophets as well as the

---

[29] Trainor, *The Quest for Home*, 94-95.

[30] Demonic possession is the Graeco-Roman nomenclature for the Jewish terminology of having an unclean spirit.

[31] J. J. Pilch, *Healing in the New Testament: Insights from Medical and Mediterranean Anthropology* (Minneapolis: Fortress, 2000), 71.

emerging Christian Evangelists, as justice or righteousness. These healing narratives were stories that informed life, as Mair indicated in an earlier quotation.[32] They held the Markan community together. The community inhabited this great story of Jesus that was shaping its culture; it lived into it; it desired that the stories might reshape the religious imaginations of members. The community would have been *lived* by these stories of healing as they sought to bring the *basileia* vision to reality in a trans- formed world. Antoinette Clark Wire says of such a telling of healing stories that

[t]he narrative tells a marvelous breakthrough in the struggle against oppres- sive restrictions on human life … – the juxtaposition of an accepted oppressive context and an extraordinary breaking out of it … The stories are structured around an extraordinary rift in a given, closed system … (and) the story affirms both a realistic, even tragic, view of the human condition and a transforming event that changes the human condition.[33]

As bearers and tellers of the Gospel story, Christians do not have to wait to hear the glimmer of hope and the stories of compassion which will emerge from Iraq, at the center of our contemporary broken world, be- fore they too are moved to act on behalf of an alternative vision. As con- temporary stories of healing and compassion emerge, they can function, together with the biblical stories of healing, to further challenge our relig- ious imaginations and to shape our Christian praxis. We do not have to add stories or invent them as Andreas thought he might have to do for Miriam. Our challenge is to find and to tell stories of healing that we might transform our broken world.

Conclusion

There is so much more that I find myself wanting to explore in relation to the telling of stories of healing in a broken world. I want to see how, what I call the final healing story in Mark's Gospel, the woman who pours healing ointment over the head of Jesus might be read in the way I have read the first two stories of healing. What social bodies are evoked by the

---

[32] Mair, "Psychology," in Freedman and Combs, *Narrative Therapy*, 32. See n. 2.

[33] A. Clark Wire, "The Structure of the Gospel Miracle Stories and their Tellers," *Se- meia* 11 (1978): 109-10.

body of Jesus overwhelmed by the death he faces.[34] I want to search further into the function of gender in the telling of these stories and to explore what its symbolic function might be. I want also to be able to reflect with my Christian communities on our life situations in dialogue with both ancient and contemporary stories of healing in order that we might determine together the healing task that is ours in our social and cultural contexts if we are Gospel communities.

Such engagement between the Gospel texts and the life of Christian communities has been sparked in many places around our globe by the work of Francis Moloney. A recent collection of his writings quoted the following words of Arundhati Roy, and they provide a fitting conclusion to this exploration of Mark's healing stories:

The Great Stories are the ones you have heard and want to hear again. The ones you can enter anywhere and inhabit comfortably. They don't deceive you with thrills and trick endings. They don't surprise you with the unforseen. They are as familiar as the house you live in. Or the smell of your lover's skin. You know how they end, yet you listen as though you don't. In the way that although you know that one day you will die, you live as though you won't. In the great stories you know who lives, who dies, who finds love, who doesn't. And yet you want to know again.[35]

---

[34] I have, in fact, explored this story further in "The Pouring Out of Healing Ointment: Rereading Mark 14:3-9," in *Toward a New Heaven and a New Earth: Essays in Honor of Elisabeth Schüssler Fiorenza* (ed. F. F. Segovia; Maryknoll: Orbis, 2003), 157-78.

[35] Arundhati Roy, *The God of Small Things* (London: Flamingo, 1997) 229; cited in F. J. Moloney, *"A Hard Saying": The Gospel and Culture* (Collegeville: Liturgical Press, 2001) 277.

14. PAULINE JUSTIFICATION AS PRESENTED BY LUKE IN ACTS 13

Joseph A. FITZMYER

For a long time NT interpreters have noted that the picture of Paul painted in the Acts of the Apostles differs somewhat from that in the extant letters that make up the uncontested Pauline corpus in the NT. This has been called "the Paulinism of Acts."[1] Sometimes the contrast between the Paul of the letters and the Paul of Acts has been exaggerated and overdrawn, and Luke has become the whipping-boy in many discussions that bear on this topic. Not always included in such discussions is the way Luke has dealt with a prime topic of Pauline teaching, viz., justification by grace through faith.

In order to clarify the issue that will be under discussion, I shall present my remarks under four headings: (i) Pauline and Lucan views of the effects of the Christ-event; (ii) Paul's view of justification; (iii) Luke's reformulation of Pauline justification; and (iv) reasons why Luke has so presented Pauline justification.

Pauline and Lucan Views of the Effects of the Christ-Event

In using the term "Christ-event," I am summing up the aspects of the ministry of Jesus of Nazareth that have to be regarded as significant for humanity. It is the complex of decisive moments of the earthly and risen life of Jesus Christ, the sum-total of the impact that Jesus has made on humanity: his passion, death, resurrection, exaltation, and heavenly inter-

---

[1] See P. Vielhauer, "On the 'Paulinism' of Acts," *PSTJ* 17 (1963): 5-17; repr. in *Studies in Luke-Acts: Essays Presented in Honor of Paul Schubert* (ed. L. E. Keck and J. L. Martyn; Nashville: Abingdon, 1966), 33-50 (cited hereinafter according to the latter publication).

cession. These are what constitute the "Christ-event," that which Jesus objectively accomplished for us ἐφάπαξ, "once and for all" (Rom 6:10).

The "effects" of the Christ-event are the different ways in which NT writers have expressed what Jesus Christ accomplished for humanity through those moments of his existence. One can catalogue such effects according to the various images or figures that different NT writers have employed to express those effects. The images differ according to the NT writers, especially those whose theological teaching is extensive and developed. Thus one can distinguish the Johannine, Lucan, and Pauline views of such effects.

The Pauline view of the effects of the Christ-event is complex; one can count at least ten such effects. One may wonder at the variety of them, but one must remember that they are all at best aspects of the one basic thing that Jesus Christ did for humanity. One can imagine that Paul conceived of the effects as a ten-sided solid figure or decahedron: when he looked at one of its panels, he called it justification; at another, salvation, and so on. In other words, Paul said: Christ Jesus has justified us, or has saved us, and so on. Such panels represent the different images or figures that Paul derived from his Jewish or Hellenistic background to describe those effects. I cannot expand now on his use of these images, but I can at least enumerate them. For Paul the effects would be justification, salvation, reconciliation, expiation, redemption, freedom, sanctification, transformation, new creation, and glorification.[2] Each of these images expresses a distinctive aspect of the mystery of Christ and of his work on behalf of humanity, but each one expresses only an aspect of the whole complex.

Just as one can synthetically present the effects of the Christ-event as Paul understood them, so too one can present the effects as Luke saw them. In this case, they are not as numerous, but they include salvation (Acts 4:12), forgiveness of sins (Luke 24:47), peace (Luke 2:14; 19:28), life (Acts 3:15; 5:20), and association with the risen Christ (Luke 23:43).[3] What is striking is that only "salvation" is an effect common to both Paul and Luke. Moreover, Luke himself never affirms that Christ Jesus "justified" us, even though he does put that effect on the lips of Paul on one occa-

---

[2] See further J. A. Fitzmyer, *Paul and His Theology: A Brief Sketch* (2d ed.; Englewood Cliffs: Prentice Hall, 1989), 59-71.

[3] See further J. A. Fitzmyer, *The Gospel According to Luke* (AB 28, 28A; Garden City: Doubleday, 1981, 1985), 221-27.

sion. These then are the different ways that Paul and Luke have summed up the effects of the Christ-event.

Paul's View of Justification

The Pauline view of justification begins in God himself, with what he calls δικαιοσύνη θεοῦ, "the righteousness of God." This phrase has two different meanings in Paul's writings. Sometimes it denotes a quality or attribute of God, his "righteousness" as opposed to his ὀργή, "wrath" (Rom 1:17-18; 3:5); and sometimes it denotes something that is bestowed on human beings (2 Cor 5:21: "that we might become the righteousness of God," i.e., that we might have a status of righteousness in God's sight). When I say that justification begins in God, I mean that δικαιοσύνη θεοῦ begins as an attribute: that quality of God that sets the process of justification in operation; it is the divine quality that sees to the justification of human sinners. The other sense of δικαιοσύνη θεοῦ expresses rather the term of the process: what human beings become as a result of what God has bestowed on them.

What God does for human beings as a result of his δικαιοσύνη is expressed by Paul as δικαιοῦν, "justify," which means that he acquits their sins and sinfulness, restoring them to a right relationship with him. For Paul conceives of the sinner as standing before the divine tribunal and hearing the verdict "not guilty." This does not mean, of course, that this verdict is passed on sinners because of anything that they themselves do. The status of righteousness is rather seen as an alien status, *iustitia aliena*, as Luther expressed it. It may now belong to sinners, but it does not belong in virtue of anything that sinners have done by their own effort. It is the righteousness that Christ Jesus has won for sinners; it is the righteousness of Christ attributed to sinners by God the judge who sits on the tribunal.

The Greek verb δικαιοῦν belongs to the class of –όω verbs, which usually express a factitive or causative nuance of the root. For instance, δηλόω, "I make clear"; δουλόω, "I make (someone) a slave"; θανατόω, "I mortify." Hence δικαιόω should mean "I make (someone) righteous."

In classical Greek, however, especially among writers such as Herodotus, Aeschylus, and Aristotle, δικαιοῦν meant "make right" or "deem right," and when used with a personal object it denoted "do someone justice," i.e., in the case of someone who has been unfair, violent, or wrong;

hence "to pass sentence against, condemn, punish (someone)."[4] That negative meaning prevailed in classical usage; only rarely does one find a positive meaning, "set right an injustice suffered," e.g., in Pindar's poetry.[5] The negative meaning hardly suits the Pauline contexts, and so one asks: In what sense is the verb δικαιοῦν meant in Pauline thinking? Normally that question is answered by saying that it is used by Paul in the declarative or delocutive sense that it often has in the Septuagint, "declare righteous."[6] The use of the verb in the Septuagint, however, is complicated, as N. M. Watson has shown: whereas the majority of instances are declarative or delocutive, there are some instances where δικαιοῦν seems to mean "make righteous," as in Isa 53:11; Ps 73:13; and other cases where the passive of δικαιοῦν is used to translate the simple *qal* of Hebrew צָדֵק, "be righteous."[7]

Patristic interpreters, both Greek and Latin, moreover, understood the verb as factitive, "make righteous." This is the meaning given by John Chrysostom (δίκαιον ποιῆσαι) and also by Augustine (*iustum facere*).[8] From such an understanding of the verb Alister E. McGrath in his noted study, *Iustitia Dei*, concluded that "righteousness, effected in justification, is regarded by Augustine as *inherent* rather than *imputed*, to use the vocabulary of the sixteenth century."[9] He also maintained that this sense of δικαιοῦν persisted throughout the early and late medieval period.[10] When, however, the meaning of δικαιοῦν was debated in the sixteenth century, two sides developed, one maintaining the traditional inherent or effective meaning of justification, and the other the meaning of imputed or declarative justification. Yet even then Philip Melanchthon was able to say, "'To be justified' means to make unrighteous men righteous or to regenerate them, as

---

[4] See Herodotus, *History* 1.100; 3.29; Aeschylus, *Agamemnon* 393; Aristotle, *Nicomachean Ethics* 5.9.2 §1136a.

[5] See Pindar, Fragment 169.3, quoted in Plato, Gorgias 484b.

[6] E.g., Exod 23:7; Deut 25:1; Ps 82:3; Isa 5:23; 43:26; 50:8. Cf. G. Schrenk, *TDNT* 2:212-14; D. R. Hillers, "Delocutive Verbs in Biblical Hebrew," *JBL* 86 (1967): 320-24; J. H. Ropes, "'Righteousness' and 'the Righteousness of God' in the Old Testament and in St. Paul," *JBL* 22 (1903): 211-27.

[7] See N. M. Watson, "Some Observations on the Use of δικαιόω in the Septuagint," *JBL* 79 (1960): 255-66.

[8] John Chrysostom interpreted δικαιοῦν as meaning δίκαιον ποιῆσαι (*In ep. ad Romanos* 8.2; PG 60.456; *In ep. II ad Corinthios* 11.3; PG 61.478). Augustine understood it as *iustum facere* (*Sermo* 292.6; PL 38.1324; *De Spiritu et littera* 26.45; 32.56; CSEL 60.199, 215).

[9] A. E. McGrath, *Iustitia Dei: A History of the Christian Doctrine of Justification* (2 vols.; Cambridge: Cambridge University Press, 1986), 1:31.

[10] McGrath, *Iustitia Dei*, 1:184.

well as to be pronounced or accounted righteous. For Scripture speaks both ways."[11]

In recent years, E. Käsemann has argued for an understanding of δι-καιοσύνη θεοῦ, as a manifestation of God's "power": "the rightful power with which God makes his cause to triumph in the world which has fallen away from him and which yet, as creation, is his inviolable possession."[12] That important nuance of "power" must not be forgotten, and when one joins to it what Isaiah wrote concerning the effectiveness of God's word (55:10-11), that the word of God that goes forth from his mouth "shall not return to me empty," the declaration of the justification of sinners becomes a powerful one that might readily entail some change in them.[13] Also in recent times one has used a "transformationist" sense of δικαιοῦν, which would mean that sinful human beings are not only declared righteous, but even made righteous. Romans 5:19 even seems to call for such an understanding: "Just as through the disobedience of one man many were made sinners, so through the obedience of one many will be made righteous." Here Paul does not use simply the passive of δικαιοῦν, but rather δίκαιοι κατασταθήσονται, which clearly involves something more than a juridical assessment. Rather, δικαιοῦσθαι, "to be justified," is seen to be the opposite of ἁμαρτάνειν, "to sin," and ὑστεροῦνται τῆς δόξης τοῦ θεοῦ, "they fall short of the glory of God" (3:23). Through justification the condition of δόξα is restored to the sinner, for "God's judgment has creative power. Declaring the sinner righteous has not only a forensic effect, but as forensic also an 'effective' meaning."[14] The formal effect of Christ's obedience has been to make humanity upright or righteous in the sight of God at the judgment seat.

No matter which sense of δικαιοῦν one uses today, however, the result is that in the sight of God sinners have become δίκαιοι, "righteous." For Paul this is a manifestation of God's righteousness "at the present time to show that he is righteous and justifies the one who puts faith in Jesus (τὸν

---

[11] See *Apology* 4.72; *BC* 117.

[12] E. Käsemann, *New Testament Questions of Today* (Philadelphia: Fortress, 1969), 168-82, esp. 180.

[13] Here one might recall the famous debate about the meaning of δικαιοῦν between (Baptist) E. J. Goodspeed, who in his translation of the New Testament rendered δι-καιοῦν, "make upright," and (Presbyterian) B. M. Metzger, who criticized him for that translation (*Theology Today* 2 [1945-46]: 561-63). Goodspeed's defence of his translation is found in "Some Greek Notes," *JBL* 73 (1954): 84-92, esp. 86-91.

[14] See K. Kertelge, *"Rechtfertigung" bei Paulus: Studien zur Struktur und zum Bedeutungsge-halt des paulinischen Rechtfertigungsbegriffs* (NTAbh 2/3; Münster: Aschendorff, 1967), 123.

ἐκ πίστεως ᾽Ιησοῦ)" (Rom 3:26). In this way, Paul can also admit that such a person has "become the righteousness of God" (2 Cor 5:21).

This teaching on justification is best presented by Paul in Rom 3:21-26, a passage that J. Reumann has well explained.[15] There Paul insists on its gratuitous character: God has done this for humanity "freely" and "by his grace" (3:24), "through the redemption that comes in Christ Jesus." He also stresses its appropriation by sinners through faith, "for all who have faith" (3:25). For Paul this "faith" is not merely an intellectual affirmation that "Jesus is Lord" (1 Cor 12:3; Rom 10:9), but rather an affirmation that must so begin, because "faith comes from what is heard" (ἡ πίστις ἐξ ἀκοῆς, Rom 10:17), yet it has to become "a commitment of faith" (ὑπακοὴ πίστεως, Rom 1:5), engaging the whole person. Faith is thus the human response to the gospel, to "the word that we preach" (Rom 10:8). This brings me then to my third point.

Luke's Reformulation of Pauline Justification

Although Luke himself never speaks of justification as an effect of the Christ-event, he does put it on the lips of Paul as he depicts him preaching to Jews in the synagogue of Pisidian Antioch. One may wonder why Luke avoids this mode of expression, especially since the formulation of an effect of the Christ-event under this image did not begin with Paul himself, even though he may have used it more than any other NT writer because of his controversy with the early Christian Judaizers seeking to impose their Jewish way of life on Gentile converts. Reumann has argued, rightly in my opinion, that "justification" or "righteousness" was already a pre-Pauline conceptualization and formulation of such an effect. It formed part of early Christian reflective *homologiai*, "credal summaries," and some evidence of it can be found in 1 Cor 1:30; 6:11; Rom 4:24-25; 3:24-26.[16] Why then did not Luke pick up and echo this mode of expression from the early community before him? We shall probably never learn for sure.

In Acts 13:16b-41, Luke depicts Paul addressing Jews and God-fearers in Pisidian Antioch with "a word of exhortation" (13:15), in which he

---

[15] See "The Gospel of the Righteousness of God: Pauline Reinterpretation in Romans 3:21-31," *Int* 20 (1966): 432-52.

[16] See J. Reumann, *"Righteousness" in the New Testament: "Justification" in the United States Lutheran-Roman Catholic Dialogue* (Philadelphia: Fortress; New York: Paulist, 1982), 26-40. See also pp. 203-5 for my reaction to some of his evidence.

mentions justification.[17] The passage in question is a missionary speech that Paul addresses to these Jews. The speech resembles in part that of Peter on Pentecost (Acts 2), especially in its use of Psalm 2 of the resurrection, and that of Stephen (Acts 7), in that it recounts some of the history of Israel as part of its argumentative buildup, thus establishing the continuity of the Church with Israel. Paul relates how God chose Israel from its Egyptian bondage and made of it a great people, how God put up with Israel for forty years in the desert, how God overthrew the Canaanites and gave Israel their land as its heritage. Later God gave the Israelites kings, Saul and then David. From the latter Jesus is descended, the Savior whom God has now sent to Israel. Those who lived in Jerusalem and their leaders failed to recognize Jesus, Paul maintains, and, in condemning him and handing him over to Pilate, they fulfilled oracles of the prophets. Luke depicts Paul continuing to say to the Jews in Antioch:

32 We too are proclaiming to you that the promise made to our ancestors has been realized: 33 God has fulfilled this promise for us, [their] children, by raising up Jesus, even as it stands written in the second psalm,
You are my son,
this day I have begotten you.
34 As proof that he raised him from the dead, who is never again to return to decay, he thus declared, 'I will give *you the covenant-benefits assured to David.'* 35 That is why he also says in another place, *'You will not allow your holy one to see decay.'* 36 For David indeed, after he had served God's purpose in his own generation, fell asleep and was buried with his ancestors, and did see decay. 37 But the one whom God raised up has not seen decay. 38 So let it be known to you, Brothers, that through him forgiveness of sin is being proclaimed to you, 39 [and] through him everyone who believes is justified from everything from which you could

---

[17] See further W. H. Bates, "A Note on Acts, 13:39," *SE VI* (TU 112; Berlin: Akademie, 1973): 8-10; F. F. Bruce, "Justification by Faith in the Non-Pauline Writings of the New Testament," *EvQ* 24 (1952): 66-77; M. F.-J. Buss, *Die Missionspredigt des Apostels Paulus im pisidischen Antiochien: Analyse von Apg 13,16-41 im Hinblick auf die literarische und thematische Einheit der Paulusrede* (Stuttgart: Katholisches Bibelwerk, 1980): 122-29; M. Dumais, *Le langage de l'évangélisation: L'Annonce missionnaire en milieu juif (Actes 13, 16-41)* (Recherches 16; Tournai/Paris: Desclée; Montreal: Bellarmin, 1976); D. Ellul, "Antioche de Pisidie: Une prédication ... trois credos? (Actes 13,13-43)," *FilNeot* 5 (1992): 3-14; C. A. J. Pillai, *Apostolic Interpretation of History: A Commentary on Acts 13:16-41* (Hicksville: Exposition, 1980); *Early Missionary Preaching: A Study of Luke's Report in Acts 13* (Hicksville: Exposition, 1979); Reumann, *"Righteousness" in the New Testament*, 141-42; D. A. de Silva, "Paul's Sermon in Antioch of Pisidia," *BSac* 151 (1994): 32-49; U. Wilckens, *Die Missionsreden der Apostelgeschichte* (WMANT 5; Neukirchen-Vluyn: Neukirchener-V., 1961), 50-55, 70-71.

not be justified by the law of Moses. 40 Beware, then, lest what was said in the prophets becomes true of you:

41 *"Look, you scoffers,*
be amazed, and then disappear!
For I am doing a deed in your days,
a deed *which you will not believe, even if someone tells you*
about it."

Verses 38-39 of this speech are the only place in all of the Lucan writings were δικαιοῦν is used in the technical sense.[18] These verses are introduced, moreover, by οὖν, "therefore," and clearly draw a hortatory conclusion,[19] but they do not follow logically from the preceding argument in the sermon; they seem to be more or less adventitiously joined to the preceding.[20] And yet, they form part of the culmination of the sermon that Paul has been addressing to the synagogue audience. John J. Kilgallen has rightly related the forgiveness of sins and justification to "the covenant-benefits assured to David" (13:34).[21] When one considers, moreover, how Luke has played on "the forgiveness of sins" thus far in Acts (2:38; 5:31; 10:43) as an effect of the Christ-event, one can understand how he now introduces this notion along with justification as covenant-benefits resulting from Christ, whom Paul is preaching. These benefits are now available to all human beings through Christ Jesus (διὰ τούτου, v. 38; ἐν τούτῳ, v. 39), precisely through him, whom God has raised from the dead. The main problem, however, remains: How is δικαιοῦν used here? Seven things have to be noted about the way Luke depicts Paul speaking of justification.

First, Luke is referring here to genuine Pauline teaching. This has to be noted, because O. Glombitza has claimed that Luke in these verses is teaching that the forgiveness of sins, which the Mosaic Law does not achieve, is accorded through the priestly work of the Messiah Jesus in Jerusalem.[22] This would be a theme akin to Heb 5:1-2, but not a reference to

---

[18] It is found in Luke 7:29, 35; 10:29; 16:15; but in each of these instances it has a different nuance. In Luke 18:14 it comes closest to the Pauline sense, but even there it is not exactly the same, because it is part of the story of the Pharisee and the Publican.

[19] See W. Nauck, "Das *oun*-paräneticum," *ZNW* 49 (1958): 134-35.

[20] See C. F. Evans, "The Kerygma," *JTS* 7 (1956): 25-41, esp. 40. Similarly Bates, "A Note," 10: a "Pauline afterthought." With this description J. Dupont disagrees; see his article, "*Ta hosia Dauid ta pista* (Ac xiii 34 = Is lv 3)," *RB* 68 (1961): 91-114, esp. 114.

[21] J. J. Kilgallen, "Acts 13,38-39: Culmination of Paul's Speech in Pisidia," *Bib* 69 (1988): 480-506.

[22] O. Glombitza, "Akta xiii. 15-41: Analyse einer lukanischen Predigt vor Juden: Ein

Pauline justification by faith. That strange interpretation of these verses, however, has found little support from other interpreters. Rather, one has to admit with P.-H. Menoud that "if it is Luke who wove the cloth of the speech at Antioch in Pisidia, more than one of the threads was spun by Paul."[23] This Menoud asserted apropos of these verses in Acts 13.

Second, Luke rightly portrays Paul emphasizing the role of Jesus' death and resurrection in the matter of justification (Acts 13:34, 37). Such a status before God comes only through Christ. This would agree with Paul's use of "freely" and "through his [i.e., God's] grace" (Rom 3:24) and also with the Apostle's assertion that Christ Jesus was "raised for our justification" (Rom 4:25; cf. Rom 5:2, 15; Gal 2:21).

Third, Luke includes the role of human faith in the justification brought about by Christ: "through him everyone who believes is justified" (Acts 13:39). This too would agree with Paul's affirmation that justification is "to be received by faith" (Rom 3:22, 25; Phil 3:9).

Fourth, just as Paul spoke of his fellow Jews seeking to be justified by "works of the law" (Gal 2:16; Rom 3:28), so too Luke refers to their striving to attain justification "by the law of Moses" (Acts 13:39).

Fifth, one sees the precise Lucan reformulation of Pauline justification in his subsuming of this notion under "forgiveness of sin." Indeed, Luke even makes ἄφεσις ἁμαρτιῶν take precedence over δικαιωθῆναι, when he says, "So let it be known to you, Brothers, that through him forgiveness of sin is being proclaimed to you, [and] through him everyone who believes is justified from everything from which you could not be justified by the law of Moses" (Acts 13:38-39). What Luke is making Paul do in these verses is to proclaim an effect of the Christ-event that Luke favors but that Paul never uses in any of his seven uncontested letters.

ἄφεσις is a word derived from an economic, financial, or even social background, either denoting the image of "remission" of debts or of charges due, or even "release" from captivity or imprisonment. In the Greek OT it translates Hebrew יוֹבֵל, "jubilee" (Lev 25:30), דְּרוֹר, "release" (Jer 41:8 [MT 34:8]); שְׁמִטָּה, "release" or "pardon" from debt (Deut 15:1). Only in Lev 16:26 does it occur in a context involving "sin," from which it developed in later Jewish writings the nuance of "pardon" or "forgive-

---

Beitrag zum Problem der Reden in Akta," *NTS* 5 (1958-59): 306-17, esp. 315-16.

[23] P.-H. Menoud, "Justification by Faith According to the Book of Acts," in his *Jesus Christ and the Faith: A Collection of Studies* (PTMS 18; Pittsburgh: Pickwith, 1978), 202-27, esp. 217.

ness," when חטאה, "sin," and חובתה, "debt," were often related as synonyms (e.g., 4QMess ar 2:17; 11QtgJob 38:2-3).

Luke himself often speaks of an effect of the Christ-event as "forgiveness of sin" (Luke 1:77; 3:3; 24:47; Acts 2:38; 5:31; 10:43; 26:18). By this image Luke shows that Christ has brought about the pardon of the sins of humanity; he has forgiven them by canceling the debt of their guilt. This notion also appears in the Deutero-Pauline writings, Col 1:14 and Eph 1:7, but in none of the uncontested Pauline letters. The closest one comes to that idea is the rare word πάρεσις in Rom 3:25c, the meaning of which is contested. πάρεσις occurs only there in the NT and never in the Septuagint. The Latin Vulgate and some ancient interpreters understood it as *remissio*, "pardon," using a meaning that is also found for it in extrabiblical Greek and adopted by some modern commentators as well.[24] Many other interpreters, however, prefer to translate it as a "passing over, overlooking," as do the RSV, NRSV, and the NIV.

The upshot is that Luke has in Acts 13:38 made Paul proclaim justification as a form of "forgiveness of sin." In reality, of course, that is what justification is supposed to entail. Yet when one tries to respect the images involved, one realizes that justification is a judicial, forensic term and does not connote the economic, financial, or social aspects of ἄφεσις.[25]

Sixth, this reformulation of justification in terms of "pardon, forgiveness, remission" also brings it about that Luke makes Paul speak of people being "justified from": ἀπὸ πάντων ὧν οὐκ ἠδυνήθητε ἐν νόμῳ Μωϋσέως δικαιωθῆναι, "from everything from which you could not be justified by the law of Moses" (Acts 13:39). The reason why Luke makes Paul so speak is that ἄφεσις, "release," dominates his way of speaking about justification.[26] This explains why the RSV translates 13:38-39, "and by him every one that believes is freed from everything from which you could not be freed by the law of Moses." Similarly, the NRSV: "by this Jesus everyone who believes is set free from all those sins from which you could not freed by the law of Moses." Why have the RSV and the NRSV

---

[24] See Phalaris, *Ep.* 81.1; Dionysius of Halicarnassus, *Antiquitates Romanae* 7.37.2; Athenagoras, *De resurrectione* 16S.68.4. Cf. J. A. Fitzmyer, *Romans* (AB 33; New York: Doubleday, 1993), 351-52.

[25] Saying this means that I agree with what Vielhauer once wrote in "On the 'Paulinism' of Acts" (p. 41), but I would not agree with everything stated in that paragraph of his, especially what he writes on p. 42.

[26] Not even Rom 6:7 (ὁ γὰρ ἀποθανὼν δεδικαίωται ἀπὸ τῆς ἁμαρτίας) has quite the same nuance as the preposition ἀπό in Acts 13:38.

avoided translating δικαιοῦν in these verses by "justify," the English verb that they normally use in Paul's letters, and substituted instead "free"? That, of course, may be a way of expressing the difference between Luke and Paul; yet it tends to obscure what Luke has done to Pauline justification.[27]

Seventh, the phrase ἀπὸ πάντων, "from everything," is also part of the Lucan reformulation, and the nuance to be associated with it has been debated. It has been understood as an instance of Lucan hyperbole, for Luke makes abundant use of πᾶς or ἅπας, "all."[28] In this case, Paul's statement would mean that Christian believers are justified from all things, whereas no such justification comes from the Mosaic Law.[29] Lake and Cadbury long ago showed that the relative clause introduced by the pronoun ὧν had to qualify πάντων, so that the Lucan sentence had to mean "forgiveness of everything – which the Law never offered."[30]

The phrase, however, has been understood to mean that Luke was saying that "one could gain partial, but not complete, justification through the Law." This formulates what has been called Luke's understanding of "the insufficiency of the Law," which H. Conzelmann maintains has to be interpreted according to Acts 15, "that it was just too great a burden" for anybody to bear.[31] In other words, Luke would be depicting Paul presenting justification through faith in Christ as a complement to the justification that comes through the Mosaic Law. If this understanding of that phrase were correct, it would be still another Lucan difference from the Pauline view. In fact, it would be a significant reformulation. As Bacon put it,

---

[27] BDAG (249) give a meaning of δίκαιον as "make free/pure," under which Acts 13:38-39 is booked, but few of the instances recorded actually substantiate that meaning. See, moreover, the article of Kilgallen, "Acts 13,38-39," 480, where the verses are properly translated. Similarly, Menoud, "Justification by Faith," 211.

[28] For other instances of such hyperbole, see Acts 1:14, 19; 2:14, 43, 44; 3:18, 24; 5:12; 8:1, 40; 9:32, 35, 40; 13:24, 44; 16:3, 15 [ms. D]); 18:23; 19:10, 17bis, 26; 21:18, 20, 21, 28.

[29] So it was understood by F. F. Bruce, *The Speeches in the Acts of the Apostles* (London: Tyndale, 1942), 12.

[30] *The Beginnings of Christianity: Part I. The Acts of the Apostles* (ed. F. J. Foakes Jackson and K. Lake; 5 vols.; Grand Rapids: Baker Book House, 1979), 4:157.

[31] H. Conzelmann, *Acts of the Apostles* (Hermeneia; Philadelphia: Fortress, 1987), 106; similarly B. W. Bacon, *The Story of St. Paul: A Comparison of Acts and Epistles* (Boston/New York: Houghton Mifflin and Co., 1904), 103 n.; Bates, "A Note," 10; Vielhauer, "On the 'Paulinism' of Acts," 42.

The doctrine is exactly that which Paul fundamentally repudiates, and which in Gal. ii. 15-21 he demonstrates against Peter to be untenable, namely, that a man may rest upon the works of the law for his general justification, and rely on the death of Christ to make up the deficiencies.[32]

However, it is merely another instance of Lucan hyperbole, and the difference from genuine Pauline teaching about justification and the Mosaic Law is not so exaggerated as Bacon, Conzelmann, and Vielhauer, and others would have us believe. For Luke means that Paul is saying that it is not at all possible to find justification through the Law of Moses.

In any case, these considerations explain how Luke has reformulated Pauline justification. In effect, Luke makes Paul sound somewhat like himself in this matter of justification. This brings me to my fourth and last point.

Why Has Luke so Presented Pauline Justification?

This transformation of Pauline teaching on justification is a factor in "the Paulinism of Acts," the notion with which we began. To account for it three further considerations have to be made. First, partly involved in this issue is the question of who the author of Acts really is and the extent to which he may have been a collaborator of Paul. For Vielhauer "the Paulinism of Acts," and in particular the way Luke has altered Pauline teaching on justification, is one of the reasons why the traditional Luke cannot have been Paul's collaborator.

Traditionally, the author of the Third Gospel and Acts has been regarded as the Luke mentioned in Phlm 24; Col 4:14; and 2 Tim 4:11. This tradition is found in several patristic writers.[33] Irenaeus, in particular, based his identification of the author with Luke on the so-called We-Sections of Acts (16:10-17; 20:5-15; 21:1-18; 27:1-28:16), because he regarded them as authored by such a companion of Paul.[34] In modern times it has become the vogue to discount that patristic tradition and to speak rather of "the Rev. Mr. Luke,"[35] whoever he may be. The current trend is

---

[32] Bacon, *Story of St. Paul*, 103 n.

[33] For the details, see Fitzmyer, *Luke*, 35-41.

[34] See *Adversus haereses* 3.14.1.

[35] So W. C. van Unnik, "Luke-Acts, a Storm Center in Contemporary Scholarship," *Studies in Luke-Acts: Essays Presented in Honor of Paul Schubert* (ed. L. E. Keck and J. L. Martyn; Nashville: Abingdon, 1966), 15-32, esp. 16.

supposed to reflect a critical way of reading the evidence about the authorship of Luke-Acts. I consider that mode of evaluation to be hyper-critical, even though I also consider Irenaeus' conclusion that the We-Sections of Acts show that Luke was the "inseparable" collaborator of Paul to be wrong. If one uses the same evidence that Irenaeus used, however, and critically examines the We-Sections, even regarding them as some sort of record of travels with Paul, one can only conclude that Luke had been a *sometime collaborator* of Paul, not an inseparable one.

Indeed, if one takes the We-Sections at face value, they reveal that the author of Acts would have been with Paul from the time of his vision at Troas of the Macedonian who summoned Paul "to come over and help us" to the end of Paul's evangelization of Philippi on his second missionary journey. For the We-Sections begin with Acts 16:10-17 and are followed by a break, after which they resume in 20:5-15, when Paul, at the end of his third missionary journey is returning to Jerusalem via Philippi. The association of the first two We-Sections with Philippi would suggest that the author of Acts stayed in that town from the middle of the second missionary journey to the end of the third missionary journey. If he did so, then the author of Acts was not present with Paul in Corinth toward the end of his second missionary journey or with him during any of the first part or middle of the third missionary journey. Yet that was precisely the time (from roughly A.D. 50 to 58) when Paul wrote all his major letters (from 1 Thessalonians to Romans). That would mean that, if Luke were indeed the author of Acts, he was not with Paul when he was battling with the Judaizers, when he wrote the Letters to the Galatians and the Romans.

Second, this raises the question about how well Luke understood Pauline teaching. Since there is no real evidence that the author of Acts ever read any of the Pauline letters,[36] it would follow that he was not very well informed about Pauline theology, even on such a capital matter as justification by grace through faith. Paul was for Luke a prominent example of an earlier generation of Christian missionaries; that is why he made him the hero of the second half of the Book of Acts, but that does not

---

[36] Some interpreters have indeed tried to maintain that he did read Paul's letters: so E. E. Ellis (*The Gospel of Luke* [CentBib; London: Nelson, 1966], 51); M. S. Enslin ("'Luke' and Paul," *JAOS* 58 [1938]: 81-91); J. Knox ("Acts and the Pauline Letter Corpus," *Studies in Luke-Acts: Essays Presented in Honor of Paul Schubert* [ed. L. E. Keck and J. L. Martyn; Nashville: Abingdon, 1966], 279-87). The evidence for that interpretation, however, is so meager that it is scarcely convincing.

mean that Luke would have been fully informed about every facet of Pauline teaching. Luke surely knew that Paul preached about justification, but he depicts Paul doing so only on one occasion, in the sermon to Jews in Pisidian Antioch. For Luke "justification" has become merely a slogan associated with Paul, but Luke understands it as "forgiveness of sins," a phrase that he also puts on the lips of Peter (Acts 2:38; 5:31; 10:43).

Third, because such Pauline teaching about justification was not without its complications, that may be part of the reason why Luke reformulates it in terms of his more usual and more easily understood teaching about "forgiveness of sins." After all, it was not only Luke who has reformulated Pauline justification in the NT. The author of the Deutero-Pauline Epistle to the Ephesians has also done so. There we read, "By grace you have been saved through faith; and this is not from you; it is the gift of God. It is not from deeds so that no one may boast. For we are his handiwork, created in Christ Jesus for good deeds that God has prepared in advance that we might live by them" (Eph 2:8-10). For the author of Ephesians it is no longer "justification by grace through faith," but "salvation by grace through faith." Here the complicated notion of justification has given way to the simpler notion of salvation, and the judaizing controversy that made Paul dwell on justification has long since been forgotten. The operative notions of grace and faith have been retained, but they are no longer associated with justification, as they were in Romans. This explains then, at least in part, why Luke has reformulated justification in Acts 13. In this regard I quote a paragraph from M. Hengel, which sums up my attitude to this whole matter. Hengel wrote:

Although he was a companion of Paul and had great respect for this unique missionary, Luke did not completely understand and assimilate Paul's theology. Those who reflect on the theological changes to be seen among once 'narrow Barthians' or 'strict Lutherans' over the past thirty years, or note how far imagination and reality have become confused in the legends about the church struggle over a period of only forty years, will be more careful in judging Luke than his strictest critics in recent decades. After all, he was a child of his time, who was still quite unfamiliar with the 'historical-critical method,' did not have the possibility of easy access to information in well-filled libraries and archives, and was even less acquainted with the strict methods of NT seminars. It is without doubt a serious failing that Luke does not take up the Pauline theology of the cross and that justification by faith alone without the works of the law takes very much a back place with him (but cf. Acts 13.38f. for Paul and 15.11 for Peter). Still, which of Paul's pupils remained completely faithful to his master's heritage?

Taking into account the so-called 'Deutero-Pauline' letters, can we not also include Luke among the 'disciples of Paul'? Those who cannot forgive him his questionable 'Paulinism' and his other 'freedoms' should at least consider how many people are proud of being the disciples of a great theological teacher and heap praise upon him, though in the meantime they have moved miles away from him. In how many cases might we not think it a blessing that the dead teacher is no longer in a position to note the errors and confusions of his pupils? Only those who are really completely without sin here can go on throwing stones at Luke because of his un-Pauline 'Paulinism.'[37]

No matter what the real explanation of this Lucan reformulation is, we have to realize that "we would hardly have understood the doctrine of [Pauline] justification very well if Acts 13:39 was all we had to go on."[38]

---

[37] M. Hengel, *Acts and the History of Earliest Christianity* (Philadelphia: Fortress, 1979), 66-67.

[38] Bates, "A Note," 10.

15. THE COMMISSIONING OF WOMEN DISCIPLES: MATTHEW 28:9-10

Timothy A. FRIEDRICHSEN

Francis J. Moloney has considered the narratives of the empty tomb and the resurrection in many of his publications. With respect to these narratives, Moloney has given a very helpful opening perspective for our discussion here: "One of the most outstanding features of the Gospels' treatment of women characters is the universal presence of women at the empty tomb, and their being first to proclaim the easter message."[1] He goes on "simply to reach back and attempt to indicate what stands behind" the versions of the four canonical Gospels.[2] According to Mark 16:8, the women remain silent, which seems to be "a uniquely Marcan twist."[3] Given that, the women must have proclaimed "something like

---

[1] F. J. Moloney, "Jesus and Woman," in *Virgo fidelis. Miscellanea di studi mariani in onore di Don Domenico Bertetto, S.D.B.* (eds. F. Bergamelli and M. Cimosa; BELS 43; Rome: Edizioni Liturgiche, 1988), 53-80, esp. 72 (for slightly different wording, see, "Jesus of Nazareth," in *Woman: First among the Faithful* [Melbourne: Dove, 1984; with introduction by T. H. Green; Notre Dame: Ave Maria Press, 1986]), 18-35). Due to Marcan priority, which Moloney accepts, the Synoptic Gospels have more than one woman at the empty tomb; John 20 mentions only Mary Magdalene. For Moloney, John is literally independent of the Synoptic Gospels; see his *The Gospel of John* (SP 4; Collegeville: Liturgical Press, 1998), 2-3.

[2] Moloney, "Jesus and Woman," 72.

[3] Moloney, "Jesus and Woman," 73. See now F. J. Moloney's commentary, *The Gospel of Mark: A Commentary* (Peabody: Hendrickson, 2002), esp. 352: "When and how does Jesus' meeting with the failed disciples, women and men, take place? The answer to that question cannot be found *in the story*, but the very existence *of the story* tells the reader that *what Jesus said would happen, did happen.*" But the meeting Jesus foretold "did not take place because of the women. As the disciples failed (14:50-52), so also the women failed (16:8). In the end, *all human beings fail* . . . but God succeeds." For a presentation both of Moloney's commentary and of J. R. Donahue and D. J. Harrington (*The Gospel of Mark* [SP 2; Collegeville: Liturgical Press, 2002]), see T. A. Friedrichsen, "Reading Mark as Mark: Two New Narrative Commentaries," *ETL* 79 (2003): 134-56.

Luke 24:34: 'The Lord has been raised' (see also I Cor 15:4-5)," which likely lies behind both Matthew's and Luke's redactions of the Marcan account.[4] Nevertheless, "[t]he proclamation of the women is not believed by the disciples. The Gospels … are remarkable in their consistent presentation of the doubt and unfaith of the disciples, both at the proclamation of the resurrection, and at the appearances (Matt 28:16-17; Luke 24:10-12, 13-35; John 20:2-10)."[5]

Given this general perspective evinced in the Gospels, which has been well laid out by Francis Moloney, I decided for the purposes of this collection of articles in his honor to turn my attention to a peculiarly Matthean addition, namely, the commissioning of the women disciples in Matt 28:9-10.[6] Moreover, there are clear structural parallels between the encounter of the women with the risen Lord in Matt 28:9-10 and the encounter of the Eleven with the risen Lord in Matt 28:16-20. After considering the texts and the presence of Matthean redaction, we will consider possible reasons why the Evangelist both created the repetition of the angel's command to the women in the words of the risen Lord and structured the latter so similarly with the commissioning of the Eleven.

The Women in Matthew 28:1-8 – Redaction of Mark 16:1-8

Although there is agreement between Matt 28:1-8 and Mark 16:1-8 in terms of the general story, there are also a considerable number of differences. The redactional character of Matthew's text in comparison to his Marcan source has been thoroughly demonstrated, thus, it need not be repeated here.[7] For the purposes of this piece, we are most interested in how the Matthean redaction develops the women characters.

---

[4] Moloney, "Jesus and Woman," 73. Despite his position on the independence of John from the Synoptics, Moloney adds, "it is also behind John's use of his Mary Magdalene tradition" (cf. below, n. 38).

[5] Moloney, "Jesus and Woman," 73.

[6] Although I will take a different tack, my interest in this text was raised by a former doctoral student, Nancy Maestri, "The Women at the Tomb" (Research paper; The Catholic University of America: 2000), 32 pages.

[7] Most especially by F. Neirynck, "Les femmes au tombeau: étude de la rédaction Matthéenne (Matt 28:1-10)," in *Evangelica. Gospel Studies – Études d'évangile. Collected Essays* (ed. F. Van Segbroeck, BETL 60; Leuven: Peeters University Press, 1982), 273-95, esp. 272-83 on Matt 28:1-8. Among others, H. Hendrickx notes that Mark 28:1-8 is "very Matthean in character" and "does not presuppose any source different from Mark 16:1-

To investigate Matthew's treatment of the women in 28:1-8, it is necessary to return briefly to the women who witnessed the crucifixion "from
afar" (ἀπὸ μακρόθεν; Mark 15:40-41//Matt 27:55-56). Matthew altered
Mark's reference to Salome by substituting "the mother of the sons of
Zebedee," who, on behalf of her sons, had asked for the places of honor
at Jesus' right and left (Matt 20:20; cf. Mark 10:35).[8] By the time of the
burial (Matt 27:57-61//Mark 15:42-47), however, only "Mary Magdalene
and the other Mary" are present; the latter Mary is most likely "the mother
of James and Joseph" of 27:56.[9] This leaves Matthew's narrative with the
requisite two witnesses.[10] Significant for the reader, however, is that these
women were not only among the first group of women named in the
Matthean narrative, but Matthew also described them as among "many
women ... who had followed Jesus from Galilee, ministering to him."[11]
The description of these women as following (ἀκολουθέω) and ministering (διακονέω; "to serve") from Galilee to the time of the crucifixion is
strongly reminiscent of the language of discipleship. Nevertheless, by
adding "many" (πολλαί) and by moving this description forward (cf. Matt
27:55 and Mark 15:41), the description has "been highlighted by the
Matthean structuring."[12]

8" (*Resurrection Narratives: Studies in the Synoptic Gospels* [London: Geoffrey Chapman,
1978], 32).

[8] W. D. Davies and D. C. Allison, Jr. note that with respect to this substitution for
the otherwise unknown Salome, Matthew would have "felt justified ... because, according to Mark, the 'many' women ... were Galileans." In addition, as she witnesses the crucifixion, "she learns the true meaning of being on Jesus' left and right. Her presence also
serves as a foil for her sons' cowardly absence" (*A Critical and Exegetical Commentary on the
Gospel according to Saint Matthew in Three Volumes.* Vol. III: *Commentary on Matthew XIX–
XXVIII* [ICC; Edinburgh: T&T Clark, 1997], 3:638).

[9] Among others, see, D. A. Hagner, *Matthew 14–28* (WBC 33B; Waco: Word Books,
1995), 859; Davies and Allison, *Matthew XIX–XXVIII*, 652.

[10] Jewish law requires two independent witnesses; see Deut 19:15. Davies and Allison
note: "not only have the disciples fled, but by this point even most of the women have
left" (*Matthew XIX–XXVIII*, 652).

[11] Unless indicated otherwise, all English translations are from the Revised New
American Bible (RNAB).

[12] E. M. Wainwright, *Towards a Feminist Critical Reading of the Gospel According to Matthew*
(BZNW 60; Berlin: Walter de Gruyter, 1991), 296. On women understood as "disciples"
by Matthew, see too, e.g., B. Witherington III, *Women in the Ministry of Jesus* (SNTSMS 51;
Cambridge: Cambridge University Press, 1984), 122-23; G. R. Osborne, "Women in Je-
sus' Ministry: Redactional Analysis of Gospels," *WTJ* 51 (1989): 259-91, esp. 275; J. Ko-
pas, "Jesus and Women in Matthew," *ThTo* 47 (1990): 13-21, esp. 20; R. H. Gundry,
Matthew: A Commentary on His Handbook for a Mixed Church under Persecution (2d ed.; Grand
Rapids: Eerdmans, 1994), 578-79; T. A. Friedrichsen, "'Disciple(s)' in the New Testa-

We can now turn to the visit to the tomb on "the first day of the week" (Matt 28:1; cf. Mark 16:2). Unlike Mark, Matthew does not have the women bring spices for the purpose of anointing the body of Jesus (cf. Mark 16:1 and Matt 28:1), which would be impossible, given that the women had seen the sealing of the tomb with "a huge stone" (Matt 27:60 adds μέγαν to Mark 15:46).[13] In addition, when compared with Mark, Matthew is even more consequent with respect to the narrative, for Jesus had been anointed in anticipation of his burial by the woman in the house of Simon the leper in Bethany (Matt 26:6-13//Mark 14:3-9). In lieu of that purpose, Matthew writes that the women have come "to see the tomb" (θεωρῆσαι τὸν τάφον). The use of θεωρέω here continues the faithful watching of the women, of whom the verb is used in Matt 27:55, as Jesus is crucified, and seems implied at the burial, for "... Mary Magdalene and the other Mary remained sitting there, facing the tomb" (Matt 27:61).[14] In addition, the return of the women "to see the tomb" may be for confirming Jesus' death, an obligation with which Matthew's Jewish readers would have been familiar.[15]

Since the women do not come to anoint the body, Matthew omits the dialogue among the women about rolling back the stone and the "delayed parenthesis" about the size of the stone (Mark 16:3-4).[16] Rather, Matthew

---

ment: Background, usage, characteristics and historicity," *Sal* 65 (2003): 717-39, esp. 725-26.

[13] This impossibility is heightened by the placement of guards at the tomb, who further seal the stone (Matt 27:62-66). Matthew never clearly indicates whether the women would have known of this, since it happens "The next day, the one following the day of preparation."

[14] Note Mark 15:47: ἐθεώρουν ποῦ τέθειται ("watched where he was laid"). Wainwright suggests that the use of θεωρέω may "be an attempt to present the women's witness in unique terminology which highlights the nature of their action, but which is also in terminology acceptable to the entire community" (*Feminist Critical Reading*, 295-96). W. Carter proposes that θεωρέω expresses comprehension and insight into what God is doing ("'To See the Tomb': Matthew's Women at the Tomb," *ExpTim* 107 [1996]: 201-5). N. Maestri correctly notes that "the statement of the angel, in v. 5 ... does not support this claim. Instead, it suggests that they expected the crucified Jesus to be in the tomb" ("Women at the Tomb," 7 n. 20).

[15] See T. R. W. Longstaff, "The Women at the Tomb: Matthew 28:1 Re-Examined," *NTS* 27 (1981): 277-82. According to D. J. Weaver, up to now the women have been powerless, "whether as a group (27:55-56) or by twos (27:61). ... In the face of Jesus' crucifixion these women are clearly as impotent as they had once been invisible," i.e., until 27:55-56 ("Matthew 28:1-10," *Int* 46 [1992]: 398-401, esp. 401).

[16] This description of the comment, ἦν γὰρ μέγας σφόδρα, comes from F. Neirynck, "The Apocryphal Gospels and the Gospel of Mark," in *Evangelica II: 1982–1991 Collected Essays* (ed. F. Van Segbroeck; BETL 99; Leuven: Peeters University Press,

(v. 2) moves immediately to an in-breaking of the divine by the addition of one of his favorite stock apocalyptic images, namely, an earthquake – a great one at that.[17] This epiphanic earthquake takes place because (γάρ) an angel descends from heaven and sits on the stone, which the angel rolls back.

The first reaction to the angel's appearance and enthronement comes from the guards (v. 4), which harkens back to Matthew's addition of the placement of guards at the tomb (Matt 27:62-66). As the earth had quaked, now the guards quake (σείω); now the guards "became like dead men," while their charge, Jesus, who had been dead, has been raised.[18] This reaction of the guards stands in sharp contrast to the faithfulness of the women.

For the rest of the scene at the tomb, Matthew follows his Marcan source more faithfully (Matt 28:5-8//Mark 16:6-8). The angel/young man assures the women that they need not be afraid/amazed (cf. μὴ φοβεῖσθε/μὴ ἐκθαμβεῖσθε), which is a "normal reaction" to an epiphany.[19] Although it is implied of the young man in Mark, Matthew explicates the angel's foreknowledge of what the women seek ("I know…"; οἶδα). Matthew reverses the next phrases found in Mark, so that the angel says, "He is not here, for he has been raised";[20] this reversal prepares nicely for the Matthean addition, "just as he said," which he has anticipated from Mark 16:7 ("as he told you"). By this, then, the angel both interprets the meaning of the empty tomb and affirms that Jesus' predictions that he would rise had come true (esp. Matt 16:21-23; 17:22-23 and 20:17-19).[21] To con-

1991), 715-67, esp. 743.

[17] In addition to the case here, in which σεισμός is added to Mark 16:4, see Matt 8:24 (+ μέγας) and 27:54 (added to Mark 4:37; 15:39, respectively; see too Matt 24:7//Mark 13:8). P. Minear notes: "This particular earthquake belongs to a long series of earthquakes in Scripture … (Exod 19:16-25; Isa 29:5-9; Jer 4:19-31). Many prophetic passages anticipate the last judgment as 'a great earthquake' (Ezek 37:1-14; Zech 14:1-8; Matthew 24; Revelation 11)" ("Matthew 28:1-10," *Int* 38 [1984]: 59-63, esp. 60-61). See, too, the interesting perspective of L. Marin, "The Women at the Tomb: A Structural Analysis Essay of a Gospel Text," in *The New Testament and Structuralism* (ed. and trans. A. M. Johnson, Jr.; PTMS 11; Pittsburgh: Pickwick, 1976), 73-96, esp. 78-79.

[18] For this double ironical twist, see, e.g., Minear, "Matthew 28:1-10," 60; Weaver, "Matthew 28:1-10," 401; Hagner, *Matthew 14–28*, 869; Davies and Allison, *Matthew XIX–XXVIII*, 666.

[19] Minear, "Matthew 28:1-10," 60.

[20] "Matthew exchanges Mark's chronological order for a logical order" (Gundry, *Matthew*, 588).

[21] For an interesting description of the angel's role, see Marin, "Women at the Tomb," 96.

firm that Jesus is not there, the angel then invites the women, "Come and see the place where he lay" (Matt 28:6b; cf. Mark 16:6c). The addition of "come" (δεῦτε) works well in Matthew's narrative, for as of yet the women had not entered the tomb.

Invitation now shifts to command (Matt 28:7) as the angel urges haste ("quickly"; ταχύ) on the part of the women to go and tell the news to the disciples:[22] "He has been raised from the dead, and he is going before you to Galilee; there you will see him."[23] Matthew concludes the angel's summary of the news with "Behold, I have told you," in place of Mark's "as he told you" (16:5), which Matthew anticipated in v. 6 (see above); this phrase "completes the angel's errand"[24] and "adds a touch of solemnity."[25]

In perfect obedience (Matt 28:8), the women departed quickly (ἀπελθοῦσαι ταχύ), and "fearful yet overjoyed, ... ran to announce this to his disciples." This, of course, is Matthew's most dramatic editing of his Marcan source with respect to the actions of the women at the empty tomb. Mark 16:8 emphasizes the failure of the women to carry the message to the disciples with a double negative, καὶ οὐδενὶ οὐδὲν εἶπαν, literally, "and they said nothing to nobody." Their failure is due to their fear, as the Marcan Gospel's concluding phrase notes: "for they were afraid" (ἐφοβοῦντο γάρ).[26] In Matthew's view, however, the women, who had been invisible and unnamed until 27:55-56, and who remained "powerless," silent–albeit faithful–watchers (cf. 27:61, too), "now become powerful players in the concluding act of Matthew's narrative, characters whose actions are crucial to the outworking of the plot itself."[27]

From Messengers to Witnesses: Matthew 28:9-10

With the explicit indication that the women set out to fulfill the charge given to them by the angel, Matthew's narrative could continue with the

---

[22] In Mark 16:7, Peter is explicitly mentioned. Davies and Allison note that "the deletion corresponds to 28:16-20, where Peter is just one of the group" (*Matthew XIX–XXVIII*, 667).

[23] Minear provides a concise paragraph on the importance of Galilee for Matthew ("Matthew 28:1-10," 61).

[24] Minear adds: "when the women have completed their errand, the same words could be used" ("Matthew 28:1-10," 61).

[25] Davies and Allison, *Matthew XIX–XXVIII*, 668; see, too, Hagner, *Matthew 14–28*, 870.

[26] Cf. Moloney, *Mark*, 352.

[27] Weaver, "Matthew 28:1-10," 401; cf. too Marin, "Women at the Tomb," 79.

appearance of the risen Jesus to the Eleven in Galilee (Matt 28:16-20), with or without the report of some of the guard to the chief priests (Matt 28:11-15), at which time a conspiracy is hatched to claim that Jesus' disciples had stolen the body – a passage that has clear apologetic intentions.[28] Matt 28:9-10 could thus be dismissed as a superfluous addition after Matthew's reworking of Mark 16:1-8.[29] Some argue, however, that Matthew has at hand a now lost ending of Mark.[30] This seems highly improbable, because Mark 16:8 can be defended as the ending intended by the Evangelist with "textual, literary, and theological arguments."[31] Matt 28:9-10, then, results from Matthean redaction, which has been thoroughly argued.[32] The focus here is again on how these verses contribute to the development of women as characters in Matthew's narrative.[33]

Matthew opens this brief scene with his well-liked phrase, "And behold" (καὶ ἰδού), which indicates something new and of importance is about to happen.[34] The risen Jesus greets the women with the common

---

[28] Treating this passage (Matt 28:11-15) is beyond the scope of this piece. Clearly the placing of guards at the tomb (Matt 27:62-66), their reaction to the earthquake and appearance of the angel (28:2-4) and their report to the chief priests (28:11-15) all serve the purpose of substantiating the claim that Jesus had been raised from the dead and to counter any rumor to the contrary.

[29] Gundry concludes that these verses are "wholly unnecessary" (see *Matthew*, 590-91).

[30] Gundry, *Matthew*, 590-91; Gundry argues that with 16:8, Mark is "starting a new pericope, the rest of which is now lost" (*Mark: A Commentary on His Apology for the Cross* [Grand Rapid: Eerdmans, 1993], 1009-12, esp.1009). He is supported by C. A. Evans, *Mark 8:27–16:20* (WBC 34B; Nashville: Thomas Nelson, 2001), 539.

[31] Moloney treats the canonical ending in "The Appendix (Mark 16:9-20)" (*Mark*, 355-62, esp. 353). Donahue and Harrington accept 16:8 as the conclusion to Mark, but treat "Later Endings (16:9-20)" (*Mark*, 462-64). Neither of these commentaries considers Gundry's proposal. I too accept Mark 16:8 as the intended ending. If one is to imagine a lost, longer ending, then is it not rather surprising that the portion of Mark that has been lost to the textual tradition just happens to begin at a point that provides a grammatically possible – albeit sudden and troubling – ending to the Gospel?

[32] Neirynck, "Les femmes," esp. 281-89; see too his "Note on Mt 28,9-10," in *Evangelica III. 1992–2000 Collected Essays* (BETL 150; Leuven: Peeters University Press, 2001), 579-84. Even Gundry sees numerous Mattheanism in Matt 28:9-10 (*Matthew*, 590-91).

[33] Gundry says Mark needs something like Matt 28:9-10 "to jolt the women out of their speechlessness," and thus this passage "had its raison d'être only in Mark. ..." (*Matthew*, 590-91). This presentation, however, finds that even without a Marcan *Vorlage*, Matthew had quite his own *raison d'être* for these redactional verses, namely, the development of the characterization of women disciples.

[34] Wainwright (*Feminist Critical Reading*, 301) notes the following general structure of Matt 28:1-10:

χαίρετε ("Hail"; RSV). The women immediately approached (προσελ-
θοῦσαι) the risen Jesus, and without the faintest hint of doubt, which will
be present among the Eleven (v. 17), the women "embraced his feet, and
did him homage"; both the women and the Eleven pay homage or
"worship" (προσκυνέω).

Matthew shifts the verb for the risen Jesus' speaking in v. 10 to "the
emphatic historic present λέγει" (literally, "says").[35] Although there is no
reference to the women being afraid – either here or at the tomb – similar
to the angel at the tomb, Jesus exhorts the women, "Do not be afraid."
Compared to the angel at the tomb (v. 7), the command of the risen Jesus
to go to the disciples differs in wording, at least in part because of the
change in speaker:

7a καὶ ταχὺ πορευθεῖσαι εἴπατε τοῖς μαθηταῖς αὐτοῦ ὅτι ἠγέρθη ἀπὸ
τῶν νεκρῶν,
10b ὑπάγετε ἀπαγγείλατε τοῖς ἀδελφοῖς μου

The urgency of the angel's command, "go quickly" is retained in the
imperative, ὑπάγετε (also translated "go" in the RNAB).[36] According to

v. 1	Setting of scene	
vv. 2-8	Καὶ ἰδοὺ σεισμός	Angel and Women
		Response
vv. 9-10	Καὶ ἰδοὺ Ἰησοῦς	Jesus and Women
		Response

She notes (301 n. 114) a more complete structural analysis provided in H. Bloem, *Die
Ostererzählung des Matthäus: Aufbau und Aussage von Mt 27,57–28,20* (Rome: Zeist, 1985),
24-25, which we need not repeat here, for the parallels are provided in the text above.

[35] Gundry, *Matthew*, 591. Might this usage indicate that these words are "an address to
the church," as Gundry proposes of its use in 9:37-38 (181)? J. C. Anderson notes that
the historic present here places the characters, narrator and implied readers into the same
temporal position, so that not only the characters, but also the implied readers are addressed ("Matthew: Gender and Reading," *Semeia* 28 [1983]: 3-27, 24). According to H.
Fleddermann, "Matthew uses the historic present to highlight the climax of a section or
to mark its christological center" ("The Demands of Discipleship: Matt 8,19-22 par. Luke
9,57-62," in *The Four Gospels 1992. Festschrift Frans Neirynck* [eds. F. Van Segbroeck, *et al.*;
3 vols.; BETL 100A-C; Leuven: Peeters University Press, 1992], 1:541-61, esp. 545; cf. n.
19 for a list of instances).

[36] In the former case, the infinitive followed by καί + imperative gives the infinitive
the force of an imperative; the urgency is also underlined by ταχύ. Nevertheless, the im-
peratival use of ὑπαγώ – "go away," "depart," "away," or "be gone" – often communicates urgency: cf. Matt 4:10; 5:24, 41; 8:4 (//Mark 1:44), 13, 32 (diff. Mark 5:13); 9:6
(//Mark 2:11); 16:23 (//Mark 8:33); 18:15 (add Q 17:3); 19:21 (//Mark 10:21); 20:4, 7,
14; 21:28; 26:18 (//Mark 14:13); 27:65. Cf. too Weaver, who locates urgency in the repetition of the angel's message by the risen Jesus ("Matthew 28:1-10," 401).

the angel, the women are to "tell" (εἴπατε) the news they have been given, whereas the risen Lord uses "report" or "announce" (ἀπαγγείλατε; flatly translated "tell" by RNAB) with the sense of being charged to do so.[37] While the angel refers to "his disciples," the risen Jesus refers to the disciples as "my brothers," which harkens back to Matt 12:48-50 (par. Mark 3:33-35) where Jesus indicates those who are truly members of his family.[38] The very appearance of the risen Jesus confirms the angel's words that Jesus had been raised, thus there is no reason to have the risen Jesus reiterate these words. Moreover, the risen Jesus wants the women to tell the disciples "to go to Galilee, and there they will see me," which likewise confirms what the angel had said. Again, the parallelism between the two is striking:

7b καὶ ἰδοὺ προάγει ὑμᾶς εἰς τὴν Γαλιλαίαν, ἐκεῖ αὐτὸν ὄψεσθε
10c ἵνα ἀπέλθωσιν εἰς τὴν Γαλιλαίαν, κἀκεῖ με ὄψονται

Finally, just as the scene at the tomb ended with an indication that the women had set out in obedience to the angel's command, Matthew again notes that the women set out to fulfill their charge with a genitive absolute construction, "While they were going" (πορευομένων δὲ αὐτῶν). This phrase also serves as a transition to the scene of the guard's report to the chief priests (28:11-15).

So, while the specifics of the charge given by the risen Jesus to the women do not add much to the angel's command, the addition of vv. 9-10 in the first place does bolster the news that the women will bring to the disciples, for now it is not only the word of the angel at the tomb, but the charge of the risen Lord himself. That is to say, the status of the women "has changed from messengers to *witnesses*, and the message that they can convey is not only that Jesus is risen, but *they have encountered the risen Jesus*."[39]

---

[37] H. K. Moulton, ed., *The Analytical Greek Lexicon Revised* (2nd rev. ed., Grand Rapids: Zondervan, 1982), s.v. "ἀπαγέλλω" 35.

[38] The reference to his disciples as "my brothers," as well as much of this passage, is quite similar to the encounter between Mary Magdalene and the risen Jesus in John 20; see Neirynck, "Les femmes," esp. 289-95. He revisited the issue in "John and the Synoptics. The Empty Tomb Stories," in *Evangelica II*, 571-97, esp. 579-88 on Matt 28:9-10 and John 20:11-18.

[39] Maestri, "Women at the Tomb," 11-12.

The Form and Structure: Matt 28:9-10 and Matt 28:16-20

The case for Matthew doing something intentional and with a larger purpose comes into sharper focus when one notes that there is also a structural similarity between the charge given to the women in vv. 9-10 and the commissioning of the Eleven in vv. 16-20. The focus here, therefore, will be on the structural similarities, for it is beyond the purposes of this article to treat Matt 28:16-20 in detail.

Matt 28:16-20 is traditionally referred to as "The Great Commissioning"; it is often considered the high point of Matthew's Gospel. Form-critically speaking, scholars find identifying the genre of Matt 28:16-20 challenging. Benjamin Hubbard discussed a number of suggestions,[40] concluding that the Old Testament offers "several points in which God commissions individuals and promises his support in the undertaking."[41] From a study of a number of such passages from the law, prophets and writings, Hubbard identifies a "*Gattung* of Commissionings,"[42] which has the following seven formal elements: Introduction; Confrontation; Reaction; Commission; Protest; Reassurance; Conclusion.[43] Hubbard identifies these elements in the 'Christophanies' of Matt 28:9-10 and 16-20 as follows:[44]

Formal Element	Verse(s)	Text
Introduction	8c	"Then they went away quickly from the tomb"
	16	The Eleven on the mountain in Galilee
Confrontation	9a	Jesus' greeting

---

[40] B. Hubbard, *The Matthean Redaction of a Primitive Apostolic Commissioning: An Exegesis of Matthew 28:16-20* (SBLDS 19; Missoula: University of Montana, 1974), esp. 2-23.

[41] Hubbard, *Matthean Redaction*, 23; he found the following two studies particularly helpful: W. Trilling, *Das wahre Israel: Studien zur Theologie des Matthäus Evangeliums* (SANT 10; München: Kösel, 3d. umgearbeitete Aufl., 1964); C. H. Dodd, "The Appearances of the Risen Christ: An Essay in Form-Criticism of the Gospels," in *Studies in the Gospels: Essays in Memory of R. H. Lightfoot* (ed. D. E. Nineham; Oxford: Blackwell, 1955), 9-35.

[42] Hubbard, *Matthean Redaction*, 25-67. See, now, Davies and Allison who quickly review suggestions made with respect to the form of Matt 28:16-20, finding Hubbard's proposal "[m]ore satisfying" than other proposals (*Matthew XIX–XXVIII*, 676; see also pp. 679-70).

[43] Hubbard offers a list, descriptions and analysis of the use of these elements in the passages he surveyed. Not every passage has all seven; nor do they always appear in the same order (*Matthean Redaction*, 62-5). Of the seven elements, the reaction and the protest are the least frequent, although one or the other appears in all the passages surveyed (see pp. 63-4).

[44] Hubbard, *Matthean Redaction*, Appendix III, 178-79; with some bracketed adaptation of my own, he also includes the "Angelophany" of Matt 28:1-8 in this appendix.

	17a, 18	"When they saw him, ... Then Jesus approached and said to them"
Reaction	9b	"They approached, embraced his feet, and did him homage."
	17b	"they worshiped, but they doubted."
Commission	10b	"Go tell my brothers..."
	19-20a	"Go, therefore, and make disciples of all nations..."
Protest	[9]	"They ... embraced his feet"
	[17b]	"but they doubted"[45]
Reassurance	10a	"Do not be afraid."
	20b	"And behold, I am with you always, until the end of the age."[46]
Conclusion	11a	"While they were going,"[47]
	[Matt 1–28][48]	

---

[45] Hubbard does not include a protest for either of these texts, but I would propose that at least a remnant of this element is present in the verses I have quoted. Certainly that the women "embraced his feet" is part of their reaction to the "confrontation," but if maintained, it would prevent them from going and announcing the message to the disciples, as well as from fully accepting the resurrection, which might be subtly indicated in that no such physical detail is present in vv. 16-20.

Similarly, although the doubt of the disciples (some or all?) is part of the reaction upon seeing Jesus, if it persists it would hinder fulfilling the commission "to make disciples" (taking μαθητεύσατε as the main verb) by going, teaching and baptizing. On whether οἱ δὲ ἐδίστασαν refers to all or some of the disciples, see the discussion in, e.g., Hagner, *Matthew 14–28*, 884-85, who opts for it referring to all of the Eleven. For reading μαθητεύσατε as the main verb of the commission, see p. 882.

[46] That the reassurance, "Do not be afraid," appears after holding on to Jesus' feet seems to support taking the latter as a remnant of the protest. Similarly, Matthew does not explicate what the disciples doubted, but since it follows seeing the risen Jesus, the reassurance in v. 20b can be understood not only as assuring the disciples that their Lord will be with them as they fulfill their mission, but also that any earlier doubt is fully laid to rest.

[47] "Although these words are part of the next pericope (the legend about the guards), they serve as a conclusion for the second epiphany by pointing out that the women did as Jesus directed them" (Hubbard, *Matthean Redaction*, 179 n. 3).

[48] Hubbard says that although 28:16-10 has no conclusion, Matthew does have a conclusion for the angelophany of vv. 1-8 and the christophany of vv. 9-10; these instances are sufficient "proof of his [Matthew's] familiarity with this element of the HB [Hebrew Bible] commissioning *Gattung*" (*Matthean Redaction*, 179 n. 2). Hubbard notes reasons for Matthew's omission of a conclusion here (see pp. 71-72). In some ways, just as the very existence of Mark's Gospel shows that the meeting between the disciples and the risen Lord did take place (see above, n. 3), Matthew's Gospel itself attests that the commission has been – or is in the process of being – carried out.

Clearly the verbal similarities between vv. 9-10 and 16-10 are not striking. Structurally, however, there is a significant correspondence between
the two texts, when analyzed in light of the literary form of a commissioning. So, while vv. 9-10 heightened the role of the women from mere
messengers of the resurrection to witnesses of the Resurrected One,[49]
these verses are also cast in the same form as the Gospel's finale, the
"Great Commissioning" of the Eleven.

Matthew's Two Commissionings and the Matthean Community

Francis Moloney has noted "two important Matthean contributions" to
the presentation of women in the Gospel narrative: 1) in the Matthean Infancy Narrative, "Matthew has shown that ... 'women' have played a decisive role in the gradual unfolding of God's salvation history, because of
their openness to his action in their lives";[50] 2) in Matt 12:46-50, the
Evangelist has rewritten Mark 3:31-35 so as to provide a setting that
"closely parallels a Jewish school," in which all those present, women and
men, who are doing the will of God are disciples, such that "Christian discipleship can admit of no culturally or historically conditioned barriers."[51]
This Matthean contribution can now be extended, for the Evangelist
has made a great contribution in the final chapters and climax of his Gospel, as this study has shown. Even though until Matt 27:55, women remain nameless and passive, at this point many women are noted and some
are named. These many women have been doing what disciples are supposed to do, following (ἀκολουθέω) and serving (διακονέω). Moreover,
even though the women watch the crucifixion "from afar" (ἀπό μακρόθεν;
Matt 27:55//Mark 15:40) and only watch – with no active role in – his
burial (Matt 27:61//Mark 15:47), the women are certainly more faithful
disciples than the men who had abandoned Jesus at the time of his arrest
(Matt 26:47-56//Mark 14:43-52). Although Matthew has thus far followed
his source, Mark, as noted above, he has at a minimum highlighted the description of the women here.

[49] Cf. Maestri, "Women at the Tomb," 11-12.

[50] Moloney, *Woman*, 47; he compares this point of view with that of Luke's, in which
"a woman," namely, Mary, plays a major role.

[51] Moloney, *Woman*, 49; On Matthew 12:46-50, esp. vv. 49b-50, Moloney notes that
Matthew offers "a description and an identification of a *disciple of Jesus*. Here we find that
Matthew lists male and female, without any sign of division or distinction: disciples are
Jesus' mother and brothers and sisters, all doing the will of the one Father" (pp. 48-9).

From the brief overviews of Matt 28:1-8 and 9-10, however, clearly Matthew has taken great care to heighten the role of the women, when compared to Mark. At the tomb, the women continue their positive role of watching (θεωρέω) and, different from the Marcan account, are quick to obey the angel and leave to carry the message they had been given to Jesus' disciples. That already would be a major development in the characterization of the women, but when the women encounter the risen Lord, Matthew shows them to have no doubt, to worship Jesus, and again, to obey the command they had been given. They now go not only to tell Jesus' disciples of the news of the resurrection, but also as eyewitnesses of the risen Jesus. Finally, they go with this message and witness as women who have been commissioned by the risen Lord, which Matthew narrates with structural similarity to the "Great Commissioning" of the Eleven.

Neither Mark nor Matthew has invented the central role of women outlined above, for a number of scholars have observed that the earliest followers of Jesus would not have created stories that rested resurrection faith on the witness of women rather than on the witness of men.[52] In the first-century Mediterranean world there were a number of attitudes concerning the reliability of women as witnesses, from totally unreliable to reliable only in matters of which they are witnesses.[53] Given that, vv. 9-10 can be seen as a way of shoring up the testimony of the women, for by these verses they are shown to be witnesses. But, as was described above, Matthew has gone above and beyond that by his redactional changes already in vv. 1-8 and his structuring of vv. 9-10 in line with vv. 16-10.

Having noted all of that, the commission given to the women is still quite limited, namely, to Jesus' brothers, whereas the commission given to the Eleven is expansive,[54] namely, to carry the teaching of Jesus to "all [the] nations" (πάντα τὰ ἔθνη).[55] During the ministry of Jesus "the lost

---

[52] See, e.g., Moloney, "Jesus and Woman," 74; Hagner, *Matthew 14–28*, 870-71.

[53] See, e.g., R. G. Maccini, *Her Testimony is True: Women as Witnesses according to John* (JSNTSup 125; Sheffield, England: Sheffield Academic Press, 1996), esp. 95. He also notes that with respect to religious matters, "[t]he intrinsic ability of women to give honest and accurate testimony is recognized in their comparatively frequent religious prophecies, prayers, songs, confessions, oaths and vows" (see p. 92). See the concise treatment in C. S. Keener, *A Commentary on the Gospel of Matthew* (Grand Rapids: Eerdmans, 1999), 698-700.

[54] Minear notes the limited and unlimited missions of the women and men, respectively ("Matthew 28:1-10," 61).

[55] I take πάντα τὰ ἔθνη to include Israel, as do Hagner (*Matthew 14–28*, 886-87) and Davies and Allison (*Matthew XIX–XXVIII*, 684).

sheep of the house of Israel" were the focus both of his mission (Matt 15:24; add Mark 7:25) and of the mission of the Twelve (Matt 10:6).[56] Given this and other aspects from the Gospel of Matthew that have already been noted, the commissioning of the Eleven in 28:16-20 fulfills Jesus' promise that he would go before the apostles to Galilee (Matt 26:32//Mark 14:28), rehabilitates those who had fled (Matt 26:47-56), and extends the Eleven's mission to πάντα τὰ ἔθνη.

The parallel structure of the commissioning of the Eleven and of the women disciples seems to point to how Matthew envisions the roles of women and men in the new community formed in faith in the risen Lord, that is, the church (ἐκκλησία; Matt 16:18; 18:17 [*bis*]). While the Eleven clearly are commissioned to "make disciples," baptize and teach all the nations, that is to bring the good news beyond the boundaries of the community, the women are commissioned by the risen Lord himself to bring the news of the resurrection to the Eleven, i.e., to those who clearly are the center of the early church's leadership. While the Eleven receive an expansive and extra-communal commissioning, it seems clear that Matthew wants to affirm the importance of the role of faithful women in the new community of faith by narrating vv. 9-10 as a commissioning; theirs is an important intra-communal commissioning, the *sine qua non* for the Eleven's expansive commissioning.[57]

For Matthew's community, which he makes clear by the impressive redaction here at the end and climax of his Gospel, *both* women and men are *both* messengers and witnesses of the resurrection. And though, relatively speaking, the women's commission is more limited than is that of the men, the women are not only the first to hear the news of the resurrection, but they are the first to witness the resurrection; moreover they go as messengers and witnesses to the Eleven, thereby keeping them on task both by proclaiming the Easter message and – to put it facetiously – by telling them "where to go."

---

[56] In Matt 10:5 the Twelve are specifically prohibited by Jesus from going "into pagan territory" or "a Samaritan town."

[57] Weaver comments: "Mary Magdalene and 'the other Mary' have now become the crucial link between the Risen Jesus and his fearful and faltering 'brothers' (28:10). No less is at stake here than the ongoing and worldwide mission …" ("Matthew 28:1-10," 401-2).

Conclusion

By way of a brief conclusion, this piece is grounded in the example that Francis J. Moloney is to students and colleagues as both a historical-critical scholar and as a contemporary believer and preacher.[58] In this piece, I have paid attention to the intentions and the narrative of Matthew in its historical setting, but have specifically looked at the role of women in Matthew, most especially at the end of his Gospel, out of my own concern for the issues contemporary Christian communities face with respect to the roles of women. Matthew's understanding of discipleship, which, as Moloney put so well, "can admit of no culturally or historically conditioned barriers,"[59] is supported by the exposition herein. Matthew's understanding was no doubt provocative in his time. It remains provocative for the Church today, because even the implied 'historical barrier' in the limitedness of the commissioning of the women cannot be used literalistically today without being unfaithful to the challenge both of the Gospel of Matthew and of the inclusiveness of Jesus' circle of disciples.

---

[58] Moloney provides a fine summary of both of these interests in his "Preface" to *The Gospel of Mark* (xvii-xviii).

[59] Cf. Moloney, *Women*, 49.

16. TABITHA OF JOPPA:
DISCIPLE, PROPHET AND BIBLICAL PROTOTYPE
FOR CONTEMPORARY RELIGIOUS LIFE

Veronica LAWSON

On the right hand side of the sanctuary, in the lower level of the Basilica of the Annunciation in Nazareth, the privileged observer comes face to face with an exquisitely carved 13th century Crusader capital. The carving depicts a larger than life figure of the apostle Peter raising his right hand over the head of a tiny miniaturized woman. The woman is Tabitha, and the carving is a narrative representation of the story found in Acts 9:36-43. Peter's eyes are raised, presumably to the heavens. Tabitha's eyes are likewise raised, not in Peter's direction, but somewhere beyond. A huge halo enclosing twelve smaller circles surrounds the head of Peter. Tabitha is veiled and halo-less. The power of God is seen to work through the figure of Peter who restores this "little woman" to life in the community. Like the text, this centuries' old carving captures a key aspect of the movement of the Lucan narrative at this point in Acts, namely the focus on the power of God working through Peter, the designated leader of the Twelve. While the diminutive figure of the woman Tabitha is clearly subordinated to that of the apostle Peter, a close reading of the text, informed by a hermeneutics of suspicion and a hermeneutics of retrieval, reveals that the story inspiring the image is her story as much as his.

The re-reading of Acts 9:36-43 offered below seeks to demonstrate that the character Tabitha is both "disciple" and prophetic presence according to the Lucan schema and that her story has the potential to function as a biblical prototype for all Christians, and in particular for those who choose the way of public commitment to the Christian life within the post-biblical ecclesial phenomenon known as Religious Life. Readers familiar with the writings of Francis J. Moloney, Salesian biblical scholar and priest, will recognize in this choice of topic the intertextual links with his publications on the subject of Religious Life. Other contributors to this volume will be paying tribute to Frank Moloney's biblical and theological scholarship in various contexts. In adding my voice to theirs, I welcome the opportunity to acknowledge his significant contribution to the development of a biblical theology of Religious Life in the post-conciliar Catholic Church. The history of that debate including an evaluation of Moloney's writings on the subject would form a worthwhile study in itself. In this context, however, a brief overview will suffice to situate the interpretive location informing the analysis to follow.

"Ask the Scriptures"

In the early to mid 1970s, Moloney was one of two prominent biblical scholars who engaged in an open dialogue that was to provide an impetus for developing new ways of imaging Religious Life. Dominican scholar and priest Jerome Murphy-O'Connor initiated the discussion in 1973 with the publication of a series of articles in *Supplement to Doctrine and Life* in which he raised the question, "What is Religious Life?"[1] His sub-title, "Ask the Scriptures" shifted the nature of the debate on Religious Life that was taking place in the period after Vatican II. To that point, few if any had thought to "ask the Scriptures" specifically, despite the clear directive of Vatican II that Religious Institutes should constantly return to the sources of Christian life and to the originating inspiration of their founders.[2]

Murphy-O'Connor's provocative writings elicited a response from Frank Moloney in subsequent issues of *Supplement to Doctrine and Life*.[3]

---

[1] J. Murphy-O'Connor, "What is Religious Life? Ask the Scriptures." *SupDL* 45 (1973). See also J. Murphy-O'Connor and others, *What is Religious Life: A Critical Reappraisal* (Dublin: Dominican Publications, 1977).

[2] The Vatican II decree on the renewal of Religious Life, *Perfectae Caritatis* (28 October, 1965), had called for "a constant return to the sources of the whole of the Christian life and to the primitive inspiration of the institutes" (*PC* 2). The first principle to guide the renewal reads: "Since the final norm of the religious life is the following of Christ as it is put before us in the Gospel, this must be undertaken by all institutes as the supreme rule." Since the phenomenon known as Religious Life did not emerge until the fourth century C.E., any search for biblical models based on direct correspondence with biblical texts or with biblical characters is anachronistic and has generally been abandoned in recent times. Rather, in line with the directives of Vatican II, Religious Institutes and congregations have looked to the originating charism(s) of their founder(s) for such models, and have discovered there new paths to reading and interpreting the biblical texts.

[3] F. J. Moloney, "Why Community?" *SupDL* 49 (1974) 19-31; "Asking the Scriptures about religious life," *SupDL* 58 (1975) 3-12.

Moloney continued to address the subject in workshops and seminars and his popular 1980 publication, *Disciples and Prophets: A Biblical Model for Religious Life*, became an invaluable resource for recovering the biblical foundations of contemporary Christian life in general and of Religious Life in particular. It found a ready audience among members of Religious Institutes, and was used in the induction of new and prospective members in a variety of cultural contexts.

In *Disciples and Prophets*, Moloney deals first with the universal call to holiness and the centrality of the "God of the Bible" in Christian life. Religious Life, as part of Christian life, participates in a loving partnership where the God of Israel and of Jesus Christ takes the initiative. For Moloney, Religious Life is a prophetic movement in the church. Its distinctiveness lies not in a qualitative difference between the lives of other baptized Christians and members of Religious Institutes but in the prophetic function of a *public* commitment to a *public* following of Jesus of Nazareth.[4]

Prophetic Dimension of Religious Life

The biblical foundation of the prophetic dimension of Religious Life addressed by Moloney in this context has been taken up more recently by Sandra M. Schneiders, I.H.M., in her monumental work, *Religious Life in the New Millenium*. In her first volume, Schneiders locates Religious Life in both its human (part one) and ecclesial context (part two). At the beginning of the latter section, she addresses questions of difference and distinctiveness. Drawing upon the insights of Abraham Heschel and Walter Brueggemann, Schneiders identifies three key elements of a prophetic vocation: participation in the divine pathos or God's view of history; proclamation (in lament, vision, and hope) or the capacity to announce the vision to both oppressor and oppressed; and willingness to suffer for the sake of justice.[5] This is precisely how Jesus of Nazareth, the prophet *par excellence*, understood and lived out his mission of announcing the Empire

---

[4] F. J. Moloney, *Disciples and Prophets: A Biblical Model for Religious Life* (London: Darton, Longman & Todd, 1980), 156-67. Moloney, 156, acknowledges the intuition of the famous Protestant scholar, W. F. Albright, who suggested an analogy between the beginnings of the prophetic movement in ancient Israel and the growth of religious life in the Christian Church in the early centuries. See W. F. Albright, *The Biblical Period from Abraham to Ezra* (New York: Harper & Row, 1963), 44.

[5] S. M. Schneiders, *Finding the Treasure: Locating Catholic Religious Life in a New Ecclesial and Cultural Context* (New York/Mahwah: Paulist Press, 2000), 138-44.

of God (cf. Mark 1:14-15), of lamenting all that was opposed to God's way of being in the world, and of giving his life for the sake of justice.

All Christians, as disciples of Jesus of Nazareth, are called to be prophets of God's reign. For Schneiders, the distinctiveness of Religious Life lies in contemplative immediacy to God expressed in lifelong consecrated celibacy and social marginality created by celibate solitude. These are "the coordinates of Religious Life as a prophetic life form in the Church."[6] Schneiders insists that Religious Institutes are not simply a "source of committed workers" for the cause of justice, but are rather a spiritual resource for the struggle. If Religious are to exercise the twofold prophetic task of criticizing (lament) and energizing (vision and hope), then social marginality must be kept in balance with their exclusive God-quest.[7] Their lament is to be "a howl of protest from the heart of the desert... the weeping of Rachel for her children who are no more (cf. Jer 31:15); ...the lament of Jesus over Jerusalem, which does not know the time of its visitation (cf. Matt 23:37-39)."[8]

While Religious live their prophetic calling as part of the Church's mission in the world, they have a particular prophetic function towards the Church: "When the Church itself becomes the problem, the spiritual life takes on a particular urgency."[9] Where the Church is faithful to its identity and mission of incarnating, proclaiming, and making present the Reign of God, the prophetic role of Religious is "to support and foster that mission... especially in areas or forums where it is difficult or impossible for others to go..."[10] Where the Church is unfaithful, however, the prophetic role of Religious is, ideally, "to challenge and confront with the word of the Gospel the apathy, compromise, and abuse of power in the community, including and especially as it is embodied in the leadership."[11] Such an exercise of their role, as Schneiders acknowledges, is fraught with danger, "laced with interior suffering and external threat." She draws attention to the struggle of Women Religious in an institutional Church emerging from a "four-hundred-year Tridentine slumber."[12] It must be noted that Schneiders does not offer a phenomenology of Religious Life as it is

---

[6] Schneiders, *Finding the Treasure*, 137.
[7] Schneiders, *Finding the Treasure*, 141.
[8] Schneiders, *Finding the Treasure*, 142.
[9] Schneiders, *Finding the Treasure*, 145.
[10] Schneiders, *Finding the Treasure*, 151.
[11] Schneiders, *Finding the Treasure*, 151.
[12] Schneiders, *Finding the Treasure*, 146.

actually lived, but rather attempts to provide a challenge and a criterion "for those called to the life and also to offer hermeneutical access to those ... who relate to religious in one way or another."[13]

While Moloney explores both discipleship and prophecy as dimensions of Religious Life, Schneiders leaves aside the notion of discipleship and addresses prophecy in greater detail and with greater urgency than does Moloney. Writing some two decades after Moloney, Schneiders considers the issues that confront Religious, especially Women Religious, "as a creative prophetic presence" in the new millenium. She notes that "immediacy to God in contemplation and solidarity with the people in struggle takes place in a cultural context that is historically particular."[14] Much of the focus in her first volume is on the characteristics of postmodernity and the challenges it poses for Religious Life today and into the future.

Acts 9:36-43

Against the backdrop of the wisdom of Moloney and Schneiders, we return to the representation of Tabitha in the first century story of Acts 9:36-43 with a view to searching out its prototypal potential, or in other words its potential as a "root-model" of faith and life for women and men Religious today.[15] The story appears towards the beginning of the second major section (Acts 8:4–11:18) of the Acts of the Apostles, the structure of which can be understood in geographical terms as a narrative movement from Jerusalem to Judaea and Samaria, and ultimately to the ends of the earth (cf. Acts 1:8).[16] The bi-partite proemium (Acts 1:1-26) has shaped the perspective from which the narrative as a whole is to be read. A rhetorical strategy of selection has operated at the outset to defocus all others and to highlight the role of "the apostles" who in this context are

---

[13] Schneiders, *Finding the Treasure*, 151-152.

[14] Schneiders, *Finding the Treasure*, 327. Schneiders' "coordinates of Religious Life" are precisely the coordinates of the life and mission of Jesus of Nazareth, in whom Religious Life is centered.

[15] On biblical texts as prototypal rather than archetypal, see E. Schüssler Fiorenza, *Bread Not Stone: The Challenge of Feminist Biblical Interpretation* (Boston: Beacon Press, 1984), 10-14. On the analogous notion of "root metaphors" see S. M. Schneiders, *Beyond Patching: Faith and Feminism in the Catholic Church* (New York: Paulist Press, 1991), 46.

[16] For a discussion on the structure of Acts, see F. O. Fearghail, *The Introduction to Luke-Acts: A Study of the Role of Lk 1,1-4,44 in the Composition of Luke's Two-Volume Work* (Rome: Biblical Institute, 1991), 73-76.

the Twelve of the Lucan Gospel, minus Judas the betrayer. The reconstituted Twelve, destined to sit on thrones judging the twelve tribes of Israel (Luke 22:30), form the nucleus of the restored Israel.[17] As the proemium and the early part of the second Lucan volume unfolds, the narrative lens tends to defocus the other apostles in their turn and to zoom in on the figure of Peter whose authority has already been established in the Gospel. He is the first named apostle of those listed in Acts 1:13. In 1:15, he assumes a dominant role by standing in the midst of the assembled believers, addressing the post-resurrection community gathered in the upper room, and instigating the process required to replace Judas. Successive episodes in the first major section of the narrative (Acts 2:1-8:3) confirm the decisive role of the Twelve and of Peter in particular in the establishment and ordering of the new community "in Jerusalem" (1:8). In 8:1-3, persecution of the nascent community in Jerusalem at the hands of Saul is the catalyst for the movement out from Jerusalem to Judaea and Samaria.

While the figures of Philip and Saul are fore-grounded in Acts 8:4-40 and 9:1-30, Peter's reappearance in 9:32 is signaled by attention to the comprehensive nature of his mission in Judaea (ἐγένετο δὲ Πέτρον διερχόμενον διὰ πάντων).[18] Three successive stories serve to demonstrate the nature of Peter's mission. Some scholars treat the first two, the healing of Aeneas in the name of Jesus Christ and the raising of Tabitha, as prelude or introduction to the more significant story of the centurion Cornelius and his household (10:1–11:18).[19] Although less extensive than the latter, both stories in 9:32-43 function to demonstrate the key role of Peter in effecting the commission of Acts 1:8 and as such are integral to the movement of the narrative. While Acts 9:15 has shown Saul being commissioned to "carry [the] name" of Jesus to the Gentiles and kings as well as to the people of Israel, the Cornelius story attests to the primacy of the Lucan Peter in bringing "the name" of Jesus to the Gentiles.[20] The

---

[17] See J. Jervell, *Luke and the People of God: A New Look at Luke-Acts* (Minneapolis: Augsburg, 1972), 75-112.

[18] On the various possible interpretations of this phrase, see F. F. Bruce, *The Acts of the Apostles* (3d ed. Grand Rapids, Mich.: Eerdmans, 1990), 246; also, C. K. Barrett, *A Critical and Exegetical Commentary on the Acts of the Apostles* (vol. 1; Edinburgh: T&T Clark, 1994), 1:479.

[19] So B. Witherington III, *The Acts of the Apostles: A Socio-Rhetorical Commentary* (Grand Rapids: Eerdmans, 1998), 327: "The material in this subsection, while not an aside, is transitional, bringing the reader back to the subject of Peter's work in preparation for the major narrative about Peter and Cornelius."

[20] Detailed discussion of the Cornelius episode, including his status as "God-fearer,"

power of God works more powerfully through the figure of Peter than through any other character in Acts, including Paul (Saul). It is not surprising therefore that the story of Tabitha, whether literary construct or historical memory or a combination of both, is made to serve the construction of the character of the leading apostle Peter as principal bearer of the name of Jesus, and prophetic wonder worker in the tradition of Jesus, Elijah, and Elisha.

Tabitha: Disciple and Prophet

There is more to Tabitha, however, and more to her story than her role as beneficiary of God's healing power mediated through God's apostle and prophet, Peter. Given the overall focus on the mission of Peter in this section of Acts, there is a surprising amount of attention paid to the figure of Tabitha. In the opening verses of the previous story (Acts 9:32-34), for example, Peter is the subject of the five main verbs, whereas in Acts 9:36, Tabitha is immediately introduced as the subject and described in some detail. Her death occasions the delegation to Lydda and Peter appears for the first time only in Acts 9:38.

Tabitha is defined at the outset in relation to place: she is a woman on the edge, a resident of Joppa (9:36). The placement of the name Joppa at the beginning of the first sentence of the pericope (ἐν Ἰόππῃ δέ τις ἦν μαθήτρια ὀνόματι Ταβιθά) underlines its significance in the narrative and creates a link with the Cornelius episode to follow where Joppa (10:8, 23, 32) appears as one of three named cities, along with Caesarea (10:1, 24) and Jerusalem (10:39). For narratologist, Ute Eisen, the characters in the narrative are "oriented to these cities, and acquire significance through particular groups of features" associated with them.[21]

Joppa was a northern Judaean port city located close to the border between Judaea and Samaria. Established as a Jewish port after Simon Maccabeus occupied it in 145 BCE (1 Macc 12:33-34; 13:11), it had remained a significant Jewish center until its destruction at the hands of the Romans in 68 CE.[22] Within Acts, the particularities of the Tabitha event

is outside the scope of this paper.

[21] U. E. Eisen, "Boundary Transgression and the Extreme Point in Acts 10:1-11:18," in *On The Cutting Edge: The Study of Women in Biblical Worlds* (eds. J. Schaberg, A. Bach, & E. Fuchs; New York: Continuum, 2003), 161.

[22] By the time Luke is narrating the story of Tabitha, the city had been in ruins for

make Joppa "the semantic place of Jews who believe in Christ and exercise justice."[23] It "constitutes a geopolitical opposition" to the port city of Caesarea which was built by Herod the Great in honor of Augustus and was thus part of the *Imperium Romanum*.[24] Caesarea, situated in northern Samaria, constitutes the final step in the progression of the witness to Jesus from Jerusalem to Judaea and Samaria. There is an element of surprise at this point in the narrative flow, however; the word spreads from Jerusalem, the center of Christian Judaism, into the surrounding territory of Judaea and beyond, not to the Samaritans in this instance, but rather to a Gentile and his family living in clearly defined Gentile space within Samaria.

Eisen insists that the "boundary is clearly laid between Jews and Gentiles" and not between Jews and Jews who believe in Christ.[25] The apostle Peter following in the footsteps of Philip effects the command of Jesus to give witness in Jerusalem, Judaea (Lydda and Joppa), and Samaria (Caesarea) where he potentially opens up the way for a witness to the ends of the earth and then returns to Jerusalem to provide an account of his mission. Some Jewish believers in Christ from Joppa (καί τινες τῶν ἀδελφῶν τῶν ἀπὸ Ἰόππης συνῆλθον αὐτῷ, 10:23) accompany Peter into Gentile space in northern Samaria. They "cross the boundary with him and later serve as witnesses in Jerusalem."[26] In narrative terms, the Judaean mission is consolidated in Joppa as a consequence of the Tabitha event (9:42). In 10:8, Joppa provides the locus for the reception of the emissaries from Caesarea, who have crossed the boundary from the other direction and proceed to direct Peter towards the Gentiles (10:22-24). The Tabitha event, situated at the culmination and highpoint of the Judaean phase of Peter's mission, on the border between Judaea and Samaria, and on the threshold of the inclusion of the Gentiles, is a liminal event in the Lucan schema.

Tabitha is one of only ten women introduced in Acts by name. The Greek translation of her Aramaic name is supplied in Acts 9:36 (μαθήτρια

---

two to three decades. See Josephus' account of its destruction and the elimination of its 8,400 inhabitants in *War* 2.508-509; 3.414-415.

[23] Eisen, "Boundary Transgression," 161. For further comment on the activities of the believing Jews in Joppa, see below.

[24] With the development of Caesarea, Joppa lost some of its influence as a Mediterranean port. For further comment on Joppa, see G. Rochais, *Les récits de résurrection des morts dans le Nouveau Testament* (Cambridge: Cambridge University Press, 1981), 148.

[25] Eisen, "Boundary Transgression," 162.

[26] Eisen, "Boundary Transgression," 162.

ὀνόματι Ταβιθά, ἣ διερμηνευομένη λέγεται Δορκάς:). The Greek
(Δορκάς) not the Aramaic form of her name is used in 9:39. Tabitha or
Dorcas stands alone among the three named beneficiaries of Peter's missionary activity (Aeneas [9:32-35], Tabitha, and Cornelius [10:1-48]) in that
the narrative depicts her as a disciple prior to Peter's visit, presupposing
an earlier evangelization of Joppa, presumably by Philip who in 8:40 is
credited with evangelizing the coastal cities from Azotus to Caesarea.[27]
Tabitha of Joppa was not among those gathered in Jerusalem and explicitly addressed in the command of Acts 1:8: "You will be my witnesses…
." She is nonetheless a resident witness to the resurrected Jesus and provides the occasion for Peter's visit to her hometown, albeit unwittingly. In
contrast, there is no indication in the previous pericope as to whether
Aeneas is a disciple or not: he is simply the recipient of Peter's healing
ministry. The third character, Cornelius, is a "devout and god-fearing
man" who comes to faith in Jesus and so implicitly becomes a disciple.

The feminine form of "disciple" (μαθήτρια) predicated of Tabitha is a
biblical *hapaxlegomenon*. In other words, Tabitha is the only woman in the
whole of the Christian Scriptures to be designated "disciple." In the later
apocryphal Gospel of Peter, μαθήτρια will be applied to Mary Magdalene.
It appears nowhere else in early Christian literature. The lack of a definite
article indicates that Tabitha is not the only disciple, or even the only female disciple, in Joppa. She is *a* disciple among others, although the subsequent narrative suggests that she has exercised a significant leadership
role among the Christian Jews, especially the widows, of Joppa.

In Luke's Gospel the term disciple is more inclusive than in the other
Synoptics where it is generally used in reference to the Twelve. In Luke
6:12, Jesus calls his disciples and chooses twelve of them to be apostles; in
6:17, he stands on the plain with "a great crowd of his disciples." Disciples in the Gospel are those who follow Jesus of Nazareth, both women
and men, the former implied in the generic plural masculine usage of the
term. The context of the first occurrence of the term in Acts (6:1) makes a
clear distinction between the Twelve and the disciples. A subsequent reference in 11:26 indicates that "Christian" had become the accepted equivalent of "disciple": "…it was in Antioch that the disciples were first called
"Christians" (χρηματίσαι τε πρώτως ἐν᾽ Ἀντιοχείᾳ τοὺς μαθητὰς Χρι-
στιανούς 11:26)." Acts 21:16-17 suggests an equivalence between disci-

---

[27] Similarly, the mention of Lydda in the Aeneas pericope has foreshadowed the reference to Lydda in the Tabitha pericope and forged a link between the two accounts.

ples (μαθηταί) and sisters and brothers (ἀδελφοι). In the post resurrection period, the disciples of the Lucan narrative are thus those who accept Jesus as the longed for messiah and are referred to variously as οἱ μαθηται, οἱ σῳζόμενοι, οἱ πιστεύοντες, οἱ ἁγίοι, οἱ ἀδελφοί, οἱ Χριστιανοί.[28]

Tabitha of Joppa is a Christian *disciple*, a Jewish woman who accepts Jesus of Nazareth as the anointed one of God and works for the realization of the *basileia* of God. She is characterized as a disciple (αὕτη ἦν πλήρης ἔργων ἀγαθῶν καὶ ἐλεημοσυνῶν ὧν ἐποίει) "devoted to good works and acts of charity" (9:36). She has fallen sick and has died; she is washed and put into an upper room. Her death is of such significance to the community that the disciples of Joppa then send two messengers with an urgent request that Peter come to Joppa. Although the reason for their request is not specified, it implies a widespread faith among the believers in Peter's power and readiness not only to effect healing cures but also to raise the dead to life in the tradition of the prophets of Israel and more particularly of Jesus of Nazareth. It also implies confidence on the part of the saints that Peter will recognize the importance of this woman to the on-going life of their community and respond to their request. Peter is taken to the "upper room" (9:39).[29] When Peter commands her to rise, she opens her eyes and, seeing Peter, she sits up (v. 40). He offers his hand and helps her to get up. She is then presented "alive" to the saints and the widows (v. 41).

Tabitha is mourned especially by "all the widows" who weep and show Peter the garments she produced "while she was with them" (Acts 9:39). Whereas the cure of Aeneas means a return to health for an individual (9:33), the resuscitation of Tabitha[30] is a restoration to discipleship of an honored and effective member of the faith community in Joppa, an aspect that is implied rather than emphasized in the narrative.

The second sentence in the story marks Tabitha out as *a prophetic presence* in Joppa. Like other named women prophets of Luke-Acts, such as Anna (Luke 2:36-38) and the daughters of Philip (Acts 21:9), no words of prophecy are attributed to Tabitha. Only the extraordinary nature of her

[28] For further discussion on the connotations of "disciple(s)" in Acts, see I. Richter Reimer, *Women in the Acts of the Apostles: A Feminist Liberation Perspective* (Minneapolis: Fortress, 1995) 34-35.

[29] See L. T. Johnson, *The Acts of The Apostles.* (SP 5; Collegeville: Liturgical Press, 1992), 178. Johnson detects here "a faint verbal echo" of the story of the widow of Sarepta (1 Kgs 17:19) who places the dead body of her son in an upper room.

[30] Richter Reimer, *Women in the Acts of the Apostles*, 41-49 explores in detail the differences between resurrection and resuscitation within the Jewish-Christian tradition.

prophetic activity is recorded. Not only does she engage in works of justice and works of mercy. She is said to be "full of" or "filled with" such activities (αὕτη ἦν πλήρης ἔργων ἀγαθῶν καὶ ἐλεημοσυνῶν ὧν ἐποίει). The term πλήρης provides intertextual links with passages in which Spirit-filled Lucan figures are described: Luke 4:1 where God's prophet Jesus is said to be "full of the Holy Spirit"; Acts 6:3 and the search for seven among the disciples who are "full of the Spirit and of wisdom"; Acts 6:5 where Stephen is chosen as one "full of faith and the Holy Spirit"; and finally the description of Barnabas in Acts 11:24 as one "full of the Holy Spirit and of faith."[31] Just as Tabitha's call to discipleship is implied rather than narrated, so too is her role as prophet implied in the assertion that she was fully engaged in works of justice and of mercy.

Ivoni Richter Reimer explores the early Jewish and Christian traditions relating to ἔργα ἀγαθά and ἐλεημοσύνη.[32] She notes that the latter is generally interpreted inadequately as "almsgiving" with its connotations of giving to the needy the scraps that fall from the tables of the rich. She argues that both ἔργα ἀγαθά and ἐλεημοσύνη denote works of justice, which are inclusive of various forms of care for the needy but which cannot be reduced to contributions from one's surplus. The semantic relationship between ἔλεος (mercy) and ἐλεημοσύνη also permits the rendering "works of mercy" for the latter. Both Hebrew and Christian scriptures present the God of Israel as a God of justice and mercy (Hos 2:19; Isa 30:18; Ps 119:156; Matt 23:23). Tabitha actualizes the justice and the mercy of God in the border town of Joppa. But she is not alone in this.

It is usually assumed that the beneficiaries of Tabitha's work are the widows who weep for her and who show her work to Peter on his arrival in the upper room. They may indeed be among the beneficiaries; they may also be co-workers who gather in Tabitha's house and, together with her, provide for the needy in the community. That these widows constitute a formal group in the Christian community at Joppa is indicated by the use of the definite article preceded by the adjective "all" (πᾶσαι αἱ χῆραι v. 39). Turid Seim rightly points out that the text does not present Tabitha as

---

[31] While the terminology differs in Luke 1:41 and 1:67, the sense in both instances is similar, even synonymous, with the use of πλήρης in Luke 4:1; Acts 6:3, 5; 11:24. In Luke 1:41 Elizabeth is said to be filled with the Holy Spirit (καὶ ἐπλήσθη πνεύματος ἁγίου) and she proceeds to utter prophetic words. In 1:67 Zechariah likewise is filled with the Holy Spirit and prophesies (ἐπλήσθη πνεύματος ἁγίου καὶ ἐπροφήτευσεν λέγων).

[32] Richter Reimer, *Women in the Acts of the Apostles*, 36-41.

a widow, although many of the commentators assume that she is.[33] Tabitha is the householder who provides a gathering place for all the widows of Joppa. While this does not mean that she is a wealthy woman, it does mean that she has the resources to host a significant group of people in her house. Like the women of Galilee (Luke 8:3), she shares her resources for the sake of the community. She embodies the Lucan ideal of Acts 2:44-45 and 4:32.

Conclusion

The trajectory from Tabitha of Joppa to contemporary Religious Life is not self-evident. It would be anachronistic to look to this story or to any other in the Christian scriptures for a direct correspondence with an ecclesial life-form that developed in the post-biblical era. Biblical stories, like biblical metaphors, provide prototypes not archetypes for those embracing new ways of living the Gospel. Moloney's study of Religious as disciples and prophets was based on this premise, with the result that *Disciples and Prophets* offered a biblical framework for conceptualizing both Christian life in general and Religious Life in particular. Sandra Schneiders has subsequently drawn upon key elements of the prophetic tradition and brought them into dialogue with the experience of living Religious Life in the new millennium. This contribution is deeply indebted to both Moloney and Schneiders. It represents a modest attempt to build on their work. Its claim is that Tabitha's story is rich in wisdom and inspiration for those who make a public commitment to a public following of Jesus of Nazareth. Tabitha's home-based activities are in no sense private activities: she is a spiritual resource for the marginalized in their daily struggle for survival. She draws on all her personal and material resources for the sake of the Gospel mission. She operates in liminal spaces: in a port city; on the border between Judaea and Samaria; on the cusp of life and death. Her commitment to the God-quest is such that she is "full of" God's mercy and justice. In other words, she gives all for the sake of mercy and justice. A close reading of certain aspects of her story, informed by a hermeneutics of suspicion and retrieval, has revealed that there is more to Tabitha than seems to have entered the imagination of the skilled medieval artisan who chiseled her image in the limestone capital at Nazareth.

---

[33] T. Karlsen Seim, *The Double Message: Patterns of Gender in Luke-Acts* (Edinburgh: T.& T. Clark, 1994), 241.

17. SEXUALITY IN
THE TESTAMENTS OF THE TWELVE PATRIARCHS AND THE NEW TESTAMENT

William LOADER

This study is dedicated in appreciation to Frank Moloney, my Melbourne colleague in New Testament on the others side of the vast Australian continent from Perth, and now half a world away, whose great passion both for excellence in scholarship and for making it more accessible has always inspired me.

The writings within the New Testament belong to a changing world with its own voices in Gentile and Jewish literature, which we sometimes faintly hear as we encounter the canonical texts. Too often such literature is cited only as parallels, tucked away in footnotes. One such parallel, regularly tucked away in footnotes to Paul's comments about sexual intercourse and prayer in 1 Cor 7:5, is the *T. Naph.* 8:7-8. Its author might rightly claim that it deserves a better airing, perhaps even a reversing of the tables with Paul's statement relegated to a footnoted parallel.

This paper will, in some sense, reverse the tables by listening directly to the *Testaments of the Twelve Patriarchs (T12)* in the area of sexuality and noting some "parallels" in the New Testament. Parallelomania, the exegetical disease of confusing similarity with dependence, is all the more to be avoided in the case of *T12*, because of the uncertainty concerning the date of the work.[1] In its present form it is clearly a Christian work, possibly from the late second century CE. It is also clearly a compilation of older

---

[1] For what follows see the review of recent research in M. de Jonge, *Pseudepigrapha of the Old Testament as Part of Christian Literature: The Case of the Testaments of the Twelve Patriarchs and the Greek Life of Adam and Eve* (SVTP 18; Leiden: Brill, 2003), esp. "Defining the Major Issues in the Study of the Testaments of the Twelve Patriarchs," 71-83; and R. A. Kugler, *The Testaments of the Twelve Patriarchs: Guides to Apocrypha and Pseudepigrapha* (Sheffield: Sheffield Academic Press, 2001), 31-38.

material, but here the difficulties start and opinions widely diverge. This makes suggestions of dependence, for instance, of NT writers on *T12* very unsure. Even in those sections of the work which contain no explicit Christian references, including all of the passages we shall consider below, we cannot determine dates nor assume that they must be non Christian, let alone pre-Christian in origin.

At most we can speak of these ethical discourses as reflecting a range of influences, primarily Jewish, including the telling and retelling of biblical stories, now read in the LXX, but also philosophical, from the world of popular Stoicism. Testaments of the patriarchs must have appeared as early as the second century BCE, at least in the form of the patriarchs addressing future generations. The fragments at Qumran of such words from the obscure Naphtali make this likely, but the extent to which what might have once existed is now present in the version of the *T12* which has survived to us is difficult to determine. The presence of some of the earlier material makes it likely that there is more. The absence of other earlier material in the present work cautions us that the developments will have been complex.

Nevertheless *T12* is a rich source for understanding how some Christians in the late second century, and probably some Jews of at least the previous century, approached some issues of ethics, not least sexuality. The present paper will not address issues of sources and traditions; nor is our concern to argue dependence either from *T12* to NT or vice versa, but to "unparallel" the parallels and give them a voice. We begin with the "footnoted parallel" to Paul, then consider the major treatment of sexuality in *T12*, namely in the *T. Reuben*, in the process noting some further parallels – from the other side of the track looking from *T12* towards the NT.

Love and Sexual Intercourse in Marriage

Paul suggested that married couples not deprive one another of sexual love except by mutual agreement for a time, to make room for prayer (1 Cor 7:5). But then they should return to "the same," lest Satan tempt them because of their likely lack of self control.[2] The "footnoted parallel"

---

[2] See my extended discussion in W. Loader, *Sexuality and the Jesus Tradition* (Grand Rapids: Eerdmans, 2005), 149-64 [forthcoming].

is regularly *T. Naph.* 8:7, where the writer speaks of a time for sexual intercourse with one's wife and a time for abstinence for the sake of one's prayer: Καιρὸς γὰρ συνουσίας γυναικὸς αὐτοῦ καὶ καιρὸς ἐγκρατείας εἰς προσευχὴν αυτοῦ.[3]

The assumption behind both texts is that abstinence from sexual intercourse in some way benefits or is appropriate to prayer. The issue is not time spent in sexual intercourse, but rather a longer span of time, measuring days or perhaps weeks, which is to be devoted to prayer and that sexual intercourse during that period is to be avoided. We are probably dealing with long established and widely held beliefs which saw holy space (and time) needing to be kept free from sexual activity. We find a comparable instance when Moses asks that the people abstain from sexual intercourse before the holy encounter at Sinai (Exod 19:15) or when David reassures the priest that his men may enter the temple because they had not engaged in sexual intercourse with women in the preceding days (1 Sam 21:5-6).[4]

The passage from *T. Naph.* invites consideration because it gives this instruction in the context of a wider statement about sexual intercourse.

(7) The commandments of the law (αἱ ἐντολαί τοῦ νόμου) are twofold (διπλαῖ) and they must be fulfilled through prudence (μετὰ τέχνης).

(8) For there is a season (καιρός) (for a man) to have sexual intercourse with his wife and a season (καιρός) to abstain therefrom (ἐγκρατείας) for his prayer:

(9) so there are two commandments (ἐντολαί) and if they are not done in their order (ἐν τάξει αὐτῶν), they bring sin. So also is it with the other commandments (ἐντολῶν).

(10) Be, therefore, wise in God and prudent, understanding the order of his commandments (τάξιν ἐντολῶν) and the laws of every activity, that the Lord will love you. (*T. Naph.* 8:7-10).[5]

---

[3] E.g., W. Schrage, *Der erste Brief an die Korinther* (4 vols; EKKNT VII; Zurich: Benziger Verlag; Neukirchen–Vluyn: Neukirchener Verlag, 1991, 1995, 1999, 2001), 2:69 n. 99; A. C. Thiselton, *The First Epistle to the Corinthians: A Commentary on the Greek Text* (NIGTC; Grand Rapids: Eerdmans; Carlisle: Paternoster, 2000), 509 n. 136; see also R. F. Collins, *First Corinthians* (SP 7; Collegeville: Liturgical Press, 1999), 257.

[4] W. Deming suggests both draw on a common tradition, showing Stoic influence and apocalyptic and wisdom concerns with sexual immorality, but without noting the issue of sexuality and holiness (*Paul on Marriage and Celibacy: The Hellenistic Background of 1 Corinthians 7* [SNTMS 83; Cambridge: Cambridge University Press, 1995], 124-26). On this see my discussion in *Sexuality and the Jesus Tradition*, 158-60.

[5] Translation by H. W. Hollander and M. de Jonge (*The Testaments of the Twelve Patriarchs: A Commentary* [SVTP 8; Leiden: Brill, 1985]) of the Greek text in M. de Jonge, *The*

The "twofold" commandments in 8:7 refer to the commandment to love God and love one's neighbor,[6] a common theme in *T12* (e.g., *T. Iss.* 5:1-2; 7:6; *T. Zeb.* 5:1; *T. Dan* 5:3; *T. Benj.* 3:3-5).[7] The same thought recurs in 8:9, which speaks of the "two commandments." μετὰ τέχνης (v. 7), translated here as "prudence," and probably focuses on deliberate planning and attention. V. 8 somewhat suddenly introduces sexual intercourse. In v. 8 the use of καιρός ("season," "time") echoes Eccl 3:1-8 LXX and the two "times" relate here to the two commandments. Devoting oneself to prayer is a way of fulfilling the first commandment to love God; having sexual intercourse with one's wife is a way of fulfilling the second commandment to love one's neighbor as oneself. V. 9 makes it clear that there is a priority of loving God over loving one's wife and all other commandments. It is a matter of getting the priority, the order (τάξιν), right (8:10).[8] Implied then, within the exposition of the order of the commandments, is a very positive statement about sexual intercourse in marriage as an act of love. Had this been found within canonical writings, we might imagine it would have generated many a fine (and healthy) sermon!

This positive attitude coheres with a generally positive approach towards marriage that *T12* assumes. Joseph, a model of sexual responsibility,[9] eventually marries a daughter of his masters (*T. Jos.* 8:3); Reuben advises men to wait for God to provide a wife (4:1b) and Issachar models this advice, taking a wife at the age of thirty, and avoiding sexual immorality before that. Similarly Isaac advised Levi to take a wife while he was still young (*T. Levi* 9:10), which he did at the age of twenty-eight (11:1; 12:5). Nowhere do we find any negative comments about marriage nor anything like the stance that Paul espoused, which affirmed the validity of marrying, but preferred singleness.

The closest New Testament "parallel" comes in Ephesians, where the

---

Testaments of the Twelve Patriarchs: A Critical edition of the Greek Text (Leiden: Brill, 1978). Elsewhere I provide my own translation, remaining close to Hollander and de Jonge, but departing from it where I believe sense requires; e.g., I translate πορνεία by "sexual immorality," rather than "impurity."

[6] So H. C. Kee, "Testaments of the Twelve Patriarchs," *OTP* 1:775-828, 814 n. 8c.

[7] See M. de Jonge, "The Two Great Commandments in the Testaments of the Twelve Patriarchs," in *Pseudepigrapha*, 141-59, who does not, however, cite *T. Naph.* 8:7 in this context nor do Hollander and de Jonge make this connection in dealing with the passage in their *Commentary*, 318-19.

[8] See 2:9 which also mentions τάξις and Καιρός, in allusion to Eccl 3:11 LXX. So Hollander and de Jonge, *Commentary*, 319.

[9] Σωφροσύνη is a key word for chastity in *T. Jos.* 4:1, 2; 6:7; 9:2-3; 10:2-3.

author also appears to apply Lev 19:18 to marital relations. There we read: "In the same way, husbands should love (ἀγαπᾶν) their wives as they do their own bodies. He who loves his wife loves himself. For no one ever hates his own body, but he nourishes and tenderly cares for it" (5:28-29). Paul is not far from this in 1 Cor 7:3-4 where in relation to sexual intercourse he argues for a mutuality based on belonging to one another and of obligation and even suggests not to fulfill sexual obligations is to rob or deprive (ἀποστερεῖτε) one another (1 Cor 7:5; cf. Exod 21:10 τὴν ὁμιλίαν αὐτῆς οὐκ ἀποστερήσει). But the Corinthian statement still falls short of love. Even Ephesians, which doubtless also has sexual intercourse in mind, turns the motivation around somewhat: if you love yourself, you should love your wife. Of course, one should not immediately assume later notions of romantic love.

What appears to be a very positive understanding of sexual relations in marriage in *T12* and a positive attitude towards marriage as part of the divine order, one that would cohere with the household instructions of Colossians and Ephesians, stands beside other statements which play down the pleasure of sexuality in marriage. *T. Iss.* 1:2–2:5 elaborates the story of the encounter between Rachel and Leah over two mandrakes (Gen 30:14-16). The story is overlaid with an interpretation according to which Rachel, far from being greedy over apples, chose abstinence from sexual intercourse. She "despised intercourse with a man and has chosen abstinence (ἐγκράτειαν)" (2:1). The Lord "saw that for the sake of children she wished to have intercourse with Jacob and not for the lust of pleasure (διὰ φιλοδονίαν)" (2:3).

Here the author expounds a widely held Stoic view that sexual intercourse is to serve procreation, never pleasure alone.[10] Within a biblical framework, refusal to procreate is a serious sin against Gen 1:28. According to *T. Jud.* 10:3-5 the angel of the Lord killed Er, and Onan met his death because they were not willing to have children by Tamar, the latter by what we would describe as *coitus interruptus*. Luke implies that one of the reasons why there will be no sexual activity in the world to come is that there will be no death and therefore no need for procreation (20:34-36).[11] By implication sexual intercourse is solely for procreation. The version in

---

[10] E.g., Musonius fr. 12; 13A; 14. Hierocles, *On Duties*, 4.28.21; reflected, for instance, in Philo, *Spec. Leg.* 3:113; *Jos* 43; Josephus, *War* 2.161; *Ap* 2.199; Justin, *Apol* 1.29. See also H. C. Kee, "Ethical dimensions of the Testaments of the XII as a clue to provenance," *NTS* 24 (1978): 259-70, esp. 265.

[11] And so the Sadducees' taunt about the woman with many husbands falls flat!.

Mark more likely reflects the view that sexual intercourse and sacred presence are incompatible (Mark 12:25).[12] This is more related to the view of *T. Naph.* 8:7 and Paul in 1 Cor 7:5, except that in the world to come the season will be permanent. The Issachar story also implies that the desire for pleasure, even in marriage, is in itself bad or, at least, to be avoided by the wise and virtuous – a Stoic commonplace. It is interesting that Paul's reticence about marriage and his preference for celibacy are not expressed in terms of avoiding such desire as though desire itself or pleasure is bad; he is prepared to concede that some with burning desire will lack self control,[13] but their decision to proceed with marriage is not, therefore, sin (1 Cor 7:9, 28, 36). In Cor 7:1-6 he does not give the impression that sexual intercourse is only natural or valid when it includes the possibility of procreation.

Women and Danger: *The Testament of Reuben* and Sexuality

Outside the island of marriage *T12* devotes much attention to the dangers of sexual immorality. It is the major theme in the first of the testaments, *T. Reuben,* and is based on two slender references in Gen 35:22 and 49:4. The texts had already spawned speculation (see *Jub.* 33:1-17).[14] In this section of the paper we shall review the relevant material in *T. Reuben,* following the order in which it is presented, in order to observe the way each element functions in its discourse.

Reuben commences his discourse with an exhortation to his descendants: "not to walk in the ignorance of youth and sexual immorality (ἐν ἀγνοίᾳ νεότητος καὶ πορνείᾳ), in which I was poured out and defiled (ἐμίανα) the bed of my father, Jacob" (1:6). The allusion is to Reuben's having sexual intercourse with Jacob's concubine.

T. Reuben 1:7-10 reports God's punishment of Reuben by striking him with an affliction for seven months in the same area of the body with which he had sinned, namely his "loins" which included his genitalia.[15]

---

[12] On this see my discussion in *Sexuality and the Jesus Tradition*, ch. 3.1.

[13] For burning desire in *T12* see *T. Jud.* 16:1; *T. Jos.* 2:2.

[14] See J. Kugler, "Reuben's sin with Bilhah in the Testament of Reuben," *in Pomegranates and Golden Bells: Studies in Biblical, Jewish, and Near Eastern Ritual, Law, and Literature in Honor of Jacob Milgrom* (Winona Lake: Eisenbrauns, 1995), 525-54. Kugler notes ambiguities in the Hebrew text which open a range of speculation.

[15] See *T. Gad* 5:10 for an enunciation of this principle.

Only Jacob's intercession averted death, which was the punishment required by the Law.[16] He spent seven years in repentance and abstinence from wine, strong drink, meat, and, perhaps, "sweet bread." None of these relates directly to sexual immorality, although the *T. Judah* makes a strong connection between wine and sexual immorality (14:1-8 and see 15:4) and the author perhaps intends an allusion to sexual passion by word play in the final item: "sweet bread," literally, "bread of desire" (cf. Dan 10:3). There need not be a link between the sin of which one repents and the items from which one abstains; they do, however, all represent physical pleasure.

The basis of sexual immorality is explained in *T. Reuben* 2:1–3:7.[17] Here, we are taken beyond the prohibiting of acts to an understanding of what lies behind them. Reuben claims that he *saw* these insights during his time

---

[16] *Jubilees* explains that the Mosaic law demanding death had not yet been revealed (*Jub.* 33:15-16). Cf. CD 5:2-4 which explains David's taking many wives on the basis that he had no access to the Law.

[17] *T. Reuben* 2. And now hear me, my children, about what I saw in my repentance concerning the seven spirits of error. Seven spirits were given from Beliar against the human being (or "man" – it is male focused) and they are the head of the works of youth, and seven spirits were given to him at creation, that in them every work of man might be done. The first is the spirit of life, with which man's constitution is created. The second is the spirit of sight, with which comes desire. The third is the spirit of hearing, with which teaching is given. The fourth is the spirit of smell, with which taste is given to draw in air and breath. The fifth is the spirit of speech, with which comes knowledge. The sixth is the spirit of taste, with which comes the consumption of meats and drinks, and through them strength is created, for in food is the basis of strength. The seventh is the spirit of procreation and sexual intercourse, with which through love of pleasure sin comes in. Therefore it is the last (in the order) of youth, because it is filled with ignorance and leads the young man as a blind man to a pit, and as an animal to a precipice.

3. Besides all these, there is an eighth spirit of sleep, with which the ecstasy of (human) nature is created and the image of death. With these spirits is mingled the spirit of error. The first, that of sexual immorality, resides in (our) natural physical make-up and (our) senses; the second is the spirit of insatiate desire in the belly; the third is the spirit of fighting in the liver and gall. The fourth is the spirit of flattery and trickery, so that through officiousness a man may appear fair. The fifth is the spirit of arrogance, so that a man may boast and be high-minded. The sixth is the spirit of lying, in destruction and jealousy to speak deceitful words, and to conceal one's words from family and relations. The seventh is the spirit of injustice, with which theft and acts of stealing come, so that one might act on the love of pleasure in one's heart; for injustice works together with the other spirits through the receiving of bribes. Besides all these, the spirit of sleep, the eighth spirit, is connected with error and fantasy. And thus every young man is brought to ruin, darkening his mind from the truth and not understanding what is in the law of God nor obeying the instruction of his fathers, just as I, too, suffered in my youth (2:1-3:8).

of repentance (2:1). *Seeing* here is more than rational reflection; it implies revelation (4:3 refers to angelic revelation about the specific psychology of women). *T. Reuben* 2:1-2 begins by mentioning seven spirits from Beliar, described as being "against human beings" (similarly *T. Gad* 6:2). These will be elaborated one by one in 3:3-6, with the spirit of sexual immorality taking first place. The other six are incidental to the theme, but the inclusion of the full list has the effect of setting what is said about sexual immorality in the context of all sin. So this is more than a warning about sexual immorality; it belongs within a much wider concern about avoiding sin and going astray morally, a wider theme in *T12*.

Before, however, we reach the elaboration of the seven spirits from Beliar, we have another list in 2:3-8, where the same word, "spirit," is used neutrally to identify life, sight, hearing, smell, speech, taste and "procreation and sexual intercourse." The effect of listing these senses here, before going on to itemize the spirits of Beliar, is to alert the hearer to the psychological context. The author of the final document thus combines different streams of thought, Stoic psychology and Jewish demonology.[18]

Each item in the first list is given an application. Of particular relevance are "sight" to which the lists adds: "with which comes desire (ἐπιθυμία)" (2:4); and "procreation and sexual intercourse" (2:8), where the author adds: "with which through love of pleasure (φιληδονίας) sin comes in." The fact that this is the final item of the list makes a neat transition to the list of spirits from Beliar, which begins with sexual immorality (3:3-8). Its position at the head of the list, like in similar lists in the NT (Mark 7:21-22; 1 Cor 6:9; cf. also Rom 13:9), doubtless reflects its priority as the greatest sin, an emphasis supported by its prominence in the LXX Decalogue where it heads the second table.[19] In 2:9 the author plays with the sequence by declaring that the last in the list of created capacities is the first evil spirit to plague youth and lead them to disaster.

It is important to note precisely where the author lays the blame. In 2:9a he refers to the spirit of procreation and sexual intercourse: "Therefore it is the last of creation, and the first of youth." He then intimates disaster: "because it (youth) is filled with ignorance (ἀγνοίας) and that

---

[18] On this see C. R. Henry, "The Testaments of the XII Patriarchs," *APOT* 1: 282–367, esp. 297; M. de Jonge, *The Testaments of the Twelve Patriarchs: A Study of their Text, Composition, and Origin* (Assen: Van Gorcum, 1953; 2d ed., 1975), 75-77; Hollander and de Jonge, *Commentary*, 93; Kee, "Ethical Dimensions," 266.

[19] See the discussion in W. Loader, *The Septuagint, Sexuality and the New Testament: Case Studies on the Impact of the LXX* (Grand Rapids: Eerdmans, 2004), 5-9, 12-24.

(αὕτη) leads the young man as a blind man to a pit and as an animal to a precipice." Already in 1:6 Reuben had associated "the ignorance of youth and sexual immorality" (ἀγνοίᾳ νεότητος καὶ πορνείᾳ). The author does not see the spirit of procreation and intercourse as evil in itself. It is God's gift.[20] It includes pleasure, but love of pleasure makes it a danger. Ἄγνοια, not the spirit, leads to disaster. The stream of psychology is more determinative in the discourse than the stream of demonology. This bears some similarity to Paul's preference for "psychology" and for personifications over demonology, especially in Romans 7 (but note the reference to Satan in 1 Cor 7:5 and Beliar in 2 Cor 6:15). Youth are prone to ἄγνοια, which is not innocent ignorance, but the result of turning away from available knowledge. Reuben's discourse is offering that kind of knowledge. Youth's problem is not that it has not yet learned, but that it does not want to learn.[21]

Before proceeding to the list of the seven spirits from Beliar the author appends an eighth spirit: sleep. Like the seven spirits of creation it is neutral, but for the author's psychology, particularly in relation to sexuality, it appears significant. The additional comment about sleep, "with which is created the ecstasy of nature and the image of death,"[22] appears to be neutral, and to be based on observation and speculation about firstly, dreaming, which takes one beyond natural experiences (ἔκστασις), and secondly, about death, for sleep and death were often compared.[23] The application appears in 3:7 where the author states that the evil spirit of sleep brings together sin and "fantasy,"[24] which may come through dreams but may also evoke conscious day dreaming.[25] The world of dreams was also the world where supernatural beings and human beings were believed to connect with each other.

All of the spirits from Beliar, which the author collectively defines as

---

[20] *Contra* J. H. Ulrichsen, *Die Grundschrift der Testamente der Zwölf Patriarchen: Eine Untersuchung zu Umfang, Inhalt und Eigenart der ursprünglichen Schrift* (Acta Universitatis Upsaliensis, Historia Religiorum 10; Uppsala: Almqvist & Wiksell, 1991), 73.

[21] On the vulnerability of youth and its blindness see also *T. Jud.* 11:1 (similarly *T. Sim.* 2:7) and 19:3-4, where it almost reads as an exoneration until one understands that ignorance is culpable (as also in *Jub.* 41:25).

[22] μεθ' οὗ ἐκτίσθη ἔκστασις φύσεως καὶ εἰκὼν τοῦ θανάτου.

[23] See Hollander and de Jonge, *Commentary*, 94.

[24] "Fantasy" seems to describe the impression or image received through the senses. See Hollander and de Jonge, *Commentary*, 95-96.

[25] Such "daydreaming" may be assumed in relation to Reuben's sleeplessness about Bilhah in *T. Reuben* 3:12 and to the women in relation to the watchers in 5:6-7.

"the spirit of error/going astray (τὸ πνεῦμα τῆς πλάνης)" mix with the spirits of creation (3:2). This is an odd mixing of categories: the spirits of creation refer to neutral capacities, not beings, whereas the spirits from Beliar assume a demonology. The underlying assumption is that human capacities are not in themselves evil, but have characteristics which evil can use/abuse. This is apparent in the description of the first of the spirits which lead astray: "The first, that of sexual immorality (πορνείας), has located itself (ἔγκειται) in (our) natural physical make-up (ἐν τῇ φύσει) and in (our) senses (ταῖς αἰσθήσεσιν)." Neither one's natural physical make-up nor the senses are evil in themselves.

Both lists show signs of being resources that the author employs for his purpose.[26] In 3:8 he returns to this purpose by noting: "And in this way every young man is brought to ruin (ἀπόλλυται)." It recalls the concern about youth in 2:2. This concluding remark seems hopeless and fatalistic, until we read on: "darkening his mind from the truth and not comprehending what is in the Law of God nor obeying the instruction of his fathers, just as I, too, suffered in my youth." The reason for the hopelessness is youth's ἄγνοια: they refuse to learn. "The truth," "the law of God" and "the instruction of fathers" are equated. The effect is to recall the exhortation to listen in 2:1 and at the beginning of the discourse in 1:5. The assumption is that youth need not be destroyed if it heeds good teaching. That is the import of 3:9, "love the truth and it will protect you" from such danger. For the author part of that truth lies also in the primitive psychology which he has just expounded.

In 3:10 we begin to move into direct exhortations, but these verses are to be understood in the light of the psychology of 2:1–3:7. The warning not to give attention to a woman's face (μὴ προσέχετε ὄψει γυναικός 10a), has many parallels both within the testaments (e.g., *T. Jud.* 12:3; 17:1; *T. Iss.* 4:4; 7:2) and beyond (e.g., Sir 9:8-9; 25:21; 42:12; Ps Sol 4:4-5). Within *T. Reuben* it finds its echo in 4:1 μὴ οὖν προσέχετε κάλλος γυναικῶν. It is best considered along with the other warnings in relation to women. Thus 3:10 continues: "Do not spend time alone with a married woman and do not concern yourself with women's matters (περιεργάζεσθε πρᾶξιν γυναικῶν)."[27] A similar warning against giving attention to women's matters (πράξεις) is found in 4:1.

---

[26] See de Jonge, *Testaments*, 75-77.

[27] Being alone in the company of a married woman is a theme taken up again in 6:2, where the instruction is applied both to women and to men (see also Prov 6:23-24; Sir 7:9).

The author reinforces these warnings with concrete illustrations and with further psychological observations. After the warning of 3:10, the author returns to the incident with Bilhah (3:11-15). Reuben saw Bilhah bathing discreetly in a covered place. Her bathing would be counted as one of the "women's matters." He sees more than her face; he sees her naked. There is almost a self-distancing in the observation in 3:12: "my mind conceiving the female nakedness" (συλλαβοῦσα γὰρ ἡ διάνοιά μου τὴν γυναικείαν γύμνωσιν). Bilhah also almost disappears as a person. Reuben does not see Bilhah naked; he sees "female nakedness."[28] The author may also be playing with words in speaking of the mind "conceiving" (συλλαβοῦσα).[29] This is much more complex than saying: I saw Bilhah naked. It reflects the author's psychology. Somewhat overstated: Reuben's mind became pregnant as a result of focusing on female nakedness. The author is not absolving Reuben of responsibility. His fault was that he turned his mind towards Bilhah. Once he had done so, the rest followed: "it did not allow me to sleep until I had committed the abomination (βδέλυγμα)."[30] While not inevitable, Reuben's subsequent action with the apparently dead drunk and naked Bilhah, was the sin which the author is seeking to counter not just with warnings against sexual immorality, but also with warnings about what gives birth to such actions.

Strikingly absent is any concern about Bilhah. Reuben raped her! It is also worth noting that the author offers no comment about Bilhah being drunk, as he might have done in the light of his warnings against drunkenness in *T. Judah*. He seems unconcerned with Bilhah's well being, moral or otherwise.[31] The sin was, as 1:6 had already announced, a sin against his father, Jacob. There Reuben described it as defiling his father's bed. This understanding is confirmed in 3:15 when it notes that after he found out Jacob had no further sexual relations with Bilhah (so also *Jub.* 33:9). This was not some kind of pique of resentment or even grief, but rather a

---

[28] In his own way Paul, too, saw danger in some forms of female nakedness for men and for angels, but within the distinctive context of holy worship (1 Cor 11:2-16); see Loader, *Septuagint*, 99-104.

[29] Cf. Jas 1:15, ἡ ἐπιθυμία συλλαβοῦσα τίκτει ἁμαρτίαν, ἡ δὲ ἁμαρτία ἀποτελεσθεῖσα ἀποκύει θάνατον.

[30] Other circumlocutions include: ἡ ἀσέβεια (3:14, 15); τὸ ἀσέβημα (6:3); τὸ ἔργον (5:3); ἡ πρᾶξις (5:6; *T. Jos.* 5:2); τὸ βδέλυγμα (also *T. Jud.* 12:8); ἡ ἁμαρτία (4:3; *T. Jud.* 14:3; *T. Jos*, 14:4); ἡ ἁμαρτία ἡ μεγάλη (1:10; *T Jud.* 14:5); ἡ ἀνομία ἡ μεγάλη (3:11).

[31] Kugler, "Reuben's sin," 533, points out her virtue in *T12* in seeking a discreet place to bathe unlike Bathsheba. Being drunk she is not even conscious (an angel must inform Jacob), so she bears no blame (535-36).

matter of impurity. She had become unclean for Jacob. As an observer of Torah Jacob must not have sexual relations with her. That would be an abomination. This thought lies behind Deut 24:1-4 and was a widely assumed to be the norm.[32] Poor Bilhah!

After returning to direct exhortation in 4:1, not to give attention to women's beauty and set one's mind on women's matters, the author offers further advice about sexuality. One should neglect it altogether, live with singleness of mind (ἁπλότητι καρδίας) and get on with work and study of the Law and keeping sheep, "until the Lord gives you a marriage partner (σύζυγον) whom he wants for you." The expression "simplicity or singleness of heart" recurs in a similar context in *T. Iss.* 4:1, which goes on to warn against lusting after what belongs to others, offering the model of one who did not expose his mind to "female beauty" (οὐ γὰρ εἶδεν ἐπιδέξασθαι κάλλος θηλείας, 4:4). Earlier Issachar extols the simple lifestyle of the farmer (LXX Gen 49:14-15) and avoidance of thoughts of sexual pleasure with women (οὐκ ἐνενόουν ἡδονὴν γυναικός): marriage will come in due time. He married at thirty (3:5). Keeping oneself busy and tired (διὰ τοῦ κόπου ὁ ὕπνος μου περιγένετο, 3:5) is seen as part of the solution for dealing with sexual passion. At the same time the passage clearly assumes that marriage is appropriate and a wife, a gift from God. *T. Levi* 9:9-10 offers similar advice.

In 4:2-4 Reuben returns to the consequences of his action: shame before his father and brothers and his continuing bad conscience, but also his good behavior since repenting. Shame is also a major motif in *T. Judah*, where the patriarch reports his shame, brought on by wine, in having sexual intercourse unawares with his daughter-in-law, Tamar. He uses it to warn future kings about surrendering their power, symbolized by the staff, girdle and diadem, to women (15:1-6). Reuben has made himself a model for any who have sinned similarly.

T. Reuben 4:5 focuses directly on sexual immorality and vv. 6-7 examine its destructive effects both for youth and for the old and noble. Motivating factors are again: the shame it brings before others and before Beliar; and that it separates people from God and leads them to idolatry (*T. Sim.* 5:3; similarly *T. Jud.* 23:2). This latter theme receives no further elaboration in *T. Reuben*. It is quite incidental to Reuben's story, but it looms very large in *T. Judah* in the form of warnings against foreign women (10:6; 11:1, 3; 14:3; 17:1; 23:2) and especially in *T. Levi*, which brings together a

---

[32] 1QapGen 20:15; *t. Sot.* 5.9; Philo, *Abr.* 98; *Lex Iulia de adulteris* of 18 BCE.

range of acts of sexual immorality, including marrying foreign wives and the exposure to idolatry (9:9-10; 14:5-6; see also *T. Dan* 5:5-6).

Verse 6 speaks of sexual immorality leading the mind (νοῦν) and understanding (διάνοιαν) astray and thus leading the youth to Hades before his time. This is similar to 2:9, but also to Reuben's description of what happened to his mind (διάνοια) in 3:12. Verses 8-10 then offer the example of Joseph. "Joseph kept himself away from every woman" (4:8). This is a variation of avoiding their company, on the one hand, and keeping oneself from engaging their beauty, on the other. This verse makes two further, important statements: "and he purified his thoughts (ἐννοίας) of all sexual immorality (πορνείας)." This statement implies controlling the imagination. It coheres with the author's psychology. The second statement belongs in the realm of shame and honor: "he found favor before the Lord and people." The author's psychology is also apparent in 4:9: "and the attitude (διαβούλιον) of his soul did not welcome (ἐδέξατο) evil desire (ἐπιθυμίαν πονηράν)." As in the NT, ἐπιθυμία is a neutral category, but becomes evil when inappropriately focused. Joseph had the capacity to welcome such desire, but chose not to. The logical conclusion follows in 4:10: "For if sexual immorality (πορνεία) has no power over your thought (ἔννοιαν), nor has Beliar." Already 4:6 had personified sexual immorality. The demonic Beliar comes in at a secondary level. In terms of 3:3 one would have to say that the spirit of πορνεία which comes from Beliar seeks control. Reuben is saying: it can be resisted. This brief reference to Joseph is interesting, because the long narrative in *T. Joseph* about his encounter with the Egyptian woman (3:1–9:5) focuses almost entirely on her various manipulations. Only at a very secondary level, almost sounding like an afterthought, do we hear from Joseph about the danger of women's beauty in 9:5, where he describes the attractiveness of her bare arms, legs and breasts and adornment. *T. Reuben* does, however, pick up the theme of women's wiles in the next section.

T. Reuben 5:1 shifts back from sexual immorality to women. Its opening statement is shocking: "Women are evil." It should not, however, be separated from its context. The sentence goes on to explain, that the author thinks they are evil because they compensate for not being as strong as men by acts of trickery, to attract (ἐπισπάσονται) them. The "Egyptian woman" of 4:8-10 was a prime example and is doubtless still in the author's mind (see also *T. Naph.* 1:6 about Rachel and, in irony, *T. Jud.* 12:7, about Tamar). The language of struggle or contest is employed in v. 2: "and whom they are not strong enough to conquer (καταγωνίσασθαι) by power, they conquer through deceit." The following verse will continue the language of warfare!

First, however, in 5:3a, the author asserts that he has received teaching from the angel of the Lord – about women's psychology.[33] Verse 5:3a expresses a fundamental premise: "Women are weaker (ἡττῶνται) than men when it comes to resisting the spirit of sexual immorality (πορνείας)" (an allusion to the spirit of sexual immorality in 3:3).[34] We find a similar statement in 6:2, where women are said to have "an incurable disease."

In 5:3b the author continues to report his alleged revelation. Women conduct war against men to take them captive in the deed of sexual intercourse (τῷ ἔργῳ αἰχμαλωτίζουσιν). The negative imagery is striking. They plot against them (μηχανῶνται κατὰ τῶν ἀνθρώπων), they deceive (πλανῶσιν), they sow poison (ἰὸν ἐνσπείρουσι), they take them captive (αἰχμαλωτίζουσιν). The means are not insignificant: through adornment (διὰ τῆς κοσμήσεως), referring possibly both to clothing and to cosmetics; and through the look or glance (διὰ τοῦ βλέμματος). Women are "evil," in the sense that they are the enemy when they act in this way. But v. 4 reassures: men are not bound to face defeat![35]

A tone of exhortation returns in 5:5: "Flee sexual immorality" (φεύγετε οὖν τὴν πορνείαν). Paul uses an identical exhortation in 1 Cor 6:18. Both are probably inspired by Joseph's flight, but Paul's concern is prostitution, Reuben's is more generally concerned with women as dangerous.[36] In what immediately follows, the author instructs men not to allow their wives and daughters to engage in such warfare against men. They should not adorn their heads and faces – otherwise they will bring eternal punishment on themselves (5:5). This is the other side of the coin from the exhortation to men not to give attention to women's faces which are their beauty (3:10; 4:1).

In 5:6-7 the author gives a version of the watchers' sin. Its focus is a psychological interpretation of the events:

For thus they [women] bewitched (ἔθελξαν) the watchers before the flood. And they [the watchers] constantly looking at them [the women] developed lust

---

[33] Cf. 2:1 and the "psychology" of 2:1- 3:7; see also the angelic revelation about women's power in *T. Jud.* 15:5-6 over kings.

[34] 1 Pet 3:7 speaks of women as the weaker vessels (ὡς ἀσθενεστέρῳ σκεύει τῷ γυναικείῳ), but not in a context of vulnerability to sexual immorality.

[35] As earlier in 3:9; 4:11.

[36] B. Rosner argues for Paul's dependence ("A Possible Quotation of Test. Reuben 5:5 in 1 Corinthians 6,18A," *JTS* 43 [1992]: 123-27).

for one another (συνεχῶς ὁρῶντες αὐτὰς ἐγένοντο ἐν ἐπιθυμίᾳ ἀλλήλων) and conceived (συνέλαβον) the deed (πρᾶξιν) in their imagination (διανοίᾳ) and changed their shape to become men and appeared to them [the women] while they were engaging in sexual intercourse with their husbands. And they [the women] lusting (ἐπιθυμοῦσαι) in their imagination (διανοίᾳ) for their fantasies (φαντασίας) gave birth to giants. For the watchers appeared to them as high as heaven in appearance (perhaps a reference to huge penises).

This remarkably constructed account parallels the deeds of the watchers and the response of the women, but the root cause are the women (cf. 1 En 8:1). As in the account of Reuben's response to "female nakedness" in 3:12, the word συνέλαβον appears with its double meaning: "conceive." As in 3:12 the mind becomes pregnant with the deed. Avoiding the notion of acts of sexual intercourse between the women and the watchers, 5:6 reports that the angels appeared to the women while they were having sexual intercourse with their husbands. Probably the author meant this to indicate sexual fantasy (the image of the watchers in their minds); perhaps he also envisaged something more supernatural (cf. 3:7). The following verse relates that the women lusted after the fantasies and as a result gave birth to giants (v. 7).

The psycho-physiology is complicated, given that in their understanding the child comes from implantation of male seed. The author must imagine that the combination of the women's lusting after these big watchers and the fact that they were at the time engaging in sexual intercourse, made it somehow easier for the angelic seed to be implanted in them. Was it that the author assumed women could only conceive if they were in a certain receptive state such as when they engaged in sexual intercourse?

There are some difficulties in v. 6 because it suggests that the initial effect on the watchers was that they lusted after each other (ἐγένοντο ἐν ἐπιθυμίᾳ ἀλλήλων) in what would have to be homosexual desire. If so, that is not in focus here. It becomes the focus in *T. Naph.* 3:3-5. There, citing the men of Sodom as following the ways of the Gentiles in altering the divine order of nature (ἐνήλλαξε τάξιν φύσεως αὐτῆς), an allusion to homosexual activity (rape in this instance), the author cites the watchers as doing the same (ἐνήλλαξαν τάξιν φύσεως αὐτῶν), although in their case no homosexual behavior is implied. Paul's argument in Rom 1:18-28, which sees homosexual actions as the result of abandoning "nature," is similar.

The following chapter maintains the emphasis on the dangers women posed (hence the οὖν "therefore"): "So keep yourself from sexual immorality (6:1)" echoes 5:5, "So flee sexual immorality." Both here and there women are in mind. Verse 1 continues: "and if you want to be pure in mind (καθαρεύειν τῇ διανοίᾳ), keep your senses (αἰσθήσεις) away from all that is female (πάσης θηλείας)." This is the author's psychology and it recalls 4:8. The senses are the vehicle through which what is seen or experienced reaches the mind. Protecting oneself from the female (note: it has become impersonal again) means protecting oneself from danger. By implication that means not doing as the watchers did: looking continuously at women; nor doing as Reuben: looking at female nakedness. It means not looking at their adorned faces and heads, their beauty, and avoiding being alone with them. Verse 2 returns to what men should teach women (see 5:5) and for a moment the author seems concerned also that women be pure in mind (ἵνα καὶ αὐταὶ καθαρεύωσι τῇ διανοίᾳ). Women should not be alone with men, because such meetings make them incurably sick (in their lust for sexual intercourse). The assumption is that women cannot help themselves and are therefore dangerous.[37] They are fundamentally flawed. Men should not be alone with women because if they engage in sexual immorality, they will be shamed.[38]

As in 4:6 we return in 6:4a to the personification of πορνεία: it has no understanding or piety. The second part of this verse then shifts rather abruptly to another possible sub-theme: jealousy, but, rather than exploit it in relation to sexual relations, the author appears to have introduced it only as a point of transition to jealously in a general sense, directed in future towards the sons of Levi. With that the author moves away from the theme of sexual immorality and does not return to it in the rest of the testament (6:5-12; 7:1-2).

Conclusion

The material considered above reflects an interesting confluence of affirmation of sexual intercourse within marriage, grounded ultimately in

---

[37] Philo cites the plural ποιήσωμεν ("let us make") of the LXX of Gen 2:18 (the Hebrew has the singular) in order to explain that others joined God in the creation of women and occasioned their being flawed (*Opif.* 75; see also *Fug.* 68-70). On Gen 3:15 LXX and insatiable female sexuality see Loader, *Septuagint*, 47-49.

[38] The sense here is that they will be shamed before Beliar; cf. 4:7 before Beliar *and other men*.

understandings of divine order and creation, with streams of thought influenced in part by prevailing Stoicism of the period, with which Jewish moral teachers found much in common. Divine order linked the two, but led to consequences sometimes reflected in a virtual misogyny, as in Sirach, Philo and *T12*, which sees women as the source of men's temptations and virtually made the arousal of sexual passion a moral failure in itself. *T12*'s hearer would understand Jesus' exposition of adultery in Matt 5:28 in this way, contrary to its likely intent.[39] Such a stance made it very difficult for men to relate openly to women and to their own sexuality.

T12 belongs in the turbulent convergence of culturally different streams of thought in which Christianity also arose. It is an important source for understanding the reflections about sexuality which were developing at the interface of Judaism and the Hellenistic Roman world and which were being taken up into the heritage of Christianity and continue their influence to the present day.

---

[39] See my discussion in *Sexuality and the Jesus Tradition*, 9-20.

INDEX OF MODERN AUTHORS

INDEX